CW01652266

BOB HEPPLE
Master of Clare College, Cambridge; Visiting Professor of Law, University College London; Barrister of Gray's Inn; Advocate of the Supreme Court of South Africa

PAUL O'HIGGINS
Vice-Master, Christ's College, Cambridge; Member of the Royal Irish Academy; Emeritus Professor in the University of London at King's College; Honorary Professor of Law, Trinity College, Dublin; Visiting Professor of Law, City University, London; Barrister of the Kings' Inns and of Lincoln's Inn

Disability, Discrimination and Equal Opportunities

A Comparative Study of the Employment Rights of Disabled Persons

BRIAN DOYLE

MANSELL

First published 1995 by
Mansell Publishing Limited, *A Cassell imprint*
Wellington House, 125 Strand, London WC2R 0BB, England
387 Park Avenue South, New York, New York 10016–8810, USA

British Library Cataloguing-in-Publication Data

Doyle, Brian
Disability, Discrimination and Equal Opportunities: Comparative Study of the Employment Rights of Disabled Persons. – (Studies in Labour & Social Law)
I. Title II. Series
331.133

ISBN 0–7201–2242–2

Library of Congress Cataloging-in-Publication Data

Doyle, Brian John.
Disability, discrimination, and equal opportunities : a comparative study of the employment rights of disabled persons / Brian Doyle.
p. cm. – (Studies in labour and social law)
Includes bibliographical references and index.
ISBN 0–7201–2242–2 : $110.00. – ISBN 0–7201–2244–9 : $40.00
1. Handicapped – Employment – Law and legislation.
2. Discrimination in employment – Law and legislation.
3. Handicapped – Legal status, laws etc. I. Title. II. Series.
K1771.D69 1995
344′.0159–dc20
[342.4159] 94–34931
CIP

Printed and bound in Great Britain by
Biddles Ltd, Guildford and King's Lynn

For my parents
Mary and Jude Doyle

CONTENTS

Preface

During 1994, the debate about the civil rights of disabled persons obtained a central role in the political agenda. The furore which surrounded the defeat of the Civil Rights (Disabled Persons) Bill momentarily threatened the career of one Government minister and threw a spotlight upon the inadequacies of the legislative process in Britain. How could a Bill which had received all-party support, had been approved by the second chamber on a previous occasion and had survived the Committee stage in the House of Commons be defeated at Third Reading by the cynical combination of procedural means and tactics? Yet the Bill's demise has ironically improved the chances that the civil rights of disabled persons eventually will be recognized in law. In the summer of 1994, the Government announced its intention to consult about a limited initiative in law reform to address the aspirations of disabled citizens to social and economic participation. While this is unlikely to assuage the demands of disability rights activists, the issues of disability, discrimination and equal opportunities are now in the forefront of public and political debate.

This study makes a small contribution to that debate by examining the role that the law might play in combating disability discrimination in the labour market and in promoting the employment rights of disabled workers. This is an area which has been much neglected in the legal literature and in the pages of employment law scholarship. The study sets itself six objectives. First, it will seek to clarify our understanding of disability and the experience of persons with disabilities in the context of employment activity. Second, it will examine the data that describe the status of disabled workers in the labour market and will assess how far their employment vulnerability or disadvantage is the result of prejudice, discrimination or lack of equal opportunities. Third, a number of different legal models addressing the employment rights of disabled persons will be described through an account of the legal position in selected comparative countries. Fourth, the study will explore how far, if at all, the comparative legal models or existing discrimination theories and laws can be applied in the reform of Britain's disabled employment legislation. Fifth, a number of inherent problems and issues for legal reform will be analysed and solutions suggested. Finally, the efficacy of using law as a means of social engineering will be assessed in the context of the present topic.

Chapter 1 explains the concepts and terminology that provide the framework for the subsequent analysis. This chapter also explores the nature, demography and experience of disability, and examines the hypothesis that disabled persons are the subject of prejudice and discrimination which infects and affects their employment status and opportunities. Chapter 2 narrates the current legal position in Britain and outlines the contemporary pressures for legal reform of disability rights in the employment field. As British employment rights have been influenced by recent developments in the European Communities, Chapter 3 surveys the state of disabled employment rights in Europe. As the main point of comparison in this study is between the law in Britain and the legal rights of disabled workers in the United States, Chapter 4 looks at the use of constitutional, federal and state laws to protect disabled workers in the USA. Chapter 5 introduces additional comparative perspectives by summarizing the position in the Canadian provincial and federal jurisdictions and under Australian Commonwealth and state legislation.

In Chapter 6 the problems of applying discrimination theory to disability are investigated. The main issue here is concern with how to define in legal terms what amounts to disability-related discriminatory actions or effects. Chapter 7 identifies the protected class and contemplates the difficulties of translating the medical and social conceptions of disability into legal terms. The question of how to accommodate the right of disabled persons to be treated fairly in the labour market with the right of employers to organize their workforce and production efficiently is tackled in Chapter 8. In this chapter, the application of the merit principle to disability discrimination laws is examined, and the formulae for ensuring fitness for work and qualification for employment are weighed. Chapter 9, a key chapter, sets out the essential ingredient of any legal reform in this area: the need to make reasonable accommodation for disabled persons. Chapter 10 returns to the British experience of the use of quotas as a means of promoting disabled employment opportunity and also probes the role of preferential treatment. The problems of how disability discrimination law is to be enforced, what remedies should be granted, what procedures followed and how the law might encourage alternative dispute avoidance and resolution are addressed in Chapter 11. Looking beyond enforcement, Chapter 12 explores how positive action, equal opportunity policies and contract compliance techniques might be recruited to the present discussion. Finally, Chapter 13 attempts a summary of the main arguments of this study and draws appropriate conclusions.

A bibliography is supplied to indicate the major materials which have influenced the preparation of this study and a fuller bibliography is appended to the original thesis. In the main, the author–date citation method is employed and the bibliography also serves as a key to cited sources. Extensive use of abbreviations and acronyms is made, so that the reader should refer to the list of abbreviations for an explanation of those which are less familiar. Legal citations and references observe the varying conventions of the different jurisdictions, but with some modifications where appropriate, and readers should refer to the usual dictionaries of legal citations to decode the less familiar references. This book is based upon the author's doctoral thesis (Doyle, 1993b) to which reference must be made for the further detailed evidence that underpins many of the arguments exposed here. Chapter 2 draws upon my earlier publications (Doyle, 1987b, 1991, 1994b), while the framework of Chapters 6 to 12 was rehearsed in Doyle (1993a, 1994a). I am grateful to the Institute of Employment Rights, the Industrial Law Society and Tolley Publishing Co. Ltd for their permission to draw upon those sources in which they own copyright.

A study of this nature cannot be completed without a number of debts of gratitude being incurred. The first and most extensive debt is that owed to my wife, Antoinette, who encouraged and cajoled me at various stages of the research, particularly during the lonely and despairing hours of writing-up. I might have given up or settled for something less ambitious without her influence. At various stages in the gestation of the original thesis and its translation into a book, my students and fellow academics offered many insights into the process of research and the substantive topic itself, although naturally they cannot be blamed for the many deficiencies of style, presentation and analysis that remain. My department provided much in the way of material assistance during the research, not least in respect of my calls upon the travel budget and equipment funds. I am grateful to the chairman of department, Professor K. P. Gee, for his support. The personnel of many libraries have answered my requests for sources and information, and provided me with temporary research accommodation at different stages of the study. I would mention in particular the librarians and staff of the Clifford Whitworth Library at the University of Salford, the John Rylands Library at the University of Manchester, the Bodleian Law Library at the University of Oxford and the Library of the Institute of Advanced Legal Studies in the University of London, as well as the British Library Document Supply Centre. I am also grateful to a number of individuals and organizations, too great to mention by name, who sent me papers and materials or responded to my requests for information. Finally, I am indebted to Professor Brian Napier (Queen Mary and Westfield College, London) and Mr Trevor Buck (University of Leicester), who acted as the external examiners of my original doctoral thesis and encouraged me to convert the thesis into the present publication.

I have attempted to state the law as I understand it as at the end of November 1994. However, in a comparative study it will be inevitable that some last minute developments may have been overlooked. Nevertheless, it is worth reporting that, during the proofs stage, the British government announced its intention to introduce a Bill to address disability discrimination in the employment field during the 1994–95 parliamentary session. It remains to be seen whether this measure will match the hopes and aspirations of disabled workers themselves.

Brian Doyle
Salford
7 December 1994

List of Abbreviations

ACT	Australian Capital Territory
ADA	Americans with Disabilities Act; Anti-Discrimination Act
ADB	Anti-Discrimination Board
AIDS	Acquired Immune Deficiency Syndrome
Alb	Alberta
Ark	Arkansas
BC	British Columbia
BFOQ	*Bona fide* occupational qualification
BFOR	*Bona fide* occupational requirement
Cal	California
Can	Canada
CFR	Code of Federal Regulations
CHR&F	Charter of Human Rights and Freedoms
Conn	Connecticut
CRE	Commission for Racial Equality
Cth	Commonwealth (Australia)
DC	District Court; District of Columbia
DDA	Disability Discrimination Act
DE	Department of Employment
DP(E)A	Disabled Persons (Employment) Act
EC	European Community (Communities)
ECJ	European Court of Justice
EEA	Employment Equity Act
EEOC	Equal Employment Opportunities Commission
EEO(CA)A	Equal Employment Opportunity (Commonwealth Authorities) Act
EOA	Equal Opportunity Act
EOB	Equal Opportunity Board
EOC	Equal Opportunity Commission
EOT	Equal Opportunity Tribunal
EP(C)A	Employment Protection (Consolidation) Act
FCA	Federal Court of Appeal
Fla	Florida
FPA	Fair Practices Act
Ga	Georgia

Haw	Hawaii
HIV	Human Immunodeficiency Virus
HPDT	Handicapped Persons Discrimination Tribunal
HPEOA	Handicapped Persons Equal Opportunity Act
HR&EOCA	Human Rights and Equal Opportunity Commission Act
HRA	Human Rights Act
HRC	Human Rights Code; Human Rights Commission
HRT	Human Rights Tribunal; Human Rights Review Tribunal
Ill	Illinois
ILO	International Labour Organisation
Ind	Indiana
IRPA	Individual's Rights Protection Act
IT	Industrial Tribunal
La	Louisiana
Man	Manitoba
Mass	Massachusetts
Md	Maryland
Minn	Minnesota
Miss	Missouri
Mo	Montana
NB	New Brunswick
NC	North Carolina
New	Newfoundland
NJ	New Jersey
NS	Nova Scotia
NSW	New South Wales
NT	Northern Territory
NWT	Northwest Territories
NY	New York
OFCCP	Office of Federal Contract Compliance Programs
Okla	Oklahoma
Ont	Ontario
OPCS	Office of Population, Censuses and Surveys
Pa	Philadelphia
PACT	Placement Assessment and Counselling Team
PEI	Prince Edward Island
Penn	Pennsylvania
Qld	Queensland
Québ	Québec
RA	Rehabilitation Act
RI	Rhode Island

SA	South Australia
Sask	Saskatchewan
SCPR	Social and Community Planning Research
Tenn	Tennessee
Tex	Texas
TUC	Trades Union Congress
UN	United Nations
USC	United States Code
Va	Virginia
Vic	Victoria
WA	Western Australia
Wash	Washington
WHO	World Health Organization
YT	Yukon Territory

1

Disability and Discrimination

INTRODUCTION

Throughout history disabled people have experienced social discrimination, segregation and exclusion. They have been characterized as incomplete or defective human beings, subjected at one extreme to neglect, persecution and death, and at the other extreme to charity, social welfare and paternalism.[1] Between these two poles lies the common experience of many, although not all, disabled persons: segregated in education, trapped by the benefits system, denied independence by health and social services, marginalized by the built environment, immobilized by the transport system, denied full participation in leisure and social activities, and disenfranchised by the political process. Disadvantage and inequality of opportunity represent the everyday experience of individuals with disabilities. Disability discrimination is institutionalized and interwoven in the fabric of our society.[2]

Persons with disabilities are especially vulnerable to discrimination and disadvantage in employment. It is true that, in some cases, the nature and severity of disability can disqualify the individual from some economic activity. For many disabled persons, entry or re-entry to the labour market is restricted by impairment or disability, lack of skills or qualifications, and income insecurity during the transition from disabled unemployment to rehabilitated employment. Nevertheless, disabled workers can be equally, if not further, handicapped by the ignorance, fear and prejudice of employers and 'able-bodied' fellow workers.[3] Entry to and participation in the labour market can be obstructed by structural and institutional barriers erected by the norms of the non-disabled world and maintained by the legacy of past discrimination. Like women and minority groups, disabled workers often experience unequal employment opportunities, limited rights at work and reduced job security. This might be the result of prejudice or ill motive on the part of employers and others in the workplace. It is more likely to be caused by employers stereotyping disabled persons and applying preconceptions about their abilities and employability. Even in the absence of such discrimination, a disability can still be a disadvantage unless employers are willing or required to take reasonable steps to accommodate disabled applicants and employees.

Recognition of this pattern of discrimination, disadvantage and lack of opportunity, which is the life menu of many disabled persons, has led several and various voices to advocate the entrenchment of basic social, economic and political rights for disabled people in law. Although there are a number of statutory and extra-statutory measures that regulate the employment of disabled persons in Britain and provide them with a degree of employment protection, there is no anti-discrimination or equal opportunities legislation outlawing employment discrimination against disabled people. Today in Britain, a person's disability, unlike a person's sex, marital status or race, may be a lawful ground upon which to base an otherwise irrational employment decision.

Disabled Britons have learned much from the disability rights and independent living movements in the USA,[4] and have subscribed to the tenets of supranational disability associations.[5] Since the 1960s, in the battle for rights and acceptance, organizations for disabled people have been displaced by organizations of disabled people, the emergence of which has been symptomatic of and instrumental in the growing confidence of disabled people in the socio-political arena.[6] Despite

> the excessive paternalism of the welfare state coupled with the absence of a strong British Civil Rights tradition [that] has caused disabled people in Britain to be relatively cautious in their choice of tactics,

since the late 1980s disabled activists have been prepared to use protests, civil disobedience and demonstrations – even at personal risk – to highlight the case for change.[7]

The justification for legislating for disabled employment rights has been advanced thus:

> Disability imposes individual and social costs. With the onset of a potentially disabling condition, an individual experiences both economic and psychic losses as he or she faces restricted

> choices. The individual may suffer pain, incur increased medical costs, lose income, and face societal prejudice. Society may lose the output of an otherwise productive worker and use its resources for medical care and rehabilitation. A firm may lose its investment in the hiring and training of that worker.[8]

International labour standards recognize this argument and furnish some support for the guarantee of disabled employment rights. In 1923, the ILO first decided to recommend to governments the adoption of compulsory disabled employment schemes:[9]

> In the ILO discussions the experts stressed the obligations owed to disabled ex-servicemen by society, the economic value of work to an injured man, the ill-effects of dependency and the need for countries to maximise their productive capacity. But they never lost sight of the fact that European war pensions were inadequate and that this made it imperative that work should be provided for the disabled men.[10]

The ILO subsequently required governments to formulate and implement policies for vocational rehabilitation and disabled employment, to promote equal employment opportunities in competitive employment and to permit positive discrimination in favour of disabled workers.[11]

The UN Declaration on the Rights of Disabled Persons expresses the right of disabled people to

> economic and social security and to a decent level of living, [and] according to their capabilities, to secure and retain employment or to engage in a useful, productive and remunerative occupation.[12]

The European Social Charter mandates signatory states 'to take adequate . . . measures to encourage employers to admit disabled persons to employment'. The EC Recommendation on the Employment of Disabled People exhorts member states to take all appropriate measures to promote fair employment and vocational training opportunities for disabled people.[13] Article 26 of the EC Charter of Fundamental Social Rights of Workers provides that:

> disabled persons, whatever the origin and nature of their disablement, must be entitled to additional concrete measures aimed at improving their social and professional integration.

> These measures must concern, in particular, according to the capacities of the beneficiaries, vocational training, ergonomics, accessibility, mobility, means of transport and housing.[14]

Furthermore, Article 2 of the Social Chapter Agreement annexed to the EC Protocol on Social Policy calls for the EC to support and complement the activities of member states in, *inter alia*, 'the integration of persons excluded from the labour market', a phrase that is capable of being applied to disabled persons.[15]

DISABILITY

Defining Disability

Three terms are central to the study of disabled persons and their experience: namely, 'impairment', 'disability' and 'handicap'. Dictionary definitions of the above labels cast only a little light upon their importance as conceptual signifiers. The most controversial of the three words is 'handicap'. This is because it is believed to have originated from the phrase 'hand i' cap' or 'hand in the cap', a description of a seventeenth century sport or game involving the action of drawing objects out of a cap.[16] The term was applied to horse-racing in the eighteenth century and came into general usage in the 1850s. In that sense it signifies:

> The extra weight or other condition imposed on a superior in favour of an inferior competitor in any athletic or other match; hence, any encumbrance or disability that weighs upon effort and makes success more difficult.[17]

Although 'handicap' is used in modern times in this latter sense, when employed in relation to persons with disabilities or impairments, it obtains a narrower, more negative connotation of disadvantage and inferiority.[18]

The medical view of disability has been the predominant one in twentieth-century industrialized democracies. This is also reflected in the terminology and etymology of disability. The WHO's classification of impairment, disability and handicap has gained widespread usage.[19] This defines handicap as:

> A disadvantage for a given individual, resulting from an

> impairment or a disability, that limits or prevents the fulfilment of a role that is normal (depending on age, sex, and social and cultural factors) for that individual.

In that context, impairment is 'any loss or abnormality of psychological, physiological, or anatomical structure or function', while disability indicates 'any restriction or lack (resulting from an impairment) of ability to perform an activity in the manner or within the range considered normal for a human being'. Little disagreement exists over the concept of impairment, which is essentially a matter of clinical judgment.

Although this classification focuses upon physical or mental impairment and its medical and functional consequences, it at least recognizes that the disadvantage experienced by persons with disabilities is also the product of society's negative reaction (or failure to react positively) towards impairment and disability. Impairments are of many causes and varying severity, and possession of an impairment does not inevitably mean that the individual is disabled or handicapped, contrary to the popular perception and conventional usage. On the other hand, disability depicts the individual's experience of a limitation in a particular activity or range of activities, but without colouring all other life functions. In contrast, handicap describes the manner in which society interacts with a disabled person and his or her impairment or disability.[20] This latter point bears out Burgdorf's observation that

> One of the most important elements in delineating who is and who is not handicapped is a social judgment; a person truly qualifies as handicapped only as a result of being so labeled [sic] by others. And the decision to impose or not to impose the *handicapped* label is ultimately grounded upon perceptions of an individual's role in society.[21]

The popular perception would probably recognize blindness, deafness or paraplegia, for example, as disabilities or impairments; in contrast, colour blindness, vertigo or other 'hidden' disabilities would probably not be so acknowledged.[22] There is no fine dividing line which can be drawn between disability and 'normality', and between capability and inability. Such lines as are drawn are necessarily arbitrary. The better view is to regard disability and able-bodiedness as being extremes on a broad spectrum or continuum of human behaviour and experience. A person may be disabled or non-disabled at different times of life and/or for different purposes or activities.

Careless and lazy use of these terms produces phraseology such as 'the handicapped' or 'the disabled'. The objection to such language is that it emphasizes or exaggerates a person's medical condition or status, or characterizes disabled individuals as tragic (or courageous or heroic) victims, unable to make a full contribution to society and, therefore, fit only as the proper recipients of charitable assistance and social welfare.[23] The nomenclature dehumanizes disabled persons and fails to accord them their proper respect as individual human beings. As a consequence, individuals with disabilities have attracted numerous derogatory sobriquets which tend to demean their status further.[24] Unless the context requires otherwise, this study will use the expressions 'disabled persons' or 'persons with disabilities' (or variations thereon), and the term 'disability' (and its co-derivative 'disabled') will be used in relation to the individuals and groups in whose support the law is mobilized. This decision reflects the growing awareness of the negative power of labels and the preference of disabled persons for descriptive language which focuses upon the individual rather than the disability.[25] In legal terms, however, the choice of nomenclature is not significant and, as will be seen, these terms are often used interchangeably without affecting their legal import. Nevertheless, it will be essential below to grasp the nettle and attempt to furnish a legal definition of the protected class.

Understanding Disability

Defining disability and its attendant terms brings us no nearer to understanding the meaning of disability. This is amply demonstrated by a survey of disabled persons themselves. When asked what the term 'disabled' meant to them, 50 per cent replied that it refers to a general restriction or restriction in personal movement.[26] Thirty per cent thought that 'disabled' referred to someone with a named disability and 21 per cent identified disability with someone who is unable to do certain types of jobs. A further 13 per cent visualized individuals who need help or who are dependent on others or cannot do things for themselves, while 10 per cent mentioned an inability to get about or around. Only 5 per cent thought that the term 'disabled' applied to someone unable to work and a further 6 per cent to someone who is unable to perform certain named activities. This research demonstrates, albeit tentatively, the difficulties of defining disability and identifying disabled persons, as well as the pitfalls of relying upon self-definition or self-perception.

Disability is often used to describe the limitations imposed by ill health or a medical condition upon an individual's normal social activities and roles.[27] Such limitations are almost invariably the product of impairments, which in turn involve a loss of mental, anatomical or physiological structure or function. The causes of such loss of structure or function might be congenital or might originate in disease or injury. The limitation in activity may be absolute, as in a case of full or partial incapacity, or relative, as in a case of reduced ability or difficulty in functioning. Nevertheless, this still does not adequately describe the concept of *disability*. It is necessary to distinguish further between limitations in *actions* and limitations in *activities*. Speaking and walking are primary examples of actions. They would be thought of as essential actions necessary to fulfil the role of a university teacher, for whom the activities of being mobile and able to communicate with students and colleagues are clearly important. None the less, those activities can be accomplished just as well by modifying or substituting the actions required. So, for example, communication can be achieved with a keyboard speech synthesizer, while mobility might be assured by means of a power-operated wheelchair. So impairment need not produce disability and, even if it does, such disability need not be a handicap.

As used in this study, disability signifies a physical or mental condition substantially modifying or limiting daily life functions without necessarily destroying the ability to work or to participate in other activities.[28] A disabled person is someone who 'is unable to perform some social role because of a mental or physical condition', where disability is 'the loss of the ability to perform socially accepted or prescribed tasks and roles due to a medically definable *condition*'.[29] The medical condition may have left the individual with residual impairments: that is, 'some physiological, anatomical, or mental loss or abnormality that persists after the condition has stabilized'.[30] In turn, the residual impairments may result in 'functional limitations', which create inability in lifting, carrying, walking and so on. Functional limitations may then result in difficulty in performing expected roles and, in that sense, a person may be 'disabled'. The concepts of mental or physical condition, impairment and functional limitation are essentially medical and can be determined by medical examination. However, the existence of disability is more elusive, 'since the inability to perform an expected or prescribed role may be due to a functional limitation as it interacts with a whole host of other factors in that person's environment'.[31] In that sense, disability is a 'socioeconomic phenomenon'.

DISABLED PERSONS

The reform of disability rights has been dogged by difficulties in identifying persons with disabilities and in measuring the disabled population. Disability is an elusive concept. The problem of whether and how to distinguish between short-term and long-term illness, temporary and permanent conditions, fleeting and chronic sickness, and disabling and non-disabling impairments has been ever present. As a result, governments have been unable to plan adequately for welfare and other services or to make appropriate provision for disabled needs within social security and public expenditure budgets. The lack of hard data has also allowed political procrastination and a denial that there is any sizeable constituency of people whose experience merits legal or administrative intervention. It is essential, therefore, that as a precondition to any reform of disabled employment rights, there should be consensus on the meaning of disability, the dimensions of the disabled population and the quality of life of persons with disabilities.

Arriving at a widely accepted delineation of the social meaning of disability does not resolve the problem of how to identify disabled persons and to gauge the magnitude of the disabled population. In fact, it exacerbates this problem, as socially defined subjects or phenomena are notoriously hard to catalogue under survey research conditions and easily elude calculation. The Herculean task of attempting to ascertain the size of the disabled population is inextricably associated with the difficulties of defining, identifying, recognizing and recording disability. For example, a recent statistical compendium of disability surveys indicated that the percentage of disabled persons in 55 countries ranged from 0.2 to 21 per cent of the general population.[32] Such findings are undoubtedly the result of figures which rely upon various and differing definitions of disability, disparate age ranges and variable methods of data collection. The purposes for which the information is collected will also inform the lack of comparability.

Survey Evidence of Disability[33]

Between 1985 and 1988, two surveys were carried out by the OPCS of disabled adults living in private households and disabled adults living in communal establishments in Britain. The surveys resulted in the publication of three pertinent reports in 1988 and 1989.[34] The OPCS research selected a relatively low threshold of disability, being defined as a restriction or lack of ability to perform normal activities, which has resulted from an impairment of a structure or function of the body or mind.[35] In 1989, separate survey research was carried out by SCPR on behalf of the Department of Employment. This set out to estimate the size and distribution of the population of persons registrable under the Disabled Persons (Employment) Act 1944 and was undertaken specifically to inform disabled employment policy and provision. A report of the research findings was published in June 1990.[36]

The OPCS surveys established an estimate of the prevalence of disability by severity and type of disability, calculating that there is a disabled adult population in Britain of some 6 million people.[37] This results in approximately 14 per cent of adults in the general population being defined as disabled.[38] It was also found that 42 per cent of all disabled adults living in private households were aged between 16 and 64 years, of which 31 per cent were aged 16–59 years, compared with 74 per cent of the general population.[39] Sub-analysis of the OPCS data leads to the conclusion that disabled adults, broadly defined, constitute 6 per cent of the economically active general population. Further analysis results in the OPCS finding that the numbers of disabled adults increase with increasing age, as does the severity of disability.[40] When gender is entered into the equation, OPCS found that women constitute approximately 60 per cent of the disabled population.[41]

The survey undertaken by SCPR found that, among adults of working age, 22 per cent had a health problem or disability (7.3 million adults).[42] This split into 14 per cent who suffered no occupational handicap as a result and 8 per cent who did (among whom 5 per cent were economically active or expected to be so in the next twelve months). It is also clear from the SCPR research that both health problems and occupational handicaps become more prevalent with increasing age.[43] The SCPR researchers estimated that persons who are occupationally handicapped and economically active represent 4 per cent of the working age population,[44] of which 3 per cent are in work or on a government scheme, and 0.8 per cent want work. It was estimated that 3.2 per cent of the working population were registrable as disabled under the 1944 Act. As a result, the SCPR research gauges the economically active, occupationally handicapped population of Britain to be 1.4 million.[45] When the SCPR statistics are examined by gender, we find that the numbers of men and women reporting health problems are roughly equal. However, slightly more men than women report that they are occupationally handicapped by their health status. The same observation is true among those who were both occupationally handicapped and economically active. The SCPR survey found that 94 per cent of economically active, occupationally handicapped respondents were white and 6 per cent were from ethnic minority groups.

The differences in the data produced by the OPCS and SCPR surveys are largely explicable by the different thresholds of disability selected for identifying respondents.[46] Both surveys confirm earlier impressions that the numbers of disabled persons have been significantly under-estimated in official statistics and that disabled people represent approximately 10–15 per cent of the population.[47] The OPCS study itself sought to make comparison with the 1985 *General Household Survey*, which was based upon limiting long-standing illness or disability. That source estimated a disability prevalence of 21 per cent in the general population, compared with 14 per cent in the OPCS research.[48] Amongst the economically active population, the *General Household Survey* found a disability prevalence rate of 14 per cent, compared with the OPCS rate of 6 per cent. Undoubtedly, part of the difference in these results can be explained by a lower definitional threshold for disability chosen for the *General Household Survey* study.[49]

DISABILITY AND THE LABOUR MARKET

Disability and Economic Activity

In the general population, an adult would expect to be economically active between the ages of 16 and 65 years old. Economic activity means that the individual is engaged in self-employed activity or earns an income through employment as an employee or is seeking to enter work either in the present or in the near future. We might also include among the economically active those who might be termed 'discouraged workers': that is, those who are not seeking work and have withdrawn *involuntarily* from the labour market, because they perceive that there is no work available for them or believe that, based upon personal past experiences, the market is not open to competition by them, for whatever reason. Evidence presented above suggests that 14 per cent of the general population can be classified as disabled (or, on a less conservative estimate, 22 per cent of adults of working age) and that as many as 42 per cent of disabled adults are of working age. Disabled persons represent approximately 4–6 per cent of the economically active adult population.

The OPCS surveys compared the working status of disabled adults with that for the general population.[50] Overall, only a minority of disabled adults are working and this compares unfavourably with the working status of adults in the general population. This disparity also widens with age and with the increasing severity of disability.[51] The OPCS studies also examined factors associated with whether or not disabled adults were in paid jobs and took a broader look at the employment status of disabled people.[52] Thirty-three per cent of men and 29 per cent of women were in paid employment, while 17 per cent of men and 11 per cent of women were unemployed. These figures superficially suggest that 31 per cent of disabled adults are in employment and between 10 and 15 per cent of disabled adults are unemployed.[53] However, these figures are based upon the conventional view of unemployment: being available for work and actively seeking work. Extrapolation from the data reveals that the true unemployment rates for economically active disabled men and women should be 27 and 20 per cent respectively.[54] Support for this analysis can be gleaned from the SCPR research. It found that 78 per cent of occupationally handicapped persons who were economically active were in work, while 22 per cent wanted to work.[55] By way of comparison, the contemporaneous 1987 *General Household Survey* showed that 77 per cent of people in the general population were in work and 15 per cent wanted work.[56]

Clearly, economic activity varies with severity of disability and with age.[57] It is also apparent that the economic activity of disabled persons, as for the general population, varies according to their socio-economic or occupational categorization and their educational or training qualifications.[58] The SCPR survey discovered that 46 per cent of the economically active, occupationally handicapped population had no formal educational qualifications, as compared with about 27 per cent of the general population.[59] Manual occupational status and low levels of qualifications tended to be associated with an increased incidence of disabled unemployment. Cross-tabulation of the OPCS survey results further demonstrated that the significant variables determining employment status of disabled persons were in rank order: severity of disability, age, occupational status, qualifications and gender. These rank-ordered factors also appear to explain the likelihood of disabled persons defining themselves as being permanently unable to work.[60]

The OPCS surveys found that 69 per cent of all disabled adults under state pension age were not working for whatever reason. Looking at this group of disabled adults, it was discovered that 73 per cent were not available for work and 27 per cent were available.[61] Some 46 per cent reported that it was impossible to do any paid work, 13 per cent did not want or need to work and 3 per cent were ill and unsure about the future. In contrast, 17 per cent had not found a suitable job, 5 per cent could do only sheltered work, 4 per cent could do only part-time work and 1 per cent were not working for some other reason. About half the disabled adults available for work were currently looking for work, but 12 per cent had stopped looking and 20 per cent had not looked at all because in their view there were no suitable jobs for someone with their disability. Ten per cent cited the general employment situation as the cause of their not looking for work and 9 per cent gave other reasons.[62] Among non-working disabled adults available for work, 78 per cent of men and 70 per cent of women thought that their disability had had some effect on the difficulty of them finding work. They were more likely to take that view if they had not looked for work or had stopped looking for work. In rank order of effect, disability was cited as affecting the type of work, working conditions, amount of work, journey to work, hours of work and attendance at work.[63]

Disability and Employment Status

As previously noted, 31 per cent of disabled adults under pensionable age were in paid employment: 14 per cent of disabled men and 10 per cent of disabled women in paid work were self-employed, and while 94 per cent of the men were in full-time work, 53 per cent of the women were in part-time work.[64] Looking at the socio-economic status of disabled persons in employment and comparing them with the general population of workers,[65] there is a close degree of congruence between the findings for the disabled working population and for the general population. The largest socio-economic group to which disabled respondents in work belonged was 'other white collar'. The SCPR survey shows that 30 per cent of respondents were so classified, compared with 33 per cent of the general population under the 1987 *General Household Survey*. It is noticeable, however, that disabled workers are more likely to be in manual occupations than their non-disabled colleagues. Among persons with a health problem with an occupational handicap, but who were in work, the SCPR survey found that 12 per cent were in professional or managerial occupations (compared with 21 per cent of the general population), 30 per cent were in other non-manual occupations (against 33 per cent), 26 per cent were classified as skilled manual (25 per cent), 25 per cent were semi-skilled workers or providing personal service (16 per cent) and 6 per cent were unskilled manual workers (5 per cent).[66]

Sub-analysis of the OPCS data unfortunately does not prove or show any meaningful relationship between socio-economic status and severity of disability. The hypothesis is that there might be a correlation between manual occupations and increasingly severe disability status, either because manual occupational groups tend to be associated with a greater incidence of ill health and disability or because a combination of disability and unemployment might force disabled workers further down the occupational hierarchy.[67] On the other hand, Martin *et al.* postulate that the more severe the disability, the less likely is it that the disabled worker will be able to fill a physically demanding manual position and the more likely he or she is to seek light office duties. Nevertheless, the majority of disabled workers themselves (68 per cent) thought that their disability had some effect upon their occupational status, in particular as regards the type of work they could do, followed by the amount of work they could do, the conditions in which they could work, their hours of work and their attendance at work. In general, for both disabled men and women, the likelihood of their disability having some effect upon their employment increased with the severity of disability.

Because the SCPR research was primarily concerned with the effects of disability upon employment, it goes a long way towards informing our understanding of the way in which health status or disability contributes to occupational handicap. Health and disability affect the chance of getting work or the type of work which can be done.[68] Clearly, physical limitations in undertaking manual work are most frequently recorded, and nearly 10 per cent of economically active, occupationally handicapped people report facing prejudice and ignorance among employers concerning disability. Among occupationally handicapped persons in work, 22 per cent admitted an incapacity to work a five-day 35–40-hour week, 12 per cent could not work a five-day week of any duration, while 20 per cent could not work a 7–8-hour day.[69] These percentages increase noticeably for those not in work but wanting to work or expecting to want work in the next year.

According to the *General Household Survey*, persons of working age in the general population experience an average of twenty-one days per year restriction of normal activities through illness or disability. In contrast, the SCPR survey found that about half the number of economically active, occupationally handicapped respondents took fewer than five days off per year for sickness or treatment, although 10 per cent took thirty days or more.[70] Some 28 per cent of respondents reported having to take regular breaks or rests during the working day because of their health or disability.[71] About three in every ten respondents recorded that they were unable to do some of the tasks that were normally part of their job and about the same number required some assistance in carrying out their job duties.[72] The need for special equipment or aids to do the job was mentioned by 8 per cent of respondents and a similar number indicated that they had special needs in gaining access to the workplace.[73] Health status or disability was also a factor affecting the quality of the work respondents felt able to obtain. Some 45 per cent thought that they could get a more skilled job but for their condition; 27 per cent thought that their chances of promotion were affected by disability.[74] Supporting the view that disability discrimination affects pay, 28 per cent believed that they were earning less than co-workers doing the same job.

Whatever their current occupational position, do disabled workers feel that their disabilities might be a disadvantage in moving jobs? Seventy-two per cent of men and 62 per cent of women thought that their disabilities would make it more difficult for them to change their employment in the future, especially as regards the type of work they could do and the conditions they could work in.[75] Once again, the severity of disability tends to influence the pessimism of response to this enquiry. Fifty-five per cent of disabled working adults opined that both their current job and their future employment prospects were adversely affected by disability, whereas only 19 per cent thought that neither would be affected.[76] Both severity of disability and occupational status influence this view. The less severe the disability and the higher the occupational status, the less likely would be the opinion that disability has an adverse effect upon present and future employment prospects.

Disability and Employment History[77]

The work histories of disabled persons may cast light upon their experience of discrimination or disadvantage. The SCPR survey found that 70 per cent of economically active but occupationally handicapped persons were in work when they first experienced the onset of ill health or disability (57 per cent remained in work now); 30 per cent were not in work at the onset of ill health or disability (25 per cent were in work now or had been in work since the onset, 3 per cent had worked prior to the onset but not since, and the remainder had never worked).[78]

> The 70% of respondents who were working at the time they first started to experience problems at work were almost equally divided between those whose problem occurred suddenly as a result of an illness (such as a heart attack), an accident or something similar (45%) and those for whom it had gradually become a problem (55%).[79]

The average length of work experience before the onset was fifteen years, and the average number of years worked in the job held at the time of onset was eight.[80] Occupationally handicapped employees in work are likely to be found in workplaces with under twenty workers (39 per cent) or fewer than 100 workers (66 per cent). However, the total size of the organization (rather than the individual workplace or site) is also a factor. Some 40 per cent of disabled workers in employment in the SCPR survey were to be found working in enterprises with a workforce of 1,000 or more employees, although 35 per cent were to be located in organizations of fewer than twenty staff.[81] The respondents indicated that their employer knew of their condition in 78 per cent of cases.

Nevertheless, in smaller organizations, it was much more likely that the onset of illness or disability would not be made known to the employer. This is obviously an important factor in whether or not the newly disabled worker retains his or her job after the onset of disability. Approximately one-third of employees were still working for their original employer, in an identical job (14 per cent), in the same job with accommodation (7 per cent) or in a different or changed job (10 per cent); the remaining 3 per cent had been off work continuously since the onset of the problem.[82] About 28 per cent had left the employer's employment for a non-health related reason and 37 per cent for a health related reason. Of this latter group, 9 per cent had been dismissed, 2 per cent pressurized into resigning and 10 per cent advised by their doctor to leave, 13 per cent had decided on their own to leave, 1 per cent took early retirement by mutual agreement and 2 per cent left for other reasons. The SCPR research shows that the chances of newly disabled employees being retained by the employer at onset of disability are in direct proportion to their length of service. Whereas only 15 per cent with under a year's service and 20 per cent with less than two years' service were retained, nearly half those with ten or more years' service were retained. The chances of being *dismissed* were also greater with less service.[83] The size of organization was also a factor in the record of being retained, with larger enterprises being more likely to try to keep the worker in employment.[84] Managerial or professional employees had a greater chance of being retained, while skilled or unskilled manual employees were least likely to be retained.[85] For those who were not retained, 23 per cent had not worked again and the remainder had taken an appreciable time to find fresh employment.[86]

Age and educational qualifications both play a part in obtaining work after the onset of disability. The older and less qualified the person, the more difficult gaining post-disability employment becomes.[87] The first job after onset of disability or after leaving the job in which the onset of disability occurred will be difficult to find. Nevertheless, in 61 per cent of cases, the newly disabled worker applied for only two or fewer jobs before re-employment. Only 9 per cent of cases required twenty or more applications before finding new work.[88] About a third of respondents got a new job in less than a month and over half had gained fresh positions in under two months.[89] Given disabled persons' natural suspicion that their disability will inform their employment opportunities, the SCPR research asked economically active, occupationally handicapped respondents whether they would declare their disability or health problem on an application form and whether they would disclose it at interview. About 60 per cent of respondents would declare their disability in an application form and only 30 per cent might not disclose their status at interview.[90]

Disability and Earned Income

There are three main ways in which disability may have financial consequences for disabled people and their families:

> First, disabled individuals may have lower incomes either because they are not able to earn as much as non-disabled people, or because they are unable to work and are therefore more likely to be dependent upon state benefits. A second consequence is that disabled people may incur extra expenditure as a result of disability resulting in less money being available to meet other needs. A third consequence may be that if help is needed from other members of the family this may affect the ability of those members to undertake paid work and thus to contribute to the family's income.[91]

Only a minority of disabled adults are in employment and receive earned income but, with the exception of the gross weekly earnings of female non-manual disabled employees and the average hourly pay of female manual and non-manual employees, there are significant differences between the earnings of disabled and non-disabled employees.[92] From comparison of hourly rates of pay, it is clear that even when patterns of working time are accounted for, disabled workers are disadvantaged.

The SCPR survey also uncovered some interesting findings on the income of occupationally handicapped persons.[93] Based upon full-time and part-time work, 60 per cent had gross weekly incomes of £100 or more, while 65 per cent would exceed this figure if earnings from partners' jobs and income from other sources were to be included. Comparing these findings with the 1989 *New Earnings Survey*,[94] whereas the median income group in the SCPR survey was £150–199 per week, the *New Earnings Survey* of the general population produced a median income group of £200–249.[95]

The differences in earnings cannot be simply explained away by the fact that disabled adults might work fewer hours than non-disabled workers. One possible explanation is that

> It would therefore appear that, within the broad categories of non-manual and manual employment, disabled men are to be found in the less well-paid jobs.
>
> The nature and severity of the disability may constrain the type of work it is possible for disabled adults to do, even among those working full-time, but other factors may also

> explain the lower earnings of disabled men . . . [We] have already seen that disabled adults of working age are on average much older than the general population, which may have implications for the type of work they do and their earnings. Another possibility is that people in lower paid occupations are more likely than others to become disabled.[96]

The researchers also speculate that the lower earnings of the least severely disabled employees are a product of shorter working hours and that the most severely disabled are in addition most likely to be found in lower paid jobs.

DISABILITY AND EMPLOYMENT DISCRIMINATION

The statistical data undoubtedly present a depressing portrait of the disabled unemployment rate, employment prospects and status, and inequality of earnings.[97] There is evidence that some of this canvas can be coloured by the direct effects of the limitations of disabling conditions. However, it is suggested that this is not a complete depiction of the experience of disability and employment. Weiss identified a number of problems faced by disabled workers in attempting to enter employment.[98] First, they must surmount physical and vocational obstacles during rehabilitation and training. Second, disabled persons must overcome the barriers presented in architectural designs and transportation systems. Third, they will encounter resistance by employers to hiring persons with disabilities. Fourth, disabled job-seekers experience self-doubt as a product of previous prejudice. Fifth, they must master the tests created by inflexible medical examinations, which many employers use without questioning their value and utility. In short, it is contended that disability-informed discrimination in many guises plays an important hand in affairs.

Nature of Disability Discrimination in Employment

Borrowing from Posner's economic analysis of sex discrimination laws, it might be possible to attempt some explanation or postulation of discrimination against disabled persons.[99] First, there may be an element of distaste for association with disabled persons, equivalent to the misogynist's distaste for women. It may be born of a fear or mistrust of disabled people, perhaps informed by images of the discriminator's own possible future, disabled by old age or disease or accident. Alternatively, it may be purely a question of aesthetics, based upon a judgment of what is normal and attractive, and predicated upon a desire to associate only with those who match the discriminator's view of what is appreciable. Second, disability discrimination may be based upon exploitation by the 'fit' of the 'unfit' or by the 'strong' of the 'weak'. Stereotypically and erroneously, disabled persons have too often been regarded as passive individuals, who have come to terms with their compromised station in life, and who will be willing to accept further compromises in their status without demur. This may provide self-justifying and reinforcing evidence for a discriminator's view that disabled persons may be exploited or treated unfavourably without a risk of complaint. Third, disability discrimination may be simply based upon ignorance of disabled persons' abilities and capacities. The discriminator is misinformed about what disabled workers can or cannot do and allows that misinformation to inform employment decisions. Fourth, even if employers are well-informed and have no discriminatory impulses,

> it may be rational for employers to discriminate against [disabled persons] because of the information costs of distinguishing a particular [disabled] employee from the average [disabled] employee.[100]

This is statistical discrimination. Fifth, the discriminator may be merely a conduit of third party discrimination. That is to say, the discriminator is merely reflecting the tastes of co-workers, other employers and customers, whose own predisposition towards disabled persons may be informed by the factors already discussed immediately above.

A crucial cause of disabled unemployment is employer attitudes and stereotyped prejudices. Discrimination against disabled persons often takes the form of prejudice. Prejudice is manifested in attitudes that distort social relationships by over-emphasis upon the characteristic of disability.[101] Prejudice feeds the stereotypical, stigmatized view of disabled persons, exaggerates the negative connotations of impairment and excludes or devalues other measures of social worth or attributes. The view of disabled persons as lesser individuals poisons their chances of full participation in employment opportunities. The assumption is that *disability* means *inability* and consequently many jobs are assumed to be beyond the capacity of disabled workers. The literature suggests that prejudice against disabled persons increases with the nature and severity of disabilities, while prejudice is strongest in respect of sensory impairments, mental disabilities, disfigurement or deformity and visible imperfections. The intensity of disability prejudice among employers is also seemingly greater than negative attitudes towards elderly persons, ethnic minorities, criminal offenders and political radicals.[102] For instance, one study suggested that personnel directors would prefer to engage former prisoners or mental hospital patients than they would an epileptic.[103]

Employers tend to justify such resistance by reference to supposed reduced productivity, unsatisfactory performance, safety problems, insurance costs and the attitudes of co-workers.[104] This is despite evidence that disabled workers' performance emulates that of their able-bodied peers.[105] For example, one study found that disabled workers had a slightly higher productivity rate and fewer disabling injuries than non-disabled workers.[106] In this study, however, disabled workers experienced slightly higher rates of absenteeism[107] and a higher rate of turnover.[108] A more recent US study found that employers rated disabled workers' performance as being average or above average when compared with that of non-disabled colleagues, and that, the more employers hired disabled applicants, the more positive their attitude towards them became.[109] Furthermore, the fear that hiring disabled workers will increase employers' liability insurance rates is not necessarily borne out, either by insurance underwriting practices or by the excellent safety record of disabled workers.[110] In the face of evidence to the contrary, however, many employers still seek to justify disability discrimination by an unfounded belief that disabled workers have a poor safety record or will cause an increase in the employer's insurance premia.[111]

In research published in 1990, Morrell solicited British employers' accounts of their experience regarding disabled persons.[112] She found that, among employers employing disabled workers, one in ten rated their level of performance as better than that of other employees, while seven in ten thought that of such workers to be comparable with that of other employees. Seventy-three per cent of employers reported that disabled employees' attendance records were about the same as or better than those of their non-disabled workers, although nearly a quarter thought that their disabled personnel took more time off than their comparators. A large majority of employers reported their perception of the attitudes of line management as being very or fairly willing to have disabled workers as part of the team (85 per cent) and the attitude of co-workers as very or fairly positive towards disabled workers (93 per cent). As many as 40 per cent of employers believed that there were no problems facing them in employing disabled persons. However, when prompted, 91 per cent of employers perceived a number of problems.[113] The unsuitability of available jobs, problems with the suitability of the workplace premises and lack of disabled applicants were the problems most frequently mentioned, although other problems anticipated included problems of getting to work (because the workplace was inaccessible) and shift working.

Disabled people may also be the victims of statistical discrimination. Johnson cites evidence to suggest that employers offer minority workers poorer employment opportunities because of a belief that they are on average less productive than majority workers. This is reinforced by employers' use of pre-employment test scores, which may be inadequate proxies for measuring productivity. In particular, Johnson asserts that

> Test scores are biased when an impairment limits test-taking skills but does not limit performance on the job for which the test is required . . . Some firms flag test results for impaired persons or waive the test requirements for their employment. Unfortunately, both solutions increase the subjectivity of the hiring decision.[114]

In the absence of objective testing methods, it is thus tempting for employers to stereotype all disabled workers as non-productive or of limited productivity, and to regard them suspiciously as a source of increased costs.[115] In addition, persons with disabilities face structural discrimination or discrimination through the erection of barriers in the social and physical environment.[116] Without accommodation of disability, disabled persons are unable to participate in many aspects of society and employment.

Evidence of Disability Discrimination

In the USA, the evidence of discrimination against disabled persons is well documented.[117] In some cases, disabled Americans also appear to experience dual discrimination because of the combination of race or gender with disability.[118] The Louis Harris studies discovered that 66 per cent of disabled persons who are not working would like to work, but that 25 per cent of disabled persons of working age reported incidents of employment discrimination.[119] Approximately one-half of those not in full-time employment felt that employers failed to recognize their capability for full-time work, while a similar proportion believed that discrimination contributed to their employment status.[120] The surveys also provided evidence that 75 per cent of employers and managers support that belief, and evidence to underpin the contrary view of many employers to the effect that increasing the employability of disabled persons is good for business.[121] Nevertheless, other reasons for the poor employment status of persons with disabilities were also offered, including unavailability of suitable positions, inability to find any jobs, lack of educational qualification, transportation problems and lack of auxiliary aids or equipment.[122] Of those in work, their disability, rather than employers' attitudes, was a barrier 77 per cent of those looking for work or unable to work.[123]

In Britain, much of the evidence concerning employment discrimination against disabled people has been anecdotal or illustrative rather than empirical and systematic. This has allowed government to deny that the employment disadvantage of disabled persons is caused by discrimination:

> Discrimination may occur on occasion – perhaps particularly where the person is mentally handicapped – but there is little evidence to suggest that unemployed disabled people generally fail to get jobs because of discrimination against them.[124]

The Department of Employment has preferred the view that many disabled persons would find it hard to gain employment because of their age, lack of education or skill, or some other social disadvantage, regardless of impairment or disability.[125] Nevertheless, during the late 1970s and early 1980s, separate inquiries undertaken by the Working Party on Integration of the Disabled and by the Committee on Restrictions against Disabled People began to establish more formal records of systematic and institutional discrimination against disabled people.[126] Other social research pointed to negative attitudes and discrimination faced by people with particular disabilities.[127]

However, two pieces of research undertaken by Scope provided methodologically sound evidence of disability discrimination in employment practices.[128] In the first study, 97 per cent of able-bodied applicants for employment received positive responses from employers, but only 59 per cent of disabled applicants.[129] In short, a non-disabled application was 1.6 times more likely to receive a positive response than an application from a disabled person. In one case, the employer's reply to the disabled applicant made indirect comments to suggest that disability had informed the employment decision:

> In this case the employer, without actually mentioning the disability, wrote that they could not consider employing her until they moved to less cramped and difficult offices in two to three months time. This was, of course, without having found out any details of the disability first.[130]

In the usual case, no reply at all was received or, at best, a standard letter of rejection which offered no reasons for the decision. Fry continues:

> Occasionally however, employers [sic] replies to the disabled candidate were more disingenuous. Two employers claimed that the disabled candidate's qualifications and experience were not what was required, while asking the able-bodied candidate with similar qualifications and experience for an interview. Another excuse given was that the position had already been filled, even though the able-bodied candidate was, at the same time, invited to an interview. One employer informed the disabled candidate that the temporary secretary who had been working with them had decided to stay. The able-bodied candidate had already been offered an interview.

These are scenarios which are readily recognizable from the experience of ethnic minorities in the labour market.

Scope repeated the research in a second study at a time when unemployment was falling and the demand for skilled labour was relatively high.[131] Using methodology, it was found that 94 per cent of able-bodied applications received positive responses, but only 61 per cent of disabled applications. In short, an able-bodied applicant was 1.5 times more likely to receive a positive response than an application from a disabled person. The similarity in the outcomes of the two studies is marked.[132] Again it was clear that many employers had based the decision to reject the disabled applicant upon 'unfounded assumptions about disability'.[133] In rejection letters and, more insidiously, in letters classified as positive responses, employers erected hurdles in the way of the disabled applicant or made assumptions about her disability which were unsupported by evidence or contrary to the facts stated in the application letter. Graham, Jordan and Lamb quote the following examples:

> It is frequently necessary for all staff to travel between the subsidiary companies using a company vehicle, attend meetings and conferences and generally be available to assist in a wide range of duties, many of which may require a degree of physical ability.[134]

And, in another reply:

> due to your disability I feel I should bring to your attention the fact that there are steps up to the building and in addition our offices are situated over three floors. A lift serves the ground and subsequent floors but not lower ground floor which is where the successful applicant will be required to work . . . *if you feel you can cope with this, please contact us.*[135]

As before, the disabled applicant would be rejected on grounds of experience, qualifications or work history, but the able-bodied applicant with an equivalent *curriculum vitae* would be permitted to proceed further into the selection process. There was a marked unwillingness to afford the disabled applicant an opportunity to show her worth or to dispel doubts at an interview. There was also evidence of the two applications being handled differently: for example, by requesting further information or requiring a *pro forma* application from the disabled applicant but not from her counterpart.[136]

An important difference between the 1986 survey and the 1990 survey was that the latter study presented evidence on the type and size of employer who discriminates. Seventy per cent of the recorded cases of disability-based discrimination were in small to medium-sized firms (up to 250 employees), but equally the small number of cases where the disabled applicant had been preferred over the able-bodied candidate were predominantly in small businesses. The industrial sectors found to produce most cases of discrimination were (in rank order): estate agency, hotel and catering, public administration, marketing, publishing, finance and entertainment.

CONCLUSION

The survey research demonstrates that disabled people or persons with health problems constitute a sizeable minority group in British society. It is estimated that approximately 6–7 million disabled adults are resident in Britain and constitute about 14–22 per cent of the general population. Between 4 and 6 per cent of the economically active population or adults of working age are classifiable as disabled. Furthermore, both the prevalence and degree of disabilities increase with age, while women represent a marginally larger proportion of the disabled population than men, at least during the main years of working capacity. The general direction of these findings appears to be in line with comparative studies elsewhere. This chapter has sought to make a connection between disability, employment status and discrimination. The evidence suggests that disabled people suffer an unemployment rate 2–3 times that of the general population and the length of disabled unemployment is likely to be greater than that for the unemployed in general. Many disabled people have withdrawn from the labour market and so are not truly economically active, although a good proportion of these are discouraged workers. Many others seek employment, but without much success or optimism. For those persons with disabilities who are in work, the picture is not necessarily rosier, as disability tends to inform occupational status and there is a consequent over-representation of disabled workers in the lower reaches of the occupational hierarchy. The ill effect of disability upon earned income is also manifest. For those who become disabled while in post, employment security is not an automatic expectation.

While there is much evidence to link disability with unemployment and impoverished employment prospects, the statistics do not prove one way or another the influence of disability-informed discrimination upon disabled employment opportunities. Indeed, disabled people themselves frequently cite their self-perceived limitations and lack of full capacity as a greater cause of their employment position than employers' attitudes or prejudice. Nevertheless, the data do raise an inference that disabled persons do not enjoy fair treatment in the labour market and this is now borne out by empirical research that suggests that employers may be acting unfavourably towards disabled job applicants and pre-judging their capabilities. The case for protective legislation to safeguard and to realize the employment expectations of disabled persons is arguably made out.

NOTES

1. Burgdorf and Burgdorf, 1975.

2. Oliver, 1985; Thompson *et al.*, 1990; Barnes, 1991; Barnes, 1992; Massie, 1994; Gooding, 1994; Liberty, 1994.

3. Lyth, 1973; Walker, 1982. The evidence to rebut ignorance and fears about employing disabled persons is plentiful. See, for example: Stevens, 1986.

4. See generally: DeJong, 1979; Scotch, 1984, 1987, 1989. The American disability rights movement in turn was inspired by the struggles of African-Americans for civil rights in the 1960s and consciously adopted many of the strategies and examples of that episode: Kriegel, 1969; Burgdorf, 1991: 427–9.

5. See, for example, Rehabilitation International's *Charter for the 80s*, whose aims include ensuring the fullest possible integration of and equal participation by disabled people in all aspects of community life: Rehabilitation International, 1981. See also the seven basic human rights to education, employment, economic security, services, independent living, culture and recreation, and political influence identified by the Disabled People's International as essential for the integration and social participation of disabled individuals: Disabled People's International, 1981; Driedger, 1989.

6. Oliver 1990; Finkelstein, 1991; Oliver and Barnes, 1991; Barnes, 1992; Shakespeare, 1993.

7. Barnes, 1992: 18.

8. Berkowitz and Hill, 1986b: 1. See also: Haveman *et al.*, 1984; Habeck *et al.*, 1985; Berkowitz and Hill, 1986a. Note also the arguments of Kavka, 1992.

9. ILO, 1923.

10. Bolderson, 1991: 45.

11. ILO Vocational Rehabilitation and Employment (Disabled Persons) Convention No. 159 and ILO Vocational Rehabilitation and Employment (Disabled Persons) Recommendation No. 168 of 1983. See also ILO Vocational Rehabilitation (Disabled) Recommendation No. 99 of 1955, which states that disabled persons should be afforded an equal opportunity to perform work for which they are qualified and to accept suitable work with employers of their choice. The Recommendation also emphasizes the abilities and work capacities of disabled persons rather than disabilities.

12. *Declaration on the Rights of Disabled Persons*, General Assembly Resolution 3447 (XXX) adopted 9 December 1975. See also UN Standard Rules on the Equalization of Opportunities for Persons with Disabilities (A/RES/48/96:20 December 1993).

13. Council Recommendation No. 86/376/EEC of 24 July 1986 on the Employment of Disabled People in the Community: OJ No. L225/43 12 August 1986.

14. Community Charter of the Fundamental Social Rights of Workers adopted by the heads of state or government of eleven members states of the EC meeting at Strasbourg on 9 December 1989.

15. The Protocol on Social Policy was part of the European Union Treaty signed at Maastricht in February 1992. Britain is not a signatory to either the Charter or the Protocol.

16. *The Oxford English Dictionary* (2nd edn, 1989. Oxford: Clarendon Press) Vol. VI at 1073. Some commentators have suggested that this phrase became corrupted as 'cap in hand' and thus the term 'handicap' became associated with begging: Barnes, 1991: 2.

17. *Ibid.* at 1074.

18. Burgdorf, 1980b: 3–4.

19. WHO, 1980.

20. Acton, 1981: 2.

21. Burgdorf, 1980b: 10 (emphasis in the original).

22. See the interesting findings of Krauss *et al.*, 1993.
23. For a review of the tensions between the medical model and the social theory of disability, see: Sullivan, 1991.
24. See, for example, the multiplicity of terms used to describe disabilities and disabled persons unearthed by Burgdorf, 1980b: 1–4.
25. Burgdorf (1980b: 5) has argued that the phrase 'handicapped person' is preferable. The word 'disabled' implies an inability to do something, whereas 'handicap' more accurately reflects the social construction of disability. Cf. West, 1991b: 13–15.
26. Research Surveys of Great Britain Ltd, 1978: Table 3.1.
27. Nagi, 1965, 1969a, b, 1991; LaPlante, 1991: 58.
28. Weiss, 1974: 457.
29. Berkowitz and Hill, 1986b: 1 and 4 (emphasis in the original), following Nagi, 1969a; Haber, 1985.
30. *Ibid.*: 6.
31. *Ibid.*: 6.
32. UN, 1990b.
33. More detailed analysis of the demography of disability may be found in Doyle, 1993b: 29–38.
34. Martin *et al.*, 1988, 1989; Martin and White, 1988. The OPCS surveys are subjected to critical analysis by Berthoud *et al.*, 1993.
35. Martin *et al.*, 1988: xi and 9. The severity of disability was measured by self-assessment on a scale of 1–10 in ten main areas of disability: locomotion, reaching and stretching, dexterity, seeing, hearing, personal care, continence, communication, behaviour and intellectual functioning.
36. Prescott-Clarke, 1990. Seventy-three per cent of economically active, occupationally handicapped respondents in the SCPR survey fulfilled the OPCS 'disabled' criteria: Prescott-Clarke, 1990: 44.
37. Martin *et al.*, 1988: Table 3.1.
38. *Ibid.*: 18.
39. Martin *et al.*, 1989: 1 and Table 2.1.
40. Martin *et al.*, 1988: 27 and Table 3.3.
41. *Ibid.*: 21–2. The OPCS surveys did not discover significant differences in the prevalence of disability among different ethnic groups.
42. Prescott-Clarke, 1990: 20.
43. *Ibid.*: Table 4.2.
44. *Ibid.*: 20. A further 0.3 per cent expected to become economically active within a year.
45. *Ibid.*: Table 4.1.
46. Both surveys also produce fascinating evidence of the types and frequency of disabilities in the general population. See Doyle, 1993b: 38–41.
47. See, for example: Sainsbury, 1970, 1973; Harris *et al.*, 1971; Buckle, 1971; Townsend, 1979.
48. Martin *et al.*, 1988: 20–1.
49. The evidence of the OPCS, SCPR and GHS surveys in Britain is supported by comparative data on the prevalence of disability and the disabled population in Australia, Canada, the European Union and the United States. The comparative evidence is explored in Doyle, 1993b: 36–8.
50. Martin and White, 1988: Table 2.15.
51. *Ibid.*: 13–14.
52. Martin *et al.*, 1989: Table 7.1.
53. The 1989 *Labour Force Survey* suggested that 21 per cent of disabled adults were unemployed, compared with 5 per cent of the general population (evidence cited in House of Commons Employment Committee, 1990a: para. 7). The Winter 1992–3 *Labour Force Survey* records that 38 per cent of working age people with a health problem or disability limiting employment were in employment: *Employment Gazette* Vol. 101, No. 8 at 434 (September 1993). Research carried out in 1982–3 estimated that 21 per cent of the unemployed in the general population were disabled (5 per cent who had registered as disabled and 16 per cent unregistered): Parker, 1983.

54. Martin *et al.*, 1989: 74. See also Moreton, 1992: 75. Although 34 per cent of all disabled adults are recorded as permanently unable to work, this does not take account of part-time or sheltered employment opportunities.
55. Prescott-Clarke, 1990: Table 5.1.
56. *General Household Survey* 1987 (1989. London: HMSO) cited in Prescott-Clarke, 1990: 31–2.
57. Martin *et al.*, 1989: 69–71.
58. *Ibid.*: Tables 7.5 and 7.6.
59. Prescott-Clarke, 1990: 36 and Table 5.8.
60. Martin *et al.*, 1989: 72–3.
61. *Ibid.*: Table 7.10.
62. *Ibid.*: Table 7.14.
63. *Ibid.*: 80.
64. *Ibid.*: 80. This compares with 43 per cent of women in the general population: *General Household Survey* 1985. In the SCPR study, among occupationally handicapped respondents in work, 85 per cent were employees and the remainder were self-employed: Prescott-Clarke, 1990: Table 10.22. This is in line with the 1986 Labour Force Survey statistics of 88 and 12 per cent respectively. About three-quarters were in full-time employment (over 30 hours per week), again in line with the general population.
65. Martin *et al.*, 1989: Table 7.20.
66. Prescott-Clarke, 1990: Tables 5.4 and 5.5 and 10.22. Prescott-Clarke (1990: 35) analyses these data and finds that there is a heavy concentration of occupationally handicapped women in clerical work and the service sector.
67. Martin *et al.*, 1989: 82.
68. Prescott-Clarke, 1990: Table 7.1.
69. *Ibid.*: Table 7.2.
70. *Ibid.*: Table 7.4.
71. *Ibid.*: Table 7.5.
72. *Ibid.*: Table 7.6.
73. *Ibid.*: Table 7.7.
74. *Ibid.*: Table 7.8.
75. Martin *et al.*, 1989: Tables 7.24 and 7.25.
76. *Ibid.*: Table 7.26.
77. For a comparative perspective, see Doyle 1993b: 64–6.
78. Prescott-Clarke, 1990: Table 10.1.
79. *Ibid.*: 97.
80. *Ibid.*: 92.
81. *Ibid.*: Table 10.23.
82. *Ibid.*: Table 10.8.
83. *Ibid.*: Table 10.9.
84. *Ibid.*: Table 10.10.
85. *Ibid.*: Table 10.11.
86. *Ibid.*: 104.
87. *Ibid.*: 105–7.
88. Extrapolation from *ibid.*: Table 10.16.
89. *Ibid.*: Table 10.17.
90. *Ibid.*: 112–3.
91. Martin and White, 1988: 1.
92. *Ibid.*: Table 3.1.
93. Prescott-Clarke, 1990: Table 9.1.
94. *New Earnings Survey* 1989 (1989. London: HMSO).
95. Prescott-Clarke, 1990: 86–8.
96. Martin and White, 1988: 17.
97. Evidence of discrimination and disadvantage suffered by disabled persons in other social spheres and activities is considered in Doyle, 1993b: 41–6.
98. Weiss, 1974: 458.
99. Posner, 1989: 1318–21.

100. *Ibid.*: 1320.
101. West, 1991b; US Commission on Civil Rights, 1983.
102. Yuker *et al.*, 1966; Bowe, 1978; Hahn, 1983.
103. Rickard *et al.*, 1963; Rickard *et al.*, 1977.
104. US Bureau of Labor Standards, 1961; *Hearings on HR 8395 Before the Subcommittee on the Handicapped of the Senate Committee on Labor and Public Welfare*, (1972) 92nd Congress, 2nd Session, 265; and further studies cited in Weiss, 1974: 458.
105. US Bureau of Labor Standards, 1961; Louis Harris and Associates, 1987: 7; National Council on the Handicapped, 1988: 15; US Commission on Civil Rights, 1983: 32.
106. US Department of Labor, 1948.
107. 3.8 days per 100 work days as opposed to 3.4 for non-disabled workers.
108. 3.6 per 100 employees compared to 2.6 per 100 non-disabled employees.
109. Zadny, 1979.
110. Evidence cited in *Georgetown Law Journal*, 1973: 1513 suggests that disabled workers have 8 per cent fewer accidents than their co-workers.
111. See for example: Flaccus, 1986b: 262–3.
112. Morrell, 1990: 13–15.
113. *Ibid.*: Table 20.
114. Johnson, 1986b: 246.
115. Schroedel and Jacobsen, 1978.
116. Rebell, 1986.
117. See, for example: Livneh, 1982; US Commission on Civil Rights, 1983.
118. Burkhauser *et al.*, 1990.
119. Louis Harris and Associates, 1986: 75 and Table 34.
120. *Ibid.*: 70 and Table 32.
121. Louis Harris and Associates, 1987: 12.
122. LaPlante (1991: 71) comments that 'most persons with activity limitation felt it was the limitation rather than employer's attitudes that prevent them from getting the type of job they desired'.
123. Louis Harris and Associates, 1987: Table 37.
124. Department of Employment, 1973: para. 40.
125. See also: Manpower Services Commission, 1979: para. 21.
126. Snowdon, 1976, 1979; Large, 1982.
127. See, by way of illustration: Bunting, 1981; British Deaf Association, 1984; Whaley *et al.*, 1986; Banking, Insurance and Finance Union, 1987; Royal National Institute for the Deaf, 1987. More recent research found that about 40 per cent of employers surveyed regarded disabled persons as unsuitable employees, a view that was most prevalent among employers with no experience of employing disabled workers: *IRS Employment Trends* No. 517 (August 1992) at 13–14; Honey *et al.*, 1993.
128. Fry, 1986; Graham *et al.*, 1990. There is also evidence that disabled persons are discriminated against in training provision by Training and Enterprise Councils: Smith, 1992a.
129. Fry, 1986: 9.
130. *Ibid.*: 14.
131. Graham *et al.*, 1990: 2.
132. Research conducted among French employers in 1989 found that highly qualified able-bodied applicants were 1.78 times more likely to receive a favourable response than their disabled counterparts, and modestly qualified able-bodied applicants were 3.2 times more likely to receive a positive response. The incidence of disability discrimination increased with company size. See: Ravaud et al., 1992. In contrast, further analysis by J. Smith (1992) suggests that disabled persons are six times more likely to be denied a job interview than are non-disabled applicants.
133. Graham *et al.*, 1990: 5.
134. *Ibid.*: 5.
135. *Ibid.*: 5 (emphasis added).
136. *Ibid.*: 6.

2

Disabled Employment Rights in Britain[1]

INTRODUCTION: TOMLINSON PRINCIPLES

Disability discrimination in employment has not been addressed in direct terms by British labour law. Post-war employment policy towards disabled people has been informed by the guiding principles enunciated by the Interdepartmental Committee on the Rehabilitation and Resettlement of Disabled Persons (the Tomlinson Committee).[2] The Tomlinson Committee recognized that 'disabled persons, given the opportunity, are capable of normal employment', and articulated 'the need for a strategy to secure for the disabled their full share, within their capacity, of such employment as is ordinarily available'.[3] This principle subsequently has been pursued primarily through measures promoting rehabilitation, retraining and job placement services for disabled people. Although these measures have had some impact on the employment prospects of disabled people, they appear as mere palliatives to the problems of disability disadvantage and may even add to the marginalization of disabled people.

In Britain, post-war employment policy has conceded to persons with disabilities only a limited recognition of a right to work. The report of the Interdepartmental Committee, although with the war disabled chiefly in mind, acknowledged that the exclusion of disabled persons from the labour force reduced productive capacity and increased social costs. Disabled persons were seen to have a justifiable claim to competitive employment rights and, given the opportunity, to be capable of normal working lives without institutional or sheltered protection.[4] Measures to promote opportunity and negate prejudice were essential, but the creation of employment for disabled workers and the extension of preference to them without regard to individual ability and production efficiency were ruled out. The Tomlinson Committee recommended the creation of a register of those handicapped in employment by disability, the reservation of certain occupations for such persons, the imposition of a disabled employment quota upon employers, a framework for vocational rehabilitation, training and resettlement services, and obligatory provisions for sheltered employment.[5] These recommendations formed the substance of the Disabled Persons (Employment) Act which was enacted in 1944,[6] although the Committee had originally envisaged that compliance with the disabled employment quota would be an employer's duty in the national interest, rather than a statutory obligation.[7]

When, a decade later, a second committee examined developments since 1944, the system was found to be sound and without need of radical change.[8] Only minor changes were effected by the DP(E)A 1958. Although the last quarter of the century has witnessed changes in the aspirations of disabled people themselves, subsequent official reviews of employment services for disabled people have rarely questioned the Tomlinson philosophy.[9] Most recently, the National Advisory Council on the Employment of Disabled People, established under the DP(E)A 1944, reviewed the Tomlinson principles. It found basic continuity in the approach to disabled employment provision and endorsed the justification for helping disabled people in the employment field.[10] The Council reiterated the fundamental principle that

> access of disabled people to training and to jobs and their development within organisations should be based on their capacities as individuals, properly and fairly assessed . . . [and that] disabled people for whom special employment provision has been arranged should enjoy the same employment rights as other workers.[11]

It recognized that there was a strong case for saying that 'legislation properly designed and applied is an essential tool, particularly when supported by persuasive action, for helping the employment prospects of disabled people'.[12]

Nevertheless, a contemporary change in emphasis in disabled employment policy away from the statutory quota scheme and towards the promotion of voluntary equal opportunity practices is illustrated by more recent developments. A previous review of the statutory quota scheme suggested that the quota should be replaced by a general statutory duty, linked to a code of practice, requiring employers to promote the employment of disabled people.[13] Although this idea was supported in some quarters, it did not attract political support.[14] A code of good practice was subsequently produced,[15] but without the statutory framework of the original proposal the code is deprived of legal status and is devoid of sanctions to underpin it. The future of the quota scheme remains under threat, nevertheless, and this is a theme which will be returned to in Chapter 10; first it will be necessary to set out the detailed provisions of the post-war legislation itself.

DISABLED PERSONS (EMPLOYMENT) ACT 1944

The employment rights of disabled workers have been considered at first hand in three respects: the statutory quota scheme, the legal requirement for corporate disability policy statements and the promotion of voluntary good practice. The DP(E)A 1944 provides a basic, although not universal, definition of 'disabled person' registrable under the Act. Employers are obliged to employ a quota of registered disabled persons, subject to exemption by permit, and to keep records of compliance. The Act also designates certain occupations as reserved for registered disabled persons. The 1944 Act further restricts the ability of employers to dismiss registered disabled employees, who also enjoy equal employment protection rights under general employment law. In particular, the unfair dismissal and redundancy rights of the Employment Protection (Consolidation) Act 1978 will be relevant.

Definition of Disability

The terms 'disabled person' and 'disablement' are instrumental in the operation of disabled employment measures. The cognate expressions 'disabled' and 'disability' have been the source of much categorization and confusion in social security law. In the context of employment law, however, the key concept is that of 'disabled person' within the meaning of section 1 of the DP(E)A 1944. A disabled person is defined there as someone who is substantially handicapped in obtaining or keeping employment because of injury, disease or congenital deformity. Disease includes a physical or mental condition arising from imperfect development of any organ.[16] An individual is also qualified as a disabled person if handicapped in undertaking work on his or her own account by reason of these causes. The employment or work in question must be of a kind which, apart from the injury, disease or deformity, would be suited to that person's age, experience and qualifications.

This broad definition of 'disabled person' embraces congenital disabilities, industrial or war injuries, accidental injuries at large and diseases or deformities (whether occupationally related or not). Suffering a loss or abnormality of a psychological, physiological or anatomical structure or function, or experiencing a restricted or reduced range of performable activities because of impairment, are necessary but insufficient criteria of the definition. The individual must be handicapped or disadvantaged in employment as a result of the impairment or disability. Furthermore, apart from the impairment or disability, the disabled person must be otherwise qualified for employment. Employment handicap must be the result of impairment or disability alone and not simply because the individual lacks the necessary training, educational qualifications or personal qualities for particular employment.

Register of Disabled Persons

An individual who satisfies the primary definition of disabled person may register under the 1944 Act as a 'person registered as handicapped by disablement'.[17] In certain cases, only registered disabled persons qualify for *certain* employment assistance and services offered by the state. Employers' obligations under the statutory quota scheme and in respect of designated employment are also imposed only in respect of registered disabled persons. A register of disabled persons is maintained by the Department of Employment.[18] An individual who satisfies the definition of disabled person may apply to be entered upon the register, provided that the disablement is likely to last for at least 12 months.[19] The applicant must also have attained the school leaving age, desire to engage in remunerative work, have a reasonable prospect of obtaining and keeping such work, and be ordinarily resident in Great Britain (unless a serviceman or merchant seaman).[20] A registered disabled person is issued with a certificate of registration, known as a 'Green Card', production of which an employer or prospective employer subject to the 1944 Act may demand.

The Disabled Persons (Registration) Regulations 1945 contain a number of grounds upon which a person may be disqualified from attaining or retaining the status of a registered disabled person.[21] Prisoners are disqualified, as are whole-time hospital patients who are unable to undertake vocational training or work. A person of habitual bad character may also be denied registration. A refusal without reasonable cause to attend or to complete vocational training, if so required, can result in the disabled person being removed from the register. A persistent refusal without reasonable cause to undertake suitable work can also result in de-registration. The duration for which a disabled person's name shall remain on the register will be determined at the time of registration.[22] A person who ceases to satisfy the conditions for registration or who otherwise comes under a disqualification may be removed from the register.[23] Once he or she is in employment, however, a registered disabled person's registration will not terminate as long as he or she retains employment with that employer. Otherwise, a registered disabled person may apply to have his or her name removed from the register at any time.[24] There is no right of appeal from a refusal to register or a decision to de-register.

Statutory Quota Scheme

Employers of a 'substantial number' of employees are under a duty to employ a quota of 'persons registered as handicapped by disablement' and to allocate vacancies for that purpose when they occur.[25] The duty is subject to some misunderstanding. Employers to whom the quota scheme applies are not in breach of duty simply by failing to maintain the quota of disabled persons in their employment. They are under no obligation to dismiss able-bodied employees and replace them with disabled persons. However, such employers shall not take, or offer to take, into employment any person other than a registered disabled person if, immediately after employing such other person, the number of registered disabled persons in their employment would be less than the specified quota.[26] The legal validity of any such engagement is not affected, but contravention of this provision is a criminal offence punishable by a fine and/or imprisonment.[27] Employers are not prevented from employing or re-employing any person if under a statutory duty to do so: for example, a reinstatement or re-engagement order made under the unfair dismissal provisions.[28] Moreover, the statutory duty does not apply to employers possessing exemption permits issued under the Act.[29] Similarly, there is no breach of duty where a transferee of a business takes into employment non-disabled employees employed by the transferor immediately before a transfer.[30]

The 1944 Act also regulates the dismissal of registered disabled persons.[31] Employers subject to the statutory quota obligations may not dismiss a registered disabled person without reasonable cause if, as a result of that dismissal, the number of registered disabled persons employed by them would be less than the specified quota. There is no minimum service qualification for protection under this enactment. Although the dismissal remains legally valid, the employer commits a criminal offence.[32] It cannot be assumed automatically that an unlawful dismissal under the 1944 Act will be an unfair dismissal under general employment protection law. While there are no general exceptions to or exemptions from this prohibition, it is provided that the Act has no effect if the dismissal would result in the employer no longer being subject to the quota obligation. So, if as a result of the dismissal there are now fewer than twenty employees in the employment, the employer cannot be liable.[33]

This last comment immediately requires explication. These recruitment and employment security obligations apply only to employers of not fewer than twenty employees.[34] For the purposes of the quota number and the total number of employees, employees working fewer than ten hours per week are disregarded and those working between ten and thirty hours per week count as half an employee.[35] The standard percentage is 3 per cent.[36] However, there is a special percentage of 0.1 per cent in respect of employment in the capacity of master or crew member of a British ship.[37] Disabled persons employed in a designated employment (reserved occupations) do not count towards satisfaction of employers' quota obligations,[38] and neither do disabled persons who have not registered under the 1944 Act. The quota percentage may be reduced for up to a year on an application of an employer whose particular circumstances suggest that it is too great.[39] Applications are renewable on the advice of a local Committee for the Employment of People with Disabilities and, from 1992, are made through Placement Assessment and Counselling Teams, which now carry out the roles previously played by Disablement Resettlement Officers, the Disablement Advisory Service and the Employment Rehabilitation Service.

Many employers would be nominally in breach of the statutory quota scheme were it not for the fact that application may be made for permits allowing employers to recruit employees who are not registered disabled persons.[40] Where a permit has been issued, there can be no breach of the recruitment restrictions of the Act. A permit will be granted if, having regard to the nature of the work to which the employer wishes to recruit, there are no available registered disabled persons (or an insufficient number) who are qualified and suitable for that work.[41] The permit may be unconditional or subject to conditions,[42] such as an undertaking that job vacancies will be notified publicly as they arise. It may refer to a specified individual or to a number of persons (a so-called 'bulk permit').

Designated and Sheltered Employment

Certain classes of employment have been designated by ministerial order as affording specially suitable opportunities for disabled employment.[43] The Disabled Persons (Designated Employments) Order 1946 nominates employment as a passenger electric lift attendant and as a car park attendant as designated employments.[44] Employers may not engage or employ in a designated employment any person other than a registered disabled person unless in pursuance of a statutory re-employment obligation or within the scope of an exemption permit.[45] Breach of this provision is a criminal offence punishable by a fine and/or imprisonment.[46] Furthermore, registered disabled persons employed in a designated employment do not count for the purpose of determining whether an employer is in compliance with the statutory quota scheme.[47] The 1944 Act also mandates the provision of facilities to enable registered disabled persons with severe disabilities, who are unable to obtain employment in the open labour market or to compete on comparable terms with able-bodied persons, to be trained and to work or be employed under special conditions of sheltered employment.[48]

Record Keeping

In order to ensure compliance with the 1944 Act, employers are obliged to keep employment records, which may be used as evidence in any prosecution under the Act.[49] Records must be kept for two years from the date to which they relate and are open to inspection. There are criminal sanctions for failure to observe these various obligations. The records must show the total number of employees, the names of those employed for not more than thirty hours per week (distinguishing those who work for fewer than ten hours), the date of engagement of every employee and the date of termination of any employee. The number and names of registered disabled persons employed must also be recorded, as well as the names of persons employed where a special percentage quota applies, every reinstated employee and every person employed under a permit. The name and date of engagement of every person employed in a designated employment must be recorded, together with separate identification of such employees who are registered disabled persons, reinstated persons or employed under a permit. If an existing employee has been moved to designated employment, the date of the move must be recorded.

COMPANIES ACT 1985

Incorporated Employers

Companies legislation requires directors of registered companies to prepare a directors' annual report, which is presented to the shareholders and the Registrar of Companies.[50] Since 1980, it must disclose, among other things, information concerning the employment, training and advancement of disabled persons.[51] Disclosure only applies to companies with an average number of employees exceeding 250 within the United Kingdom in each week of the previous financial year.[52] A failure to comply with this requirement is a criminal offence and any director of the company at the relevant time may be liable to a fine.[53] It is a defence, however, to show that all reasonable steps were taken to comply with the requirement.[54]

The statement in the directors' report must describe what policy has been applied for giving full and fair consideration to applications for employment by the company made by disabled persons, having regard to their particular aptitudes and abilities.[55] The company's practice in continuing the employment of, and in arranging appropriate training for, employees who have become disabled during the time of their employment with the company must be outlined. This applies as much to disabilities whose causation is unrelated to employment as to work-related disabilities. Information must also be given about company policy on the training, career development and promotion of disabled employees in the company. Part One of the Code of Good Practice, which is addressed to directors and senior managers, makes suggestions for setting objectives for the employment of disabled persons. The

Code also provides guidance on the devising, implementation and monitoring of employers' policies towards disabled workers.

A company is not explicitly required to have a policy in respect of the employment of disabled persons; nor is it expected that any policy should be made operational. The directors' report needs only to contain a statement describing *such* policy as the company *has applied* during the financial year. It is merely implicit that the directors should give consideration to the company's policy on disabled employment, and it does not appear permissible merely to state that the company has applied no policy at all. Nevertheless, this has led to some fairly anodyne statements appearing under this heading in directors' reports.[56]

Public Sector Employers

The provisions of the Companies Act apply only to incorporated employers, although their spirit is equally applicable to other employers. The adoption and implementation of disabled employment policies by public sector employers can nevertheless be fraught with difficulties. Local government law requires that every appointment of a person to a paid office or employment by a local authority or parish or community council must be on merit.[57] While this is made expressly subject to any obligations under the 1944 Act, it might undermine the policy of a few local government employers who have pursued short-term policies of recruiting only disabled persons to advertised vacancies. An exception made in respect of the 1944 Act only permits merit to be ignored as an appointment criterion in respect of *registered* disabled persons and only as long as the employer remains below the statutory quota.

Some public sector employers have used 'contract compliance' as a tool of disabled employment policy. This drafting technique makes it a condition of a supply or works contract, granted to a contractor by a public sector employer, that the contractor should observe good employment practices in respect of its workforce. This might include, for example, an insistence that the contractor comply with the quota obligations of the 1944 Act. However, the provisions of Part II of the Local Government Act 1988 prohibit local and other public authorities from including such non-commercial considerations in public supply and works contracts.

EXTRA-STATUTORY MEASURES

Disabled Employment Schemes and Services[58]

Within the framework provided by the 1944 Act and subsequent legislation are a number of statutory and extra-statutory schemes and measures concerned with advancing the employment status of disabled persons. The newly formed PACTs based in Job Centres provide help to disabled job-seekers and liaise with employers and other organizations, as well as administering the statutory quota scheme. PACTs also promote vocational rehabilitation and training.[59] Further encouragement, advice and assistance is given by PACTs to employers to improve disabled employment policies and practices. Sheltered employment and sheltered placement provision is made for people with severe disabilities who are unable to obtain or secure employment in the open labour market. Various special schemes provide financial or practical help and encourage employers to make reasonable accommodations for disabled workers, although research demonstrates that awareness and usage of these special schemes is unacceptably low.[60] Mainstream government employment and training programmes are also open to disabled persons.

Employers who engage a disabled person may have doubts about the disabled employee's ability to meet the full requirements of the job or to perform to the expected level of productivity. Such doubts are not always justifiable and many job descriptions and requirements are not always strictly related to the needs of the job. This may be addressed by discussion with the disabled employee and any mentor. One solution to this problem might be to engage the disabled employee on a trial period. The Job Introduction Scheme encourages this by paying a grant towards the remuneration of a disabled worker employed by an employer for a six-week trial period. The scheme only applies to a position which is expected to last for at least six months after the trial period. The employer must pay the disabled employee the normal rate for the job during the trial period. The grant is payable upon the completion of a trial period approved under the scheme before it commenced. Provision is made for a *pro rata* payment if the trial period is shortened for whatever reason. Sickness absence of one to three weeks will not count under the scheme, although the trial period may be extended. Such absence for more than three weeks will normally terminate the trial period, subject to the employer's wishes.

The Department of Employment also provides practical and financial assistance to employers to encourage the recruitment of disabled workers. With effect from 1994, many of the schemes run by the Department are to be replaced by a new and unified scheme entitled the Access to Work scheme.

Code of Good Practice

The Code of Good Practice on the Employment of Disabled People was originally issued by the Manpower Services Commission in November 1984. A revised version of the Code was issued by the Department of Employment in March 1993. Research indicates that the Code has been received by about one-fifth of employers, although within those establishments penetration of the Code to different levels of management appears to be good.[61] Among employers who are aware of the Code, opinion of its contents is highly favourable. Unlike other codes of practice in employment law, the Code of Good Practice is a voluntary standard. It does not enjoy statutory underpinning nor does it have the force of law. Nevertheless, it furnishes guidance for employers who wish to develop disabled employment policies, to comply with the relevant law and to introduce best practice in employing disabled workers. The Code of Good Practice is also a source of information about financial and other assistance available to promote disabled employability. It furnishes employers with valuable advice on the recruitment and selection of disabled employees.[62] Especial attention is paid to job descriptions and requirements, methods of recruitment, selection procedures, interviewing and health screening. The Code also seeks to heighten employers' awareness of their statutory obligations under the 1944 Act and employment protection legislation.

EMPLOYMENT PROTECTION LEGISLATION AT LARGE

Disabled employees must qualify for and may participate in statutory employment rights upon an equal basis with their non-disabled colleagues. In the absence of specific protective legislation, however, there is nothing to prevent an employer giving less favourable treatment to disabled persons on the grounds of their disabilities.

Wages

Under the previous wages councils law, employers could be permitted to pay disabled workers, otherwise subject to a wages order, less than the statutory fixed minimum rate.[63] This provision was repealed in 1986.[64] In the absence of a relevant wages order guaranteeing minimum wages, the law does not prevent employers having differential rates of remuneration for disabled and able-bodied employees, unless this is the product of sex-based discrimination contrary to the Equal Pay Act 1970. In any event, from 1993 the statutory minimum wage machinery has been dismantled following the repeal of its statutory underpinning.[65]

Health and Safety

Both at common law and under the Health and Safety at Work etc. Act 1974 employers have a duty to ensure the safety of their employees and others in the workplace. This duty includes an obligation to provide safe fellow employees. Although there is no evidence to suggest that disabled employees have an inferior safety record in comparison with other employees, some consideration should be given to the health and safety implications of employing disabled persons. PACTs and the Employment Medical Advisory Service of the Health and Safety Executive advise on the health and safety implications of employing persons with particular disabilities. The Code of Good Practice is also a source of reference on this point.[66]

The employer's duty of care towards the disabled employee is instructive. If an employee with a known disability has been engaged, the employer must consider whether any adjustments should be made to that employee's working conditions so as to provide a safe workplace, a safe system of work, and safe plant and equipment.[67] In the circumstances peculiar to that disabled employee, the fact that the employee might be under a greater risk of injury or a risk of a further disabling injury should be contemplated.[68] The employer's obligations to other employees (and third parties) must be considered. If the evidence supports a conclusion that a disabled employee cannot fulfil the functions of a job (or otherwise work alongside colleagues) without being a danger to others, then it may be permissible to move the employee to other work or, in the extreme, to dismiss.[69]

The employee's duty under the 1974 Act to have regard for his or her own safety and that of others raises a further issue. It is suggested that a disabled employee who concealed a disability or did not disclose a deteriorating disability might be in breach of this provision. Although unlikely to result in a criminal prosecution of the employee, this would be both a justifiable reason for dismissal and grounds for defending any personal injury claim which the employee might bring against the employer.

Dismissal

Disabled persons, whether registered under the 1944 Act or not, are likely to enjoy better protection from arbitrary dismissal by reliance upon the unfair dismissal provisions in Part V of the 1978 Act. Indeed, a registered disabled employee may be entitled to special consideration by an employer, including reflection upon any personal circumstances, before a decision to dismiss is taken.[70] However, to enjoy statutory protection from unfair dismissal under the 1978 Act, the disabled employee must have two years continuous employment with the dismissing employer. In this case, the employer must have a reason capable of justifying the dismissal and must have acted fairly in deciding to dismiss in reliance upon that reason.[71] The House of Lords decision in *Polkey* v *AE Dayton Services Ltd*[72] underlines the importance of adopting a fair procedure when dismissing any employee.

An employer who has engaged an employee with a known disability (or retained a newly disabled employee) should be slow to dismiss for incompetence. In these circumstances, the employee's disability must be taken into account. If the employee is performing to the level of capability reasonably to be expected of a person with that disability, then the employer might not be able to justify the dismissal. On the other hand, if, once the disability has been accounted for, the employee's performance is below the expected standard, then, provided the employer applies a fair procedure for handling the dismissal, termination of employment may be defensible.

Employees whose health or disability status makes them a safety risk to themselves or their colleagues might be dismissed fairly on grounds of 'capability' or 'some other substantial reason' provided the employer has acted reasonably in deciding to dismiss.[73] While disability does not inevitably result in ill health absenteeism, if an employee's disability or health status does lead to absences from work, then the employer is entitled to act upon the evidence. The usual procedural steps for handling an ill health dismissal should be taken.[74] Nevertheless, a disabled employee might be entitled to a degree of sympathetic treatment, especially if the disability or health problem is job-related or was known to the employer at engagement.[75] In any event, an employer should consider what, if any, alternative employment is available.[76]

It will be only in exceptional circumstances that an employee's disability will be a relevant factor when deciding to dismiss on the grounds of conduct. A disabled employee subject to a disciplinary dismissal is entitled to the same procedural safeguards as any other employee. The redundancy of a disabled employee is likely to be both a reasonable cause of dismissal under the 1944 Act and a justifiable reason for dismissal under the 1978 Act. In both cases, however, the employer should ensure that the same criteria for selection for redundancy are being applied to disabled and able-bodied employees. The Code of Good Practice recommends that employers should consider redeploying redundant disabled employees within the undertaking or assisting them to find employment elsewhere.[77] In the absence of an agreed procedure or universally recognized practice, the fact that an employee is a registered disabled person is a personal circumstance which might be taken into account and given a little weight in the employee's favour when redundancy selection is being undertaken.[78] This does not necessarily mean, however, that a disabled person should be given automatic preference when retaining employees during a restructuring or redundancy situation.[79]

Employers should give particular care and attention to the question of how to deal with employees who become disabled while in their employment. The Code of Good Practice recommends that employers should attempt to retain the newly disabled employee in suitable employment. There might be good second order reasons for doing so. If the cause of the disability is job-related, then retention of the employee in paid employment will be an important factor in reducing any personal injury compensation the employer (or its insurer) might have to pay. In some cases, however, the employer might have no option but to terminate the employment of the newly disabled worker. Such a dismissal can be justified on the grounds of 'capability' and will be a fair dismissal if the employer has acted reasonably in all the circumstances.

PRESSURE FOR REFORM

At first sight, a bare account of disabled employment legislation in Britain might leave a favourable impression of the employment prospects and job security of disabled persons. However, as will be explored in more detail in Chapter 10, the 1944 framework of law is fundamentally flawed and pressure for reform has become irresistible. Reviews of the quota legislation during the 1970s and 1980s appear to posit three fundamental questions.[80] First, should the employment of disabled persons be provided for entirely by voluntary means, or is some form of statutory protection necessary? Second, if statutory protection is necessary should this be in the shape of a quota scheme or some modification thereof? Third, if any form of quota scheme is unacceptable, what other form of statutory protection would be appropriate?

Voluntarism or Regulation?

In 1981, the possible elements and implications of a mainly voluntary approach to disabled employment opportunities were examined.[81] This would include a major programme aimed at educating employers about the ways in which disabled persons could be more effectively integrated into employment. It was believed that

> this kind of policy is the best way of capitalising on the existing goodwill of employers and creating an atmosphere in which positive practices towards disabled people's employment will be developed.[82]

This would be supplemented by existing advice services in Job Centres and employment offices, and by special schemes to provide financial assistance for disabled persons and employers. Also proposed was the development of a code of practice setting out clear guidelines on all aspects of the employment of disabled workers and indicating the proportion of employees who should be disabled individuals.[83] However, it was doubted whether the voluntarist approach would work without statutory support.[84]

Research in 1978 indicated that disabled people, especially those who were registered as disabled and unemployed, strongly supported the retention of special legislation, even with the weaknesses of the existing system.[85] Thirty-five per cent thought that special legislation was the most useful means of helping disabled persons in the labour market, although the remaining 65 per cent favoured special employment services, employer subsidies, publicity and information campaigns or other voluntarist measures in varying degrees.[86] However, when given a free policy choice without prioritization, disabled respondents overwhelmingly supported special laws to help disabled people find and keep work (92 per cent).[87] The same research indicated that, if disabled people had a choice as to the form that special legislation would take, 39 per cent favoured quota legislation, 37 per cent wanted anti-discrimination laws and 22 per cent opted for legal obligations upon employers to publish policy and records.[88] Nevertheless, some 86 per cent of disabled persons in the 1978 survey favoured retention of the quota scheme with modifications and reforms.[89]

Anti-discrimination Legislation?

The 1978 survey also solicited disabled respondents' views on the introduction of anti-discrimination legislation. Eighty-three per cent of respondents favoured or strongly favoured laws that would give individual disabled people the opportunity to take action against being unfairly treated by employers because of disability.[90] If such legislation was to be introduced, 87 per cent of disabled individuals believed that it should apply to both those seeking work and those in work.[91] Anti-discrimination legislation for disabled persons had not been seriously considered in official circles until the 1979 review of the quota.[92] In its 1981 review of the quota, the MSC returned once again to what it now termed 'equal opportunities legislation'.[93] The MSC thought that such a new initiative would highlight the needs of disabled persons and increase public awareness of their problems. Such legislation, unlike the quota, could also protect disabled employees once in employment. Most importantly,

> It would be compatible with the philosophy of the Tomlinson Committee, since it would afford disabled people the right to treatment on the same terms as able-bodied people.[94]

Furthermore, it might induce employers to re-examine employment policies, thus benefiting all disabled persons, regardless of registered status.

Nevertheless, the view was taken that such legislation would assist persons with lesser disabilities more than those with more serious disabilities. Furthermore, it was feared that increased litigation would increase the antagonism of employers toward disabled persons. It was specifically feared that frivolous or malicious complaints would bring the law into disrepute and that the complaints system necessary to make the legislation work would require considerable resources. In particular, it was thought unlikely that disabled individuals would wish to expose themselves to a detailed examination of their medical status by a tribunal or court.[95] There was also concern that anti-discrimination law would produce disputes about whether an individual's disability was an inherent handicap in relation to a particular job and the official thinking was that

> discrimination may be justified in some instances when a person's medical history or a reduction in his working capacity mean that his employment would pose a particular risk.[96]

This is an issue which will be returned to later.

Perhaps crucially, there was insufficient evidence of disability discrimination that would justify such legislation. Direct comparisons with other forms of social discrimination were rejected.[97] No recommendation for anti-discrimination legislation covering disability was forthcoming.[98] Politicians also felt unable to support anti-discrimination legislation, believing there to be a 'fundamental difference' between disability and race or sex and the effect these factors have upon the ability to do a job.[99] Instead, a 1981 report recommended that there should be a general statutory duty upon employers obliging them to 'take reasonable steps to promote equality of employment opportunity for disabled people', linked to a code of practice, in a model similar to that in health and safety law.[100] It was proposed that it should be a criminal offence not to comply with this statutory duty. However, it was envisaged that every effort would be made to resolve problems without recourse to litigation and that few cases would go beyond the stage of exhortatory visits to employers whose policies were deficient.[101] In unresolved or persistent cases of breach, there might be a conciliation stage followed by the issuing of an improvement notice. Only if improvement was not forthcoming would a prosecution be put in train.

Triumph of Voluntarism

The Government's attitude to special legislation for disabled workers in Britain has been ambivalent. The problem is that, until comparatively recently, the Government has refused to recognize the phenomenon of discrimination against disabled people. Some concession that the disadvantage experienced by disabled workers in the labour market might transcend the limitations of disability was made in the 1990 consultative document. There it stated that 'Mistaken attitudes to or misconceptions about disability (and about older workers) by some employers and others in society will need to be challenged'.[102] However, it was clear that the role of legislation in tackling such attitudes and misconceptions was to be a limited one. The consultative document restated the Government's commitment to remove 'unnecessary burdens on employers which may inhibit job growth' and indicated that retained legislation in the employment field must be necessary to promote policy objectives, be effective and be acceptable to the taxpayer and businesses.[103]

That consultative document on disabled employment policy acknowledged that anti-discrimination legislation

> would have the advantage of sending positive messages to employers about people with disabilities and of putting enforcement into their hands. It would also bite on areas other than recruitment. However, a major difficulty is that disability, unlike race or sex, can be relevant to job performance and what to some might seem like discrimination may in reality be recruitment based on legitimate preferences and likely performance.[104]

This final observation is a constant theme in official reactions to the pressure for anti-discrimination law. In reality, however, it does not withstand close scrutiny. Even in sex and race discrimination, the ability to do the job is a relevant factor and employers are allowed to discriminate upon the basis of merit or ability. If a disabled person is refused an employment opportunity because he or she cannot perform the work or is ill-suited to the job, that is not unlawful discrimination and it is not proposed that it should be so.

The consultative document also contended that

> An anti-discrimination law would be complex to draft and

> uncertain in its application. There is a danger that faced with a law uncertain in its application, employers would become more reluctant to hire people with disabilities.[105]

The first part of this argument is a peculiar kind of special pleading, where the wish is father to the thought. It is a self-serving argument that leads to the deliberate drafting of ambiguous and opaque legislation in order intentionally to thwart the aims of reform. It flies in the face of the evidence in later chapters, in which successful examples of disability discrimination legislation in the USA, Canada and Australia are presented. The argument is also contradicted by the testimony of practising employment lawyers in Britain, who see no such difficulties in devising and writing such legislation.[106] The second part of the contention does have some mileage in it. Undoubtedly new laws prohibiting employment discrimination on the grounds of disability will not be actively courted by employers and business. Certainly, laws that are inadequately drafted will cause confusion and might create difficulties for their intended beneficiaries. However, with careful and well-intentioned draftsmanship, there is no evidence that discrimination laws have made employers more reluctant to hire women and ethnic minorities, and this is not the parallel experience of disability discrimination laws elsewhere.

The political view, having taken evidence and heard the reactions to the 1990 consultation exercise, concluded that the Government

> should explore urgently the possibility of equal opportunities legislation for the employment of people with disabilities and report to Parliament on its potential effects and costs in the labour market.[107]

However, early in 1993 the Prime Minister responded that

> We have no plans to introduce generalized anti-discrimination legislation because we foresee problems in both approach and implementation. However, as I have made clear in the past, we are continuing to work to eliminate unjustified discrimination against people on the ground of their disability. We believe that this is best achieved by education and persuasion backed up by targeted legislation to address specific problems.[108]

It seemed likely, therefore, that it would require a change of government before any equal opportunities legislation addressing disabled employment rights would be enacted in Britain. Both the Labour Party and the Liberal Democratic Party have indicated support for such legislation at various times.

Attempts at Law Reform

Despite the situation outlined above, since 1982 there have been numerous attempts to introduce, by means of private members' bills, anti-discrimination legislation covering disabled people. The enactment by the US Congress in July 1990 of the Americans with Disabilities Act gave British disability rights advocates renewed inspiration to attempt similar legislation in this country.[109] In the 1991–2 session the Civil Rights (Disabled Persons) Bill was first presented,[110] patently fashioned after the American model. For the first time, a comprehensive and carefully drafted proposal for disability discrimination legislation was before Parliament. Despite cross-party support the Bill failed to obtain a Second Reading in the House of Commons, ironically being talked out by a Conservative backbench MP who was himself a person with a record of disability.[111] The Bill was promptly reintroduced in the House of Lords,[112] but failed to make progress with the intervention of the General Election.[113] The Bill was again reintroduced in the 1992–3 parliamentary session,[114] and passed all stages of the legislative process in the House of Lords, even surviving a procedural error on Third Reading.[115] The Bill was sent to the House of Commons, where it was presented for First Reading, but it made no further progress.[116] However, in order to keep the initiative, the sponsors of the Bill subsequently presented three further Bills applying to Northern Ireland, Scotland and Wales,[117] but these also fell on stony ground.

The Civil Rights (Disabled Persons) Bill was reintroduced in the House of Commons in the 1993–4 session.[118] Upon a groundswell of support for the Bill's principles, the draft legislation made sound progress, passing through its Committee stage for the first time in the lower chamber.[119] However, at the Report stage of the Bill, the Government contrived to defeat the measure. It was revealed for the first time that the Government had costed the Bill as requiring up-front expenditure of £17 billion, with on-going costs of £1 billion per year.[120] Although admitting that these compliance estimates were based upon implementation within five years, covered all aspects of the proposed law (and not simply the employment provisions) and ignored any cost–benefit analysis, the Government clearly sought to make the proposals unattractive to its own backbenchers. The Bill first ran out of parliamentary time when numerous amendments were tabled (allegedly with the assistance of Government draftsmen) and was then subsequently defeated on the floor of the House by procedural means.[121] Subsequent attempts to resurrect the Bill in the House of Lords and House of Commons have been unsuccessful to date.[122]

The furore that surrounded the defeat of the Civil Rights (Disabled Persons) Bill momentarily threatened the tenure of the Minister for Disabled People, Mr Nicholas Scott. However, he survived the controversy surrounding his supposed role in the Bill's demise, but at the expense of promising Government-sponsored legislation of a less ambitious nature. In July 1994, he issued a consultation paper which invited views upon the desirability of selective legislation addressing discrimination in the employment field (among others).[123] This is unlikely to produce reforming law of the depth and breadth desired by disability rights activists.

CONCLUSION

Britain's reliance upon a statutory quota scheme as the main vehicle for the legal regulation of disabled workers' rights has in practice meant that disabled people's employment aspirations rest upon frail foundations. The failure of the quota in terms of both observance and enforcement will be seen as a salutary lesson for those who advocate the reservation of employment for minority groups. As a result, the British system of disabled employment rights now relies heavily upon extra-statutory measures, government exhortations and employer goodwill. It is the triumph of voluntarism over regulation. Nevertheless, as has been recounted, the pressures for reform have been building up over the past decade and, if the quota is incapable of being made operable, then there are many who would favour the introduction of equal treatment legislation and equal opportunity requirements covering disabled persons. Inevitably, British disability rights activists look abroad for inspiration. In recent years, British employment law has been fundamentally revised by the harmonizing effects of EC law. Accordingly, in the following chapter we look to the continent and to the Community to see what lessons, if any, can be learned for the development of disabled employment laws in this country.

NOTES

1. This chapter draws upon Doyle 1987a, b, 1991, 1994a, b.
2. Tomlinson, 1943.
3. *Ibid.*: para. 71.
4. *Ibid.*: para. 9.
5. *Ibid.: passim.*
6. DP(E)A 1944 amended principally by the DP(E)A 1958.
7. Tomlinson, 1943: para. 77.
8. Piercy, 1956.
9. Manpower Services Commission, 1978, 1982, 1986.
10. National Advisory Council on the Employment of Disabled People, 1986.
11. *Ibid.*: paras 5.9 and 5.10.
12. *Ibid.*: para. 6.6.
13. Manpower Services Commission, 1981.
14. *The MSC Report on Review of the Quota Scheme – Memorandum by the National Advisory Council on Employment of Disabled People* (evidence to the House of Commons Employment Committee) and reproduced in House of Commons Employment Committee, 1981: 38–9. See also *idem*, 1981: paras 14–19 and *idem*, 1982. The Committee was particularly concerned at the problems of defining disability, the identification of disabled persons by employers and the enforcement of the general duty.
15. The Code of Good Practice on the Employment of Disabled People was originally prepared and issued by the Manpower Services Commission in 1984 and is now published by the Employment Department.
16. DP(E)A 1944 s 1(2).
17. *Ibid.*: s 6(3).
18. *Ibid.*: s 6(1). Regulations have been made under s 6(2) and (4) appertaining to registration and the register: Disabled Persons (Registration) Regulations 1945 (SR&O 1945 No. 938, as amended by SR&O 1946 No. 262 and SI 1959 No. 1510).
19. *Ibid.*: s 7(2)(a). In cases of dispute, the application is referred to a district advisory committee for determination: s 7(2)(b). This will be the local Committee for the Employment of People with Disabilities.
20. *Ibid.*: s 7(1) and the Disabled Persons (Registration) Regulations 1945.
21. The authority for these grounds of disqualification derives from *ibid.*: ss 7(1) and 8(2).
22. *Ibid.*: s 8(1).
23. *Ibid.*: s 8(3). Removal will only occur after a reference to a local advisory committee for recommendations.
24. DP(E)A 1958 s 2(2).
25. DP(E)A 1944 s 9.
26. *Ibid.*: s 9(2). As to the interpretation of references to taking into employment, see: s 13(2).
27. *Ibid.*: ss 13(5) and 9(6). Note s 9(7) which contains provisions relating to prosecution.
28. *Ibid.*: s 9(3) and see EP(C)A 1978 s 69.
29. *Ibid.*: s 9(4).
30. *Ibid.*: s 13(2)(b).
31. *Ibid.*: s 9(5).
32. *Ibid.*: ss 13(5) and 9(6) and (7).
33. *Ibid.*: s 9(5).
34. *Ibid.*: s 9(1). The Act does not bind the Crown. The Act also only applies to employment relationships which are in the nature of a contract of service or of apprenticeship: s 13(1).
35. Disabled Persons (General) Regulations 1945 (SR&O 1945 No. 1558, as amended by SR&O 1946 No. 1256) made under DP(E)A 1944 s 13(3). The ascertainment of the quota number is determined by the rules of calculation set out in s 10(4).
36. DP(E)A 1944 s 10(2)(a). The standard percentage is fixed by the Disabled Persons

(Standard Percentage) Order 1946 (SR&O 1946 No. 1258) made under s 19(3) after consultations with both sides of industry.

37. *Ibid.*: s 10(2)(b). The special percentage is fixed by the Disabled Persons (Special Percentage) (No. 1) Order 1946 (SR&O 1946 No. 236) made under s 10(3). The Minister may fix a special percentage for employment in any trade or industry (or part thereof) where there are distinctive characteristics with respect to its suitability for the employment of disabled persons.

38. *Ibid.*: ss 9(2), 9(5), 10(4) and 10(6).

39. *Ibid.*: ss 10(5) and 10(6); Disabled Persons (General) Regulations 1945.

40. *Ibid.*: ss 9(4) and 11(1); Disabled Persons (General) Regulations 1945.

41. *Ibid.*: s 11(1).

42. *Ibid.*: s 11(2).

43. *Ibid.*: s 12(1).

44. SR&O 1946 No. 1257 made under DP(E)A 1944 s 12.

45. DP(E)A 1944 s 12(2) and (3).

46. *Ibid.*: s 12(4).

47. *Ibid.*: s 9(2).

48. *Ibid.*: s 15.

49. *Ibid.*: s 14 and the Disabled Persons (General) Regulations 1945.

50. Companies Act 1985 s 234.

51. The obligation to disclose such information derives from the Companies (Directors' Report) (Employment of Disabled Persons) Regulations 1980 (SI 1980 No. 1160) made under Companies Act 1948 s 454(1) and in force on 1 September 1980.

52. Companies Act 1985 Sch 7, para. 9.

53. *Ibid.*: s 234(5).

54. *Ibid.*: s 234(6).

55. *Ibid.*: sch 7, para. 9.

56. Doyle, 1987b.

57. Local Government and Housing Act 1989 s 7.

58. This section draws upon publications of the Employment Department describing its services to disabled people. See also: Thompson, 1986; Barnes, 1991; Berthoud *et al.*, 1993.

59. Berthoud *et al.*, 1993: 39

60. Morrell, 1990.

61. *Ibid.*

62. Code of Good Practice paras 5.1–5.21.

63. Wages Councils Act 1979 s 16.

64. Wages Act 1986 s 32(2) and Sch 5.

65. Trade Union Reform and Employment Rights Act 1993 s 35.

66. Paras 4.2, 4.3 and 6.3.

67. *Qualcast (Wolverhampton) Ltd* v *Haynes* [1959] AC 743 (HL).

68. *Paris* v *Stepney Borough Council* [1951] AC 367 (HL).

69. *Harper* v *National Coal Board* [1980] IRLR 260 (EAT).

70. *Seymour* v *British Airways Board* [1983] ICR 148 (EAT).

71. EP(C)A 1978 s 57.

72. *Polkey* v *AE Dayton Services Ltd* [1988] AC 344 (HL).

73. *Harper* v *National Coal Board* [1980] IRLR 260 (EAT); *Converform (Darwen) Ltd* v *Bell* [1981] IRLR 195 (EAT).

74. *Shook* v *Ealing London Borough Council* [1986] ICR 314 (EAT).

75. *Kerr* v *Atkinson Vehicles (Scotland) Ltd* [1974] IRLR 36 (IT).

76. *Garricks (Caterers) Ltd* v *Nolan* [1980] IRLR 259 (EAT).

77. Paras 6.10 and 6.12.

78. *Hobson* v *GEC Telecommunications Ltd* [1985] ICR 777 (EAT); *Forman Construction* v *Kelly* [1977] IRLR 468 (EAT).

79. *Seymour* v *British Airways Board* [1983] ICR 148 (EAT).

80. Manpower Services Commission, 1981: para. 6.2.

81. *Ibid.*: Chapter 7.

82. *Ibid.*: para. 7.2.

83. *Ibid.*: para. 7.7.
84. *Ibid.*: paras 7.10 and 7.11.
85. *Idem*, 1979: para. 68.
86. Research Surveys of Great Britain Ltd, 1978: Table 9.12.1.
87. *Ibid.*: Table 9.11.1.
88. *Ibid.*: Table 9.9.1.
89. Manpower Services Commission, 1979: para. 75.
90. Research Surveys of Great Britain Ltd, 1978: Table 9.8.1.
91. *Ibid.*: Table 9.8.2.
92. Manpower Services Commission, 1979: paras 78–81.
93. *Idem*, 1981: para. 8.20.
94. *Idem*, 1979: para. 79.2.
95. *Idem*, 1981: para. 8.22. Very pertinently in the context of this study, it was believed that individual litigation would have a limited effect beyond the circumstances of the individual case.
96. *Idem*, 1979: para. 80.2.
97. *Idem*, 1981: para. 8.22.
98. *Ibid.*: para. 8.23. Perhaps significantly, it was thought that the legislation would require an equal opportunities commission to support it and the civil servants felt unable to recommend such a body be established in the light of the lack of conclusive evidence, the then economic situation and the current public expenditure policy.
99. House of Commons Employment Committee, 1981: para. 23.
100. Manpower Services Commission, 1981: paras 8.24 and 8.25. The obligation would be to give disabled persons full and fair consideration for all vacancies, to retain newly disabled employees where reasonable and practicable, and to provide full and fair opportunities for the career development of disabled persons.
101. *Ibid.*: paras 8.29 and 8.30.
102. Department of Employment, 1990: 16.
103. *Ibid.*: 35–6.
104. *Ibid.*: para. 5.14.
105. *Ibid.*: para. 5.15.
106. Law Society Employment Law Committee, 1992.
107. House of Commons Employment Committee, 1990a: para. 23.
108. HC Deb Vol. 217 col 485 (Mr J Major, Prime Minister) 22 January 1993.
109. Aided by the compelling arguments of writers such as: Bynoe *et al.*, 1991; Campbell and Heginbotham, 1991; Barnes, 1991, 1992; Cunningham, 1993.
110. HC Bill 24 (1991–2).
111. HC Deb Vol. 200 col 280 (1st reading 4 December 1991; HC Deb Vol. 202 cols 1235–63 (2nd Reading 31 January 1992: debate adjourned while Mr R. Hayward MP was addressing the House).
112. Civil Rights (Disabled Persons) (No. 2) Bill: HL Bill 49 (1991–2).
113. HL Deb Vol. 535 col 346 (1st reading 6 February 1992); HL Deb Vol. 535 cols 1473–96 (2nd Reading 21 February 1992).
114. Civil Rights (Disabled Persons) Bill: HL Bills 13, 25 and 29 (1992–3).
115. HL Deb Vol. 537 col 711 (1st Reading 1 June 1992); HL Deb Vol. 538 cols 79–108 (2nd Reading 15 June 1992); HL Deb Vol. 538 cols 846–51 (Committee 1 July 1992); HL Deb Vol. 539 cols 295–305 (Report 15 July 1992); HL Deb Vol. 539 cols 1516–34 (3rd Reading 4 November 1992); HL Deb Vol. 540 col 80 (Message from House of Commons 9 November 1992); HL Vol. 540 cols 329–30 (3rd Reading Amendment (Privilege) made 12 November 1992).
116. HC Bills 79 and 82 presented for First Reading (5 November 1992), withdrawn and represented for First Reading (9 and 12 November 1992). It is believed that the Bill has been blocked by Government whips: 'News in Brief', *The Times*, Saturday 27 February 1993 at page 2. The Bill has cross-party support, as evidenced by over 300 MPs signing Early Day Motion 330, which recognizes the necessity of anti-discrimination legislation and calls for the early introduction of a CRDP Bill.
117. Civil Rights (Disabled Persons) (Northern Ireland) Bill (HC Bill 210: 1st Reading 16

June 1993); Civil Rights (Disabled Persons) (Scotland) Bill (HC Bill 216: 1st Reading 23 June 1993); Civil Rights (Disabled Persons) (Wales) Bill (HC Bill 215: 1st Reading 24 June 1993).

118. HC Bills 16 and 91.

119. HC Deb Vol. 234 col 1298–9 (1st Reading: 16 December 1993); HC Deb Vol. 239 col 520–80 (2nd Reading: 11 March 1994); HC Deb Vol. 240 col 529 (money resolution: 24 March 1994); Standing Committee C (30 March 1994 and 12–13 April 1994).

120. HC Deb Vol. 242 col 1001 (Mr N. Scott, Minister for Disabled People) 6 May 1994.

121. HC Deb Vol. 242 col 960–1017 (6 May 1994) and HC Deb Vol. 243 col 1077–102 (20 May 1994).

122. HL Bill 68. See also: HC Bills 153, 154 and 159.

123. Department of Social Security, 1994. Compare the Labour Party's proposals in: Commission on Social Justice, 1994.

3

Disabled Employment Rights in the European Community and Its Member States

INTRODUCTION

Broadly speaking, approximately 30 million or one in ten Europeans are disabled in the sense that they are restricted in or unable to perform an activity or function considered normal for a human being because of physical, sensory, mental or psychological impairment.[1] As in Britain, so in the other member states of the European Community (EC), disabled people of working age face higher rates and longer periods of unemployment, and suffer sweeping social and economic disadvantages. In Germany, for example, there are estimated to be some 1.38 million disabled persons, of whom 37.5 per cent are of working age. Some 1.017 million disabled persons are estimated to be in the German labour market, of which 80 per cent were employed under a statutory quota scheme, 7 per cent were otherwise employed, and 13 per cent were unemployed.[2] Undoubtedly, statistics of this nature are repeated across the Community and they can be partly explained by prejudice and unreconstructed negative attitudes among employers and in the labour market generally.[3] Architectural, environmental and occupation barriers also explain in part the unequal status of the disabled European citizen.

The development of a so-called 'Social Europe' during the period since the mid-1970s holds out some prospect that disabled workers' rights could be secured by Community-wide initiatives. EC intervention has had a marked effect upon the use of law to redress inequalities that are the product of occupational segregation along gender lines. In particular, it has ensured that women workers enjoy a degree of protection and redress in the diverse areas of: equal pay; equal treatment in employment, social security and occupational pension schemes; pregnancy, maternity and child care rights; and, most recently, sexual harassment in the workplace.[4] European workers and participants in the labour market have also benefited from action taken in respect of collective redundancies, acquired rights, employer insolvency, employment information, and health and safety in general.[5] While these advances might indirectly improve the lot of disabled employees, it has often been noted that EC law has largely by-passed the employment problems of minority groups. If EC law has barely scratched the surface of race discrimination, for example, what prospects are there that disabled persons will enjoy even formal equality under a market order?

EUROPEAN COMMUNITY LAW

Social Action Programmes and Disabled People[6]

The early steps of the EC on the path towards better services and opportunities for disabled persons were witnessed in the 1970s. In 1974 the Community established an initial action programme to promote the vocational rehabilitation of disabled persons.[7] In the same year, the Community initiated its first social action programme, under which the European Social Fund was established to support vocational training for open employment, with disabled persons recognized as a priority group.[8] Other activities were also begun, especially in respect of research and social security provision.[9] In 1981, the UN International Year of Disabled People, the European Parliament adopted a Resolution on the economic, social and vocational integration of disabled persons.[10] This was followed by an influential opinion on the problems of disabled people from the Economic and Social Committee.[11] The Resolution pointed a way forward and demonstrated a concern for the rights of disabled people above and beyond rehabilitation. As the International Year ended, and stimulated by these earlier contributions, the Community agreed a new action programme on disabled people for the next four years.[12]

In the event, the first action programme lasted for six years from 1982 to 1987. It covered a wide and inclusive range of disabilities and focused upon two areas. These two areas have continued to be at the forefront of Community action in this field: first, employment, vocational training and rehabilitation; second, environmental factors, including mobility, transport, access to buildings and facilities, and housing. The focus of this study is employment and, fortuitously, employment was also the obvious choice for policy initiatives by the EC Commission in respect of disabled people. So it was that the EC Recommendation on the Employment of Disabled Persons emerged from the first action programme.

EC Recommendation on the Employment of Disabled Persons

The Council of Ministers adopted the Recommendation on the Employment of Disabled People in the EC in 1986.[13] Daunt records that the decision to bring forward a weak instrument such as a Recommendation, rather than a constraining measure such as a Directive, was taken by the Commission against the advice of its legal service. He notes that:

> The argument put forward . . . was that a draft Directive on the employment of disabled people, brought forward at a time of high unemployment throughout the Community, would encounter insuperable difficulties in the Council, so that either it would never get through or it would be adopted after considerable delay and in such a truncated form as to be virtually useless. A Recommendation on the other hand would have a fair chance of being adopted within a reasonable time, its weakness of form being also compensated by a relative richness of content; moreover, it would always be possible to bring forward a draft Directive at a later stage, which by focusing on points where the member states had evidently failed to carry out the terms of the Recommendation would have a much better chance of success.[14]

Nevertheless, despite this concession and the careful groundwork that had been done to establish the statistical, socio-economic and legislative basis of the proposals,[15] the Council 'did all it could at all stages of the process to weaken its content, especially on the question of employment quotas'.[16] In contrast, the European Parliament (with the noticeable exception of the British Conservative parliamentarians) was highly critical of the weakness of the Recommendation's form and content.[17]

The Recommendation is addressed to the member states and requires them to take all appropriate measures 'to promote fair opportunities for disabled people in the field of employment and vocational training' (Article 1). This principle of fair opportunity is applicable to access to employment and training, retention in employment or training, protection from unfair dismissal and opportunities for promotion and in-service training. The Recommendation expects governments to adopt policies to assist disabled people: in particular, by taking steps to eliminate negative discrimination and to provide for positive action (Article 2). Annexed to the Recommendation are guidelines for a framework for positive action to promote the employment and vocational training of disabled people.

The elimination of discrimination involves five recommended actions (Article 2(a)(i)–(v)). First, governments should review existing law and extra-legal provisions to ensure that they do not contradict the principle of fair opportunity regardless of disability. Second, member states are urged to take 'appropriate measures to avoid as far as possible dismissals linked to a disability'. Third, the principle of equal treatment in employment and training should admit only exceptions justifiable by reference to incompatibility between work-related activities and a particular disability. Fourth, the use of testing before, during and after training should be designed to avoid disadvantaging candidates with disabilities. Fifth, governments should provide disabled persons with means of redress or of establishing their rights 'in accordance with national law and practice'. The mandating of positive action on behalf of disabled persons is noteworthy. The Recommendation envisages that member states should fix 'realistic percentage targets' for the employment of disabled workers in both public and private enterprises having a *minimum* workforce of fifteen to fifty employees (Article 2(b)(i)). It is expected that 'Measures should also be adopted for making these targets public *and achieving them*' (my emphasis). It is recommended that guidelines or codes of good practice for the employment of disabled persons should be adopted, while governments should encourage employers to take measures corresponding with the spirit of such guidelines or codes (Article 2(b)(ii) and (iii)).

Although the Recommendation sets out a number of *desiderata* for the employment rights of disabled employees, its legal effect is limited. First, the British Government is of the view that existing statutory and extra-statutory measures in Britain already meet the principle of fair opportunity established by the Recommendation.[18] The Department of Employment points to the 1944 Act and to the employment protection regime established by unfair dismissal law as particular evidence of this, although the Department recognizes that the Recommendation goes wider than existing legislation in Britain. Second, it should be borne in mind that, under Article 189(5) of the Treaty of Rome, Recommendations do not have binding force. However, in *Grimaldi* v *Fonds des Maladies Professionnelles,*[19] the European Court of Justice has ruled that Recommendations, while not conferring directly enforceable rights upon individuals, are to be taken account of by domestic courts, particularly for clarifying other provisions of national or EC law. Nevertheless, it seems likely that the European Court's ruling only applies where the national legislation in question has been adopted in order to implement the Recommendation. Given the British Government's view that the Recommendation merely reflects existing legal and extra-legal standards in Britain, disabled persons will be unable to seek much comfort from the *Grimaldi* case or the Recommendation itself.

EC Charter of Fundamental Social Rights

Although EC Recommendation 1986 urges member states to take all appropriate measures to promote fair opportunities for disabled people in the field of employment and vocational training, in the absence of anti-discrimination or equal opportunities legislation the expectation of disabled employees to equality of employment opportunity rests upon frail foundations. Temporary hopes that stronger legal measures would emerge from EC social policy were raised in December 1989 when the member states of the EC agreed the text of a Charter of the Fundamental Social Rights of Workers. Article 26 of the Charter expresses the entitlement of disabled persons 'to additional concrete measures aimed at improving their social and professional integration'. Among other things, these measures are to give particular attention to 'vocational training, ergonomics, accessibility [and] mobility'. At first sight, this broad statement of the social rights of disabled persons appeared to have inevitable consequences for disabled employees. However, the detailed implementation of the principle here espoused had to await the adoption of Directives and other legal instruments under the action programmes which underpinned the Charter. As will be seen shortly, little has materialized that offers a prospect of 'hard law' promoting the employment rights of disabled persons. Nevertheless, it will be apparent that disabled people at least had a toehold upon the social policy agenda of the Community and that the social action programme, the Recommendation and the Social Charter held out some promise of legal recognition of disabled employment problems.

Subsequent Developments

In 1987 proposals were pressed for the establishment of a second action programme to promote the social and economic integration and independent living of people with disabilities.[20] The second action programme was established in 1988 under the title 'HELIOS'.[21] The HELIOS programme, like its predecessor, set out to take some policy initiatives, to further co-operation with and support for disability-related projects, and to disseminate information about disability issues. The main policy initiative taken was to follow up progress on the 1986 Recommendation. A report was published in July 1988 containing accounts of progress in each of the 12 member states and a comparative analysis.[22]

The report contains much of interest and is extremely informative. However, it fails to give a true indication of the impact of the 1986 Recommendation in the 12 member states because, by relying upon national reports, it takes the form of updating statements of national measures and policies, and provides little evidence of whether new initiatives have been taken *because* of the Recommendation. In reading the separate national reports, one suspects that the Recommendation, as a weak Community instrument, has had little direct influence upon legal and extra-legal action on behalf of disabled people in the member states since 1986. Rather, the Recommendation provides a convenient peg upon which to hang such new developments as have occurred. Nevertheless, the report furnishes a comprehensive account of the employment status of disabled persons in the Community and of the various statutory and voluntary measures taken to assist them. It strengthens the case for special legislation to eliminate negative discrimination and to encourage positive action.

It is clear from the 1988 report that the 1986 Recommendation has achieved little that would not have already been proposed by individual governments. As much seems to have been recognized by the Council of Ministers in its response to the Commission's report.[23] Daunt summarizes this view thus:

> The Council is also surprisingly honest in its assessment of how little the Recommendation itself has in reality achieved.

It has, we are told, 'contributed to a review' and 'encouraged new measures' in accordance with its spirit. Even more disarmingly, 'it has offered a Community reference framework for national measures that were being prepared when it was adopted'. It would be difficult to find words which demolish more skilfully than that any faith we may have in the effectiveness of *non-constraining* supranational instruments in the social field.[24]

However, the Council's conclusions do contain a direct invitation to the Commission to bring forward proposals to ensure better co-ordination and greater consistency between the various measures already in place in the member states. This has been interpreted as an invitation to legislate for a Directive on the employment rights of disabled persons, an invitation that has so far been ignored.[25]

Subsequently, the action programme underpinning the Social Charter has provided a fresh impetus to the economic integration of disabled people. First, it provides the basis for a third action programme addressing the rights and circumstances of disabled Europeans: HELIOS II. The third action programme covers the period 1992–6 and was adopted in February 1993.[26] HELIOS II has attracted 37 million ecu (approximately £29.5 million) for the duration of the programme. Like its predecessors, however, it focuses upon exchange of information, promoting co-operation between member states and appropriate organizations for the social integration of disabled persons, and continues the dialogue with disability bodies.

Second, the Charter action programme has led to a draft Directive tackling the mobility requirements of disabled workers.[27] Although the draft Directive springs from Article 26 of the Charter, its legal basis is Article 118A of the EEC Treaty, which allows the Council to legislate in the occupational health and safety field.[28] The preamble to the original proposal made it clear that the draft Directive was designed to assist workers with reduced mobility to gain access to employment and to reduce the hazards of their travel to work.[29] The measure was thus a peculiar equal opportunities instrument dressed up in the language of a health and safety regulation. However, the amended proposal less ambitiously seeks to facilitate 'the safe travel of workers with reduced mobility to and from their place of work'. This appears more like a safety initiative and less like an equal opportunities agenda. If adopted,[30] the draft Directive will apply to a worker 'with reduced mobility', meaning a person 'who has special difficulty in using public transport *for his occupational activities* owing to a serious handicap of a physical or mental origin' (Article 2(a) with emphasis supplied). The italicized portion of this quotation was added to the original drafting and has the effect of limiting the reach of the draft Directive, which is clearly not intended as a comprehensive transport reform. Nevertheless, member states will be required to take steps to ensure that means of transport are provided that are accessible and interchangeable, and to facilitate the transport of disabled workers (Article 3).[31] These steps will include informing, advising and training disabled workers and transport staff to ensure that disabled workers can travel safely and are able to use the provided transport (Article 4).[32] Where a worker with reduced mobility cannot travel without a companion or other form of assistance, governments must ensure that additional transport costs are not incurred (Article 5).[33]

An Annex to the draft Directive lays down in broad detail the minimum requirements that the public transport systems must meet. It is clear from this source that accessibility includes the provision of transport services of sufficient number, frequency and timetabling. Safe access to transport facilities should be guaranteed by appropriate methods, such as lowered floors, lifting platforms, mobile ramps, folding platforms or personal assistance by trained staff. The Annex states that at least 'one entrance/exit must be designed to allow workers with reduced mobility to board/alight from the mode of transport safely' and there must be compatibility between the means of transport and the corresponding infrastructure to ensure safe access and egress. Inside transport vehicles, the needs of disabled passengers must be accounted for, particularly in respect of reserved seating, corridors, and toilet and washing facilities. Appropriate signs should be used to indicate accessibility of transport for workers with reduced mobility and to give notice of stops.

The Community's momentum in establishing the social and economic integration of persons with disabilities in the new Europe has been slowed. In the following section consideration is given to the measures the individual member states have taken to recognize disabled workers' rights to legal protection.

MEMBER STATES OF THE EUROPEAN COMMUNITY

The development of rehabilitation, resettlement and employment rights for disabled Europeans post-1945 has been influenced by four main factors.[34] First, the immediate post-war years witnessed a prolonged economic boom and produced labour market conditions in which there was a severe shortage of labour. This provided the impetus for policies designed to find ways of employing disabled persons, who now became a prized commodity in the workforce. Second, the development of the welfare state led to greater financial provision being made for those disabled by industrial and other accidents. The costs of a comprehensive compensation scheme led many countries to seek ways of rehabilitating and resettling disabled individuals in the vocational context. Third, the efforts of voluntary and other organizations actively involved with disabled people raised the profile of individuals with disabilities in society and changed the perception of the majority towards this minority. Slowly, but perceptively, employers and others have come to see that disabled persons are not simply passive recipients of charity but individuals capable of making a contribution in their own right and entitled to do so. Fourth, with the ending of the economic boom of the 1950s, disabled people came to recognize the fickleness of labour market conditions and that economic forces alone could not deliver basic social rights. So it was, from the 1960s onwards, that disabled Europeans began to import the lessons of the independent living and civil rights movements in the USA. As in Britain, so in Europe have we seen the growth of organizations of disabled people campaigning for fundamental disability rights.[35]

The majority of the twelve member states of the Community have adopted legal instruments (in some cases, constitutional instruments) which *expressly* refer to the right of disabled persons to equal treatment or recognition in employment.[36] The exceptions are Britain, Denmark, France, Ireland and Luxembourg. The EC Commission has commented:

> The explicit affirmation of the right to equal treatment is necessary to balance existing policies which place all the effort on the individual and present the elimination of the disability (or of its implications) as the solution to the problem of

> occupational integration. The right to equal treatment puts these policies on a new track and establishes a balance between personal effort and adaptation of the social and vocational environment. It prevents the disabled person from being excluded from certain rights and benefits solely on grounds of his [*sic*] disability, and implies a right to facilities to prevent the disability from becoming an obstacle to occupational integration. Affirmation of the right to equal treatment thus reverses the current underlying philosophy, which is one of assistance.[37]

The equal treatment principle is frequently observable as imbuing access to vocational training and rehabilitation services. However, its application in respect of access to employment opportunities is more variable throughout the member states. More often than not, the application of the equal treatment principle to disabled employment opportunities is expressed in a voluntarist framework of state-provided vocational rehabilitation, training and resettlement services, complemented by state-sponsored policies designed to educate and persuade employers,[38] and supported by state-provided financial assistance, subsidies, aids and equipment.

We now turn to examine the main components of *legal* measures in respect of disabled employment rights in the 11 remaining member states of the EC.[39] This account relies upon secondary sources.[40]

Belgium

In Belgium, until 1 January 1991, co-ordination of national policy on the employment of disabled persons was in the hands of the National Fund for the Social Resettlement of the Disabled.[41] On that date the National Fund was wound up and its functions were transferred to the National Sickness and Invalidity Insurance Institute and to three community-based organizations. The relevant law on the employment rights of disabled persons applied to physically disabled individuals whose effective employment capacity was reduced by at least 30 per cent (20 per cent in the case of mental disability).[42] However, with the decentralization of disabled employment policy, the concept of disability measured by degree has been abandoned. Disability is now recognized by the effect that an impairment has upon social and vocational integration.

National provision is made for private sector employers, employing no fewer than twenty persons, to employ disabled workers as a quota obligation.[43] However, this provision is not in force, although this was to be fixed by Royal Order. In the public sector, a number of jobs in the civil service and certain semi-public bodies are reserved for disabled persons,[44] and local authorities must apply a quota of one out of every fifty-five full-time positions in favour of disabled persons.[45] A disabled applicant for public employment must demonstrate fitness for work and that he or she constitutes no danger to the health or safety of himself or herself or others.[46] If a disabled person is rejected for a position in public employment, the National Fund for the Social Resettlement of the Disabled had to be informed of the grounds for rejection. This function now devolves to the community-based successors of the National Fund.

Belgian disabled employees enjoy no particular protection from dismissal and must rely upon the general principles of unfair dismissal law or collective bargaining arrangements. However, some essential measures to promote disabled employment opportunities have been adopted. First, employers who engage a disabled worker are entitled to a wage subsidy for up to one year.[47] A wage subsidy has also been provided for by national collective bargaining, which establishes the principle that disabled workers are entitled to a guaranteed minimum wage equivalent to that fixed by bargaining or custom.[48] Second, a contribution may be made to the provision of a suitably fitted work bench or to the costs of tools and working clothes.[49] Third, a loan may be made to an employer if merited by the circumstances of the employment of a disabled person.[50] More recently, a new decree has insisted that employers of an average maximum of 100 workers must take steps to adapt the job of a newly disabled worker or enable that worker to perform another job.[51] The employer is obliged to employ the worker under a contract of indefinite duration for at least one year from the recommencement of work. A wage subsidy may be payable, subject to a medical examination of the employee and a medical report justifying the subsidization.

Denmark

Denmark does not operate a quota scheme nor does it have a legislative definition of disability. It is not surprising, therefore, that disabled persons enjoy no particular additional protection under Denmark's law of dismissal, and there is no obligation on an employer to re-employ a newly disabled existing employee.

Nevertheless, disabled persons are given priority access to certain jobs in public authorities, subject to the duties of such jobs being within the capacities of disabled persons.[52] Such jobs may not be filled until the recruitment of a disabled person has been considered and negotiated with the placement services.

France

The French quota scheme applies across the public and private employment sectors to undertakings employing at least twenty staff.[53] The scheme applies to workers recognized as disabled, regardless of the extent of disability, by the Board for the Guidance and Occupational and Social Rehabilitation of Disabled Workers,[54] and to victims of industrial accidents resulting in a permanent partial disability of 10 per cent or greater. Recipients of disability pensions are also covered if their working capacity has been reduced by two-thirds or more. From 1991, the quota is set at 6 per cent of full-time or part-time positions (having increased in steps from 3 per cent since 1988). A severely disabled person, and those disabled persons being trained by the employer, count as 1.5 workers for the purpose of calculating compliance with the quota obligation.

Employers may be exempted from the quota scheme in a number of ways. First, an employer might sub-contract production or the provision of services with sheltered workshops or other designated centres of disabled employment. Second, through collective bargaining, French employers might provide plans in respect of disabled persons covering recruitment, integration, training, adaptation to technological change or retention during redundancies. Third, an employer might be exempted from the quota system by paying an annual contribution of up to 500 times the minimum hourly pay per non-employed disabled person to the Development Fund for the Occupational Integration of Disabled Workers. This last exemption also forms the basis for penalizing employers who wilfully fail to comply with the quota. For each unfilled quota place, such employers are required to pay an amount equal to the voluntary annual contribution plus a 25 per cent premium. French law provides no particular protection from dismissal for disabled employees, but the employment contract of a worker injured in the workplace is suspended until he or she is restored to full capacity.

In 1990, France introduced additional legislation to protect sick and disabled workers.[55] Through an amendment to Articles 187 and 416 of the Penal Code, criminal sanctions and civil proceedings can be used to address discrimination against persons and employees informed by their health status or disability. An employer may not dismiss or take action short of dismissal against employees on the grounds of their health, disability or habits. Such dismissals or actions are treated as null and void, and a defendant is punishable by imprisonment of two months to one year and/or a fine of 2,000–20,000 francs. The exceptional case is where an employee's incapacity to continue work has been certified by a doctor. So an inability to work or continued absenteeism will constitute non-discriminatory grounds. The law also extends to an employer's refusal to recruit someone because of his or her state of health or disability.

Germany[56]

German employment law requires employers with a workforce of at least 16 employees to maintain a quota of disabled employees of at least 6 per cent.[57] Failure to comply with the quota obligation results in a civil penalty of 200 Deutschmarks per month (since 1990) for every job not filled by a disabled person and, in serious cases of breach, a criminal fine of up to DM5,000 might be exacted. The proceeds of this penalty are ploughed back into positive disabled employment policies pursued by the state.[58] The quota obligation applies to both the private and public sectors. A disabled person is an individual who suffers from a functional disability (*Behinderung*), which affects his or her capacity for social integration, as a consequence of the effects of an irregular physical, mental or psychological condition. The disability must have a duration of at least six months and limit functional freedom of ability by at least 20 per cent. To qualify under the quota law as a disabled person (*Schwerbehinderten*), disability is measured at 50 per cent or more, whatever the actual effect upon life activities. A disabled person who is unable to find or retain employment without assistance, and whose disability is measured at 30 per cent or more, is also treated as disabled (*gleichstellte*). An individual's status as a qualifying disabled person is decided upon by federal pension officers upon application for a card known as an *Ausweiss*. Disputes about a person's disability status are heard by a social court rather than a labour court.

A disabled person may only be dismissed after careful consideration of means of avoiding dismissal (for example, by reasonable accommodation), and only then with authorization from the relevant authorities. Under German unfair dismissal law, the fact that an employee becomes disabled does not constitute a valid reason for dismissal. In the case of the onset of disabilities, the worker is entitled to expect reintegration in the employer's workplace as a result of the quota scheme, assuming that suitable employment opportunities exist. German employers' legal obligations are amplified and explained by a code of good practice.

Inevitably, problems for the German legal system in general, and for disability laws in particular, have been created by the unification of the former German Federal Republic and the German Democratic Republic (GDR). In a recent regional labour court decision,[59] it was held that where a public institution takes over an institution of the former GDR, but fails to make adequate provision for the employment of the quota of disabled persons formerly employed under the obligations of GDR law, each case has to be decided separately as to whether or not the refusal to employ is based on a reasoned use of discretionary powers. Otherwise, the disabled employees have a right to continued employment. Furthermore, the legal provisions making it obligatory for public authorities to employ a quota of disabled persons do not infringe the principle of equal treatment in Articles 12(1) and 33(2) of the German Constitution (*Grundgesetz*).

Greece

The term 'disabled person' is regarded as a pejorative one in Greece, and the phrase 'persons with specific needs' is preferred.[60] Such individuals are defined as:

> persons between the ages of 15 and 65 who have a limited capacity for occupational activity deriving from any permanent impairment or deficiency of a physical or mental nature.

There was a legally established quota of 3 per cent of 'persons with specific needs' operating in both the public and private sectors; however, this was raised to 5 per cent in 1991.[61] The quota applies to undertakings and departments employing at least fifty workers. Curiously, the law provides that disabled persons shall be recruited as lawyers in public bodies employing at least three lawyers, and 20 per cent of vacant positions for ancillary staff in the public sector are to be reserved for disabled persons.[62] Also in the public sector, 5 per cent of vacant posts must be reserved and all vacant telephonists' jobs are reserved for blind applicants.[63] Disabled persons are also entitled to six extra days paid annual holiday.[64]

Ireland

In the Irish Republic, a disabled person is defined by reference to a disadvantage for a given individual resulting from an impairment or disability which limits or prevents the accomplishment of a role that is normal for the individual concerned. Since 1977, a 3 per cent quota of disabled persons has applied to the public service as a matter of government decision. In order to seek the benefits of the quota scheme, a disabled person must be registered with the National Rehabilitation Board as a person who, because of disability, is substantially disadvantaged in obtaining or retaining employment. The quota scheme does not apply to private employers. Otherwise, Irish law is wholly silent upon the question of disabled workers and their rights.[65]

Italy[66]

The Italian quota programme applies to 'sheltered' workers. This is a broad category that includes disabled persons, widows, orphans and refugees.[67] A disabled person for this purpose is one whose capacity for work is diminished as a result of physical, mental or sensory impairment, whether the cause of impairment is congenital or otherwise.[68] A system of registration is in existence. The quota scheme requires employers with over 35 employees to engage 15 per cent of the workforce from the pool of 'sheltered' workers and approximately 12 per cent of engagements must be applied to disabled persons. Within that quota, there is a specific quota rate for different categories of disabled person, with provision for virement between different categories. The categories include the war disabled, disabled civil servants, occupationally disabled persons with up to one-third work incapacity, non-occupationally disabled persons with similar work incapacity, and deaf mutes. Blind persons attract reserved occupations as telephonists, masseurs and masseur-physiotherapists. An employer who cannot integrate a disabled worker into the workplace (for example, because of production or environment) must recruit other 'sheltered' workers instead. Breach of the quota scheme results in a fine, the proceeds of which are directed to vocational training. A disabled worker may be dismissed if, because of disability, he or she is unable adequately to carry out the duties of employment. Under the quota scheme, dismissal of a disabled worker on health grounds is only allowed if there is a danger to the safety of the installation or a risk to co-workers' health.

Luxembourg

Disabled employment law in Luxembourg applies to disabled persons who have suffered war disabilities, industrial accident and physical, mental or psychological impairment. In terms of their aptitude to obtain and retain employment, taking account of previous work experience, their capacity must be reduced by at least 30 per cent. The Luxembourg quota system applies in both the private sector and public employment. In the private sector, employers with over fifty staff must apply a 2 per cent quota of disabled employees, while employers with twenty-five to fifty staff must give priority to disabled applicants for suitable positions.[69] A disabled person identifies himself or herself as an intended beneficiary of the quota legislation by registration. In the public sector, the quota reserves a minimum of 2 per cent of jobs for disabled persons who can meet statutory training and admission criteria. Breach of the quota law is subject to a maximum fine of 10,000 Luxembourg francs. Luxembourg's dismissal law does not extend particular protection to disabled persons. However, a worker disabled at work is entitled to be given priority in re-engagement.

Reform of the 1959 law was proposed in 1989 by extending the coverage of the quota to persons with mental or sensory disabilities and increasing the public sector quota to 5 per cent. It was also proposed that in the private sector all enterprises with twenty-five personnel must employ at least one disabled employee; for companies with at least fifty staff the quota would be 2 per cent and for companies with over 300 employees the quota would be 4 per cent.[70] However, it was not until 1991 that reform in these terms was achieved.[71] In addition, the 1991 law prohibits the payment of wages to disabled workers lower than legally or collectively agreed provisions, unless there is proof that their performance is less than an able-bodied worker, in which case they may be paid in proportion to performance.

The Netherlands

The Dutch law on the employment of disabled persons requires both sides of industry, through collective bargaining or acting in concert, to adopt measures of occupational reintegration with the objective of ensuring that employers maintain a 5 per cent quota of disabled workers.[72] Since 1 July 1989, employers who have failed to satisfy these requirements are obliged to employ disabled persons as between 3 and 7 per cent of their workforce. The quota varies according to sector, industry or public service department. A failure to observe the quota will result in periodic levies on defaulting employers, while those exceeding the quota will qualify for financial assistance. The beneficiaries of these measures are persons in receipt of disability benefits or pensions and those benefiting from special measures for carrying out their work. The Dutch legislation envisages a number of alternative means by which employers can satisfy their obligations to disabled workers. These include the establishment of retraining and re-employment measures, redefining job standards so as to avoid exclusion of disabled applicants, reserving jobs for disabled persons, making adaptations to work positions and making other accommodations to promote disabled employability, considering alternative work and reassignment, and making use of state-provided funds to compensate for the costs of accommodation, including wage dispensation regulations. Dutch employees may not be dismissed on ill health grounds, without the agreement of a regional employment office, where the illness lasts for over two years. Account must be taken of possible accommodations in the workplace, including reassignment to other work. Judicial interpretation of these provisions ensures that a partially incapacitated worker cannot be dismissed if he or she is able to carry out the work within his or her capacities. If not so capable, the worker may volunteer for other work commensurate with his or her disability and the employer must make a reasonable offer of alternative duties.

Portugal

Portugal has not adopted a quota scheme, but has preferred to promote disabled employment opportunities through education, persuasion, employment measures and financial assistance. Article 71 of the Constitution of the Portuguese Republic provides:

> The State is committed to pursue a national policy for the prevention, treatment, rehabilitation and integration of disabled people, to develop pedagogic methods whereby society may be made aware of the duty to respect and assist the disabled and assume responsibilities for the effective exercise of their rights, without prejudice to the rights and duties of parents or guardians.

Generally speaking, a disabled person is an individual who, as a result of an injury, deformity or infirmity, whether congenital or acquired, is permanently impaired in relation to his or her occupation. However, employers of more than twenty workers are required to give priority to the re-engagement of workers permanently incapacitated by an accident at work. Employers of more than ten employees are required to retain in employment any industrially injured worker with temporary incapacity of less than 50 per cent. Otherwise, dismissal of a disabled person may only take place for good cause and disabled employees are given preference for retention during redundancies.[73]

Spain

Positive action on behalf of disabled Spaniards in the labour market takes the form of a quota scheme. Public and private enterprises employing more than fifty permanent employees are subject to a 2 per cent quota of *registered* disabled persons.[74] The quota is enforced by the Labour and Social Security Inspectorate and non-compliance is an administrative infringement punishable by a fine. The law applies to disabled persons whose capacity for integration into working life is diminished by a foreseeably permanent impairment of physical, psychological or sensory abilities. In addition, discrimination is forbidden in recruitment or employment because of a reduction in physical, psychological or sensory capacity, provided the worker can perform the job and otherwise meet its requirements. An infringement of this prohibition may be visited with a fine of between 50,000 and 500,000 pesetas. Any regulation, collective agreement, contract or unilateral decision that discriminates against disabled persons in any or all aspects of employment is null and void. In the public sector, and especially in the civil service, disabled persons enjoy the general protection of the principle of equal treatment, and selection on merit and ability. However, in principle, 3 per cent of civil service posts are reserved for disabled staff.[75] Workers who suffer a permanent, but partial, disability are entitled to be re-employed by the employer, if necessary with accommodation for his or her residual capacity.[76] If the worker regains full capacity, he or she is entitled to be re-engaged in the first vacancy in the relevant job category.

CONCLUSION

The primary legal tool employed to assist disabled people in the labour markets of the European countries is a quota system. By the mid-1980s, most European disabled quota schemes were following the path of the British quota: a path of under-achievement and non-enforcement. The exceptional case was the German scheme, which is generally agreed to be a relative success, and which gives the lie to the assertion made by British employers that quotas are not compatible with commercial competitiveness. Since then, however, other countries – most notably France, the Netherlands and Greece – have taken fresh initiatives to introduce new quota obligations or to strengthen existing quota provisions. The central feature of these recent developments is the fact that these quota schemes apply in both the public and the private sectors. It seems fruitless to expect private sector employers to meet compulsory quotas unless the public sector, with whom the private sector is increasingly in competition, is similarly obligated and can demonstrate the lead in good practices.

While EC law has largely failed to provide a supranationally imposed solution to unequal treatment of disabled workers, individual member states' attempts to protect disabled persons in the labour market present some evidence of how a fresh approach to disability rights might be informed in Britain. The use of public sector quotas, a greater willingness to enforce those quotas and the imaginative use of fines and/or levies to deter or punish transgression or subsidize other positive policies seem worth a second glance. However, there is little empirical evidence readily available, beyond civil servants' national reports, to gauge how successful these European models really are in practice. The suspicion remains that, as in Britain, legal instruments fashioned nearly a century ago and in the unusual combination of circumstances resulting in the aftermath of world war – labour shortages and the influx of large numbers of war disabled ex-service personnel into local labour markets – have long ceased to serve their purpose. With the exception of France, European states have yet to embrace legislation that enshrines the anti-discrimination principle and, as in Britain, voluntary action on disabled employment appears to be favoured over legal regulation by most European governments.

The prospects for a Community-level equal treatment directive for the benefit of disabled persons are not good.[77] As was noted in Chapter 1, Article 2 of the Social Chapter Agreement annexed to the EC Protocol on Social Policy calls for the EC to support and complement the activities of member states in, *inter alia*, 'the integration of persons excluded from the labour market'. While this is capable of being applied to disabled persons, the ambit of this laudatory phrase has yet to be determined. Furthermore, Britain is not a signatory to the Protocol, although it is part of the European Union Treaty signed at Maastricht in February 1992. While the health and safety competence of the EC might provide a future platform for Community legislation for the rights of disabled workers, any *social policy* initiatives in that regard will undoubtedly be the subject of British abstention. It is not surprising, therefore, that British disability rights activists have been fascinated by developments in the USA since the mid-1970s. In the following chapter, the application of discrimination theory and law to disabled persons under US constitutional, federal and state jurisdictions is examined.

NOTES

1. Mangin, 1983; European Communities (EC), 1991, 1993.
2. Commission of the EC, 1988: 7.
3. See, for example: Ravaud *et al.*, 1992 (cited in the previous chapter).
4. See: Council Directives 75/117, 76/207, 79/7, 86/378, 86/613, 92/85 and Commission Recommendation 92/131.
5. See: Council Directives 75/129, 77/187, 80/987, 89/391, 91/533 and 92/56.
6. This section draws heavily upon Daunt, 1991: Chapter 2.
7. Council Resolution of 27 June 1974 establishing the initial Community action programme for the vocational rehabilitation of handicapped persons: OJ C 80/30 (9 July 1974). The legal basis for Community competence in this arena would appear to be Articles 128 and 235 of the Treaty of Rome.
8. Council Resolution of 21 January 1974 concerning a social action programme: OJ C 13/1 (12 February 1974). Moreton argues that only a relatively small proportion of funds has assisted disabled people in Britain. He points out that in 1989–90 the UK Government's special schemes for disabled persons consumed £400 million, while European Social Fund financing in the same area amounted to less than 10 per cent of this figure: Moreton, 1992: 77.

9. Daunt, 1991: 10.
10. Resolution of the Parliament of 11 March 1981 concerning the economic, social and vocational integration of disabled people in the EC: OJ C 77/27 (6 April 1981).
11. Opinion of the Economic and Social Committee of 18 April 1981 on the situation and problems of the handicapped: OJ C 230/38 (10 September 1981). See also: Economic and Social Committee of the EC, 1981.
12. Resolution of the Council and Representatives of the Governments of the Member States of the EC of 21 December 1981 on the social integration of disabled people: OJ C 347/1 (31 December 1981). The Resolution was influenced by a Communication of the Commission to the Council of 14 November 1981 entitled *The social integration of disabled people – a framework for the development of Community action:* OJ C 347/14 (31 December 1981).
13. Council Recommendation of 24 July 1986 on the employment of disabled people in the EC (86/379/EEC): OJ L 225/43 (12 August 1986).
14. Daunt, 1991: 22.
15. See in particular the background studies prepared for the Commission: Rouault, 1978; Mangin, 1983; Commission of the EC, 1984; Croxen, 1984; Vogel-Polsky, 1984; Albeda, 1985.
16. Daunt, 1991: 23. The legal basis of the Recommendation is Article 235 of the Treaty of Rome (supplementary powers of the Community to act on a unanimous proposal).
17. The opinion of the European Parliament is expressed at OJ C 148/84 (16 June 1986).
18. Department of Employment, 1986.
19. [1990] IRLR 400 (ECJ).
20. COM(87) 342 of 20 July 1987.
21. Council Decision of 18 April 1988 establishing a second Community action programme for disabled people (HELIOS): OJ L 104/38 (23 April 1988). HELIOS stands for Handicapped People in the European Community Living Independently in an Open Society.
22. Commission of the EC, 1988.
23. Conclusions of the Council of 12 June 1989 on the employment of disabled people in the Community: OJ C 173/1 (8 July 1989).
24. Daunt, 1991: 151–2 (emphasis in original).
25. *Ibid.*: 152.
26. Council decision establishing a third Community action programme to assist disabled people (HELIOS II 1993-1996): OJ L 56/30 (9 March 1993).
27. Proposal for a Council Directive on minimum requirements to improve the mobility and the safe transport to work of workers with reduced mobility: OJ C 68/7 (16 March 1991) as amended by OJ C 15/18 (21 January 1992).
28. See: Commission of the EC, 1992.
29. This was also restated in Article 1. The European Parliament previously resolved that mobility should be seen as essential in finding and retaining suitable employment for disabled persons: OJ C 281/85 (19 October 1987).
30. Progress has been painfully slow. The Commission proposal was tabled in February 1991. The Economic and Social Committee gave its opinion in July 1991 and there was a first reading in the European Parliament in December 1991. The amended proposal was re-tabled in January 1992 but has made virtually no headway in discussion by the Council of Ministers since.
31. The means of transport covered by this mandate include public transport, transport provided by an employer and special transport services for disabled persons: Article 2(b).
32. It is envisaged that Articles 3 and 4 must be implemented by 31 December 1999: Article 8(a).
33. This presumably addresses the need for concessions in respect of carers and favourable treatment of guide dogs or palliative devices (such as wheelchairs). It is proposed that this part of the draft Directive be operational by 31 December 1993 (and not 1994 as originally proposed): Article 8(b) as amended. This deadline is clearly no longer realistic.
34. Daunt, 1991: 6–8.
35. One such European example is the *Groupement des Intellectuels Handicapés Physiques,* later retitled as the *Groupement pour L'Insertion des Personnes Handicapées Physiques* (the Association for the Integration of Physically Disabled Persons), in France. Another example is Italy's *La Lega per il Diritto al Lavoro degli Handicappati* (the National League for the Right to

Work of the Handicapped). For an account of the work of the National League in campaigning for a right to work for disabled people, see: Tudor, 1989.

36. Commission of the EC, 1988: 71 and Table 2.

37. *Ibid.*: 71.

38. The use of codes of good practice as a substitute for legal measures appears to be almost ubiquitous.

39. Britain is excluded from this discussion because of the full treatment given to it in Chapter 2. Three new members will join the EC in 1995 (Austria, Finland and Sweden) but are not included in the present account. Sweden's disability laws are surveyed in Lunt and Thornton (1993), while a short description of the position in Austria and Finland can be found in WHO (1990).

40. Commission of the EC, 1988, 1992; *European Industrial Relations Review*, 1988; UN, 1990a; WHO, 1990; Council of Europe, 1990; Daunt, 1991; Lunt and Thornton, 1993. See also (1993) *Social Europe* Supplement 1/93.

41. Established under the Law of 28 April 1958.

42. Law of 16 April 1963 on the social reclassification of disabled persons (the Social Resettlement of the Disabled Act 1963) gazetted in *Moniteur Belge*, 23 April 1963.

43. *Ibid.*: s 21. In principle, the law applied to disabled persons who had registered with the National Fund for the Social Resettlement of the Disabled.

44. Royal Order of 19 November 1976 (*Moniteur Belge*, 19 January 1977). Originally 600 posts were so reserved, but since 1977 1,200 jobs are set aside for this purpose. See also: Royal Order of 5 January 1976 (*Moniteur Belge*, 29 August 1972) and Royal Order of 11 August 1972 (*Moniteur Belge*, 3 March 1976).

45. Royal Order of 23 December 1977 (*Moniteur Belge*, 13 January 1978) and Royal Order of 6 March 1978 (*Moniteur Belge*, 25 March 1978).

46. Royal Order of 1 December 1964 (*Moniteur Belge*, 4 December 1964).

47. Ministerial Decree of 23 January 1968, as amended (*Moniteur Belge*, 3 February 1968).

48. Collective Labour Agreement No. 26 of 23 April 1977, upon which the force of law has been conferred by Royal Order of 11 March 1977. See further: Ministerial Decree of 3 February 1977 (*Moniteur Belge*, 23 February 1977).

49. Ministerial Decree of 17 March 1965, as amended (*Moniteur Belge*, 20 March 1965).

50. Ministerial decree of 17 November 1965 (*Moniteur Belge*, 3 December 1965).

51. Royal Order of 13 December 1991. This came into force on 20 December 1991.

52. By a decree of the Ministry of Labour of 18 December 1985.

53. Law No. 87-517 of 10 July 1987. This replaces legislation dating back to 1924 and 1957. Under the 1957 law, the quota had been set at 10 per cent and affected employers of at least eleven workers. General employment policy towards disabled persons is set out in the Disabled Persons (Policy) Act (Law 75-534 of 30 June 1975).

54. A disabled worker is a person whose chances of obtaining or holding a job is reduced by inadequacy or reduction of physical or mental capacities.

55. Law No. 90-602 of 12 July 1990 concerning the protection of persons against discrimination by reason of their health or handicap. Reported in *European Industrial Relations Review* (September 1990) at page 7 and in (1990) *Le Monde*, 18 April. The law is gazetted in *Journal Officiel de la République Française*, 13 July 1990 at 8272. I am grateful to Ian Bynoe, formerly Legal Director of MIND, for a copy of the legislation, and to Adina Halpern (formerly legal assistant at MIND) for her notes of translation of the measure. I remain responsible for any infelicities in recording the substance of this law.

56. In addition to the sources cited above, this sub-section draws upon: Brooke-Ross and Zacher, 1983; Brooke-Ross, 1984; Jochheim, 1985; Rasnic, 1992.

57. *Erstes Gesetz zur Änderung des Schwerbehindertengesetzes, 1989, Bundesgesetzblatt*, I 1110; *Gesetz zur Sicherung der Eingliederung Schwerbehinderter in Arbeit, Beruf und Gesellschaft*, 1986, *Bundesgesetzblatt*, I 1421, *ber* 5.1550.

58. It is reported that in 1983 some DM230 million was paid by way of penalty by three-quarters of the employers who are bound by the quota scheme and that the remaining quarter employed far more disabled workers than their quota obligation: WHO, 1990: 129.

59. Case No. 12 Sa 56/92 [1993] *Neue Justiz* 192 (*Landesarbeitsgerich Berlin*).

60. Law 1648 of 1986.

61. Joint Decision 30965 of the Ministers of National Defence and of Labour (14 May 1991).
62. Law 1648 of 1986.
63. Law 1735 of 1987.
64. Ministerial Decree 2065/89.
65. However, the Irish Congress of Trade Unions has adopted a Disabled Person's Charter asserting the right to meaningful training and employment without discrimination or stereotyping: *European Industrial Relations Review* No. 189 (July 1990) at page 7. However, during 1994 consideration was being given to the introduction of disability discrimation legislation.
66. This account also draws upon Tudor, 1989: 42–4.
67. Act No. 482 of 2 April 1968. The Act consolidates pre-existing legislation from as early as 1940.
68. The Act makes fine distinctions and appears to exclude 'civil invalids' suffering from *mental* disability (Article 5), whereas such exclusion does not apply to war, service or work invalids. In a warning judgment, the Italian Constitutional Court indicated that the constitutional legality of this exclusion was doubtful: *Riganti, Zucchetti and Cannata* v *Plada Plasmon spa and Fontana Luigi di Veduggio spa* (Decision No. 1088 of 1988) (1989) I *Foro Italiana* 980 and (1991) 9 ILLR 113. Subsequently, the exception has been declared unconstitutional by the Court: (Decision No. 50 of 2 February 1990) (1990) II *Rivista Italiana di Diritto del Lavoro* 269 and (1992) 10 ILLR 71. This decision has legislative effect, but reforming legislation was passed in 1992 (Act No. 104 of 5 February 1992).
69. Act of 28 April 1959.
70. *European Industrial Relations Review* No. 184 (May 1989) at page 7.
71. Law of 12 November 1991.
72. Disabled Workers Employment Act 1986 (*Wet Arbeid Gehandicapte Werknemers*). Research into the attitudes of Dutch employers towards the new law showed that about two-thirds of employers did not want to recruit any more disabled persons and about one-fifth said that they would not employ any disabled person: *European Industrial Relations Review* No. 176 (September 1988) at page 7.
73. Legislative Decree No. 84/76 of 28 November 1976.
74. Registration is with an employment office. The legislation is contained in Act 13/82 of 7 April 1982 on the social integration of disabled people and derives its power from Article 49 of the Spanish Constitution of 1987, which reflects Spain's commitment to the Universal Declaration of Human Rights.
75. Royal Decree 198 of 1987.
76. Royal Decree 1451/83 of 11 May 1983.
77. But see Commission of the EC, 1994: 38–9 and Waddington, 1995.

4

Disabled Employment Rights in the United States

INTRODUCTION

The enactment of employment rights for disabled persons in the United States must be placed in the context of a society whose constitution commits it to the principles of equality and human dignity. Title VII of the Civil Rights Act 1964 established the principle of non-discrimination and equal treatment in employment irrespective of race, colour, gender, nationality and religious belief.[1] Women also enjoyed protection from sex-based discrimination in employment remuneration under the Equal Pay Act and Fair Labor Standards Act.[2] However, none of these civil rights measures protected disabled people. Prior to the Rehabilitation Act 1973 (RA 1973), legislation affecting disabled persons had been piecemeal: securing services and assistance for disabled people, rather than civil rights, or targeting only certain sections of the disabled constituency.[3] Moreover, the law and the legal system often conspired against the best interests of disabled persons.[4]

Constitutional Protection

Part of the difficulty for disabled persons trying to achieve basic civil rights through litigation was the absence of a convenient legal peg upon which to hang an argument. Litigation based upon constitutional arguments presented only partial success.[5] The Fourteenth Amendment's guarantee of equal protection and due process of law has been used as a basis to challenge employment discrimination generally and disability discrimination in particular. In principle, the equal protection analysis should apply to disabled employment opportunities. Nevertheless, there are few cases in which the analysis has been applied successfully to disabled persons.[6] Indeed, the Supreme Court specifically rejected the contention that classifications that disadvantaged individuals with mental retardation should be subjected to heightened judicial scrutiny under the equal protection clause.[7] Due process theory has been more fertile ground. The Fourteenth Amendment provides that no state shall 'deprive any person of life, liberty, or property without due process of law'. The denial of an employment opportunity by a public agency should fall within the scope of this formula, requiring the plaintiff to be accorded procedural due process, with an opportunity for notice and a hearing.[8] While the formula may protect disabled persons while *in* employment, a disabled applicant *for* employment has no property interest capable of protection.[9]

A further constitutional argument in support of disabled employment rights could be mounted under the Thirteenth Amendment. This provides that 'Neither slavery nor involuntary servitude . . . shall exist within the United States'. Although clearly designed to liberate the black slaves after the Civil War, it has been argued that the amendment can be utilized to assist other oppressed peoples.[10] The Thirteenth Amendment, unlike the Fourteenth Amendment, applies both to state action and to private acts of discrimination. Its obvious application in respect of disabled persons is to regulate forced labour practices in state institutions, but the contention is that it is broad enough to address employment discrimination against disabled persons generally. This expansive interpretation of the Thirteenth Amendment remains untested.

State Legislation

Many commentators turned to see whether state laws and constitutions could be recruited to assist disabled persons achieve civil rights.[11] Weiss observed at least four weaknesses in the coverage of state law.[12] First, state laws provided only uncertain remedies for disability-based employment discrimination. Second, they often relied upon the rather passive enforcement strategies of local civil rights commissions, and thus were not strictly enforced. Third, such laws were 'uneven in scope and quality', especially in defining disability and the protected class. Fourth, many disability discrimination laws contained exceptions which arguably codified many of the existing prejudices that disabled persons have to encounter. For example, a refusal to hire a disabled applicant might often be justified by reference to safety grounds, the well-being of the disabled person or inconvenience to co-workers, as well by contentions equating disability and inability. Weiss commented that

> The problem with these exceptions is that they focus on disability as a classification to justify discrimination. The purpose of fair employment laws should be to force the employer to focus on the capacity of the *individual* to do the job regardless of the class to which he belongs.[13]

The point about these exceptions is that, if they existed in any case, the plaintiff would not be qualified for the job and thus would not have been discriminated against on an irrational ground; yet it was not thought necessary to write such exceptions into anti-discrimination laws in general.

In a later survey, Flaccus found that 49 states had enacted some law prohibiting private employment discrimination against disabled people.[14] Unlike with Title VII of the Civil Rights Act, the majority of the states applied the law to nearly all employers, regardless of the size of their workforces. Nevertheless, Flaccus concluded that state laws were restrictive in other ways. The definition of disability (or 'handicap') was frequently very narrow. Many statutes required the disabled person to be able to perform all aspects of the job in order to qualify for protection from discrimination. It was also common for such statutes to omit any requirement of reasonable accommodation on the employer. The efficacy of remedies provided for disability discrimination was also in doubt. Flaccus concluded that, taking all factors into account, only twelve states adequately addressed the problem of employment discrimination against disabled people in private employment.[15] She commented that, 'where state and federal coverage overlap, the federal statutes are generally more helpful to the handicapped person than the state statutes'.[16] She argued that Title VII would be the logical provision upon which to construct a federal prohibition on employment discrimination against disabled persons. Only two refinements would be needed: an ability to work requirement and a reasonable accommodation requirement.

FEDERAL REHABILITATION ACT 1973

Despite several bills that attempted to amend Title VII of the Civil Rights Act 1964 to include disabled people,[17] it was not until the RA 1973 that the civil rights of disabled people were addressed and, even then, in a limited manner.[18] The main body of the Act was concerned with reforms of federal and state vocational rehabilitation programmes. The civil rights component was relegated to three sections comprising miscellaneous provisions. Nevertheless, it was an Act that broke the mould that shaped orthodox thinking on disabled people and triggered a powerful movement for comprehensive disability rights. Because the legislation was modelled on race and sex discrimination legislation, disability became a legally acknowledged civil rights issue. The Act took a cross-disability approach in recognizing the common social problems encountered by people of varying and various disabilities. In adopting an imaginative and broadly conceived definition of disability, the Act comprehended the argument that disability is often a social construct rather than a purely medical status. By bringing disabled people within the protection of the anti-discrimination principle, the law conceded that disadvantage and handicap are the products of society's attitudinal and structural barriers, and less the result of personal limitations caused by impairment and disability.

Title V of the 1973 Act specifically addresses disabled employment discrimination in federal employment (section 501), by federal contractors (section 503) and in programmes or activities receiving federal assistance (section 504). These provisions are underpinned by administrative regulations. The section 501 regulations are published by the EEOC as part of the general provisions fostering equal employment opportunities in federal government,[19] whereas the section 503 regulations are those proclaimed by the OFCCP to ensure compliance with the affirmative action obligations of government contractors.[20] The US Department of Justice has been designated as the federal department responsible for co-ordinating the implementation of section 504. The co-ordinating regulations apply to federal departments or agencies empowered to extend federal financial assistance,[21] and they in turn must issue regulations consistent with the Department of Justice model in order to implement section 504 in respect of the programmes and activities to which they provide assistance.[22]

Section 501

Section 501(b) requires the executive branch of the federal government – in its role as an employer – to develop and implement affirmative action plans for the hiring, placement and advancement of disabled persons.[23] The affirmative action plan must be submitted to the Inter-agency Committee on Employees who are Individuals with Disabilities and to the EEOC. A valid plan must describe the extent to which the special needs of disabled employees are being met, as well as the methods being used to achieve this objective. Once adopted, a disability affirmative action plan has to be updated annually. It is subject to annual review by the EEOC, which may approve it if satisfied that the plan contains sufficient assurances, procedures and commitments to provide adequate employment opportunities for disabled individuals.[24]

The section has been interpreted as including a non-discrimination component, although this is not made explicit in the statutory language.[25] Consequently, federal agencies must structure their procedures and programmes so as to afford equal employment opportunities for disabled individuals, and federal employers' actions in this regard are subject to judicial review. The regulations enacted to implement section 501 provide that federal agencies shall give full consideration to the hiring, placement and advancement of qualified disabled persons and shall not discriminate against them, and that the federal government 'shall become a model employer of handicapped individuals'.[26] Federal employers are mandated to make reasonable accommodations for disabled persons, unless this would impose undue hardship on the operation of programmes, and this has been construed as requiring the taking of measures that involve more than a *de minimis* cost.[27] The use of discriminatory employment criteria or pre-employment enquiries is also regulated,[28] while federal employers must not discriminate against qualified disabled applicants or employees by allowing their facilities to be physically inaccessible.[29]

Compliance with section 501 is enforced by the EEOC. The EEOC section 501 regulations require federal employers to adopt procedures for handling disability discrimination complaints. The section provides the exclusive remedy for federal employees subjected to disability discrimination, so that, for example, there are no separate causes of action for breaches of constitutional rights or the infliction of a tort.[30] Section 505(a)(1) extends identical remedies, procedures and rights to federal employees who are the subject of disability discrimination claims, as apply to federal employees with sex or race discrimination claims under Title VII.[31] This provision also allows a court to order an equitable or affirmative action remedy, subject to the reasonableness of the cost of any necessary workplace accommodation and the availability of alternative, appropriate relief.

Section 503

Section 503 introduces statutory contract compliance as a tool for ensuring disabled equal employment opportunities.[32] Regulations that cover federal contractors under section 503 have been enacted by the Office of Federal Contract Compliance Programs.[33] This section has also been interpreted as implying a non-discrimination component, although this is not made explicit in the statutory language.[34] Section 503 extends the non-discrimination principle, as it applies to disabled persons, into the private sector by using the federal government's purchasing power in such a way as to improve disabled employment opportunities.[35] Where section 503 does apply, every relevant contract with the federal government must incorporate a provision requiring the federal contractor, when employing persons to carry out the contract, to take affirmative action to employ and advance in employment qualified disabled persons.[36]

Any employer contracting with the federal government is required to take affirmative action to employ and advance disabled persons if the value of the contract exceeds $10,000. This provision covers procurement contracts for goods or services and construction contracts. It also applies to any similar sub-contracts that exceed $10,000 and that are entered into by a federal contractor in order to carry out the main contract.[37] Although transactions involving less than $10,000 are not covered by section 503, federal agencies and contractors must not procure supplies or services in less than usual quantities in order to avoid section 503 obligations.[38] There is a presumption that section 503 should apply to open-ended contracts and indefinite quantity contracts, unless there is reason to believe that the amount to be ordered under the contract in any one year will not exceed $10,000.[39] The commercial scope of the affirmative action obligation is equally wide,[40] but does not include employment contracts or federally assisted contracts.[41] The provisions of section 503 may be waived by executive action in the national interest with respect to any contract.[42] There is also a national security exemption.[43]

A disabled individual who believes that he or she has been the subject of a violation of the affirmative action clause in a federal contract may complain to the Department of Labor under section 503(b).[44] The Department will investigate the complaint, through the OFCCP, and take action accordingly.[45] If the investigation uncovers a breach of section 503, conciliation is attempted before a formal hearing disposes of the complaint.[46] The OFCCP may order a federal contractor to comply with an affirmative action clause and to remedy an instance of discrimination by, for example, making an employment offer and paying lost wages. In addition, the OFCCP might seek judicial enforcement of the relevant contractual provision by seeking an injunction in the ordinary courts. Furthermore, progress payments due under a contract may be withheld, the contract terminated and/or the contractor debarred from receiving future contractual opportunities.

Section 504

Section 504 prohibits discrimination against otherwise qualified disabled individuals in all programmes and activities administered by recipients of federal financial assistance.[47] The section 'was enacted with little debate and most likely little understanding of its critical role in the development of civil-rights policy'.[48] This prohibition against disability-based discrimination also applies to programmes or activities conducted by any federal agency. The section is amplified by federal regulations promulgated under the Act.[49] The Supreme Court originally limited coverage of section 504 by reducing its scope to the actual programmes and activities for which the employer was receiving federal financial assistance, rather than the whole of the recipient's enterprise.[50] The scope of programmes and activities is now broadly defined to include 'all of the operations of' relevant entities.[51] It seems reasonably clear after *Consolidated Rail Corporation* v *Darrone*[52] that section 504 does permit a private right of action, but compensatory relief (as opposed to injunctive or equitable relief) is not always available.[53]

Under the model regulations, the concept of discrimination is explained and the classification of 'handicap' expanded. The regulations recognize the need to eliminate architectural, communicational and other barriers, and to take affirmative action to ensure the application of the non-discrimination principle in the disability context. The preamble to the model regulations makes this clear:

> There is overwhelming evidence that in the past many handicapped persons have been excluded from programs entirely, or denied equal treatment, simply because they are handicapped. But eliminating such gross exclusions and denials of equal treatment is not sufficient to assure genuine equal opportunity. In drafting a regulation to prohibit exclusion and discrimination, it became clear that different or special treatment of handicapped persons, because of their handicaps, may be necessary in a number of contexts in order to ensure equal opportunity . . . These problems have been compounded by the fact that ending discriminatory practices and providing equal access to programs may involve major burdens on some recipients. Those burdens and costs . . . provide no basis for exemption from section 504 or this regulation . . . But it is also clear that factors of burden and cost had to be taken into account in the regulation in prescribing the actions necessary to end discrimination and to bring handicapped persons into full participation in federally financed programs and activities.[54]

This explains the underlying theory which informs all subsequent disability rights legislation. The application of the non-discrimination principle to disability discrimination will be explored in greater detail in Chapter 6.

There are three concepts which are common to sections 501, 503 and 504: the definition of the protected class, an ability to work requirement and the need to make reasonable accommodation. These concepts are next outlined.

Individual with Handicaps

As originally drafted, the RA 1973 protected the employment rights of the 'handicapped individual'. Amendments made in 1992 substituted the term 'individual with a disability'. The Americans with Disabilities Act 1990, discussed later in this chapter, also uses the expression 'individual with a disability'. This reflects the growing awareness in the USA of the negative power of labels and the preference of disabled persons for descriptive language which focuses upon the individual rather than the disability. In legal terms, however, the choice of nomenclature is not significant and these terms are interchangeable without affecting their legal import. Numerous amendments to the definitional section have been made since 1973.[55]

For the purposes of the anti-discrimination provisions of the 1973 Act, the protected class embraces any person who has a physical or mental impairment which substantially limits one or more of such person's major life activities, or has a record of such impairment, or is regarded as having such impairment.[56] The definition does not extend to protect individuals currently engaging in the illegal use of drugs where an employer discriminates because of such use. However, rehabilitated drug users, participants in supervised drug rehabilitation programmes and persons erroneously treated as drug users are protected, provided they are not currently using illegal drugs.[57] Individuals who are alcoholics are also excluded from protection if their current use of alcohol prevents them from performing their employment duties or would pose a direct threat to property or safety while in employment.[58] Excluded from the Act's protection too are individuals with a currently contagious disease or infection which constitutes a direct threat to the health and safety of others or which results in their inability to perform the duties of the job.[59]

The definition of an 'individual with a disability' is amplified by the model regulations, which also illustrate the disabilities covered by the section.[60] A 'physical impairment' is defined as:

> any physiological disorder or condition, cosmetic disfigurement, or anatomical loss affecting one or more of the following body systems: neurological; musculoskeletal; special sense organs; respiratory, including speech organs; cardiovascular; reproductive, digestive; genitourinary, hemic and lymphatic; skin; and endocrine;

while a 'mental impairment' constitutes 'any mental or psychological disorder, such as mental retardation, organic brain syndrome, emotional or mental illness, and specific learning disabilities'. A person who has a 'record of . . . impairment' is explained as one who 'has a history of, or has been misclassified as having, a mental or physical impairment that substantially limits one or more major life activities',[61] while a person who is regarded as having an impairment is one who:

> (A) has a physical or mental impairment that does not substantially limit major life activities but that is treated . . . as constituting such a limitation; (B) has a physical or mental impairment

> that substantially limits major life activities only as the result of the attitudes of others toward such impairment; or (C) has none of the [physical] impairments defined . . . but is treated . . . as having such an impairment.[62]

The term 'major life activities' is illustrated as meaning 'functions such as caring for one's self, performing manual tasks, walking, seeing, hearing, speaking, breathing, learning, and working'.[63] It is clear from the Department of Labor's section 504 regulations, and the OFCCP's section 503 regulations, that persons are 'substantially limited' in a major life activity if, because of their disability, they are likely to experience difficulty in securing, retaining or advancing in employment.[64] The qualification of a *substantial limitation* upon a major life activity is not otherwise explained in the scheme of regulations.

Otherwise Qualified Standard

A complainant under section 504, as well as satisfying the definitional requirements of being an individual with disability, must also be 'otherwise qualified' within the meaning of the legislation. The implementing regulations explain that, in the context of employment, this denotes 'a handicapped person who, with reasonable accommodation, can perform the essential functions of the job in question'.[65] So an inability to perform non-essential elements of a job should not disqualify a disabled person from protection. In *Southeastern Community College* v *Davis*,[66] the Supreme Court held that an otherwise qualified disabled person 'is one who is able to meet all of a program's requirements in spite of his handicap'. In *Alexander* v *Choate*,[67] the Supreme Court explained that the Davis decision did not mean that an employer might not be required to make reasonable accommodation so as to assist a disabled person to become otherwise qualified. What was required was a balancing between the rights of disabled persons to social integration and the legitimate interests of employers to preserve the integrity of their undertakings and activities.

Section 503 also contains an explicit 'otherwise qualified' requirement. However, the regulations promulgated under section 503 take a slightly different approach. They require the disabled person to be capable of performing the particular job, with reasonable accommodation, but at the same time insist that any qualifications should be job-related and consistent with business necessity and safety.[68] Section 501 does not contain an 'otherwise qualified' condition, but the implementing regulations assume that the non-discrimination principle only applies to qualified handicapped persons.[69] Again, the concept of being 'otherwise qualified' means that the individual can, with or without reasonable accommodation, perform the essential functions of the job without endangering the health or safety of the individual or others but, in addition, must also meet the experience and/or educational requirements of the position or the criteria for appointment under one of the special appointing authorities for disabled persons.[70]

Reasonable Accommodation

The 'otherwise qualified' standard is somewhat ameliorated by the imposition of a duty upon employers to make reasonable accommodation.[71] Thus, disabled persons might qualify for protection in a number of ways. First, they might be able to perform all the elements of the job without accommodation. Second, without accommodation, they might be able to perform all the elements of the job, except those which are non-essential. Third, they might be able to perform all the elements of the job with reasonable accommodation. Fourth, they might be unable to perform all the elements of the job, despite reasonable accommodation, yet be able to perform the essential elements with reasonable accommodation.

The term 'reasonable accommodation' is not defined in the Department of Justice model section 504 regulations. They simply provide that:

> A recipient [of federal funds] shall make reasonable accommodation to the known physical or mental limitations of an otherwise qualified handicapped applicant or employee unless the recipient can demonstrate that the accommodation would impose an undue hardship on the operation of its program.[72]

However, the Department of Health and Human Services section 504 regulations exemplify reasonable accommodation as including:

> Making facilities used by employees readily accessible to and usable by handicapped persons, and . . . job restructuring, part-time or modified work schedules, acquisition or modifi-

cation of equipment or devices, the provision of readers or interpreters, and other similar actions.[73]

The Department of Labor section 504 regulations are to like effect,[74] as are the regulations under section 501.[75]

AMERICANS WITH DISABILITIES ACT 1990

Although the 1973 statute ensured that the civil rights of disabled people were at least recognized in law, it was a far from complete framework for disabled equal employment opportunities. First, it applied only in the public sector to employment by the federal government, under federal contracts and in organizations receiving federal funding or assistance. It did not purport to tackle directly the employment rights of disabled persons in the private sector. Second, there were some doubts about whether the Act provided a private right of action to an aggrieved individual. Third, judicial interpretation of the statute often narrowed the protection available under it to disabled workers. Fourth, and finally, the scope and impact of remedies for breach of the federal law were limited. Nevertheless, by the late 1970s and early 1980s, the USA had a federal and state legal framework within which questions of disability discrimination could be addressed. Disability had thereby become a civil rights issue.

Background to Reform

Weicker recounted how the lack of disabled civil rights in private employment, public accommodations, transport, and state and local activities and services led to pressure for new civil rights legislation.[76] Calls were made for the amendment of the Civil Rights Act 1964 to include disabled persons as a protected class.[77] Between 1979 and 1987, a number of Bills were introduced into Congress with a view to extending the Civil Rights Act 1964 to disabled persons.[78] However, all this activity failed to bear fruit. Perhaps the turning point was the year of 1984. Then the National Council on the Handicapped,[79] re-established as an independent federal agency to review federal laws and programmes affecting disabled persons, received repeated evidence of disability discrimination.[80]

Such evidence was reinforced by survey data, which also demonstrated support for a new civil rights initiative.[81] Meanwhile, much energy had to be expended to maintain the civil rights already achieved by disabled people under the RA 1973 and amending legislation was passed to overturn Supreme Court decisions unfavourable to the civil rights of disabled people.[82] Finally, in its first and landmark report in 1986, the Council recommended far-reaching legislative reform to prohibit comprehensive disability discrimination.[83]

The full civil rights of persons with disabilities and their claims to equality under the law were eventually recognized by the enactment of the Americans with Disabilities Act 1990 (ADA 1990).[84] A draft Bill contained in the second report of the National Council on the Handicapped in 1988 formed the basis of the ADA Bill first introduced into Congress in April 1988.[85] The original Bill addressed broad types of prohibited discrimination, including employers' practices, and then described broad forms of prohibited discrimination universally applicable to employers, service providers, housing operators, transportation concerns, etc. There were no separate employment provisions in the Bill, so that employment-specific measures would be left to regulations to be issued under the statute.[86] The second ADA Bill took a different approach and was structured according to distinctive issues, such as employment, allowing sophisticated and differential treatment of each.[87] It was introduced into Congress in May 1989. After much debate and modification,[88] the ADA 1990 was eventually signed into law on 26 July 1990.

Aims and Objectives of the Legislation

The Act prohibits discrimination on the ground of disability in employment, housing, public accommodations, education, transport, communications, recreation, institutionalization, health services, voting and access to public services.[89] Although this study is primarily concerned with disability discrimination in employment, the impact on disabled persons of architectural barriers and lack of access to public transport should not be overlooked in consideration of equal employment opportunity. The ADA requires all new public transport to be accessible to disabled people and existing public rail systems must be made accessible during the course of time. Architectural barriers in existing buildings must be removed where 'readily achievable' or alternative steps can be taken to ameliorate the effect of the barrier. New construction projects (and alterations to existing buildings) must be designed and built to be accessible to persons with disabilities. Rights to mobility and physical access are now seen as essential elements of the right to work.

The avowed intention of the ADA 1990 is to provide 'a clear and comprehensive national mandate for the elimination of discrimination against individuals with disabilities'.[90] To that end, the Act furnishes 'clear, strong, consistent, enforceable standards' confronting disability-based discrimination, while it seeks to ensure that the federal government plays a central role in enforcing those standards.[91] In a magisterial phrase, the ADA 1990 strives

> to invoke the sweep of congressional authority, including the power to enforce the fourteenth amendment and to regulate commerce, in order to address the major areas of discrimination faced day-to-day by people with disabilities.[92]

As legislation fashioned upon the model of Title VII of the Civil Rights Act 1964,[93] the ADA has been described as

> the most comprehensive piece of disability rights legislation ever enacted, and the most important piece of civil rights legislation since the 1964 Civil Rights Act. This legislation will transform the landscape of American society, and will have a profound effect on what it means to be disabled.[94]

In the words of one commentator, as 'equality commands respect for the diverse cultures of our land, so the ADA also demands accommodation to the varied ways disabled people live their lives'.[95] However, nothing in the Act engineers equality of employment outcomes, reverse discrimination in favour of disabled individuals, or the mandating of quotas. Although the ADA is an emancipating statute for disabled people, in one view it is also an extension of civil rights for all Americans. A former Attorney-General of the United States, instrumental in the passage of the Act, argued that all citizens stand to benefit from *any* extension of civil rights in favour of minority groups by enabling a wider contribution to the well-being of the economy and society at large.[96] The Act has thus been designated as 'social legislation to end barriers, not an instrumentality for continuous and acrimonious litigation'.[97]

Interpreting the Legislation

The application and interpretation of the ADA are assisted by four sources. The first two are contained within the Act itself. They consist of a recital of Congressional findings and a statement of the legislative purpose.[98] The third source is the legislative history of the ADA as contained in a number of Congressional committee reports on the passage of the ADA through the parliamentary process.[99] Although the substantive provisions of the 1990 Act were more comprehensive than those of the RA 1973, Congress charged the EEOC with the task of drafting implementing regulations. Regulations were published on the first anniversary of the Act being signed into law and have subsequently been codified.[100] These regulations, having the force and effect of law, and being issued by the EEOC under powers delegated by the Act, represent the fourth source of application and interpretation.[101]

In addition, it is expressly provided that the ADA is not to be interpreted as providing standards inferior to those already set by the RA 1973 and its regulations.[102] The ADA does not pre-empt the RA 1973. Equally, the 1990 Act does not limit any other federal, state or local law which provides an equal or superior degree of protection to disabled workers.[103] This would appear to apply to both legislative and common law protection. The EEOC makes it clear that an employer may not argue that a lesser anti-discrimination standard under a state law excuses a failure to meet a higher standard under the ADA and vice versa.[104] It is clear that compliance with the RA 1973 and state fair employment laws will not necessarily assure compliance with the ADA 1990. The ADA will be interpreted in the light of precedents and regulations under the RA 1973 and applies a standard at least as stringent as the earlier law (if not more so).

Employment Provisions of the ADA 1990 Outlined[105]

The employment provisions in Title I of the ADA came into force on 26 July 1992. The ADA 1990 prohibits a 'covered entity' from discriminating against qualified individuals with disabilities. For this purpose, a 'covered entity' means 'an employer, employment agency, labor organization or joint labor-management committee'.[106] Until July 1994, only employers who employed twenty-five or more employees were within the scope of the ADA 1990, but subsequently all employers of fifteen or more employees must take cognizance of this law.[107] Employers were effectively given a two- to four-year period in which to prepare for the new legal regime, while the federal authorities were given a breathing space in which to prepare the detailed regulations and technical assistance plans which underpin the legislation.

Until the ADA, federal law provided little or no protection from disability discrimination in employment in the private sector. As has been seen, Title V of the RA 1973 applied only to federal employers, federal contractors and recipients of federal funds. Nevertheless, the employment provisions in Title I of the ADA are largely derived from the standards set by section 504 of the RA 1973 and its supporting regulations. Section 504 may have lacked the broad application of the ADA, but the 1990 statute effectively extends the existing federal provision into the private sector. Title I of the ADA addresses disability discrimination in private employment, but does so by borrowing from the non-discrimination concepts of section 504 of the RA 1973. In particular, employers in both the federal and private sectors must now make 'reasonable accommodation' for qualified disabled individuals, subject to an 'undue hardship' defence.

Meaning of Disability

In order to enjoy the protection of the ADA 1990, a person must have a 'disability' within the meaning of the statute. The Act defines 'disability', with respect to an individual, as:

> (A) a physical or mental impairment that substantially limits one or more of the major life activities of such individual; (B) a record of such impairment; or (C) being regarded as having such an impairment.[108]

These are terms which are almost identical to the definition of 'handicap' under the relevant provisions of the RA 1973. As noted before, the use of the word 'disability' rather than 'handicap' reflects modern terminology preferred by disabled persons themselves and nothing of substance hangs on the change of phraseology. The definition is broad and no attempt is made to list possible disabilities.[109] The key concept is that of an 'impairment'. The EEOC regulations define 'physical or mental impairment' as meaning:

> (1) any physiological disorder or condition, cosmetic disfigurements, or anatomical loss affecting one or more of the following body systems: neurological; musculoskeletal; special sense organs; respiratory, including speech organs; cardiovascular; reproductive; digestive; genitourinary; hemic and lymphatic; skin; and endocrine; or (2) any mental or psychological disorder, such as mental retardation, organic brain syndrome, emotional or mental illness, and specific learning disabilities.[110]

The temptation to list exhaustively the kinds of conditions which will be counted as impairments is also resisted in the regulations.

It is not enough to demonstrate the existence of an impairment. It must also be shown to present a substantial limitation on one of the individual's major life activities.[111] Once again, the concept of 'major life activities' is not defined in the Act, but the regulations state that this means functions such as walking, seeing, hearing, speaking, breathing, learning, working, caring for one's self and carrying out manual tasks.[112] A 'substantial limitation' on a major life activity may be measured in two ways.[113] First, individuals are 'substantially limited' if they are unable to perform a major life activity which an average person could perform. Second, and alternatively, individuals may be 'substantially limited' if significantly restricted as to the condition, manner or duration under which they can perform a major life activity as compared to an average person. Three factors are relevant: (a) the nature and severity of the impairment; (b) the actual or expected duration of the impairment; and (c) the actual or expected permanent or long-term impact of the impairment.[114]

Individuals who have 'a physical or mental impairment that substantially limits one or more of the major life activities of such individual' are expressly covered. Persons with a 'record of . . . an impairment' (as already defined) are also within the statute's purview. This protects a person who has a history of impairment or who has been misdiagnosed or misclassified as so impaired.[115] The ADA also includes individuals who are 'regarded as having . . . an impairment'. This means that the person in question:

> (1) has a physical or mental impairment that does not substantially limit major life activities but that is treated . . . as constituting such a limitation; (2) has a physical or mental impairment that substantially limits major life activities only as a result of the attitudes of others toward such impairment; or (3) has

> none of the impairments defined . . . but is treated . . . as having such an impairment.[116]

All three branches of the definition of the protected class are imported from the equivalent provisions of the RA 1973 and its supporting regulations.

For the purposes of the employment provisions of the ADA, disabled individuals within the Act's protection do not include individuals 'currently engaging in the illegal use of drugs', if that is the basis upon which an employer has discriminated.[117] Individuals with 'psychoactive substance use disorders' resulting from current illegal use of drugs are expressly excluded from the classifications of 'disability'.[118] The term 'use' includes possessing or distributing illegal drugs. However, rehabilitated drug users (or participants in a supervised rehabilitation programme) are not excluded from the definition of disabled person provided they are no longer engaging in drug use.[119] Similarly, an individual who is erroneously regarded as engaging in the use of illegal drugs is not excluded from qualifying as a disabled person. Nevertheless, the ADA does permit employers to adopt or administer reasonable policies or procedures designed to ensure that rehabilitating or rehabilitated drug users are no longer engaging in the illegal use of drugs.[120] This might include workplace drug testing (which, for this purpose, does not constitute a medical examination triggering the rules which apply thereto), although Congress was careful to clarify that the legislation is not intended to encourage, prohibit or authorize drug testing or the making of employment decisions based thereupon.[121] An employer can lawfully prohibit the illegal use of drugs and the use of alcohol in the workplace and adopt requirements that employees shall not be under the influence of alcohol or engage in the illegal use of drugs in the workplace.[122]

A further group of individuals are expressly outside the legislation.[123] Transvestitism, homosexuality and bisexuality are not classified as disabilities under the ADA. Similarly, certain other conditions are not treated as within the meaning of disability: transsexualism, paedophilia, exhibitionism, voyeurism, gender identity disorders (not resulting from physical impairments), other sexual behaviour disorders, compulsive gambling, kleptomania or pyromania. Burgdorf comments:

> These exclusions seem wholly inconsistent with the overall tenor of the Americans with Disabilities Act, which encourages participation and decision-making based upon individualized

> determinations of actual ability and not preconceived assumptions and stereotypes . . . it is arguable that the members of Congress relied upon nothing other than their own negative reactions, fears and prejudices in fashioning the list of excluded classes.[124]

Such exclusions are not found explicitly in comparable laws of other jurisdictions, although it is possible that judicial activism will regard these classifications as beyond the reach of disability discrimination legislation.

Qualification for Employment

Not all disabled persons otherwise within the scope of the ADA 1990 are protected from employment discrimination. The subject of discrimination must be 'a *qualified* individual with a disability'.[125] This is denoted by an individual with a disability who, 'with or without reasonable accommodation, can perform the essential functions of the employment position that such individual holds or desires'.[126] In deciding what functions of a job are 'essential', consideration is to be given to the employer's judgment, so that the court must not simply substitute its view for that of the employer; but, equally, the employer's view is not determinative of the issue. The existence of a written job description prepared in advance of recruitment and selection is to be considered evidence of the job's essential functions.[127] The use of the word 'essential' suggests that the law is concerned with job tasks which are fundamental rather than marginal.[128] The EEOC regulations under the ADA assist employers to understand their obligations as far as 'essential functions' are concerned. A job function might be regarded as essential if: (a) performance of the function is the reason the position exists at all; or (b) performance of the function could only be redistributed among a limited number of employees; or (c) the position has to be filled by someone with particular expertise or ability to perform what is a highly specialized function.[129]

Anti-discrimination Principle

The prohibition on discrimination applies to all aspects of the employment relationship. The Act provides that

> No covered entity shall discriminate against a qualified individual with a disability because of the disability of such individual in regard to job application procedures, the hiring, advancement, or discharge of employees, employee compensation, job training, and other terms, conditions, and privileges of employment.[130]

The EEOC regulations expand this prohibition in order to outlaw discrimination in the following areas:

> (a) Recruitment, advertising, and job application procedures; (b) Hiring, upgrading, promotion, award of tenure, demotion, transfer, layoff, termination, right of return from layoff, and rehiring; (c) Rates of pay or any other form of compensation and changes in compensation; (d) Job assignments, job classifications, organizational structures, position descriptions, lines of progression, and seniority lists; (e) Leaves of absence, sick leave, or any other leave; (f) Fringe benefits available by virtue of employment, whether or not administered by [the employer]; (g) Selection and financial support for training . . . ; (h) Activities sponsored by [employers], including social and recreational programs; and (i) Any other term, condition, or privilege of employment.[131]

A particular issue with regard to insurance benefits arises here. The ADA 1990 allows a degree of latitude to existing insurance practices which are otherwise consistent with state laws, but this flexibility must not be used to circumvent the purpose of the legislation.[132] This means that insurers must determine a disabled person's insurability solely according to actuarial principles or claims experience. An employer cannot refuse to hire a qualified applicant because its employer's liability insurance policy does not cover that person's particular disability or because the engagement would lead to increased insurance premia. Similarly, an employer will need to be careful in considering a disabled employee's eligibility for an occupational health or pension scheme.

What is meant by 'discriminate' here? The Act provides an inclusive definition.[133] An employer must not limit, segregate or classify job applicants or employees in a way that adversely affects their opportunities or status because of their disability.[134] For example, it would be unlawful to segregate disabled employees in a separate work area. Employers must not participate in a contractual or other arrangement or relationship – such as with an employment agency, trade union, pension scheme or training organization – that has the effect of subjecting a qualified applicant or employee with a disability to prohibited discrimination.[135] The use of 'standards, criteria or methods of administration' that have the effect of discrimination on the basis of disability or that perpetuate the discrimination of others who are subject to common administrative control will amount to unlawful discrimination.[136] Employers and others must not discriminate against a qualified individual because of that individual's known relationship or association with a disabled person.[137] For example, an employer who provides health insurance benefits which cover employees' dependants may not reduce an employee's entitlement to such benefits simply because he or she has a disabled dependant. Similarly, an employer who refused to hire an applicant with a disabled child would be discriminating unlawfully if that refusal was based upon an assumption that the applicant may be absent from work periodically to look after the child.[138]

The use of qualification standards, employment tests or other selection criteria will amount to discrimination if they screen out disabled applicants, unless they are job-related and consistent with business necessity.[139] Employment tests must be selected and administered carefully so as to ensure that the test results accurately reflect the skills, aptitude or other factors which the tests purport to measure and not the impaired sensory, manual or speaking skills of an individual with such disabilities.[140] In other words, employment tests must only measure what they purport to measure. Shaller and Rosen comment that, as a result, a heavy burden is imposed on employers to demonstrate the job-relatedness and business necessity of selection criteria which have a disparate impact upon disabled applicants and to show that there are no reasonable alternatives which would not so discriminate.[141] If employers know that an applicant has a disability which impairs manual, sensory or speaking skills, they must consider whether a reasonable accommodation should be made in the administration of the test, and an applicant may be asked whether such an accommodation is necessary.[142]

Medical Examinations and Inquiries

The Act augments the meaning of unlawful discrimination by extending it to include medical examinations and inquiries.[143] Job applicants may not be subjected to medical examinations or pre-employment inquiries to identify their status as a disabled person or to discover the extent of any disability.[144] However, pre-employment inquiries are permitted to the extent necessary to ascertain an applicant's ability to do the job.[145] Nevertheless, once an employment offer has been made to an applicant, but before employment has begun, the employer may make it a condition of employment entrance that the applicant submit to a pre-placement medical examination.[146] Such a pre-placement medical examination is lawful, provided that all new employees would be subject to it regardless of disability.

Once in employment, disabled employees are safeguarded from being required to undergo medical examination, or respond to inquiries, designed to elicit information about their disabled status.[147] Such examinations or inquiries are lawful, however, if job-related and consistent with business necessity.[148] This does not prevent voluntary medical examinations or the compilation of voluntary medical histories as part of an occupational health programme in the workplace; nor does it prevent employers checking an employee's ability to carry out job-related functions.[149] The information gleaned from a pre-placement or post-placement examination must be treated as a confidential medical record and used only in accordance with the spirit of the legislation. Exceptionally, supervisors and managers may be party to the findings of the examination if there are any consequent restrictions on a disabled worker's work or duties, or accommodation is proposed. Similarly, first aid and safety personnel may need to be given disability-specific information about an individual if the need for emergency treatment might arise.[150]

Duty to Make Reasonable Accommodation

Borrowing a concept from section 504, the ADA deems it to be discrimination if an employer fails to make reasonable accommodations to the known physical or mental limitations of an otherwise qualified disabled applicant or employee.[151] A person is qualified for employment if he or she can perform the essential functions of the job with or without reasonable accommodation.[152] Although the term 'reasonable accommodation' is not substantively defined in the body of the Act, it is a concept borrowed from the section 504 regulations and illustrated within the ADA 1990:

> The term 'reasonable accommodation' may include – (A)

> making existing facilities used by employees readily accessible to and useable by individuals with disabilities; and (B) job restructuring, part-time or modified work schedules, reassignment to a vacant position, acquisition or modification of equipment or devices, appropriate adjustment or modifications of examinations, training materials or policies, the provision of qualified readers or interpreters, and other similar accommodations for individuals with disabilities.[153]

The EEOC regulations under the ADA define reasonable accommodation as the making of modifications or adjustments in the application process and workplace environment which ensure that disabled applicants are not discriminated against on the basis of disability and that they enjoy employment privileges and benefits equal to other employees.[154] An employer may not deny employment opportunities to a qualified disabled person where the denial is based upon the need to make reasonable accommodation.[155] Therefore, employers are obliged by law reasonably to accommodate disabled persons.

Under the RA 1973, the duty to provide reasonable accommodation is subject to an 'undue hardship' exception, although this was not defined in the Act or its regulations.[156] Similarly, an exception is made under the ADA if the employer can demonstrate that the accommodation would impose an undue hardship on the operation of the business.[157] 'Undue hardship' is judged by the test of whether the accommodation would require significant difficulty or expense, taking into account various factors.[158] The factors to be considered include the nature and cost of the necessary accommodations; the overall financial resources of the facility; the overall financial resources of the employer and the number, type and location of the employer's facilities; and the type of operations of the employer, including the composition, structure and functions of the workforce, and the geographic separateness, administrative or fiscal relationship of the facilities in question.[159] The burden of proof will be upon the employer to demonstrate undue hardship.[160] The employer is simply in a better position to know what the job involves, to assess the options for accommodation, to apply the experience of other employers in like circumstances or to seek the advice of specialist agencies.

Defences

It is implicit in the Act and explicit in the ADA regulations that, in cases of direct discrimination or unequal treatment, an employer's action may be justified as motivated by a legitimate, non-discriminatory reason. For example, the dismissal of a disabled employee on the grounds of misconduct or incompetence is a defensible dismissal because it is not an employment decision based upon disability.[161] An employment decision or the use of qualification standards, tests or selection criteria which screen out disabled persons might be defended on the basis of reasoning which is job-related and consistent with business necessity. However, it must be shown that no reasonable accommodation could be made that would enable the disabled person to perform the required essential functions of the job.[162]

Employers may discriminate against otherwise qualified disabled individuals if the individuals pose a direct threat to the health or safety of themselves or other individuals in the workplace. In other words, employers may use freedom from future safety risk as a qualification standard.[163] A direct threat to health or safety means that there must be a significant risk of substantial harm which cannot be eliminated or ameliorated by reasonable accommodation.[164] The determination of a direct threat to health or safety must be made on a case-by-case basis and must be predicated upon the individual's *present* condition.[165] The regulations, but not the Act, envisage that this defence may operate where the disabled person's *own* health or safety is directly threatened. Many disabled persons and disability rights organizations argued against the inclusion of this expanded defence in the regulations, reasoning that it promoted paternalism and negative stereotyping.[166] In the event, those arguments were unsuccessful.

A number of defences are implicit in the legislation but made explicit in the regulations. First, it is a defence to disability discrimination based upon a refusal or failure to make a reasonable accommodation that the accommodation would pose an undue hardship for the employer's business.[167] Second, an employer may defend a uniformly applied standard, criterion or policy which indirectly discriminates against disabled persons by showing it to be job-related and consistent with business necessity, and not amenable to reasonable accommodation.[168] Third, an employer might be able to defend a discriminatory employment decision or action on the grounds that it is required, necessitated or prohibited by federal law or regulation, unless the defence is a mere pretext, or the other law or regulation does not actually compel the discriminatory action, or that law can be complied with in a non-discriminatory way.[169]

Particular provision is made for jobs involving food handling. The Secretary of Health and Human Resources is mandated to publish a list of infectious and communicable diseases which are transmitted through food handling.[170] An employer may discriminate against disabled individuals whose disability consists of a listed infectious or communicable disease and where there is a risk of the disease being transmitted through food handling. Clearly this only applies where the job in question involves food handling. Before the defence can be relied upon, the employer must show that the risk cannot be eliminated by reasonable accommodation.[171] This means that an employer may refuse to assign or continue to assign a disabled person with a listed infectious or communicable disease to a job involving food handling, unless reasonable accommodation can eliminate the risk of transmission. This was an amendment made to the ADA during its passage through Congress, but arguably adds little to the application of the general principle that a risk to the health or safety of others renders an individual unqualified.[172]

The amendment was prompted by the prospect of hardship for restaurants and other food retailers required to protect the civil rights of HIV-infected persons. Although there is no evidence that this disease is transmissible through food handling, it was the potential for public misperception which led to the compromise amendment. This is a curious example of a particular provision in a statute, generally designed to eliminate discrimination based upon ignorance, being shaped by a desire to accommodate misunderstanding. The debate and amendments surrounding this provision almost obstructed the passage of the ADA 1990. The fear of the restaurant and catering industry was that customers would boycott establishments where it was known or suspected that an HIV-positive employee was working. It also raises the question of how far an employer can take account of customer preference when deciding to discriminate on the ground of disability. Just as customer preference for female flight attendants did not justify scx discrimination,[173] it is doubtful whether this would be a defence to disability discrimination.

CONCLUSION

The US legislation provides a template for comprehensive disability discrimination legislation that may serve as a pattern for similar legislative interventions to protect the civil rights of disabled people in other countries. It is clear that the Act and its supporting regulations have already excited much attention in other jurisdictions. In Britain, for example, disability rights reformers both within and outside the legislature have held up the American experience as a paradigm for future British developments and, as was noted in Chapter 2, attempts have been made to introduce draft legislation in Britain that is directly modelled upon the ADA 1990. While the US framework is undoubtedly one that merits close examination, reformers should take care lest they attempt a transplant of an experiment that might not fit the British experience. As a direct descendant of Title VII of the Civil Rights Act 1964, from which the British sex and race discrimination legislation can also trace its pedigree, it is tempting to assume that the ADA 1990 can be imported into the British jurisdiction with only minor adjustments and amendments. This may prove to be true, but it should be remembered that British anti-discrimination statutes have developed subsequently in quite different ways from their American counterparts, despite their common genetic heritage. Accordingly, before examining further the lessons of the ADA 1990 for disabled employment rights in Britain, it is proposed to look for additional examples of legal approaches to disability discrimination in Australia and Canada.

NOTES

1. 42 USC s 2000e.
2. 29 USC ss 201-219.
3. *Georgetown Law Journal*, 1973: 1502.
4. Burgdorf and Falcon, 1980: 319 and 325.
5. McClure, 1978; Burgdorf and Falcon, 1980; Schoenfeld, 1980.
6. *Duran* v *City of Tampa* (1977) 430 FSupp 75 and (1978) 451 FSupp 954 (MD Fla); *Washington* v *Davis* (1976) 426 US 229; *King-Smith* v *Aaron* (1970) 317 FSupp 164 (WD Penn), reversed at (1972) 455 F2d 378 (3rd Circ); *Parolisi* v *Board of Examiners of City of New York* (1967) 285 NYS2d 936; *Heumann* v *Board of Education of City of New York* (1970) 320 FSupp 623 (SD NY).
7. *Cleburne* v *Cleburne Living Center* (1985) 473 US 432.

8. *Board of Regents* v *Roth* (1972) 408 US 564; *Perry* v *Sindermann* (1972) 408 US 593.

9. *Duran* v *City of Tampa* (1977) 430 FSupp 75 and (1978) 451 FSupp 954 (MD Fla); *Bevan* v *New York State Teachers Retirement System* (1973) 345 NYS2d 921 (SC NY); *Gurmankin* v *Costanzo* (1977) 556 F2d 184 (3rd Circ); cf *Coleman* v *Darden* (1977) 13 EPD 6788 (DC). See further: Richman, 1978; Sluzas, 1981.

10. Burgdorf and Falcon, 1980: 355–60.

11. Bassen, 1977; Nicolai and Ricci, 1977; Leap, 1979; *Law and Contemporary Problems*, 1982; Sales *et al.*, 1982; Flaccus, 1986a and 1986b; Kaufman, 1987; Perlin, 1987; Collins, 1988.

12. Weiss, 1974.

13. *Ibid.*: 462, n. 29 (emphasis in original).

14. Flaccus, 1986a, b.

15. Flaccus, 1986b: 321.

16. *Ibid.*: 265.

17. *Ibid.*: 263.

18. Pub L No. 93-112, 87 Stat 355 (1973) as amended and codified in 29 USC ss 701, 706, 791, 793 and 794. See generally: Cook, 1977; Richards, 1985; Percy, 1989; Drimmer, 1993.

19. 29 CFR Part 1613.

20. 41 CFR Part 60-741.

21. 28 CFR Part 41. See: Scotch, 1984.

22. For example: 29 CFR Parts 32 and 33 (Department of Labor); 45 CFR Parts 84 and 85 (Department of Health and Human Services); 28 CFR Part 42 (Department of Justice).

23. 29 USC s 791(b).

24. Regulations governing equal employment opportunity in federal government have been promulgated at 29 CFR s 1613.201 *et seq.* See also: 39 CFR s 255.1 *et seq.* and 5 CFR ss 720.301–720.307.

25. Mayerson, 1991b: 501. See: *Gardner* v *Morris* (1985) 752 F2d 1271 (8th Cir); *Ryan* v *Federal Deposit Insurance Corporation* (1977) 565 F2d 762 (DC Cir); *Rhone* v *US Department of the Army* (1987) 665 FSupp 734 (ED Mo); *Di Pompo* v *West Point Military Academy* (1991) 770 FSupp (SD NY).

26. 29 CFR s 1613.703.

27. 29 CFR s 1613.704; *Prewitt* v *US Postal Service* (1981) 662 F2d 292 (CA Miss).

28. 29 CFR ss 1613.705 and 1613.706.

29. 29 CFR s 1613.707. A building or facility is deemed accessible if in compliance with the Architectural Barriers Act 1968. Where necessary, federal employers must make reasonable accommodation in order to make the workplace accessible and avoid leasing buildings that are inaccessible: *Rose* v *US Postal Service* (1983) 566 FSupp 367 (DC Cal) reversed 774 F2d 1355; *Bey* v *Bolger* (1982) 540 FSupp 910 (DC Pa).

30. *Boyd* v *US Postal Service* (1985) 752 F2d 410 (CA Wash); *Connolly* v *US Postal Service* (1984) 579 FSupp 305 (DC Mass); *Rattner* v *Bennett* (1988) 701 FSupp 7 (D DC) *Di Pompo* v *West Point Military Academy* (1991) 770 FSupp (SD NY).

31. 29 USC s 794(a)(1).

32. 29 USC s 793(a).

33. 41 CFR Part 60-741.

34. *Moon* v *US Department of Labor* (1984) 747 F2d 599 (11th Cir) *certiorari denied* (1985) 471 US 1055; *EE Black Ltd* v *Marshall* (1980) 497 FSupp 1088 (D Haw). See: Mayerson, 1991b: 501.

35. *Rogers* v *Frito-Lay Inc* (1977) 433 FSupp 200 (DC Tex), *affirmed* 611 F2d 1074, *certiorari denied* 101 SCt 246, 449 US 889.

36. 41 CFR s 60-741.4. The clause may be incorporated by reference, but is deemed to be part of the contract, whether or not it is an express term and whether or not the contract is in writing: 41 CFR s 60-741.22–.23.

37. 41 CFR s 60-741.2. The prime contractor and sub-contractor must include an affirmative action clause in the sub-contract either expressly or by reference: 41 CFR s 60-741.20.

38. 41 CFR s 60-741.3(a)(1).

39. 41 CFR s 60-741.3(a)(2).

40. 41 CFR s 60-741.2.

41. 41 CFR s 60-741.2.

42. 31 CFR s 202.1 *et seq.*
43. 41 CFR s 60-741.3(b)(2).
44. 29 USC s 793(b).
45. 41 CFR s 60-741.26.
46. 41 CFR s 60-741.28.
47. 29 USC s 794(a). See generally: Tucker, 1989a.
48. Jones, 1991b: 29.
49. See, for example: 28 CFR Part 41 (Department of Justice); 29 CFR Part 32 (Department of Labor); 45 CFR Part 84 (Department of Health and Human Services).
50. *Grove City College* v *Bell* (1984) 465 US 555; *Consolidated Rail Corporation* v *Darrone* (1984) 465 US 624; *US Department of Transportation* v *Paralyzed Veterans of America* (1986) 106 SCt 2705.
51. 29 USC s 794(b) as amended in 1988.
52. (1984) 465 US 624.
53. *Alexander* v *Choate* (1985) 469 US 287. *Cf* 42 USC s 2000e-5(g) and *Griggs* v *Duke Power Co* (1971) 401 US 421.
54. 45 CFR Part 84 (preamble).
55. The current version of the relevant definitional section may be found in 29 USC s 706(8).
56. 29 USC s 706(8)(B). The definition in the ADA 1990 is in virtually identical terms: 42 USC s 12102(2). A similar definition is to be found in the various regulations: 28 CFR s 41.31(a); 29 CFR s 32.3; 29 CFR s 1613.702(a); 41 CFR s 60-741.2; 45 CFR s 84.3(j)(1).
57. 29 USC s 706(8)(C)(i), (ii) and (22).
58. 29 USC s 706(8)(C)(v). This provision purports to apply only to ss 793 and 794.
59. 29 USC s 706(8)(D).
60. 28 CFR s 41.31(b)(1); 29 CFR s 32.3; 29 CFR s 1613.702(b); 41 CFR s 60-741.2; 45 CFR s 84.3(j)(2)(i). See *School Board of Nassau County, Florida* v *Arline* (1987) 480 US 273 in which the Supreme Court makes a broad interpretation of the definition of a handicapped individual.
61. 28 CFR s 41.31(b)(3); 29 CFR s 32.3; 29 CFR s 1613.702(d); 41 CFR s 60-741.2; 45 CFR s 84.3(j)(2)(iii).
62. 28 CFR s 41.31(b)(4); 29 CFR s 32.3; 29 CFR s 1613.702(e); 41 CFR s 60-741.2; 45 CFR s 84.3(j)(2)(iv). Transvestitism is not a 'handicap': Pub L 100-430 s 6(b)(3), 42 USC s 3602 (note) overturning *Blackwell* v *US Department of Treasury* (1986) 639 FSupp 289 (D DC); nor is sexual orientation or preference: *Blackwell* v *US Department of Treasury* (1987) 830 F2d 1183.
63. 28 CFR s 41.31(b)(2); 29 CFR s 32.3; 29 CFR s 1613.702(c); 41 CFR s 60-741.2; 45 CFR s 84.3(j)(2)(ii).
64. 29 CFR s 32.3; 41 CFR s 60-741.2 and Appendix A. The Department of Labor regulations and the OFCCP regulations focus upon life activities which affect employability, including communication, ambulation, self-care, socialization, education, vocational training, employment, transportation, adapting to housing and others.
65. 28 CFR s 41.32; 45 CFR s 84.3(k)(1). The Department of Labor s 504 regulations are worded slightly differently, but to the same effect: 29 CFR s 32.3.
66. (1979) 442 US 397 at 406.
67. (1985) 469 US 287 at 300.
68. 41 CFR ss 60-741.2 and 60-741.6(c).
69. 29 CFR s 1613.703; *Stevens* v *Stubbs* (1983) 576 FSupp 1409 (D Ga) (protection is afforded only to those who can do the job in spite of handicap, rather than those who could do the job but for handicap).
70. 29 CFR s 1613.702(f).
71. 28 CFR ss 41.32 and 41.53; 29 CFR s 32.3; 29 CFR ss 1613.702(f) and 1613.704; 41 CFR ss 60-741.2 and 60-741.6(d); 45 CFR s 84.3(k) and 84.12.
72. 28 CFR s 41.53. See to like effect: 45 CFR s 84.12(a).
73. 45 CFR s 84.12(b).
74. 29 CFR ss 32.3 and 32.13.

75. 29 CFR s 1613.704. The section 503 regulations do not amplify the meaning of reasonable accommodation.

76. Weicker, 1991. See also Flaccus, 1986a. For an analysis of disability rights policy prior to 1990, see: Percy, 1989; Drimmer, 1993.

77. White House Conference on Handicapped Individuals, 1977; Peck, 1983; Burgdorf and Bell, 1984.

78. Jones, 1991a: 472; 1991b: 27.

79. Subsequently renamed as the National Council on Disability. See: 29 USC s 781.

80. National Council on the Handicapped, 1988.

81. Louis Harris and Associates, 1986, 1987. The Harris polls found that three-quarters of disabled Americans supported anti-discrimination and civil rights legislation for disabled people: Louis Harris and Associates, 1986: 112.

82. The Civil Rights Restoration Act 1987 overturned *Grove City College* v *Bell* (1984) 465 US 555. The Handicapped Children's Protection Act 1986 overturned *Smith* v *Robinson* (1984) 468 US 992, while the Air Carrier's Access Act 1988 reversed *US Department of Transportation* v *Paralysed Veterans of America* (1986) 477 US 597.

83. National Council on the Handicapped, 1986. See also, to like effect: Presidential Commission on the Human Immunodeficiency Virus Epidemic, 1988.

84. As amended by the Civil Rights Act 1991 and codified as amended at 42 USC s 12101 *et seq.* The ADA 1990 drew upon the RA 1973 and the disability provisions of more recent general civil rights legislation in the shape of the Civil Rights Restoration Act 1987 and the Fair Housing Amendments Act 1988. See generally: Tucker, 1989b, 1992; Weicker, 1991; West, 1991a; Jones, 1991a, b.

85. National Council on the Handicapped, 1988.

86. Senate Bill 2345 (100th Congress, 2nd Session, 1988). In this Bill, the obligation to make reasonable accommodations for a disability was not subject to the 'undue hardship' standard of section 504, but rather the question was whether the essential nature of the employer's business would be fundamentally altered or its existence threatened.

87. Senate Bill 933 and House of Representatives Bill 2273 (101st Congress, 1st Session, 1989).

88. For a history of negotiations and compromises which led to the eventual enactment of the ADA 1990 see: Feldblum, 1991a, c. As to the constitutional implications, see: Mikochik, 1991b.

89. For an overview of the non-employment provisions of the ADA 1990 see: Burgdorf, 1991; Cook, 1991; Tucker, 1992. For a broader perspective upon the Act and its underlying policies, see the various contributions in West, 1991c.

90. 42 USC s 12101(b)(1). For a detailed analysis of the Act, see: Bureau of National Affairs, 1990 and Colker, 1995.

91. 42 USC s 12101(b)(2),(3).

92. 42 USC s 12101(b)(4).

93. The remedies and procedures of the Civil Rights Act 1964 are applicable to any violation of the employment provisions of the ADA: 42 USC s 12117(a) incorporating ss 705–10 of the Civil Rights Act 1964 (42 USC ss 2000e-4 to 2000e-9).

94. Mayerson, 1991a: 1.

95. Mikochik, 1991a: 372.

96. Thornburgh, 1991. For example, the EEOC has calculated that the ADA regulations would result in productivity gains of more than US$164 million: Jones, 1991a: 498.

97. Thornburgh, 1991: 384.

98. 42 USC s 12101.

99. US Senate, 1989; US House of Representatives, 1990a, b.

100. 29 CFR Part 1630 promulgated under 42 USC s 12116.

101. Shaller and Rosen (1991: 405) comment that the regulations fail to provide specific rules or guidance on many key issues, including the Act's effect on existing collective agreements, insurance, workers' compensation, and burdens of proof.

102. 42 USC s 12201(a); 29 CFR 1630.1(c)(1).

103. 42 USC s 12201(b); 29 CFR 1630.1(c)(2). See: Rains, 1992.

104. 29 CFR s 1630.1 Appendix.

105. See generally: Postol and Kadue, 1991.
106. 42 USC s 12111(2); 29 CFR 1630.2(b).
107. 42 USC s 12111(5); 29 CFR s 1630.2(e). It is estimated that the ADA 1990 will cover 3.9 million business establishments and 666,000 employers: Creasman and Butler, 1991: 52.
108. 42 USC s 12102(2); 29 CFR s 1630.2(g). LaPlante (1991: 57) comments that 'persons who consider themselves disabled but are not considered by others to be so are implicitly included in the ADA definition'. This is doubtful, for reasons explored in Chapters 6 and 7.
109. Congress did illustrate what disabilities might be included (Jones, 1991a: 479): orthopaedic impairments, visual impairments, speech impairments, hearing impairments, cerebral palsy, epilepsy, muscular dystrophy, multiple sclerosis, human immunodeficiency virus infection, cancer, heart disease, diabetes, mental retardation, emotional illness, specific learning disabilities, drug addiction and alcoholism.
110. 29 CFR s 1630(h).
111. 42 USC s 12102(2); 29 CFR s 1630.2(g).
112. 29 CFR s 1630.2(i). Two further activities were referred to as major life activities in a Department of Justice Memorandum – procreation and intimate personal relations – thus encompassing AIDS and HIV as possible impairments: Memorandum of Acting Assistant Attorney General, Office of Legal Counsel, Department of Justice, 27 September 1988.
113. 29 CFR s 1630.2(j)(1).
114. 29 CFR s 1630.2(j)(2). There are additional considerations in respect of substantial limitations on working (discussed in Chapters 7 and 8): 29 CFR s 1630.2(j)(3).
115. 29 CFR s 1630.2(k). Under the ADA regulations, the fact that someone has been classified as disabled under some other statute, regulation or programme does not give rise to a presumption that they satisfy the definition of disabled for ADA purposes: 29 CFR s 1630.2(k) Appendix.
116. 29 CFR s 1630.2(l).
117. 42 USC ss 12114(a); 29 CFR s 1630.3(a). The term 'illegal use of drugs' is defined in 42 USC s 12111(6)(A); 29 CFR s 1630.3(a)(2). The term 'drug' means a controlled substance, as defined in s 202 of the Controlled Substances Act: 42 USC s 12111(6)(B); 29 CFR s 1630.3(a)(1). See also: 42 USC s 12210(a) and (d).
118. 42 USC s 12211(b)(3).
119. 42 USC s 12114(b); 29 CFR s 1630.3(b). See also: 42 USC s 12210(b).
120. 42 USC ss 12114(b) and 12210(b); 29 CFR s 1630.3(c). There are special rules covering transportation workers: 42 USC s 12114(e); 29 CFR s 1630.16(c)(2).
121. 42 USC s 12114(d); 29 CFR s 1630.16(c)(1).
122. 42 USC s 12114(c); 29 CFR s 1630.16(b).
123. 42 USC ss 12208 and 12211; 29 CFR s 1630.3(d) and (e).
124. Burgdorf, 1991: 452 and 519. He suggests that the exclusion of these groups was part of the political bargaining designed to placate vocal critics of the legislation at large. Burgdorf is thus critical of legislating 'by consensus': Burgdorf, 1991: 520.
125. 42 USC s 12112(a); 29 CFR s 1630.4 (emphasis added).
126. 42 USC s 12111(8). The ADA regulations are more expansive: 'Qualified individual with a disability means an individual with a disability who satisfies the requisite skill, experience, education and other job-related requirements of the employment position such individual holds or desires, and who, with or without reasonable accommodation, can perform the essential functions of such position': 29 CFR s 1630.2(m). Cf. 45 CFR s 84.3(k)(1).
127. 42 USC s 12111(8); 29 CFR s 1630.2(n)(3).
128. 29 CFR s 1630.2(n)(1).
129. 29 CFR s 1630.2(n)(2).
130. 42 USC s 12112(a).
131. 29 CFR s 1630.4.
132. 42 USC s 12201(c); 29 CFR s 1630.16(f).
133. 42 USC s 12112(b).
134. 42 USC s 12112(b)(1); 29 CFR s 1630.5.
135. 42 USC s 12112(b)(2); 29 CFR s 1630.6.
136. 42 USC s 12112(b)(3); 29 CFR s 1630.7.

137. 42 USC s 12112(b)(4); 29 CFR s 1630.8. The employer must know both of the association and of the other's disability.
138. Shaller and Rosen, 1992: 407.
139. 42 USC s 12112(6); 29 CFR s 1630.10. The term 'qualification standards' means: 'the personal and professional attributes including the skill, experience, education, physical, medical, safety and other requirements established by a covered entity as requirements which an individual must meet in order to be eligible for the position held or desired': 29 CFR s 1630.2(q).
140. 42 USC s 12112(b)(7); 29 CFR s 1630.11 (unless it is those very skills that the tests purport to measure).
141. Shaller and Rosen, 1992: 420.
142. 29 CFR s 1630.11 Appendix.
143. 42 USC s 12112(1).
144. 42 USC s 12112(2)(A); 29 CFR s 1630.13(a).
145. 42 USC s 12112(2)(B); 29 CFR s 1630.14(a).
146. 42 USC s 12112(3); 29 CFR s 1630.14(b).
147. 42 USC s 12112(4)(A); 29 CFR s 1630.13(b).
148. 42 USC s 12112(4)(A); 29 CFR s 1630.14(c).
149. 42 USC s 12112(4)(B); 29 CFR s 1630.14(d).
150. 42 USC s 12112(3)(B), (3)(C) and (4)(C); 29 CFR s 1630.14(b), (c) and (d). Information may also need to be made available to government officials carrying out compliance inspections in respect of the Act.
151. 42 USC s 12112(b)(5)(A); 29 CFR s 1630.9(a). Cf. 45 CFR s 84.12(b).
152. 42 USC s 12111(8); 29 CFR s 1630.2(m).
153. 42 USC s 12111(9); 29 CFR s 1630.2(o). Cf. 45 CFR s 84.12.
154. 29 CFR s 1630.2(o)(1). Employers must provide reasonable accommodation to ensure equal opportunity in the application process, to enable disabled persons to perform essential job functions (sufficient to meet the job-related needs of the disabled individual), and to permit disabled employees equal participation in the benefits and privileges of employment (such as the use of canteens, rest areas etc.): 29 CFR s 1630.2(o) Appendix and s 1630.9 Appendix.
155. 42 USC s 12112(b)(5)(B); 29 CFR s 1630.9(b).
156. See, for example: 45 CFR s 84.12(a).
157. 42 USC s 12112(b)(5)(A); 29 CFR s 1630.9(a).
158. 42 USC s 12111(10)(A); 29 CFR 1630.2(p)(1). The ADA regulations explain that an accommodation which would be unduly costly, extensive, substantial, disruptive, or that would fundamentally alter the nature or operation of the business would constitute 'undue hardship': 29 CFR s 1630.2(p) appendix.
159. 42 USC s 12111(10)(B); 29 CFR s 1630.2(p)(2).
160. *Prewitt* v *US Postal Service*, 662 F2d 292.
161. 29 CFR s 1630.15(a) and Appendix. Employment decisions based upon reasoning that an employer's insurance policy does not cover disability or that the employment of a disabled person will lead to increased insurance or workers' compensation costs are not considered to be founded upon legitimate, non-discriminatory reasons.
162. 42 USC ss 12112(b)(6) and 12113(a); 29 CFR ss 1630.15(b)(1) and 1630.15(c).
163. 42 USC s 12113(b); 29 CFR s 1630.15(b)(2).
164. 42 USC s 12111(3); 29 CFR s 1630.2(r)
165. 29 CFR ss 1630.2(r) and Appendix.
166. Shaller and Rosen, 1992: 430.
167. 42 USC ss 12111(10) and 12112(b)(5); 29 CFR s 1630.15(d).
168. 29 CFR s 1630.15(c).
169. 29 CFR s 1630.15(e) and Appendix.
170. 42 USC s 12113(d)(1).
171. 42 USC 12113(d); 29 CFR s 1630.16(e).
172. Jones, 1991a: 482.
173. Under Title VII of the Civil Rights Act 1964: *Diaz* v *Pan American World Airways* (1971) 442 F2d 385 (5th Cir).

5

Disabled Employment Rights in Canada and Australia

INTRODUCTION

Given its cultural and geographical proximity to the USA, and its shared common law history with Britain, Canada represents an alternative source of comparative material of interest. Despite the similarities of their legal cultures, discrimination law in the USA and Canada has developed in quite distinct ways. The anti-discrimination principle in Canada emerges as a component part of legislation protecting human rights in general. In contrast, Australian anti-discrimination legislation is closely patterned on the British sex and race discrimination statutes. Given the influence of the US Civil Rights Act upon the shape of the British legislation, Australian law in this area shares a common ancestry whose roots can be traced back to the US Supreme Court's seminal decision in *Griggs* v *Duke Power Co.*[1] The result is that Australian disability discrimination laws drew heavily upon the US Rehabilitation Act 1973 for basic concepts and drafting language.[2] However, there are significant differences between the US and Australian models, as well as within the various Australian paradigms themselves. Accordingly, the Australian experience is an additional point of comparative reference, but first the Canadian models will be explored.[3]

CANADA

Constitutional Protection

As a result of the 1982 repatriation of the Canadian Constitution, the Canadian Charter of Rights and Freedoms provides a constitutional framework within which the rights of all Canadians are cloaked with legal protection.[4] The key provision, in the context of the present discussion, is section 15 of the Charter, which provides:

> (1) Every individual is equal before and under the law and has the right to the equal protection and equal benefit of the law without discrimination and, in particular, without discrimination based on . . . *mental or physical disability.*
> (2) Subsection (1) does not preclude any law, program or activity that has as its object the amelioration of conditions of disadvantaged individuals or groups including those that are disadvantaged because of . . . *mental or physical disability.*[5]

In the words of one commentator, by virtue of this enactment Canada has 'conferred on its disabled citizens perhaps the most comprehensive statements of human rights to be found in any nation in the world'.[6] However, despite this optimistic view, it is clear that the Charter is only a catalyst for change and that the chemistry of disability rights requires further legal ingredients in order to prevent discrimination and promote equality of opportunity.[7] In practice, therefore, the Charter is less important than the human rights codes and statutes of the Canadian federal and provincial jurisdictions.

The failure of Canadian common law to fashion a remedy for social discrimination mirrors the experience of the common law in Britain.[8] Even the enactment of the Canadian Bill of Rights in 1960, guaranteeing fundamental civil liberties and protection from legally sanctioned discrimination, omitted to address discrimination by reason of disability. Instead the lead was taken in the years after 1960 by provincial legislatures enacting human rights statutes. In the federal jurisdiction, however, the Canadian Human Rights Act, first enacted in the mid-1970s, now includes disabled persons within its compass.

Canadian Human Rights Act

The Canadian Human Rights Act espouses the principle of individual equal opportunity without discrimination.[9] The purposive section of the Act provides:

> The purpose of this Act is to extend the laws in Canada to give effect, within the purview of matters coming within the

> legislative authority of Parliament, to the principle that every individual should have an equal opportunity with other individuals to make for himself or herself the life that he or she is able and wishes to have, consistent with his or her duties and obligations as a member of society, without being hindered in or prevented from doing so by discriminatory practices based on . . . [*inter alia*] disability.[10]

The Act proscribes a number of grounds of discrimination and prohibits certain discriminatory practices. Disability is one of the proscribed grounds of discrimination.[11] For this purpose, 'disability' denotes 'any previous or existing mental or physical disability and includes disfigurement and previous or existing dependence on alcohol or a drug'.[12]

The Act addresses both direct and indirect employment discrimination. It is a discriminatory practice for an employer to base an employment decision upon an individual's disability. This covers all incidents of the employment relationship by providing:

> It is a discriminatory practice, directly or indirectly, (a) to refuse to employ or continue to employ any individual, or (b) in the course of employment, to differentiate adversely in relation to an employee, on a prohibited ground of discrimination.[13]

This extends to both unintentional and adverse effect discrimination.[14] The Act has been interpreted as covering constructive dismissals, as well as extending to protect an individual working for the defendant employer while technically the employee of a third party,[15] and to an individual who was an army cadet enrolled on a three-week parachuting course.[16] The prohibition on discriminatory practices also extends to employment application forms and advertisements.[17] Discriminatory employment policies and practices are described as follows:

> It is a discriminatory practice for an employer . . . (a) to establish or pursue a policy or practice, or (b) to enter into an agreement affecting recruitment, referral, hiring, promotion, training, apprenticeship, transfer or any other matter relating to employment or prospective employment, that deprives or tends to deprive an individual or class of individuals of any employment opportunities on a prohibited ground of discrimination.[18]

For example, a failure to consider reassignment of a newly disabled employee to other work may be discriminatory.[19]

An employer might defend an employment decision based on disability if it can be shown to have been informed by the need for a '*bona fide* occupational requirement'.[20] There must be an honest, genuine requirement which is real and substantial, and which is related to the actual duties of the job.[21] A *bona fide* occupational requirement will include a need to avoid posing a significant safety risk to the disabled individual, fellow employees and others.[22] An employer will clearly need to rely upon medical evidence rather than uninformed assumptions.[23] However, provided the assessment of the evidence is made in good faith, it is the employer's judgment which ultimately seems to count.[24]

The Canadian Human Rights Act permits a degree of positive action in favour of disabled persons. An employer may adopt and implement a policy or plan to prevent, to eliminate or to reduce disadvantages that are likely to be or are suffered by disabled individuals.[25] The Canadian Human Rights Commission is charged with making general recommendations concerning the objectives of such initiatives and with providing advice and assistance in connection therewith.[26] A proposal to adapt services, facilities, premises, equipment or operations to accommodate the needs of disabled persons may be submitted to the Commission for approval as appropriate for meeting the needs of disabled persons. Once it is approved, the implementation of the plan contained in such a proposal will not constitute grounds for a complaint of disability discrimination in respect of matters within the scope of the plan.[27] Provision is made for the enactment of regulations prescribing standards of accessibility to services, facilities or premises.[28] Where these standards are met, access cannot constitute the basis for a complaint of disability discrimination, but a variation from the regulatory standard is not automatically deemed to be evidence of discrimination. Furthermore, where an employer seeks approval to implement a plan to accommodate the needs of disabled persons, the fact that it does not meet the regulatory access standards is not a sufficient ground for rejecting the plan.[29]

Employment Equity Act

The federal Employment Equity Act 1985 (EEA) was enacted to promote equal employment opportunities in the workplace and to take positive action to promote the employment rights of certain designated minorities, including disabled persons.[30] The purposive intent of the statute is:

> to achieve equality in the work place so that no person shall be denied employment opportunities or benefits for *reasons unrelated to ability* and, in the fulfilment of that goal, to correct the conditions of disadvantage in employment experienced by . . . *persons with disabilities* . . . by giving effect to the principle that employment equity means more than treating persons in the same way but also requires *special measures and the accommodation of differences.*[31]

The principle of 'employment equity' recognizes that it is not enough to prohibit discrimination in the form of unequal treatment of disabled persons; special measures and reasonable accommodation are also required.

The Act is addressed to employers who employ 100 or more employees and who are engaged in federal work, or a federal undertaking or business.[32] It applies to 'designated groups', which includes 'persons with disabilities', but without further definition in the statute. However, regulations made under the Act define 'persons with disabilities' as persons who:

> (i) have any persistent physical, mental, psychiatric, sensory or learning impairment; (ii) consider themselves to be, or believe that an employer or a potential employer would be likely to consider them to be, disadvantaged in employment by reason of an impairment referred to in subparagraph (i); and (iii) for the purposes of section 6 of the Act, identify themselves to an employer, or agree to be identified to an employer, as persons with disabilities.[33]

The principle of employment equity as it applies to disabled persons requires employers covered by the legislation to identify and eliminate employment practices resulting in discriminatory employment barriers, and to institute positive policies and practices (including reasonable accommodation) to promote the proper representation of disabled persons in employment positions in proportion to their representation in the workforce or the employer's catchment area or labour market.[34] This process must be carried out in consultation with bargaining agents or employee representatives. Employment practices authorized by law do not need to be eliminated and, when taking positive action to ensure proportional representation of disabled persons, the employer may define the appropriate labour market by reference to geography or skills and qualifications.

The Act requires the employer to prepare an annual plan which sets goals to be achieved in implementing employment equity and a timetable within which the goals are to be achieved.[35] The employer must file an annual report with the Minister of Employment and Immigration indicating: the employer's industrial sector, location, total workforce and number of disabled persons employed; what occupational groups the employer has and the degree of representation of disabled persons in each occupational group; the salary ranges of employees and the degree of representation of disabled persons in each range (and sub-division); and the number of employees hired or engaged, promoted and terminated (whether retired, resigned or dismissed, but not including temporarily laid off or absent by reason of illness, injury or labour dispute), with the degree of representation of disabled persons in those numbers.[36] A failure to comply with this reporting requirement is a criminal offence punishable under section 7 by a fine of up to $50,000. Copies of these reports are sent to the Canadian Human Rights Commission, are open to public inspection, and are also consolidated and analysed for parliamentary scrutiny.[37]

Following the initiatives taken in the Employment Equity Act, the federal government has implemented the Federal Contractors Programme. An employer with over 100 employees who bids for federal contracts for the supply of goods and services valued at at least $200,000 must observe the principle of employment equity in its workforce. The sanctions available where the principle is being ignored include the eventual exclusion of that employer from tendering for federal contracts. The Department of Employment and Immigration has the right to review the employer's records in order to assess efforts being made, levels of compliance and results achieved.

Canadian Provincial Jurisdiction

In Canada, large sectors of private employment remain unregulated by federal human rights legislation, while private employers might be indifferent to employment equity principles unless contracting with organs of the federal government. Accordingly, for many disabled Canadians, the protection from employment discrimination and the promotion of employment rights will be determined by provincial laws. The employment rights of disabled persons in the Canadian provinces of British Columbia,[38] Manitoba,[39] New Brunswick,[40] Newfoundland,[41] Nova Scotia,[42] Ontario,[43] Prince Edward Island,[44] Saskatchewan[45] and Yukon Territory[46] are generally addressed by a series of Human Rights Codes or Human Rights Acts. In Alberta the source of protection is the Individual's Rights Protection Act,[47] in Québec it is the Charter of Human Rights and Freedoms,[48] and in the Northwest Territories the law is to be found in the Fair Practices Act.[49] Such legislation constructs an omnibus anti-discrimination framework which applies, *inter alios*, to disabled persons and, *inter alia*, to employment.

The human rights legislation of many of the Canadian provinces recognizes the inherent dignity, equality and inalienable rights of all persons regardless of their status. The influence of the Universal Declaration of Human Rights is evident, as is that of the Canadian Charter of Rights and Freedoms. This debt is acknowledged, for example, in the preamble to Manitoba's Human Rights Code.[50] The preamble recognizes the right of individuals to be treated on the basis of personal merit and to enjoy equal opportunity. To protect this right, unreasonable discrimination must be restricted, stereotypes or generalizations must be challenged, and reasonable accommodations must be made for those with special needs. The Manitoba legislature notes that past discrimination has resulted in serious disadvantage and that affirmative action and special programmes must be designed to overcome historic disadvantage. Education is also seen as essential to eradicate discrimination based on ignorance, and human rights protection must take precedence over provincial law. Furthermore, the Canadian Supreme Court, in a series of judgments, has recognized the quasi-constitutional nature of provincial human rights codes. They take precedence over other legislation in the absence of contrary indications and must be purposively interpreted so as to give effect to their anti-discrimination edict, and statutory exceptions will be given a narrow construction.[51]

British Columbia was the first jurisdiction to protect the rights of disabled people when, in 1977, the provincial Supreme Court held that a general prohibition against discrimination 'without reasonable cause' extended to a physically handicapped plaintiff.[52] The New Brunswick legislation was the first to be amended in 1976 to add physical disability as an explicit discriminatory ground, and subsequently all provincial jurisdictions have moved to include individuals with physical disabilities within the protected class. The addition of mental disability to human rights legislation followed during the 1980s. As a result all provincial jurisdictions now address the question of discrimination against persons with physical or mental disabilities. The identification of disability as an unlawful ground of discrimination varies from province to province, and specific examples of this difference will be discussed in Chapter 7.

As in the other major common law countries, the legal concept of discrimination in Canada is largely derived from the disparate treatment and adverse impact analysis of the US Supreme Court in *Griggs* v *Duke Power Co.*[53] That analysis is so well understood in North America that the Canadian provincial human rights statutes usually merely enact a general prohibition on employment discrimination on account of disability. However, there is some embellishment of the basic concept of discrimination in some of the provinces. Similarly, having identified the meaning of discrimination and the identity of the protected class, most Canadian human rights statutes then define the scope of prohibited employment discrimination. This varies from province to province in the breadth of its description, and the prohibition on disability-based employment discrimination is expressed in a number of ways. These issues will be discussed in Chapter 6. However, one distinctive feature is worth mentioning here. A prohibition on disability-based discrimination in employment remuneration is implicit in many of the provincial statutes. Separate equal pay provisions are to be found elsewhere in Canadian provincial human rights legislation, but are nearly always concerned with gender-based pay discrimination. As terms and conditions of employment are invariably covered by the anti-discrimination principle in any case, separate protection from disability-related pay discrimination might appear otiose. However, in some provinces, such discrimination is addressed explicitly and is not restricted to sex-based discrimination.[54]

Only the Northwest Territories province fails to make explicit provision for a defence of *bona fide* occupational qualification or requirement.[55] A general defence is also made available under Alberta law if the discriminator can show 'that the alleged contravention was reasonable and justifiable in the circumstances'.[56] In Ontario, for instance, there is no discrimination if a disabled person is 'incapable of performing or fulfilling the essential duties or requirements' of employment because of disability, subject always to any accommodation without undue hardship.[57] Furthermore, there is no constructive (indirect) discrimination if the requirement, qualification or factor is 'reasonable and *bona fide* in the circumstances' *and* 'the needs of the group of which the person is a member cannot be accommodated without undue hardship', taking into account 'the cost, outside sources of funding . . . and health and safety requirements'.[58] Saskatchewan law makes it clear, however, that an occupational qualification does not include one which is 'based on assumptions of the comparative employment characteristics' of physically disabled persons in general or which is based on 'stereotyped characterizations' of physical disability,[59] and may not be based on 'the preferences of co-workers, the employer, clients or customers'.[60] Furthermore, exclusively non-profit organizations primarily engaged in serving the interests of disabled persons may employ or give preference only to disabled persons if 'the qualification is a reasonable and *bona fide* qualification because of the nature of the employment'.[61]

Several provinces allow affirmative action or preferential treatment on behalf of disabled persons.[62] In Nova Scotia, for example, a programme or activity may be exempted from the anti-discrimination measures if there is a *bona fide* reason to do so and, furthermore, the Act does not affect any law, programme or activity whose object is the amelioration of the conditions of disadvantaged persons.[63] The Ontario Code does not prevent the implementation of any special programme

> designed to relieve hardship or economic disadvantage or to assist disadvantaged persons or groups to achieve . . . equal opportunity or that is likely to contribute to the elimination of discrimination.[64]

Any organization primarily engaged in serving the interests of disabled persons may employ only disabled persons, or give them employment preference, if being disabled is a 'reasonable and *bona fide* qualification because of the nature of the employment'.[65] The Code employs a measure of contract compliance to address employment discrimination. It is an implied term of every government contract (and sub-contract) that the right to equal treatment in employment without discrimination on the ground of disability shall not be infringed during the performance of that contract.[66] A similar provision applies in respect of government grants and loans.[67] Breach of the implied term shall be grounds for the cancellation of the contract (or grant or loan) and may justify a refusal to enter into further contracts with the discriminator (or make further grants or loans thereto).[68]

AUSTRALIA

In Australia, the regulation of employment discrimination in general, and of discrimination on the grounds of disability in particular, is derived from statutory intervention at the levels of the Commonwealth and the individual states of the Australian federation.[69] Much of the relevant legislative activity took place during the 1970s and 1980s. The regulation of sex and race discrimination was in the vanguard of legal reform. Laws to address disability discrimination were subsequently enacted, but were usually grafted on to the pre-existing legal framework. As in the case of the Canadian provinces, some (but not all) of the Australian states have taken the lead in legislating for change, and Commonwealth or federal laws have then followed. Early federal legislation dealt specifically with sex and race discrimination, and the Commonwealth enacted further laws committing the federal government to the promotion of equal opportunities and the protection of human rights in the public sector. However, it was not until 1992 that the federal government addressed directly the problem of disability-based discrimination and so it is appropriate to begin with an overview of state law.

The application of the anti-discrimination principle to disabled persons first occurred in 1981 in the states of New South Wales[70] and South Australia.[71] Victoria followed suit in 1982[72] and Western Australia in 1988.[73] Queensland[74] and the Australian Capital Territory[75] did not enact such laws until 1991, while the Northern Territory did not act in this field until 1992.[76] The development of state legislation regulating disability-related employment discrimination has been evolutionary and reform has been organic. New South Wales took the lead in this area, while South Australia and Victoria added to and developed the nascent principles and concepts of disability discrimination law. Western Australia borrows heavily from the pattern established by these three states, perhaps adding one or two flourishes and novelties of its own. Much the same can be said of the remaining states to have legislated on this topic. Accordingly, the account which follows focuses exclusively upon the legislation of the four pioneer states and the more recent federal enactments.

AUSTRALIAN STATE LEGISLATION

New South Wales

The (NSW) ADA 1977 outlaws direct discrimination or less favourable treatment on the ground of physical impairment.[77] The formula for identifying direct discrimination will be familiar to British labour lawyers used to the employment of that concept in section 1 of the Sex Discrimination Act 1975 and the Race Relations Act 1976. However, what amounts to discrimination based on a person's physical impairment is amplified to include discrimination based on a characteristic generally appertaining to or imputed to disabled persons with a particular physical impairment. The statute gives a specific example of what would constitute characteristic-related discrimination.[78] Less favourable treatment of a visually impaired person because of his or her actual or potential use of a guide dog is deemed to be treatment on the basis of a disability-related characteristic. Indirect disability discrimination is also unlawful.[79] This involves the imposition of an unreasonable requirement or condition, with which a substantially smaller proportion of disabled persons than non-disabled persons can comply, and with which the particular complainant cannot comply. Once again, this is similar to the concept of indirect discrimination in British sex and race discrimination law. Thus discrimination by the application of facially neutral criteria, which have an adverse impact upon disabled persons, is also prohibited.

The protection from direct and indirect discrimination on the ground of physical impairment applies to physically handicapped persons. Who is a 'physically handicapped person' for this purpose? This is someone who

> as a result of having a physical impairment to his body, and having regard to any community attitudes relating to persons having the same or substantially the same physical impairment as that person and to the physical environment, is limited in his opportunities to enjoy a full and active life.[80]

In this context, a 'physical impairment' means

> any defect or disturbance in the normal structure and functioning of the person's body whether arising from a condition subsisting at birth or from illness or injury, but does not include intellectual impairment.[81]

Despite that rider, discrimination against intellectually disabled persons is also prohibited under the New South Wales legislation. Part IVB of the Act, which deals with discrimination on the ground of intellectual impairment, was introduced in 1982 and is a mirror image of Part IVA. The protected class is defined by reference to 'intellectually handicapped persons', meaning persons who 'as a result of disabilities arising from intellectual impairment, [are] substantially limited in one or more major life activities'.[82] An intellectually impaired person is one who experiences 'any defect or disturbance in the normal structure and functioning of the person's brain, whether arising from a condition subsisting at birth or from illness or injury'.[83] In the leading case of *Kitt* v *Tourism Commission*,[84] an epileptic was held to be intellectually impaired under the Act because epilepsy arises from a defect in a person's brain, although epileptics usually consider themselves to be *physically* disabled.

What types of employment discrimination against physically and intellectually disabled persons are circumscribed? Section 49B prohibits discrimination in recruitment and selection,[85] employment offers, terms and conditions of employment, promotion, training or transfer opportunities, and any other employment benefits. Discriminatory dismissals are also outlawed, as is any other detrimental action informed by disability.[86] Section 49Q contains mirror provisions in respect of intellectually disabled applicants and employees.

As has been noted, the language and structure of these sections is clearly derived from that of the British sex and race discrimination legislation. However, with regard to disability, there the comparison ends. In determining who should be offered employment, an employer is permitted to discriminate on the ground of disability if:

> with respect to the work required to be performed in the course of the employment or engagement concerned, it appeared to the employer . . . on such grounds as, having regard to the circumstances of the case, it was reasonable to rely, that the . . . handicapped person, because of his . . . impairment – (a) would be unable to carry out that work; or (b) would, in order to carry out that work, require services or facilities which are not required by persons who are not . . . handicapped persons and which, having regard to the circumstances of the case, cannot reasonably be provided or accommodated by the employer.[87]

Thus an employer may refuse to employ a disabled person whose disability disqualifies him or her from doing the job, or who would only be able to perform the work with the assistance of *unreasonable* accommodations.

An employer may also discriminate on the basis of disability in the terms of an employment offer, in employment terms and conditions generally, and in access to promotion, transfer, training or other employment benefits:

> in respect of any determination by the employer . . . of any terms or conditions relating to the . . . handicapped person that are reasonable having regard to . . . (a) any limitation or restriction that the . . . handicapped person's . . . impairment would or does impose on his ability to carry out the work required to be performed in the course of the employment or engagement concerned; (b) any services or facilities which would be or are required by the . . . handicapped person in order to carry out the work referred to in paragraph (a) and which would not be or are not required by persons who are not . . . handicapped persons.[88]

Again, this means that an employer may allow a disability, or the limitations and requirements of a disabled person, to be a factor in making employment decisions and extending employment opportunities. The combined effect of sections 49I(1) and 49I(2) is a manifest failure to incorporate a clear requirement of reasonable accommodation of disabled persons in the workplace. The implications of this flaw in policy or drafting were confirmed in *Jamal* v *Secretary, Department of Health*,[89] the leading case interpreting the NSW disability discrimination provisions. This case is discussed in detail in Chapter 9.

Part IXA of the Act deals with equal opportunity in public employment and was introduced by the 1980 amendments. It applies to government departments, public authorities and the police force.[90] The provisions of this part of the Act were extended to physically disabled persons in 1984. In the present context, its objects are:

> (a) to eliminate and ensure the absence of discrimination in employment on the grounds of . . . physical impairment; and (b) to promote equal employment opportunity for . . . physically handicapped persons [in public employment].[91]

Section 122J requires public sector employers to whom it is addressed to prepare and to implement an equal employment opportunity management plan in order to achieve those objects. The plan must be sent to the Director of Equal Opportunity in Public Employment, with whom an annual report must also be filed.[92] The plan must include provisions relating to: the devising of policies and programmes by which those objects are to be achieved; communication of such policies and programmes; collection and recording of appropriate information; review of personnel practices (including recruitment techniques, selection criteria, training and staff development programmes, promotion and transfer policies and patterns, and conditions of service) with a view to identifying discriminatory practices; setting of goals or targets against which the success of the management plan may be assessed; other means of evaluating the policies and programmes; revision and amendment of the management plan; and appointment of persons to implement these provisions.[93] Provision is made for references to the NSW Anti-Discrimination Board where a plan is unsatisfactory, for investigations to be made and for the power to direct the amendment of a management plan.[94]

South Australia

The scope of unlawful discrimination in this state is defined in terms very similar to those in the (NSW) ADA 1977.[95] Part V of the Act prohibits discrimination on the ground of impairment against applicants and employees. In this context, 'impairment' means intellectual or physical impairment.[96] Under the Act, 'physical impairment' denotes:

> (a) the total or partial loss of any function of the body; (b) the *total or partial* loss of any part of the body; (c) the malfunctioning of any part of the body; or (d) the malformation or disfigurement of any part of the body, *whether permanent or temporary* but does not include an intellectual impairment or mental illness.[97]

Until 1989, intellectual impairment was not covered by the Act, but this omission has now been cured by the addition of a bespoke definition. The definition of 'intellectual impairment' extends to 'permanent or temporary loss or imperfect development of mental faculties (except where attributable to mental illness) resulting in reduced intellectual capacity'.[98]

What constitutes discrimination on the ground of impairment? In section 66 of the Act, direct and indirect discrimination appear in their now familiar guises, except that the standard of unfavourable treatment, rather than less favourable treatment, is preferred as the badge of discrimination. Discrimination on the ground of past or presumed impairment is included, while discrimination based upon disability characteristics (actual or presumed) is also caught. Notably, discrimination also occurs through unreasonable refusal to accommodate disability or unfavourable treatment because such accommodation would be required. Particular protection is afforded to visually impaired or hearing-impaired persons by outlawing discrimination motivated by the fact that the person possesses or is accompanied by a guide dog.[99] A discriminator treats another unfavourably on the basis of a particular attribute or circumstance if the discriminator treats that other person less favourably than in identical or similar circumstances the discriminator treats, or would treat, a person who does not have that attribute or is not affected by that circumstance.[100]

The employer's main defence is contained in section 71(2), which provides that there will be no disability-based discrimination if

> the person suffering from the impairment is not, or would not be, able – (a) to perform adequately, and without endangering himself or herself or other persons, the work genuinely and reasonably required for the employment or position in question; or (b) to respond adequately to situations of emergency that should reasonably be anticipated in connection with the employment or position in question.

This is a version of the 'otherwise qualified' or '*bona fide* occupational requirement' test observable in the disability statutes of the North American jurisdictions. It is noticeable that it expressly incorporates a safety risk defence. Furthermore, discriminatory rates of salary, wages or other remuneration payable to persons who have impairments are not rendered unlawful.[101] Disability-based discrimination arising because premises, as constructed, are inaccessible to disabled persons, or because the owner or occupier fails to ensure that the premises are accessible to such persons, is not unlawful.[102] On the other hand, schemes or undertakings for the benefit of persons who have a particular impairment are lawful, thus permitting a degree of positive discrimination.[103]

Victoria

The Victorian statute renders unlawful certain kinds of discrimination and promotes equality of opportunity between persons of different status. It outlaws employment discrimination 'on the ground of status or by reason of . . . private life.'[104] This applies to the determination of employment offers, terms of employment offers, refusal or deliberate omission to offer employment, and denial of access to a guidance programme, an apprenticeship training programme or other occupational training or retraining programme.[105] Furthermore, it is unlawful to deny or limit access to opportunities for promotion, transfer or training or to any other benefits connected with employment, and to dismiss an employee or subject an employee to any other detriment, by reason of a prohibited ground.[106]

Discrimination on the ground of 'status' includes discrimination because of impairment.[107] For this purpose, 'impairment' means:

> (a) total or partial loss of a bodily function; (aa) the presence in the body of organisms causing disease; (b) total or partial loss of a part of the body; (c) *malfunction of a part of the body*; and (d) malformation or disfigurement of a part of a body – and includes – (e) in relation to a person with a past or present impairment an impairment which presently exists or existed in the past but has now ceased to exist; and (f) an impairment which is imputed to a person.[108]

As the words in italics above show, an impairment includes a malfunction of a part of the body. This is defined to include 'a mental or psychological disease or disorder' and 'a condition or malfunction as a result of which a person learns more slowly than persons who do not have that condition or malfunction'.[109] It does not matter whether the impairment arose before or during the employment, and whether or not the impairment was apparent before employment or only became apparent during employment.[110]

The criteria for identifying discrimination are set out in section 17. First, direct discrimination is described in familiar comparison-driven terms.[111] The comparison called for here must be based upon relevant circumstances which 'are the same, or are not materially different' in the two cases being compared.[112] Second, less favourable treatment is discriminatory if

> by reason of a characteristic that appertains generally to persons of the status or with the private life of the other person; or . . . by reason of a characteristic which is generally imputed to persons of the status or with the private life of the other person.[113]

Third, there is indirect discrimination, where

> (a) the first-mentioned person imposes on that other person a requirement or condition with which a substantially higher proportion of persons of a different status or with a different private life do or can comply; (b) the other person does not or cannot comply with the requirement or condition; and (c) the requirement or condition is not reasonable.[114]

In case there was any doubt, the Act provides that it is not discriminatory to select 'the person who is, irrespective of impairment, best suited to perform the duties relevant to the employment'.[115]

A number of exceptions to the Act are outlined. The Act does not apply to small employers employing fewer than four employees.[116] Unusually, discrimination on the ground of impairment is permitted where the employment is for the purposes of dramatic performances, entertainment, artistic or photographic work and where persons with an impairment are required for reasons of authenticity.[117] Discrimination authorized or required by Australian Commonwealth or Victorian law is allowed, as it is if pursuant to a lawful agreement or arrangement relating to industrial relations.[118] Discrimination on the ground of impairment, with respect to persons of a particular impairment, is permitted in the provision of services for the promotion of the welfare or advancement of those persons, if those services can most effectively be provided by a person of the same impairment.[119] Section 39(f) permits 'the exclusion of any person from a *bona fide* programme, plan or arrangement designed to prevent or reduce disadvantage suffered by a particular class of disadvantaged persons'.

The employer's main defences under the Act are provided by section 21(4)(g)–(i). First, discrimination on the ground of impairment is lawful if the plaintiff would be unable to perform adequately the reasonable requirements of the job with or without special services or facilities which cannot reasonably be made available.[120] In deciding this question, the plaintiff's past training, qualifications and relevant experience (and, where appropriate, employment performance) must be taken into account. This is the Victorian version of the 'otherwise qualified' or '*bona fide* occupational requirement' standard. Second, the section also incorporates a separate safety risk defence, which allows the employer to discriminate on the ground of an impairment which raises a risk of injury to the plaintiff or others in the workplace.[121] Section 39(da) also gives a general exemption to 'discrimination on the ground of impairment where the discrimination is reasonably necessary to protect public health.' Third, discrimination in employment terms or conditions is permitted to take account of any limitations in working capacity or any accommodations made to enable a disabled employee to work. This last exception also permits disability-based discrimination in terms and conditions in accordance with collective bargaining arrangements.[122]

The Victorian legislation is very tightly drafted and gives only grudging protection to disabled workers facing employment discrimination. The Law Reform Commission of Victoria has proposed that the exception relating to the employment of people who create a risk of injury to themselves or others should be restricted to cases where the employer cannot, by adopting reasonable measures, reduce the risk to a level similar to that of other employees.[123] This is the conflict between sections 21(4)(g) and 21(4)(h). Reasonable accommodation should apply in both situations. The Commission also proposes that it should be unlawful to ask for information which might provide a basis for discrimination, unless it is for a non-discriminatory purpose. In multiple reason discrimination, the Commission proposes either a causation test or a significant factor test. A further report by the Commission says that there is no evidence that the costs of complying with the Act are unreasonable.[124] It also rejects the argument that there should be a *freedom* to discriminate. The Commission recommends that the Act should specifically refer to a failure to accommodate a special need. It is recommended that section 39(da) should be extended to allow for a significant risk to a person's health, safety or property to be an exception.

Western Australia

Western Australian legislation was established by the state 'to promote equality of opportunity in Western Australia and to provide remedies in respect of discrimination on the grounds of . . . impairment'.[125] Its objects include the elimination, so far as is possible, of discrimination against persons on the ground of impairment in work, and the promotion of recognition and acceptance within the community of the equality of all persons regardless of their impairment.[126] This is to be achieved by Part IVA of the Act, which was inserted in 1988 to deal with discrimination on the ground of impairment.

The Act prohibits direct and indirect disability discrimination using the formulae with which we are now quite familiar.[127] The definition of 'impairment' for these purposes is also worth reproducing:

> (a) any defect or disturbance in the normal structure or functioning of a person's body; (b) any defect or disturbance in the normal structure or functioning of a person's brain; or (c) any illness or condition which impairs a person's thought processes, perception of reality, emotions or judgment or which results in disturbed behaviour, whether arising from a condition subsisting at birth or from an illness or injury and includes an impairment which presently exists or existed in the past but has now ceased to exist.[128]

In employment, the prohibition on discrimination extends to: the arrangements made for determining employment offers; the determination of who should be offered employment; the terms or conditions on which employment is offered; the terms or conditions of employment; the access to opportunities for promotion, transfer or training, or other employment benefits; and dismissal, or the subjecting of an employee to any other detriment.[129]

A novelty of the Western Australian legislation is that employment application procedures are also specifically regulated, as section 660 provides:

> it is unlawful . . . to request or require . . . information (whether by way of completing a form or otherwise) that persons who do not have an impairment would not, in circumstances that are the same or not materially different, be requested or required to provide.

However, an employer may discriminate against a person on the ground of the impairment if the disabled person is not otherwise qualified for the job or would require accommodations which would impose unjustifiable hardship on the employer. The statute establishes the lawfulness of such disability-informed discrimination where:

> it is reasonable for the employer . . . to conclude, on such grounds having regard to the circumstances of the case and having taken all reasonable steps to obtain relevant and necessary information concerning the impairment it is reasonable for the employer . . . to rely on, that the person with the impairment because of that impairment – (a) would be unable to carry out the work required to be performed in the course of the employment or engagement concerned; or (b) would, in order to carry out that work, require services or facilities that are not required by persons who do not have an impairment and the provision of which would impose an unjustifiable hardship on the employer, principal or person.[130]

What constitutes 'unjustifiable hardship' requires account to be taken of all relevant circumstances of the particular case, including any benefit or detriment likely to accrue or be suffered, the nature of the impairment, the financial circumstances of the employer, and the estimated expenditure required to be made.[131]

An employer may also discriminate in employment terms and conditions that

> are reasonable having regard to either or both of the following – (a) any limitation or restriction that the impairment would or does impose on the person's ability to carry out the work required to be performed in the course of the employment or engagement concerned; or (b) any services or facilities that would be or are required by the person with the impairment in order to carry out the work referred to in paragraph (a) and that would not be or are not required by persons who do not have an impairment.[132]

The limitations of this form of wording are discussed in Chapter 9. On the other hand, a degree of positive action is encouraged. Employers are permitted to take measures which are intended to achieve equality where their purpose is:

> (a) to ensure that persons who have an impairment have equal opportunities with other persons in circumstances in relation to which provision is made by this Act; or (b) to afford persons who have an impairment access to facilities, services or opportunities to meet their special needs in relation to employment, education, training or welfare.[133]

The Act further contains a number of genuine occupational qualification exceptions similar to those found in Victoria.[134] Also excluded is the provision of services promoting the welfare of impaired persons where those services can most effectively be provided by a person with the same impairment. Finally, state government departments and public authorities are obliged to devise and implement equal employment opportunity programmes. Such public sector employers are under a statutory duty to eliminate employment discrimination based upon impairment and to ensure its continued absence.[135]

AUSTRALIAN COMMONWEALTH LEGISLATION

Human Rights and Equal Opportunity Commission Act

Although the Australian Commonwealth had legislated to control racial discrimination in the 1970s and gender discrimination in the 1980s,[136] it was not until the 1990s that disability discrimination was first addressed. Prior to these recent developments, the civil rights of disabled persons were barely recognized in federal law. The Human Rights and Equal Opportunity Commission Act 1986 ratified and incorporated the UN Declaration on the Rights of Mentally Retarded Persons 1971 and the Declaration on the Rights of Disabled Persons 1975.[137] The Act also recognized the doubtful legality of social and employment discrimination based upon any distinction, exclusion or preference made on prohibited grounds or having the effect of nullifying or impairing equality of opportunity or treatment in employment or occupation.[138] Regulations were made under the Act declaring any distinction, exclusion or preference made on the ground of medical record, impairment, or physical, mental, intellectual or psychiatric disability as discrimination.[139] Imputed and previous disabilities or impairments were similarly embraced. Impairment was defined as:

> (a) total or partial loss of a bodily function; or (b) the presence in the body of organisms causing disease; or (c) total or partial loss of a part of the body; or (d) malfunction of a part of the body; or (e) malformation or disfigurement of a part of the body.[140]

However, the Act did not give disabled persons significant rights of action or remedies for disability discrimination. Rather, the Act provided a statutory framework in which the newly established Human Rights and Equal Opportunity Commission could treat disability discrimination as a subject for research, policy-making and the occasional investigation and conciliation of complaints received by it. The work of the Commission in this regard led indirectly to the eventual enactment of Commonwealth disability discrimination laws in 1992.[141]

Disability Discrimination Act

The (Cth) Disability Discrimination Act 1992 (DDA 1992) received constitutional assent on 5 November 1992 and came into force in the following year.[142] It sets out to eliminate disability-based discrimination in employment, existing laws and the administration of Commonwealth laws and programmes.[143] The Act applies throughout Australia and to both private and public sector employment, yet operates concurrently with state laws.[144] The Act will prevail as far as any state law is inconsistent with it, but where a complaint has been instituted under state anti-discrimination legislation, action under Commonwealth law is excluded.[145] The objects of the Act are:

> to ensure, as far as practicable, that persons with disabilities have the same rights to equality before the law as the rest of the community; and . . . to promote recognition and acceptance within the community of the principle that persons with disabilities have the same fundamental rights as the rest of the community.[146]

The Act prohibits both direct and indirect discrimination on the ground of disability, in terms which are by now quite familiar.[147] The concept of disability-informed discrimination also expressly includes less favourable treatment because the disabled person uses palliative or therapeutic devices or auxiliary aids, or is accompanied by an interpreter, reader, assistant, carer or guide/hearing dog.[148]

The definition of 'disability' for the purposes of the Act is one of the most extensive in the Australian jurisdiction.[149] It includes past, present and imputed disabilities but, somewhat uniquely, it also includes a disability which may exist in the future, perhaps anticipating discrimination informed by genetic screening. Disability status is also found where a person possesses bodily organisms capable of causing disease or illness, thus preventing discrimination against carriers or persons with benign or stable viral infections. The potential application of this definition to someone who is HIV-positive, but otherwise healthy, is apparent. However, the Act does not render unlawful discriminatory acts in relation to disabilities which are comprised of infectious diseases and where it is reasonably necessary to discriminate to protect public health.[150]

In regulating disability discrimination in employment, Part 2 of the Act encompasses the usual areas of employment decisions and processes in which discrimination occurs: recruitment and selection, employment offers, terms and conditions, opportunities for promotion, transfer and training, other employment benefits, dismissal and any other detriment.[151] However, in prohibiting disability discrimination, Part 2 of the Act also applies to protect a complainant from discrimination based upon the disability of any of the complainant's associates.[152] The interpretation section provides that 'associate', in relation to a person, includes:

> (a) a spouse of the person; and (b) another person who is living with the person on a genuine domestic basis; and (c) a relative of the person; and (d) a carer of the person; and (e) another person who is in a business, sporting or recreational relationship with the person.[153]

Significantly, the legislation also incorporates a detailed 'otherwise qualified' standard which provides a defence to disability discrimination. The disabled person must be able to carry out the 'inherent requirements' of the job.[154] The employer, in making the judgment of whether a disabled person is so capable, is permitted to take into account the individual's record of relevant training, qualifications, experience and employment performance, together with any other reasonably relevant factors. In addition, if the disabled worker could only satisfy the inherent requirements of the job with the assistance of services or facilities which would not be required by a non-disabled worker, an employer may discriminate if the provision of such accommodation would impose 'unjustifiable hardship' on the employer.[155] In assessing what constitutes unjustifiable hardship, all the relevant circumstances are to be accounted for, including any benefit or detriment likely to accrue to or be suffered by any persons concerned and the effect of the disability on any person concerned. The financial circumstances of the employer will be relevant, as will be the estimated amount of expenditure required for the accommodation.[156]

Like most, if not all, examples of disability discrimination laws, the Commonwealth legislation does not seek to regulate reverse discrimination. In other words, unlike sex and race discrimination laws, the legislation is not framed in terms which prohibit discrimination against persons without disabilities and in favour of disabled persons. The language of the statute might be sufficient to reach that conclusion, but the Act makes this clear. It is not unlawful to do an act that is reasonably intended to ensure that persons who have a disability have equal opportunities with other persons.[157] Furthermore, disabled persons may be afforded goods or access to facilities, services or opportunities to meet their special needs in relation to employment.[158] The Act also allows positive discrimination to the advantage of disabled persons in respect of grants, benefits or programmes to meet their special needs.[159]

Moreover, the Act contains a number of miscellaneous provisions which are worthy of note. First, disability harassment of a disabled person or a person with a disabled associate is expressly unlawful.[160] Second, it is a criminal offence to victimize an individual who exercises his or her rights under the legislation.[161] Third, it is a similar criminal offence to incite the commission of an unlawful act or offence under the legislation.[162] Fourth, discriminatory advertisements are regulated by the criminal law and the penalty for a transgression is a fine of up to $1,000.[163]

Equal Employment Opportunity (Commonwealth Authorities) Act

Like many state governments in Australia, the Commonwealth government has acted to promote equal opportunity in public sector employment. The (Cth) Equal Employment Opportunity (Commonwealth Authorities) Act 1987 was passed to require certain Commonwealth public service authorities to promote equal opportunity in employment for women and persons in designated minority groups.[164] This includes persons with physical or intellectual disabilities.[165] The relevant public authority employers are required to develop and implement equal employment opportunity programmes.[166] An equal employment opportunity programme should be designed to ensure that appropriate action is taken by the public sector employer in question to eliminate employment discrimination by it against women and persons in designated groups in relation to employment matters and to promote equal opportunity.[167] The discrimination which must be confronted includes discrimination by which a physically or mentally disabled person is treated less favourably than a non-disabled person because of disability.[168] However, discrimination is permitted if it is essential for the effective performance of employment duties and nothing in the legislation requires any action incompatible with the principle that employment matters should be dealt with on the basis of merit.[169]

Section 6 of the Act deals with the content of an equal employment opportunity programme. Employees must be informed of the contents of the programme and of the results of any monitoring and evaluation of it. Relevant employers are obliged to confer responsibility for the development, implementation and review of a programme on a senior manager. Consultations with recognized trade unions concerning a programme must take place, while employees of the authority, particularly persons in designated groups, are also entitled to be consulted. The programme should provide for the collection and recording of employment statistics and information relating to the authority. The statistics must include the number of persons in designated groups, and the types of jobs undertaken by (or job classifications of) them. The employer's policies and practices must be considered and examined to identify their contribution to discrimination and any pattern of lack of equal opportunity. Objectives to be achieved by the programme must be set, and the quantitative and other indicators against which the effectiveness of the programme is to be assessed must be established.

The implementation of the programme is required to be monitored and evaluated, while the achievement of its objectives must be appraised. The effectiveness of the programme has to be measured by comparing statistics and information (required to be collected and recorded) with the indicators against which the effectiveness of the programme is to be judged. Public sector employers must take any action necessary to give effect to their programmes and regard is to be had to a programme when exercising powers in relation to employment matters.[170] The Act makes provision for the lodging of annual programme reports with the responsible minister or Public Service Board.[171] Special reports may be requested. The minister or Board may make recommendations after considering an annual programme report. Relevant ministers are allowed to give directions to an authority with respect to its obligations under the Act and the Board may issue guidelines.[172]

CONCLUSION

The Australian experiment with disability discrimination legislation would appear to offer the most direct comparative model from which British reformers might take consolation. Designed upon the British archetype of sex and race discrimination laws, the Australian statutes have incorporated disability and other suspect grounds within a conceptual framework that will be readily familiar to British employers, politicians and lawyers. This would suggest that the Australian variant upon the British paradigm could be readily transplanted by the amendment and consolidation of British race and gender discrimination statutes so as to include disability as a prohibited ground of discrimination here. However, it will be apparent from the account in this chapter, and in the analyses that follow in the chapters below, that the Australian model of anti-discrimination legislation has created complex and unwieldy laws. In particular, the effort to fit disability into a formula devised to address the problems and disadvantages of women and racial minorities has often strained the interpretation of laws designed to achieve too many simultaneous purposes. As a result, the rights and expectations of disabled persons have been done a disservice. The 'liberal promise' of anti-discrimination legislation has singularly failed to deliver employment opportunities for disabled Australians.[173] Moreover, mandatory equal opportunity planning, affirmative action and monitoring in respect of minority groups has been limited to the public sector (at least, in respect of disabled people) with apparent little effect.[174]

At first sight, the Canadian human rights approach to disability discrimination is of a qualitatively different order to the civil rights approach of the US disability legislation or the anti-discrimination regulations of British sex and race legislation. However, upon closer scrutiny, it is clear that the framework and concepts of Canadian human rights codes are closely related to the ingredients of discrimination laws in other common law jurisdictions. Moreover, the language of the human rights approach to discrimination and equal opportunity would appear to raise a legislative commitment to the positive protection of disabled people and the promotion of their employment rights. The tenor and spirit of Canadian legislation is exhortatory and purposive, and might seem to admit little room for narrow or mean-spirited interpretation. Nevertheless, as will also be seen below, the Canadian judiciary have often failed to give effect to the emancipatory drafting of both federal and provincial human rights legislation. It is not surprising, therefore, that disability rights activists in Canada during the past decade have despaired at the achievement of disability rights via the conduit of human rights codes, and instead have begun to place more reliance upon employment equity laws, contract compliance requirements and affirmative action legislation.

NOTES

1. (1971) 401 US 424.
2. Waters, 1990: 380–4. Indeed, one of the leading cases under the legislation of one of the Australian states acknowledges an influential debt to the American law: *Jamal* v *Secretary, Department of Health* (1988) 14 NSWLR 252 (NSW CA) *passim.* See: Astor, 1988.
3. A more detailed exposition of Australian and Canadian disability discrimination law has been attempted in Doyle, 1993b: Chapters X and XI. This chapter draws from that source and some of that detail informs the remaining chapters in this monograph.
4. Canadian Constitution (Constitution Act 1982) Part I.
5. Emphasis added. See: Tarnopolsky, 1983; Lepofsky, 1992. For a discussion of the position of disabled people under the Charter, see: Lepofsky, 1983, 1985; Lepofsky and Bickenbach, 1985; Rioux, 1994.
6. Hahn, 1987: 365. Hahn presents an interesting discussion of the political processes by which disabled people were eventually included within the Charter. See also: Poirier, 1991.
7. See generally: Tarnopolsky and Pentney, 1985 and supplements. Most recently, the Canadian Supreme Court has appeared to require plaintiffs under the Charter to show that they are not differently situated from those who are not harmed by alleged discriminatory actions or measures: *Hess* v *Regina* [1990] 2 SCR 906. Lepofsky (1992: 181) comments that: 'To disabled persons seeking equality under section 15, this would entail an unfair constitutional presumption of their difference from able-bodied persons'. See also: *McKinney* v *Board of Governors of the University of Guelph* [1990] 3 SCR 229 (correlating age with ability and stereotyping the elderly with incapacity).
8. Lepofsky, 1992: 168.
9. (Can) HRA (RSC 1985 c H-6, as amended by RSC 1985 (1st Supp) c 31 and SC 1986 c 40). The Act came into force on 12 December 1988. The Act was first enacted as SC 1976–77 c 33. Further amendment is expected in 1995, with the possibility of an express reasonable accommodation requirement and explicit recognition of indirect discrimination.
10. *Ibid.*: s 2.

11. *Ibid.*: s 3(1).
12. *Ibid.*: s 25. For example, an HIV-infected person has been treated as within the Act's protection: *Fontaine* v *Canadian Pacific Ltd* (1989) 89 CLLC para. 17,024 (Can) HRC; (1991) 91 CLLC para. 17,008 (Can) FCA.
13. *Ibid.*: s 7. See also s 9, which deals with discrimination by trade unions and employee organizations. Disability-based discrimination in pension funds or plans is prohibited by s 21.
14. *Bhinder* v *Canadian National Railway Co* (1985) 23 DLR (4th) 481 (Can) SC.
15. *Fontaine* v *Canadian Pacific Ltd* (1989) 89 CLLC para. 17,024 (Can) HRC; (1991) 91 CLLC para. 17,008 (Can) FCA.
16. *Attorney-General of Canada* v *Rosin* [1991] 1 FC 391, (1991) 91 CLLC para. 17,011 (Can) FCA.
17. (Can) HRA s 8.
18. *Ibid.*: s 10. See also ss 12 and 14 prohibiting the harassment of an individual on a prohibited ground and the publication of discriminatory notices. See further s 59 (prohibiting victimization of individuals exercising rights under the Act).
19. *Boucher* v *Correctional Services of Canada* (1988) 9 CHRR D/4910, (1988) 88 CLLC para. 17,000 (Can) HRT; cf. *Rivard* v *Department of National Defence* (1990) 90 CLLC para. 17,018 (Can) HRT; *Villeneuve* v *Bell Canada* (1985) 85 CLLC para. 17,016, (1986) 86 CLLC para. 17,016 (Can HRT), affirmed (1987) 9 CHRR D/5093 (Can FCA).
20. (Can) HRA s 15(a). This section also includes exceptions based on the age of an individual (e.g. in respect of retirement or pensions).
21. *Ward* v *Canadian National Express* (1982) 82 CLLC para. 17,012 (Can) HRT; *Husband* v *Canadian Armed Forces* (1994) 94 CLLC para. 17,014 (Can) FCA. The defence has been made out in a number of cases which are discussed in more detail in Chapter 8.
22. *De Jager* v *Department of National Defence* (1986) 86 CLLC para. 17,017 (Can) HRT; cf. *Canadian Pacific Ltd* v *Canadian Human Rights Commission* (1985) 85 CLLC para. 17,025 (Can) HRC, (1987) 40 DLR (4th) 586 (Can) FCA; *Rodger* v *Canadian National Railways* (1985) 85 CLLC para. 17,019 (Can) HRT.
23. *Erikson* v *Canadian Pacific Express & Transport Ltd* (1987) 87 CLLC para. 17,005 (Can) HRT.
24. *Forseille* v *United Grain Growers Ltd* (1985) 85 CLLC para. 17,024 (Can) HRT; cf. *Cinq-Mars* v *Les Transports Provost Inc.* (1987) 88 CLLC para. 17,002 (Can) HRT.
25. (Can) HRA s 16(1).
26. *Ibid.*: s 16(2). The Commission was established under Part II of the Act and is given various powers and duties in respect of enforcement, research, education, review and reform.
27. *Ibid.*: s 17. A reasoned notice must be issued when an application is not granted: s 17(4). Provision is made for rescission of approval and for opportunities of concerned parties to make representations before decisions are made under ss 17–18: s 19.
28. *Ibid.*: s 24.
29. *Ibid.*: s 19(2).
30. RSC 1985 (2nd Supp), c 23, which came into force on 12 December 1988. Extension of federal employment equity principles is expected to be proposed in 1995.
31. EEA 1985 s 2 (emphasis added).
32. *Ibid.*: s 3.
33. Employment Equity Regulations 1986 (SOR/86-847, as amended by SOR/90-454). The definition quoted is contained in s 3(b) of the Regulations. The 'purposes of section 6 of the Act' are discussed below.
34. EEA 1985 s 4. See further: Employment Equity Programs Exclusion Approval Order 1989 (SOR/89-30); Employment Equity Programs Regulations 1989 (SOR/89-30).
35. *Ibid.*: s 5(1). The employer must retain a copy of the plan for at least three years following the year to which the plan refers: s 5(2).
36. *Ibid.*: s 6(1). The accuracy of the report must be certified and signed by the employer and records used in compiling the report must be retained for at least three years: s 6(2) and (3). See further: Employment Equity Regulations, 1986.
37. *Ibid.*: ss 8–10.
38. (BC) HRA (SBC 1984 c 22 as amended by 1985 c 51, 1989 c 40 and 1989 c 53).
39. (Man) HRC (RSM 1987 c H175 as enacted by SM 1987 c 45).

40. (NB) HRA (RSNB 1973 c H-11 as amended by SNB 1976 c 31, 1979 c 41, 1983 c 30, 1985 c 30, 1986 c 4, 1986 c 6, 1986 c 8, 1987 c 6 and 1987 c 26).

41. (New) HRC (RSN 1990 c H-14 derived from SN 1988 c 62).

42. (NS) HRA (RSNS 1989 c 214 as amended by SNS 1991 c 12).

43. (Ont) HRC (RSO 1990 c H19). See: Ontario Human Rights Commission, 1990. See also (Ont) Employment Equity Act 1993 (SO 1993 c 35) in force from September 1994 and covering disable persons.

44. (PEI) HRA (RSPEI 1988 c H-12 as amended by SPEI 1989 c 3).

45. (Sask) HRC (SS 1979 c S-24.1 as amended by 1980–81 c 41, 1980–81 c 81 and 1989 c 23).

46. (YT) HRA (SYT 1987 c 3). It contains a small bill of rights in Part 1 of the Act, but Part 2 of the Act contains wide-ranging prohibitions on discrimination.

47. (Alb) IRPA (SA 1972 c 2 and revised at RSA 1980 c I-2 as amended by SA 1985 c 15, 1985 c 33, 1988 c E-10.2, 1990 c 23, 1991 c S-0.5).

48. (Québ) CHR&F (RSQ 1977 c C-12 as amended by SQ 1978 c 7, 1979 c 63, 1980 c 11, 1980 c 39, 1982 c 17, 1982 c 21, 1982 c 61, 1989 c 51, and 1990 c 4).

49. (NWT) FPA (RSNWT 1988 c F-2), effective on 15 July 1991, replaces the former Fair Practices Ordinance (RSNWT 1974 c F-2).

50. (Man) HRC preamble. Cf. the preamble to (Alb) IRPA; (NB) HRA; (NS) HRA; (NWT) FPA; (Ont) HRC; (PEI) HRA; (Québ) CHR&F. See also: (NS) HRA s 2; (Sask) HRC s 3; (YT) HRA preamble and s 1.

51. *Ontario Human Rights Commission* v *Etobicoke* [1982] 1 SCR 202; *Ontario Human Rights Commission* v *Simpson-Sears Ltd* [1985] 2 SCR 536. See Lepofsky, 1992: 172.

52. *Jefferson* v *BC Ferries Service* (1977) unreported. See: SBC 1973 c 119.

53. (1971) 401 US 424.

54. (PEI) HRA s 7; (Québ) CHR&F ss 46 and 56; (YT) HRA s 14.

55. (Alb) IRPA ss 7(3) and 8(2). Cf. the almost identical language in (New) HRC s 9(1). See also: (Man) HRC s 14; (NB) HRA ss 3 and 6; (NS) HRA s 6; (PEI) HRA ss 6(4)(a) and (b), 11 and 14; (Québ) CHR&F ss 18.1 and 20; (YT) HRA s 9(a) and (d). In British Columbia see (BC) HRA ss 6, 8(2)(b) and 8(4) and, for example, *Cook* v *Noble, Prysianziuk, Ministry of Human Resources, and Tranquille Hospital* (1983) 83 CLLC para. 17,020 (BC HRC). In Saskatchewan, see (Sask) HRC s 16(7) and s 1(b)(i)–(iii) of the 1979 Regulations under the Saskatchewan Human Rights Code: Sask Reg 216/79 as amended by Sask Reg 258/79 and Sask Reg 144/91.

56. (Alb) IRPA s 11.1. This defence did not protect an employer who dismissed an employee with AIDS where there was no evidence of any risk of social transmission of the disease: *STE* v *Bertelsen* (1989) CLLC para. 17,017 (Alb HRC). See also: (NS) HRA s 6(f).

57. (Ont) HRC s 17.

58. (Ont) HRC s 11(1)(a) and (2). Consideration is to be given to any standards prescribed by regulations for assessing what is undue hardship: s 11(3). There is also no constructive discrimination if the apparent infringement is otherwise excused under the Code: s 11(1)(b).

59. (Sask) HRC Reg s 1(b)(iv) and (v). See *Davison* v *St Paul Lutheran Home* (1991) 91 CLLC para. 17,017 (Sask). The subsequent history of this case, concerned with whether obesity is a disability, is disposed of in Chapter 7.

60. (Sask) HRC Reg s 1(b)(vi).

61. (Sask) HRC s 16(10).

62. (BC) HRA s 19; (Man) HRC s 11; (PEI) HRA s 20; (YT) HRA ss 7, 10 and 12. Québec's affirmative action provisions are the most far-reaching and are discussed in Chapter 12 below: (Québ) CHR&F ss 86 *et seq.*

63. (NS) HRA ss 6(i) and 9. The Act does not affect *bona fide* plans, schemes or practices of mandatory retirement: s 6(h).

64. (Ont) HRC s 14(1). Whether a special programme satisfies the conditions of this provision may be determined by the Ontario Human Rights Commission: s 14(2).

65. (Ont) HRC s 24(1)(a).

66. (Ont) HRC s 26(1). Manitoba also permits contract compliance techniques: (Man) HRC s 56(1).

67. (Ont) HRC s 26(2).

68. (Ont) HRC s 26(3).

69. For a general discussion of, and critical perspective upon, Australian anti-discrimination legislation see: Thornton, 1990. Note also New Zealand's Human Rights Act 1993 which borrows from the Australian models and covers disability.

70. (NSW) Anti-Discrimination Act (No. 48 of 1979) Parts IVA and IVB as amended by the ADA 1980-1985. See in general: Scutt, 1977; Partlett, 1977; Anti-Discrimination Board (NSW), 1977 and 1981. For a discussion of the NSW experience in regulating disability discrimination, see: Nothdurft and Astor, 1986. With effect from August 1994 the disability provisions of the (NSW) ADA have been extensively amended by the (NSW) ADA 1994. This account has been unable to address these reforms.

71. Equal Opportunity Act (EOA) 1984 (SA) No. 95 of 1984, as amended by the EOA Amendment Act 1989 ((SA) No. 68 of 1989). Disability rights were first addressed in the Handicapped Persons Equal Opportunity Act 1981 (SA) No. 56 of 1981. For the pre-1981 position see: Committee on Rights of Persons with Handicaps (South Australia), 1978. Few cases were reported under this Act, but one such case demonstrated the legislative intention to control employer assumptions about the capabilities and reach of employees with disabilities: *Garton* v *Hillcrest Hospital* (1984) AILR para. 240 (SA HPDT).

72. Originally via the Equal Opportunities (Discrimination Against Disabled Persons) Act 1982 (Vic) Act No. 9843, amending OA 1977 (Vic) Act No. 9025. The law is now contained in the EOA 1984 (Vic) Act No. 10095, as amended by the EO(A)A 1985 ((Vic) Act No. 10247) and further amended by the Health (General Amendment) Act 1988 ((Vic) Act No. 48 of 1988). In addition, in the Victorian civil service, all employees must receive fair and equitable treatment in employment regardless of, *inter alia*, physical disability: (Vic) Public Service Act 1974.

73. EOA 1984 (WA) No. 83 of 1984, as amended by the EO(A)A 1988 ((WA) No. 40 of 1988).

74. Anti-Discrimination Act (Qld) No. 85 of 1991, as amended by the Anti-Discrimination Amendment Act 1992 ((Qld) No. 59 of 1992. See also: (Qld) Equal Opportunity in Public Employment Act 1992 ((Qld) No. 10 of 1992.

75. Discrimination Act 1991 (ACT) No. 81 of 1991.

76. Anti-Discrimination Act (NT) No. 80 of 1992.

77. (NSW) ADA 1977 s 49A(1). See: *Clinch* v *Commissioner of Police* (1988) AILR para. 169 (NSW EOT). Note the recent developments recorded in note 70 above.

78. *Ibid.*: s 49A(2).

79. *Ibid.*: s 49A(3).

80. *Ibid.*: s 4(1).

81. *Ibid.*: s 4(1).

82. *Ibid.*: ss 49P and 4(1).

83. *Ibid.*: s 4(1).

84. (1987) EOC para. 92-196 (NSW EOT); (1987) 11 NSWLR 686 (NSW SC). See: Astor, 1988.

85. In *Clinch* v *Commissioner of Police* (above) there was a breach of s 49B(1)(c) by virtue of the employer's standing instruction requiring prospective employees to have vision in both eyes.

86. (NSW) ADA 1977 s 49B(3) excludes the application of the non-discrimination principle in respect of private households, employers employing up to five employees and private educational authorities. The remaining sections of Part IVA extend the anti-discrimination principles to discrimination against contract workers and to discrimination by partnerships, trade unions, qualifying bodies and employment agencies.

87. *Ibid.*: ss 49I(1) and 49X(1). In *Clinch* v *Commissioner of Police* (above), as the employer had not examined the applicant, a defence made out under s 49I could not succeed. The respondent was ordered to give further consideration to the applicant. Subsequently the complaint was dismissed: (1989) AILR para. 372(16); (1988) EOC para. 92-262.

88. *Ibid.*: ss 49I(2) and 49X(2).

89. (1986) AILR para. 433 and (1986) EOC para. 92-162 (NSW EOT); (1987) AILR para. 280 (NSW SC); (1988) 14 NSWLR 252 (NSW CA).

90. (NSW) ADA 1977 s 122B.

91. *Ibid.*: s 122C.
92. *Ibid.*: ss 122J(6) and 122L.
93. *Ibid.*: s 122J(2).
94. (NSW) ADA 1977 ss 122M-122S.
95. (SA) EOA 1984 s 67(2) The Act also extends to discrimination against agents and contract workers and within partnerships, as well to associations and qualifying bodies. The Act does not apply to employment within a private household.
96. *Ibid.*: s 5 (as amended).
97. *Ibid.*: s 5 (the words in italics were added by the 1989 amendments).
98. *Ibid.*: s 5 (as amended).
99. In addition, (SA) EOA 1984 s 88 provides that: '(a) it is unlawful to impose any condition or requirement that would result in a person who is blind or deaf, or partially blind or deaf, being separated from his or her guide dog; and (b) a person who imposes any such condition or requirement shall, in addition to any civil liability that might be incurred under this Act, be guilty of an offence and liable to a penalty not exceeding $1,000.'
100. (SA) EOA 1984 s 6(3) (as amended).
101. *Ibid.*: s 79.
102. *Ibid.*: s 84.
103. *Ibid.*: s 82.
104. (Vic) EOA 1984 s 21. The Act extends to discrimination against agents and contract workers, within partnerships, and by professional and other organizations, qualifying bodies and employment agencies.
105. *Ibid.*: s 21(1).
106. *Ibid.*: s 21(2).
107. *Ibid.*: s 4(1).
108. *Ibid.*: s 4(1). The definition has been applied to capture a variety of disabilities: *MacLeod* v *State of Victoria* (1987) AILR para. 285 (Vic EOB): diabetes; *Campbell* v *FH Productions* (1984) AILR para. 178 (Vic EOB): back injury; *O'Neil* v *Burton Cables P/L* (1986) AILR para. 435 (Vic EOB): acute back condition; *Urie* v *Cadbury Schweppes P/L* (1987) AILR para. 283 (Vic EOB): knee injury and childhood record of rheumatic fever.
109. *Ibid.*: s 4(1).
110. *Ibid.*: s 21(3).
111. *Ibid.*: s 17(1) (as amended).
112. *Ibid.*: s 17(2).
113. *Ibid.*: s 17(4).
114. *Ibid.*: s 17(5).
115. *Ibid.*: s 21(4)(k). However, a disabled applicant must be given fair consideration and should only be rejected on capability grounds if there has been an individual assessment or medical examination: *O'Neil* v *Burton Cables P/L* (above).
116. *Ibid.*: s 21(4)(f). Employment 'in domestic or personal services in or in relation to the home of the employer' is also exempted, as are private households: *Ibid.*: ss 21(4)(a) and 21(4)(j).
117. *Ibid.*: s 21(4)(b). It must have been intended only to provide for this exception to ensure uniformity of approach with the other grounds of unlawful discrimination, in particular with sex and race discrimination.
118. *Ibid.*: s 21(4)(d).
119. *Ibid.*: s 21(4)(e).
120. *Ibid.*: s 21(4)(g). For a criticism of this aspect of the Victorian legislation, see: Johnstone, 1989.
121. *Ibid.*: s 21(4)(h).
122. *Ibid.*: s 21(4)(i).
123. Law Reform Commission of Victoria, 1989, 1990a.
124. Law Reform Commission of Victoria, 1990b.
125. (WA) EOA 1984 preamble.
126. *Ibid.*: s 3. The Act extends to discrimination against commission agents and contract workers, and by partnerships, professional or trade organizations, qualifying bodies and employment agencies.

127. *Ibid.*: s 66A.
128. *Ibid.*: s 4(1) (as amended). Section 66U provides for regulations to be made to exclude particular infectious diseases from the scope of the Act. It is understood that no regulations have been made.
129. *Ibid.*: s 66B(1) and (2).
130. *Ibid.*: s 66Q(1).
131. *Ibid.*: s 4(4).
132. *Ibid.*: s 66Q(2).
133. *Ibid.*: s 66R.
134. *Ibid.*: s 66S.
135. *Ibid.*: ss 140–5.
136. (Cth) Racial Discrimination Act 1975 and Sex Discrimination Act 1984.
137. (Cth) No. 125 of 1986. See (Cth) HR&EOCA 1986 s 3 and Schs 4 and 5.
138. *Ibid.*: s 3(1).
139. HR&EOC Regulations 1989 (SR 1989 No. 407) reg 4.
140. *Ibid.*: reg 3.
141. Human Rights Commission (Australia), 1985; Ware and Neale, 1986; National Council on Intellectual Disability, 1989.
142. (Cth) No. 135 of 1992. For the background to the Act see: Ronalds, 1990, 1991; Commonwealth Disability Anti-Discrimination Legislation Committee, 1991; Shelley, 1991; Wightman, 1991; Parliament of the Commonwealth of Australia, 1992; Tyler, 1993.
143. *Ibid.*: s 3(a).
144. *Ibid.*: ss 4(1) and 12-13.
145. McCarry, 1989.
146. (Cth) DDA 1992 s 3(b) and (c). The Act also applies to accommodation, education, access to premises, clubs and sport, provision of goods, facilities, services and land.
147. *Ibid.*: ss 5(1) and 6. It is sufficient that disability is one of the reasons, whether or not dominant or substantial, for the discriminatory act: s 10.
148. *Ibid.*: ss 7–9.
149. *Ibid.*: s 4(1).
150. *Ibid.*: s 48.
151. *Ibid.*: s 15(1) and (2). The Act also applies to discrimination against commission agents and contract workers, within partnerships, and by qualifying bodies, trade unions, employers' associations and employment agencies. The statute does not apply to domestic employment: s 15(3).
152. *Ibid.*: s 15(1) and (2).
153. *Ibid.*: s 4(1).
154. *Ibid.*: s 15(4)(a).
155. *Ibid.*: s 15(4)(b).
156. *Ibid.*: s 11.
157. *Ibid.*: s 45(a).
158. *Ibid.*: s 45(b).
159. *Ibid.*: s 45(c).
160. *Ibid.*: ss 35 and 36.
161. *Ibid.*: s 42. The offence is punishable by imprisonment of up to six months.
162. *Ibid.*: DDA 1992 s 43.
163. *Ibid.*: s 44.
164. (Cth) No. 20 of 1987.
165. (Cth) Public Services Act 1922 s 7(1) (as amended).
166. (Cth) EEO(CA)A 1987 s 5. Under Part 3 of the (Cth) DDA 1992, state and Commonwealth departments, public authorities and instrumentalities providing goods, services or facilities may prepare and implement action plans to achieve the objectives of that Act.
167. *Ibid.*: s 3(1). A relevant authority is one employing forty or more employees in Australia.
168. *Ibid.*: s 3(1). The scope of employment discrimination includes recruitment procedures, selection criteria, promotion and transfer, training and staff development, and conditions of service.
169. *Ibid.*: ss 3(2) and 3(4).

170. *Ibid.*: s 7.
171. *Ibid.*: ss 8–11.
172. *Ibid.*: s 12.
173. Thornton, 1990: 244 *et seq.*
174. *Ibid.*: 232–3 and 242–3.

6

Defining Disability Discrimination

INTRODUCTION

In the major common law countries, the legal concept of discrimination is largely derived from the disparate treatment and adverse impact analysis of the US Supreme Court in *Griggs* v *Duke Power Co.*[1] That analysis is so well understood in the North American jurisdictions that discrimination legislation merely enacts a general prohibition on employment discrimination on account of disability, with hitherto little further explication. Burgdorf remarks that, 'On their faces, many federal civil rights statutes constitute little more than broad directives that "Thou shalt not discriminate" '.[2] Thus the (US) ADA 1990 lays down as a 'general rule' that 'No covered entity shall discriminate against a qualified individual with a disability because of the disability of such individual'.[3] The statute then continues by indicating what this anti-discrimination edict requires of employers in practice.

The British sex and race discrimination legislation, in contrast, spells out the equivalent concepts of direct and indirect discrimination. For disability rights reform, it might be thought sufficient, therefore, to take the framework of the British discrimination statutes, add the terms 'disability' and 'disabled person' where appropriate, and supply a definition of the newly protected class. Where employers discriminate because of disability by treating disabled persons less favourably than others, the existing concept of direct discrimination would be sufficient. Where disabled persons are treated less favourably than others because they cannot comply with a requirement with which a substantially higher proportion of non-disabled persons can comply, and the requirement is not justifiable in the circumstances, indirect discrimination would arise. However, disability discrimination gives rise to additional questions and reservations, so that it will be necessary to provide a more expansive definition of discrimination if disability rights are to be enacted here.

DIRECT DISABILITY DISCRIMINATION

Although the expression 'direct discrimination' is not used in the British sex and race discrimination statutes, it labels a concept that is reasonably well understood in that context.[4] Direct discrimination occurs where a person treats a member of the protected class less favourably than he or she treats or would treat someone who is not a member of the protected class and where the less favourable treatment is on the ground of class membership. The idea of direct disability discrimination has been made explicit in the Australian anti-discrimination legislation. In New South Wales, for example,

> A person discriminates against a physically handicapped person on the ground of his physical impairment if, on the ground of... his physical impairment... he treats him less favourably than in the same circumstances, or in circumstances which are not materially different, he treats or would treat a person who is not a physically handicapped person.[5]

In South Australia, direct discrimination means *unfavourable* treatment because of a person's disability.[6] In the North American jurisdictions, the prohibition of direct disability discrimination is implicit in the general interdiction against disability-related discriminatory acts. The (US) ADA 1990 defines discrimination as including:

> limiting, segregating, or classifying a job applicant or employee in a way that adversely affects the opportunities or status of such applicant or employee because of the disability of such applicant or employee.[7]

The Canadian Human Rights Act addresses both direct and indirect discriminatory practices,[8] while the Ontario legislation states that everyone 'has a right to equal treatment with respect to employment without discrimination' because of disability.[9] In the Yukon Territory, discrimination by unfavourable treatment is prohibited,[10] while in Québec, everyone has the right to 'full and equal recognition and exercise of his/her human rights and freedoms, without distinction, exclusion or preference based on disability',[11] and in Manitoba, discrimination manifested in differential treatment not based upon personal merit is unlawful.[12]

However direct disability discrimination is defined, there are a number of common problems in the interpretation of the concept. The first problem is to show that the less favourable or unfavourable or differential treatment is owing to disability. Discrimination 'because of' disability requires the making of a causal connection between the discriminatory act and the complainant's disability. So a refusal to employ a disabled person may be defensible if that person is not qualified for the position or another applicant was better placed on merit. For example, in *Garton* v *Hillcrest Hospital*,[13] a blind employee on switchboard duties had increasingly exercised supervisory duties. The employee applied to be reclassified on the basis of these duties but this was refused. Subsequently, an internal advertisement for a new post as switchboard coordinator appeared and a job specification was published. The employee ranked either equal to or ahead of the other applicant for this post in terms of job performance and seniority, but the selection panel was swayed by the other applicant's potential for advancement. It was held that the employee had been less favourably treated by reason of his blindness. The interviewing panel had assumed that he was incapable of performing a specific duty of the job, even though that duty did not appear as part of the job specification. The employer also failed to make out the defence that special equipment or assistance would be required, and could not be reasonably provided, as this had not even been considered and no aspect of the job seemed to call for such assistance.

A second problem concerns that of multiple causes. In the USA, the RA 1973 applied only to prohibit discrimination 'solely by reason of handicap'. This form of wording gives rise to problems where disability discrimination is adulterated by other causes and motives that may have played a lesser or greater role in determining the plaintiff's employment opportunities. In principle, it would seem sufficient for a cause of action that a person's disability has contributed to the detrimental employment decision being challenged and that the presence of a prohibited ground in the employer's reasoning should taint that decision with illegality. It is remarkable that the (US) ADA 1990 dispenses with the words 'solely by reason of' disability, and other jurisdictions have consciously drafted the law so as to address the issue of multiple cause discrimination. In South Australia, for example, it is sufficient that disability was one of a number of grounds for the impugned action, provided that it was 'a substantial reason for the act'.[14] In Victoria, judicial interpretation has led to the view that disability need not be the dominant reason for the discrimination.[15] The model provision is that in the Australian Commonwealth statute, providing that it is sufficient that disability is one of the reasons, whether or not dominant or substantial, for the discriminatory act.[16]

The third problem with direct disability discrimination is whether the motive or purpose or intention of the discriminator is relevant. Some acts of disability discrimination are undoubtedly unintentional, others are not motivated by prejudice, and others still may have been informed by good intentions or benign purposes. In British sex and race discrimination cases, intention, motive and purpose are not ingredients of direct discrimination.[17] Discrimination is not a fault-based concept. The only question is whether the complainant would have received the same treatment as the comparator but for his or her status (i.e. but for disability). In Canada, human rights legislation has been interpreted as extending to unintentional discrimination,[18] while the US Supreme Court interpreted section 504 of the Rehabilitation Act 1973 as not requiring proof of discriminatory intent and accepted that evidence of indirect discrimination or disparate impact would also establish prima facie discrimination.[19] In contrast, in *Department of Health* v *Arumugam*,[20] the (Vic) EOA 1984 was not interpreted as prohibiting unconsciously motivated discrimination. The reversal of this ruling has been proposed.[21]

The Victorian illustration raises the question: should this be left to judicial interpretation? In British Columbia, for example, the intention of the discriminator is explicitly an irrelevant consideration when a question of disability discrimination arises.[22] In contrast, in the Australian case of *Jamal* v *Secretary, Department of Health*,[23] there was an egregious attempt to introduce the concept of *mens rea* into disability discrimination law, so that an employer could only be 'guilty' of disability discrimination if he or she acted intentionally and was motivated by the complainant's disability. Although the final appellate court rejected the idea that the legislature had imported any notion of guilt or intention or deliberate action into the legislation, *Jamal* demonstrates that direct discrimination can be mistakenly interpreted as intentional discrimination.

A fourth problem concerns the degree and nature of less favourable treatment. Because direct discrimination calls for a comparative approach to the treatment of the complainant and a comparator, it will always be possible to find some differences in the treatment given. Clearly, trivial differences in treatment can be ignored, perhaps on the basis of *de minimis non curat lex.*[24] However, the difficulties of comparing like with like may be less easily dismissed. This is a fifth problem: the difficulty of making a comparison. Because of the legacy of segregation, a disabled complainant might find it difficult to select an 'able-bodied' comparator. In *Clinch* v *Commissioner of Police,*[25] for example, the plaintiff had lost his right eye in a childhood accident. He had applied for a position with the police force. The police force had a standing instruction requiring prospective employees to have vision in both eyes. The police force refused to employ the plaintiff, although there was a doubt about whether there had been a formal application or merely an informal inquiry. A tribunal considered that it might be necessary to show that the police had employed another person instead of the applicant to determine whether there had been discrimination in a denial of employment. No mention of a comparison with a hypothetical person was made and this is in line with general discrimination jurisprudence.[26]

The comparability requirement raises a sixth problem. Must the circumstances in which the complainant and comparator are being compared be comparable? British discrimination law requires the relevant circumstances of the two cases to be the same or not materially different,[27] and this is also expressed to be the case in Australian disability discrimination law,[28] although South Australian law was deliberately amended so as to exclude such a requirement.[29] In fact, disability will almost certainly be a material difference in every case. Disability can create differences in the way in which a disabled person can do the work in question. Many cases of disability-related employment discrimination could fall at the first hurdle, therefore, because a disabled plaintiff's disability would destroy the basis of comparison with the able-bodied comparator. Thus, it becomes imperative that disability discrimination statutes should contain a reasonable accommodation mandate, and that such reasonable accommodation should not be a materially different circumstance for the purposes of comparison with a non-disabled comparator.[30] This point is examined further in Chapter 9.

INDIRECT DISABILITY DISCRIMINATION

Like 'direct discrimination', the term 'indirect discrimination' is not used in discrimination legislation itself. Indirect or 'adverse impact' or 'effects' discrimination derives from the reasoning of the US Supreme Court in *Griggs* v *Duke Power Co.*[31] As we understand this concept in Britain, indirect discrimination occurs where the defendant applies a requirement or condition, which is applied equally to all, but with which only a considerably smaller proportion of members of the protected class, as compared to the proportion of members of other classes, can comply and their inability to comply is to their detriment. The discriminator has a defence if he or she can demonstrate that the requirement or condition is justifiable apart from its discriminatory effects.[32] The Australian discrimination statutes generally adopt this formula.[33]

The concept of adverse impact or indirect discrimination pervades North American discrimination law. The (US) ADA 1990 makes this clear in several respects. For example, the use of qualification standards, employment tests or other selection criteria that tend to screen out disabled persons is discriminatory, unless job-related and consistent with business necessity.[34] In Canada, human rights law encompasses adverse effects discrimination, either by virtue of judicial interpretation,[35] or by virtue of statutory provision. For example, in Ontario, 'constructive discrimination' (a concept broadly similar to indirect discrimination) arises where

> a requirement, qualification or factor exists that is not discrimination on a prohibited ground but that results in the exclusion, restriction or preference of a group of persons who are identified by a prohibited ground of discrimination and of whom the person is a member.[36]

Yukon Territory terms 'any conduct that results in discrimination' as 'systematic discrimination', as does Manitoba,[37] while Québec explicitly outlaws effects discrimination.[38]

The case law in the comparative jurisdictions does not reveal any particular problems in the operation of indirect discrimination in the disability context. However, the experience of the British sex and race discrimination statutes suggests that, if disability laws were to be enacted in Britain, there would be some issues that would affect the efficacy of such new provisions. First, indirect discrimination depends upon showing that some requirement or condition has been applied. Generally unfavourable circumstances will not suffice. The (US) ADA 1990 illustrates the types of discriminatory hurdles that might constitute indirect discrimination.[39] American employers may not participate in contractual or other arrangements (for example, with an employment agency, trade union, training organization or fringe benefits provider) that have the effect of subjecting disabled persons to discrimination. The use of standards, criteria or methods of administration having the effect of discrimination on the basis of disability or perpetuating the discrimination of others who are subject to common administrative control is prohibited. Furthermore, the use of qualification standards, employment tests or other selection criteria that screen out or tend to screen out disabled individuals would be caught, unless shown to be job-related and consistent with business necessity. American employers must select and administer tests concerning employment in the most effective manner to ensure that, when such tests are administered to disabled job applicants or employees with impaired sensory, manual or speaking skills, such test results accurately reflect the skills, aptitude or whatever other factors such test purports to measure, rather than reflecting the impaired sensory, manual or speaking skills of the employee or applicant, except where such skills are the factors that the test purports to measure.

A second problem concerns how flexibly the courts will be prepared to apply the concept of indirect discrimination to disabled persons. For example, the application of a requirement that employees must work full-time can be expected to have a disproportionate impact upon some disabled persons. In one sense, such persons *could* comply with this requirement, but their disability might prevent them from doing so in practice. A narrow approach to the 'ability to comply' ingredient of indirect discrimination could serve to exclude disabled persons from its protection.[40] Moreover, too narrow an approach to what constitutes a requirement or condition could result in many hurdles faced by disabled persons being discounted for the purposes of indirect discrimination. For example, many disabled job applicants will have had insufficient experience of employment because of previous discrimination. Would an employer's preference for work experience be a 'requirement' or might it be interpreted merely as a desirable factor that does not operate as an absolute bar to employment?[41]

A third issue arises in respect of the mathematics of indirect discrimination. What statistical pools of comparators must be chosen to show the disproportionate impact of a requirement or condition upon a disabled person, and what level of disproportionate impact is necessary? This has been problematic under race and sex discrimination law.[42] Although the survey evidence described in an earlier chapter goes a long way towards improving our knowledge of disabled persons and the labour market, we still possess insufficient data about local labour markets and the numbers of qualified disabled workers within them. The need to demonstrate disproportionate impact upon disabled persons will prove to be the most difficult aspect of challenging employers' requirements or conditions via indirect discrimination theory.

OTHER FORMS OF DISABILITY DISCRIMINATION

Victimization

Discrimination by way of victimization is a common feature of all forms of employment discrimination and in all jurisdictions.[43] It involves treating the complainant less favourably than another person would be treated in the same circumstances because the complainant has relied upon, or brought proceedings under, or made allegations of contraventions of, discrimination legislation against the victimizer or another person, or has given evidence or information in connection with such proceedings.[44]

Harassment

In Britain and the USA, harassment as a form of discrimination was developed out of the principles of direct and indirect discrimination, especially in the area of sexual harassment.[45] A number of disability statutes in the jurisdictions being studied expressly outlaw harassment of disabled persons,[46] but there seems no reason why harassment should not be otherwise judicially recognized. Disability harassment, with its likely emphasis upon offensive remarks and behaviour, would seem to have much in common with racial harassment, although like sexual harassment it represents a form of power abuse or bullying.

Cases of disability harassment appear only rarely in the law reports. In one such example, *Gosh* v *Domglas Inc.*,[47] an injured worker, who had been assigned to sedentary tasks after returning to work from injury, was harassed by his supervisor and a co-worker. They made jokes about his condition, mimicking and drawing attention to his resultant limp. The relevant manager knew of the harassment but failed to stop it. A complaint of disability discrimination was upheld. The supervisor was ordered to pay $3,000 general damages, the co-worker $1,500 and the manager $2,000 for the harassment claim. The employer was held jointly and severally liable and was ordered to pay $1,000 general damages. In another such case, *Boehm* v *National System of Baking Ltd*,[48] an employee with a learning disability was subjected to adverse remarks about his mental abilities by a production manager, causing the employee to leave work and not return. A complaint of constructive dismissal failed, as the employer had asked the employee to return to work and should have had an opportunity to redress the problem, but damages for harassment were awarded.

Characteristics Discrimination

Discrimination against disabled persons often takes the form of applying disability stereotypes to individuals with disabilities and judging them accordingly. This is statistical discrimination; so-called because, relying upon imperfect knowledge, the employer applies mean statistics to individual cases. In order to deal with this form of discrimination, the law must prohibit less favourable treatment that is informed by a characteristic that appertains generally to, or is generally imputed to, disabled persons. This is a feature of Australian disability discrimination law and has no counterpart in Britain.[49] So a general rule that excluded from employment a whole class of persons (such as diabetics or epileptics) because some members of that class may not be suitable would be unlawful discrimination.[50] A classic example of statistical discrimination (or discrimination by characteristics), which is often written into disability legislation, would be unfavourable actions taken by an employer against a visually impaired person on the assumption that the person has or may be accompanied by a guide dog.[51] A further illustration would be actions taken on the ground that the complainant required to use a palliative or therapeutic device or auxiliary aid, such as a wheelchair.[52] Discrimination should also be regulated if less favourable treatment of a disabled person is informed by the fact that he or she is accompanied by an interpreter, reader, assistant or carer.[53]

Discrimination by Association

Evidence submitted to the US Congressional hearings on the ADA 1990 suggested that disability-related discrimination touches the lives of those beyond the people with disabilities themselves. In one anecdotal instance, an employee was dismissed from a job that she had held for many years because her son, who had contracted AIDS, lived with her.[54] In Canada and the USA, it is common to find that discrimination against a person because of that person's actual or presumed association with a disabled individual is also unlawful.[55] The outlawing of such discrimination in Australia is less usual, although such provision is made under Commonwealth law.[56]

DISABILITY DISCRIMINATION AND EMPLOYMENT PRACTICES

Once the concepts of disability discrimination have been identified, it is necessary to prescribe the scope of prohibited discrimination. First, in what fields of human activity is the anti-discrimination principle to operate? Like the British sex and race discrimination statutes, Australian and Canadian discrimination legislation intervenes in employment, education, and the provision of goods, services, facilities and premises. The (US) ADA 1990 regulates discrimination against disabled citizens in employment, public services, transportation, commercial facilities, public accommodations (such as hotels, theatres, shops, schools etc.) and telecommunications. It builds upon the (US) RA 1973 and earlier related laws that addressed educational, architectural and health services barriers to disabled persons. Second, assuming that discrimination in the employment field is a high priority for redress, at which parties should the legislation be directed? Again, the common practice in the jurisdictions being studied is to ensure that employers, partnerships, self-employed parties, trade unions, employers' associations, employment agencies and training or qualifying bodies are within the compass of the law's reach. Third, and most pertinently for present purposes, what practices and activities in the employment field are to be regulated?

Australian legislation, like its British sex and race discrimination model, generally applies to discrimination in recruitment and selection arrangements, terms of employment offers, refusals or omissions of employment offers, employment terms and conditions (including pay), access to opportunities for promotion, transfer or training, access to other benefits, facilities or services, dismissal or other detriment.[57] In Canada, the answer to this latter question varies from province to province. In the Yukon Territory, for example, 'no person shall discriminate . . . in connection with any aspect of employment or application for employment'.[58] Alberta's law applies to refusals to employ or to continue to employ any person, and discrimination with regard to employment or any term or condition of employment.[59] In Saskatchewan, the right to engage in an occupation is protected.[60] Québec applies the non-discrimination principle to hiring, apprenticeships, probationary periods, vocational training, promotion, transfer, displacement, laying-off, suspension, dismissal and conditions of employment.[61] Manitoba protects the opportunity to participate, or to continue to participate, in an employment or occupation, its customs, practices and conditions, as well as training, advancement, promotion, seniority, remuneration or other employment compensation,[62] and any other benefit, term or condition of the employment or occupation.[63] In seeking to comply with the prohibition upon employment discrimination, Manitoban employers must take care not to penalize other employees by terminating their employment, reducing their wages or other benefits, or changing customs, practices and conditions of their employment to their detriment.[64] Some provinces even make separate provision for pay discrimination, without limiting it to gender-based pay differentials.[65]

The (US) ADA 1990 commands a general prohibition against disability discrimination with regard to job application procedures, the hiring, advancement or discharge of employees, employee compensation, job training and other terms, conditions and privileges of employment.[66] The regulations under the (US) RA 1973 and ADA 1990 further apply the non-discrimination principle to recruitment, advertising, job application procedures, hiring, upgrading, promotion, award of tenure, demotion, transfer, lay-off, termination, right of return from lay-off and rehiring.[67] Rates of pay, any other form of compensation and changes in compensation are also covered, as are fringe benefits available by virtue of employment (whether or not administered by the employer). An employer may not discriminate on the grounds of disability in respect of job assignments, job classifications, organizational structures, position descriptions, lines of progression, seniority lists, leaves of absence, sick leave or other leave. Selection and financial support for training (including apprenticeships, professional meetings, conferences and related activities) and selection for leave of absence to pursue training are also affected. Finally, the regulations encompass employer-sponsored activities (such as social or recreational programmes) and any other term, condition or privilege of employment.[68]

In providing such detail, American disability discrimination law differs from civil rights laws in general by giving specific illustrations of what amounts to such discrimination. Supporters of the ADA wished the legislation to be as specific as possible and to be not reliant upon the subsequent issuing and content of administrative regulations. The ADA simply adopted and adapted many of the provisions already tried and tested under the RA 1973 regulations. Many aspects of disability discrimination are not readily apparent and certainly benefit from being made explicit. Feldblum gives a number of practical examples, many of which are taken from the legislative history of the Act.[69] An employer would discriminate by placing disabled workers in a separate, segregated part of the workplace. Paying disabled employees less than other workers undertaking equivalent work would be unlawful. An employer who sends a disabled employee on a training course provided by a third party would be transgressing the law if the course or its location were inaccessible to a person with disabilities. The same logic would apply to the employer's selection of a hotel or conference centre for an annual retreat or convention for the workforce. In both these latter examples, the employer would be expected to make reasonable accommodation of the employee's disabilities, subject to the undue hardship defence. The employer would have to take reasonable steps to select accessible training courses or locations. Discrimination would also occur if the employer had works rules which excluded employees from bringing their own equipment or aids to work. This might screen out, for example, wheelchair users or visually impaired persons who rely upon guide dogs. A job qualification criterion that employees should have a driving licence will also tend to screen out some disabled persons and could amount to discrimination if unjustifiable.

Canadian case law illustrates how an employer's employment policies and practices might transgress the non-discrimination requirement. For example, a failure to consider reassignment of a newly disabled employee to other work may be discriminatory. In *Boucher* v *Correctional Services of Canada*,[70] discrimination was found where a prison officer with nervous depression related to job stress was dismissed owing to his inability to fulfil his duties, but where the employer failed to consider him properly for a transfer to the position of driver for which he had applied. In contrast, in *Rivard* v *Department of National Defence*,[71] a soldier who incurred a knee injury which prevented him remaining in his present position was lawfully dismissed, despite seeking reclassification as an administrative clerk, where the evidence was that the sought-after reassignment still required the physical abilities of an active service soldier. However, reassignment need only be considered if the employee has actually *applied* for a transfer. In one case,[72] discrimination was found where the employer had not made a proper attempt to assess the employee's ability to perform the functions of a job, but had dismissed on a general assumption about the effect of a disability. However, there was no discrimination by simply failing to consider a reassignment to work for which the employee was suited but for which the employee had not applied. By way of further example, the adoption of reasonable policies on alcohol-dependent employees will usually be fair, but the employer must follow that policy carefully in order to avoid discrimination. In *Niles* v *Canadian National Railway*,[73] the employee was an alcoholic who became unable to perform his work. In accordance with the employer's policy, he was suspended and informed that he would be reinstated when capable of handling his responsibilities. After an alcohol rehabilitation programme, the employee asked to return to work seven months later. The employer refused, being unconvinced that the employee was no longer alcohol-dependent. The employee's subsequent dismissal was found to be unlawful by a federal tribunal because, although the employer's alcohol policy was fair and reasonable, it had not been correctly applied in this case. On appeal, a federal appellate court said that the employer's insistence that the employee should demonstrate ability to fulfil all the requirements of the job upon return from rehabilitation was adverse effects discrimination.

PRE-EMPLOYMENT SCREENING

Pre-employment screening for disability gives rise to additional opportunities for employment discrimination. Such screening may take the form of health-related questions in employment application forms, health questionnaires administered as part of the recruitment and selection process, or medical examinations insisted upon as a precondition of employment. Medical information gleaned in these ways is often used for making adverse employment decisions against people for trivial reasons, such as allergies, colour blindness and obesity,[74] and in respect of the mildest of conditions that bear no relationship to the requirements of the job.[75] In respect of pre-employment screening, both employer and disabled person have necessary and legitimate concerns:

> The concern of people with disabilities is to get a fair chance to demonstrate their abilities for a particular job before an employer is informed about a disability that is irrelevant to a job. The concern of employers is to be allowed to assess whether an applicant or employee is qualified for, or remains qualified for a particular job.[76]

Disabled persons who reveal their disability status in response to a question on an application form or pre-employment questionnaire, and who subsequently do not receive a job offer, may never know whether they have been rejected because of their disability or because of a deficient curriculum vitae, a poor interview performance or any number of other imponderables.[77] 'Many people with disabilities are often denied jobs because their disability is identified early in the application process and that fact taints the remainder of the application process'.[78]

Uses and Misuses of Pre-employment Screening

With the advent of genetic screening techniques, the possibilities also exist for eliminating from employment consideration those whose genetic traits predict an increased risk of future disease or injury.[79] A number of genetic conditions may lead to an increased risk of disease through certain occupational exposures.[80] For example, sickle cell anaemia may lead to splenic infarctions and sudden death at high altitude, thus restricting work at altitude or where there is relatively limited oxygen. This may restrict employment involving flying, mine work or diving.[81] There is also the possibility of a biochemical reaction with the gene, thus limiting work in the chemical industry. The human leucocyte antigen (HLA) system has been linked statistically with numerous diseases and may be related to occupational exposure. Such diseases include bladder cancer, asbestosis, silicosis and pneumoconiosis. Consequently, HLA-typing has increasing importance in identifying high-risk workers. On the other hand, the importance of non-occupational environmental factors must not be under-estimated. Such factors include the increased risk of disease based on innate characteristics, such as age, race and ethnicity, sex and reproduction, and familial factors, or the increased risk based on geography or behaviour (such as diet, tobacco smoking, alcohol use, medical drugs and radiation, and general lifestyle). An individual's overall health and physical condition can contribute to the risk of occupational illness. Occupational exposure to toxins may also significantly affect sensitivity to further occupational exposures and increase risk accordingly. Hypersensitivity and chromosome aberrations are also contributors to occupational disease.

Nevertheless, Rothstein concludes that

> The conclusiveness and predictive value of current medical evidence varies widely . . . Where employers use unreliable criteria, extensive screening unfairly denies employment opportunities to entire classes of people. Even where the evidence supports a finding of increased risk, medical screening by employers threatens to create two classes of workers, one containing disease-resistant employees, the other containing potentially productive but unemployable individuals who have genetic or other subclinical anomalies. The gaps in our medical knowledge make it difficult to respond to this prospect. Our national labor policy faces two potentially inconsistent goals: making job opportunities available to those persons capable of doing the work, while preventing job-related diseases.[82]

Apologists for pre-employment health screening argue that employing disabled workers increases insurance costs, endangers safety compliance, results in higher rates of turnover, absenteeism and sick leave, and creates a greater potential for civil liability. Rothstein counters that,

> Despite their widespread use, pre-employment medical examinations can be grossly inaccurate in attempting to screen for high-risk workers. Several studies confirm that employee selection procedures that do not use pre-employment physical examinations are as accurate in identifying high risk workers.[83]

Whatever the merits of these respective arguments, where employment decisions are taken following screening for disability, applicants or employees may never know whether their disability has informed a determination of their employment opportunities.

Pre-employment health screening is apparently widespread in the USA.[84] A medical examination between the selection and placement stages of the recruitment process is frequently a condition of engagement. Rothstein notes that in the USA most employers regularly record health information about new employees through the use of pre-employment medical questionnaires (61 per cent of employees of small employers, 82 per cent of employees of medium employers and 98 per cent of employees of large employers).[85] While employment applications rarely request detailed medical information, a medical examination is frequently a condition of employment. Rothstein states that the use of medical examinations is confined to the post-selection, pre-placement stages of recruitment, ostensibly to match the employee with the most suitable job.[86] In most cases these medical examinations are not required by health and safety legislation. Although British employers do not use medical screening to the same extent,[87] Morrell found, in a survey of British employers, that just over half had specific application form questions on health, while 10 per cent had medical examinations for every recruit and a further 14 per cent for certain recruits.[88] Medical examinations seemed to be used to follow up health information revealed on application forms or for senior positions and/or positions likely to be covered by occupational health insurance.

A test of the efficacy of discrimination law is its ability to control pre-employment screening.[89] Disability discrimination law must regulate such screening in application forms, in medical questionnaires and examinations, and in interview questions and inquiries. Pre-employment screening for disability is specifically controlled in several Canadian provinces.[90] In the USA, under the Rehabilitation Act 1973, the section 504 regulations prohibited pre-employment medical examinations and inquiries designed to discover whether an applicant was a disabled person or the extent of his or her disability, except to determine ability to perform job-related functions.[91] The section 503 regulations permitted federal contractors to require selective pre-employment medical examinations, unless this had the effect of unjustifiably screening out qualified disabled applicants.[92] However, such protections were piecemeal and not universal. Tighter controls are now in place in the USA under the ADA 1990.[93] In Australia too, pre-employment screening for disability and health status is likely to transgress state and federal disability discrimination laws, unless it is demonstrated to be relevant to the work in question (for example, on safety grounds).[94]

Pre-employment Screening and the Law in Britain

In Britain, concern that employers might discriminate on the grounds of disability might lead a disabled person to conceal the fact of disability during the recruitment and selection process. Unless the employer has solicited information about health or disability status, perhaps by appropriate questions on an application form, the non-disclosure of a disability is unlikely to lead to immediate legal implications. Except when the disabled employee is registered under the 1944 Act, he or she will have little employment protection in any case during the first two years of service. If the employee deliberately has concealed disability from the employer during pre-employment screening, then this might be grounds for termination of employment once the disability becomes apparent. On general principles, the employee has obtained employment by an actionable misrepresentation. Under unfair dismissal law, the dismissal is capable of justification by reference to capability or 'some other substantial reason' and might be fair provided a reasonable procedure has been followed.[95] Otherwise, there is no redress for a disabled applicant or employee who believes that he or she has been discriminated against on the basis of health information or medical screening. Pre-employment screening controls in Britain, therefore, would need to be written upon a *tabula rasa*. Sex and race discrimination law does not provide an appropriate paradigm. Accordingly the experience of the US regulation of disability screening and medical examinations would need to be prayed in aid.

Pre-employment Screening and the Law in the United States

The US experience suggests a number of points for consideration. First, the use of medical examinations as a means of screening out disabled persons from employment would need to be regulated.[96] Such curbs should apply to all applicants and employees, regardless of disability. Employers would be prohibited from conducting a medical examination of any employment applicant, except for the single purpose of ascertaining ability to perform functions which are job-related.

Second, once an offer of employment has been made, a medical examination could be required before the new recruit commences employment duties. In that case, the employer could make the employment offer conditional upon the results of the medical examination.[97] There is nothing in the American provisions that requires employers to show that the examination or inquiries are related to essential job functions.[98] However, if a job offer is withdrawn following such an examination, the employer will need to demonstrate that the examination results are not based upon exclusionary criteria which screen out or tend to screen out disabled applicants or, if so, that they are job-related and consistent with business necessity and no reasonable accommodation could be made.[99] Rothstein suggests that to make out business necessity, the employer will have to show: that the examination, test or procedure is job-related; that it has high predictive value and is the best that is feasible to use; that it indicates that there is a strong likelihood of the applicant developing a serious injury or illness in the near future and that this likelihood is a significant variation from the general employee population; that the discriminatory decision was based on an individualized determination of fitness; and that no reasonable accommodation will permit the individual to perform the necessary job functions.[100]

Third, safeguards would have to be built into the use of post-selection, pre-placement medical examinations, which should only be permitted if all successful applicants are subjected to such a medical examination. Taken literally, this could require employers to administer the same medical examination to all new recruits regardless of whether they were manual, white collar or managerial employees. However, the legislative history of the ADA 1990 makes it plain that the same medical examination need only be required of all new recruits in a particular job category.[101] Moreover, there would be nothing to prevent an employer from requiring disabled applicants to submit to a more extensive medical examination than others.

Fourth, once in employment, employees would not be required to undergo a medical examination at the behest of the employer, except to ascertain an employee's continuing ability to perform job-related functions.[102] Under the American statute, medical examinations and inquiries during employment are permissible provided that they are both 'job-related and consistent with business necessity'. This phrase was designed to ensure that the standard required under the ADA 1990 matched the jurisprudence of section 504 of the Rehabilitation Act 1973 and not that of the disparate impact standard under Title VII after the Supreme Court decision in *Wards Cove Packing Co.* v *Atonio.*[103] As a result, the burden of proof is on the employer to show that any medical examinations or inquiries of employees measure actual ability to perform the essential functions of the job, with reasonable accommodation if necessary.[104] If an employee's actual performance in employment indicates that he or she is no longer qualified or able to do the job, with reasonable accommodation, he or she may be dismissed without any suggestion of unlawful discrimination. The ADA allows employers to make periodic medical examination and inquiry to establish the employee's ability to work, provided the twin tests of job-relatedness and business necessity are satisfied.[105] It is irrelevant that the employer does not intend to penalize the employee. The employee is entitled not to have a disability identified, with the consequent risk of stigma, unless it interferes with the ability to do the job. Where an examination or inquiry is validly undertaken, it may be required of a specific individual, and there is no need to show that such examinations or inquiries are required across the workforce (in contrast with pre-employment testing and questions).

Fifth, *voluntary* medical examinations may be conducted (and *voluntary* medical histories compiled) as part of an occupational health programme.[106] Feldblum records that it was never intended to prohibit voluntary medical examinations, so this provision was inserted to meet the concerns of businesses and for the avoidance of doubt.[107] However, it follows from general principles that occupational health schemes must be open to all employees without distinction based upon disability or health status.

Sixth, where medical examinations and inquiries are acceptable under the legislation – whether during recruitment and selection or in employment – safeguards are built in to ensure the confidentiality and proper use of the medical information which has been solicited. Any information obtained from a lawful medical examination regarding the medical condition and history of a disabled person should be collected and maintained on separate forms and in separate medical files. Such information should be treated as a confidential medical record and in accordance with the anti-discrimination principle.[108] Thus, the results of a medical examination cannot be used to withdraw an employment offer, unless the examination demonstrates that the applicant is not qualified to do the work. However, the employer may inform supervisors and managers of any necessary restrictions on the work or duties of a disabled person and of any necessary accommodations. Furthermore, when appropriate, the employer may inform first aid and safety personnel where an employee's disability might require emergency treatment or necessitate the taking of special precautions.

Seventh, subjecting applicants or employees to a medical examination is not the only means that employers have used to screen out disabled employees. Application forms and pre-employment questionnaires frequently solicit the medical history of applicants and may be used to reach employment decisions which disadvantage persons with disabilities.[109] Such inquiries also occur face-to-face during the course of an interview or selection procedure. Employers should be prohibited from making inquiries of any applicants or employees as to whether they are persons with a disability. Similarly, employers may not inquire as to the nature or severity of a disability. In both cases, however, such inquiries may be made for the sole purpose of ascertaining an applicant's ability to perform job-related functions.[110] For example, an individual with one arm, who applies for a position as a parcel deliverer, might be asked how he or she would lift parcels from the delivery vehicle and carry them to the point of delivery, with or without accommodation. Clearly, an employer cannot disguise a question in the following terms: 'Do you have any disabilities which would prevent you performing the following job-related functions?'[111]

Eighth, these controls could create difficulties for 'equal opportunity' employers monitoring the profile of job applicants and the composition of the workforce. Such questions are permitted by the section 504 regulations if they are designed to promote remedial action to remedy past discrimination, or voluntary action to overcome conditions which have limited participation by disabled persons, or affirmative action pursuant to section 503.[112] The ADA omits any reference to voluntary questions about disability. This omission has been explained as the consequence of the dynamics of the legislative process and, in particular, by congressional concern to write a law and not a regulation.[113] The EEOC felt unable to contradict the statutory language, so that the drafting of the ADA regulations does not allow for the gathering of voluntarily supplied information about job applicants' disabilities, except for employers covered by section 503.[114] Feldblum opines that this lacuna is not necessarily to be regretted.[115] She argues that employers who wish to promote remedial or affirmative action for disabled individuals would do better to use outreach techniques to identify and encourage disabled applicants to apply for jobs. For example, contact might be made with rehabilitation agencies, independent living centres or local disability organizations. Furthermore, many disabled persons are better assisted towards equal employment opportunity by the general prohibition on pre-employment questionnaires, inquiries or examinations which identify all and any past or present medical conditions. However, in the present writer's view, if disability discrimination is to be addressed in the future by equal opportunity laws that require policy-making, targets and goals, positive action and monitoring techniques, then some compromise between the right of the individual to privacy of status and the need of the employer to collect statistics will need to be forged.

From the above analysis, it can be seen that the North American legislation imposes a two-step framework on the use of medical examinations and inquiries by, first, restricting their use at the stage of application and recruitment while, second, allowing employers more freedom once a job offer has been made. Feldblum states that this allows disabled persons to isolate what influence, if any, their disability had upon the employment process, but enables employers to test whether a particular disabled individual could meet the ability-to-work standard.[116] Feldblum observes that the

> restriction on the use of medical examination and inquiry results, together with potential liability for unwarranted disclosure of medical information, may convince many employers not to require broad-range medical examination and inquiries.[117]

Employers might see the sense of tailoring medical examinations to obtain only such information as has job-related relevance and to reduce the amount of confidential information in employers' possession that might lead to an inadvertent breach of privacy. On the other hand, employers might still prefer to have as full a medical profile of their employees as possible in order to assist in any potential personal injury or occupational compensation claim in the future.

CONCLUSION

Any thoughts that existing British discrimination laws could be amended simply to include disability as a prohibited ground are ill-conceived. The nature of disability-informed discrimination is such that the legislation will have to be expansive as to the definition and descriptions of possible unlawful actions or consequences. In particular, special attention must be given to the issue of discrimination by association or on the basis of characteristics and to regulation of pre-employment screening. The US, Canadian and Australian models all provide raw materials that could be combined to produce a definition of discrimination fit for its purpose in the context of a law designed to protect the employment rights of disabled persons. However, the problem of defining disability discrimination is perhaps less challenging than the problem of identifying who is a member of the newly protected class. This issue is considered in the following chapter.

NOTES

1. (1971) 401 US 424.
2. Burgdorf, 1991: 413.
3. 42 USC s 12112(a).
4. Sex Discrimination Act (SDA) 1975 s 1(1)(a); Race Relations Act (RRA) 1976 s 1(1)(a).
5. (NSW) ADA 1977 s 49A(1)(a). See also: (Vic) EOA 1984 s 17(1); (WA) EOA 1984 s 66A(1); (Cth) DDA 1992 s 5(1).
6. (SA) EOA 1984 s 66(a).
7. 42 USC s 12112(b)(1).
8. (Can) HRA s 7.
9. (Ont) HRC s 5(1).
10. (YT) HRA s 6.
11. (Québ) CHR&F s 10.
12. (Man) HRC s 9.
13. (1984) AILR para. 240 (SA HPDT): a complaint under s 49(5) (SA) HPEOA 1981.
14. (SA) EOA 1984 s 6(2).
15. *Campbell* v *FH Productions* (1984) AILR para. 178 (Vic EOB); but see Law Reform Commission of Victoria, 1989, 1990a, b.
16. (Cth) DDA 1992 s 10.
17. See, for example: *Equal Opportunities Commission* v *Birmingham City Council* [1989] 1 All ER 796 (HL); *James* v *Eastleigh Borough Council* [1990] ICR 554 (HL).
18. *Bhinder* v *Canadian National Railway Co.* (1985) 23 DLR (4th) 481 (Can SC).
19. *Alexander* v *Choate* (1985) 469 US 287. Under Title VII, a complainant of disparate treatment is required to show that the employer had an unlawful motive or intended to discriminate: *Furnco Construction Co.* v *Waters* (1978) 438 US 567 and *Texas Community Affairs* v *Burdine* (1981) 450 US 248. Unintentional discrimination will be caught, if at all, by

disparate impact theory: *Griggs* v *Duke Power Co.* (1971) 401 US 424. However, it is doubted whether the US Supreme Court is making a distinction other than requiring a disparate treatment complainant to show that his or her race or sex (or disability) was causally connected to the complained of action or omission. In other words, there is a similar 'but for' test of direct discrimination.

20. [1988] VR 319.

21. Law Reform Commission of Victoria, 1989, 1990a, b. The Commission recommends that motive should be expressly irrelevant, but that unconscious discrimination should not be included.

22. (BC) HRA s 13(1.1). See also: (Man) HRC s 9(3).

23. (1986) EOC 92-162 (NSW EOT); (1986) EOC 92-183 (NSW SC); (1988) 14 NSWLR 252 (NSW CA).

24. See the British sex discrimination cases of *Automotive Products Ltd* v *Peake* [1977] ICR 968 (CA) and *Jeremiah* v *Ministry of Defence* [1980] ICR 13 (CA).

25. (1988) AILR para. 169 (NSW EOT).

26. The problem of the hypothetical comparator has also featured in British equal pay law: *Meeks* v *National Union of Agricultural and Allied Workers* [1976] ICR 785 (CA); *McCarthys Ltd* v *Smith* [1979] ICR 785 (CA), [1980] ICR 672 (ECJ and CA).

27. SDA 1975 s 5(3); RRA 1976 s 3(4).

28. (NSW) ADA 1977 s 49A(1); (Vic) EOA 1984 s 17(2); (WA) EOA 1984 s 66A; (Cth) DDA 1992 s 5(1).

29. (SA) EOA 1984 s 66.

30. See to this effect, for example: (WA) EOA 1984 s 66A(2). In *Jamal* v *Secretary, Department of Health* (1988) 14 NSWLR 252 (NSW CA) the same result was eventually achieved via judicial interpretation of the provisions of the (NSW) ADA 1977.

31. (1971) 401 US 424.

32. SDA 1975 s 1(1)(b); RRA 1976 s 1(1)(b).

33. (NSW) ADA 1977 s 49A(3); (SA) EOA 1984 s 66(b); (Vic) EOA 1984 s 17(5); (WA) EOA 1984 s 66A(3); (Cth) DDA 1992 s 6.

34. 42 USC s 12112(b)(6).

35. *O'Malley* v *Simpson-Sears Ltd* [1985] 2 SCR 536 (Can SC); *Bhinder* v *Canadian National Railway Co.* (1985) 23 DLR (4th) 481 (Can SC) interpreting the (Can) HRA. See: McKenna, 1992.

36. (Ont) HRC s 11(1).

37. (YT) HRA s 11; (Man) HRC s 9(3).

38. (Québ) CHR&F s 10.

39. 42 USC s 12112(b).

40. See, for example, the narrow approach taken in the British sex discrimination case of *Turner* v *Labour Party* [1987] IRLR 101 (CA).

41. As was the case in the race discrimination case of *Perera* v *Civil Service Commission* [1983] ICR 428 (CA).

42. See, for example: *Jones* v *University of Manchester* [1993] ICR 474 (CA)

43. See, for example: (Can) HRA s 59; (PEI) HRA s 15. Under Australian Commonwealth disability law it is a criminal offence to victimize an individual who exercises his or her rights under the legislation. The offence is punishable by imprisonment of up to six months: (Cth) DDA 1992 s 42.

44. SDA 1975 s 4; RRA 1976 s 2. Victimization also includes circumstances where the victimizer has acted because he or she knows or suspects that the victimized party has done or intends to do any of the protected acts.

45. *Porcelli* v *Strathclyde Regional Council* [1986] ICR 564 (Court of Session); *De Souza* v *Automobile Association* [1986] ICR 514 (CA).

46. See, for example: (Can) HRA s 12; (Man) HRC s 19; (Ont) HRC s 5(2); (Québ) CHR&F s 10.1; (YT) HRA s 13; (Cth) DDA 1992 ss 35 and 36. Disability harassment is expressly dealt with under the (US) ADA 1990: 42 USC s 12203(b).

47. (1992) 92 CLLC para. 17,039 (Ont HRC).

48. (1987) 87 CLLC para. 17,013 (Ont HRC).

49. (NSW) ADA 1977 s 49A(1)(b) and (c); (SA) EOA 1984 s 66(c); (Vic) EOA 1984 s

17(4); (WA) EOA 1984 s 66A(1)(b) and (c). See also the similar provision under at least one Canadian provincial statute: (Man) HRC s 9(1)(b).

50. See, for example: *Cooper* v *Ford Motor Co of Australia Ltd* (1987) AILR para. 284 (Vic EOB).

51. (NSW) ADA 1977 s 49A(2); (SA) EOA 1984 s 66(e); (WA) EOA 1984 s 66A(4). The same logic should apply to hearing dogs or other animals trained to assist the disabled person: (Cth) DDA 1992 s 9(1). It is common to provide that the inclusion of this form of discrimination does not affect a disabled person's liability, if any, for injury, loss or damage caused by a guide dog.

52. (WA) EOA 1984 s 66A(1)(d); (Cth) DDA 1992 s 7. Discrimination based upon the use of palliative devices is also unlawful under some Canadian provincial statutes: (Québ) CHR&F s 10.

53. (Cth) DDA 1992 s 8.

54. US Senate, 1989: 8; US House of Representatives, 1990a: 30; Burgdorf, 1991: 419.

55. (Man) HRC s 9(1)(a) and (d); (NS) HRA s 5(1); (Ont) HRC s 12; (PEI) HRA ss 1(1)(d) and 13; (YT) HRA s 6.

56. (Cth) DDA 1992 s 15(1) and (2). It might be possible to argue that the concept of discrimination by association is implicit in discrimination statutes. In Britain, for example, direct discrimination on racial grounds has been held to cover discrimination on the basis of another party's race: *Zarczynska* v *Levy* [1979] ICR 184 (where the EAT found in favour of a white employee dismissed for refusing to obey an employer's order to discriminate against black persons). See also: *Showboat Entertainment Centre Ltd* v *Owens* [1984] ICR 65 (EAT).

57. See: SDA 1975 s 6 and RRA 1976 s 4. See further: (NSW) ADA 1944 s 49B; (SA) EOA 1984 s 67; (Vic) EOA 1984 s 21; (WA) EOA 1984 s 66B; (Cth) DDA 1992 s 15.

58. (YT) HRA s 8(b). This also applies 'in connection with any aspect of membership in or representation by any trade union, trade association, occupational association, or professional association': s 8(c).

59. (Alb) IRPA s 7(1). See to like effect: (BC) HRA s 8(1); (NB) HRA s 3(1); (New) HRC s 9(1); (NWT) FPA s 3(1); (PEI) HRA s 6(1).

60. (Sask) HRC s 9. This is then amplified in the usual terms: (Sask) HRC s 16(1).

61. (Québ) CHR&F s 16. Furthermore, employees have a general right to fair and reasonable conditions of employment which have a proper regard for health, safety and physical well-being: (Québ) CHR&F s 46.

62. Including salary, commissions, vacation pay, termination wages, bonuses, reasonable value for board, rent, housing and lodging, payments in kind, and employer contributions to pension funds or plans, long-term disability plans and health insurance plans.

63. (Man) HRC s 14(1) and (2).

64. *Ibid.*: s 14(12). The implication is that the Code requires a levelling up of employment standards and conditions rather than a levelling down.

65. See for example: (PEI) HRA s 7; (Québ) CHR&F s 19; (YT) HRA s 14.

66. 42 USC s 12112(a).

67. 28 CFR s 41.52(c); 29 CFR s 1630.4; 45 CFR s 84.11(b).

68. *Ibid.*

69. Feldblum, 1991c: 90–2.

70. (1988) 9 CHRR D/4910, (1988) 88 CLLC para. 17,000 (Can) HRT.

71. (1990) 90 CLLC para. 17,018 (Can) HRT.

72. *Villeneuve* v *Bell Canada* (1985) 85 CLLC para. 17,016, (1986) 86 CLLC para. 17,016 (Can) HRT; affirmed (1987) 9 CHRR D/5093 (Can FCA).

73. (1991) 91 CLLC para. 17,018 (Can) HRT; (1992) 92 CLLC para. 17,031 (FCA).

74. Rothstein, 1983: 1422. See also: Craft *et al.*, 1980; Hadler, 1986.

75. For example, lower back weaknesses: Rockey *et al.*, 1979. See also: Stickler and Sebok, 1992.

76. Feldblum, 1991c: 97.

77. Feldblum, 1991a: 531.

78. US Senate, 1989: 39; US House of Representatives, 1990a: 72. Cited in Feldblum, 1991a: 533.

79. Canter, 1984; Gostin, 1991; Rothstein, 1992a, b; Wilkie, 1993.

80. Rothstein, 1983; Canter, 1984.

81. Rothstein (1983: 1444) records that New Jersey law specifically prohibits employment discrimination based on an individual's 'atypical hereditary cellular or blood trait' (thus covering sickle cell and cystic fibrosis): NJ Stat Ann s 10:5-5(y). Sickle cell trait is also protected under Florida, Louisiana and North Carolina law: Fla Stat Ann s 448.075; La Rev Stat Ann ss 23:1001:1004; NC Gen Stat s 95-28.1.

82. *Ibid.*: 1381–2.

83. *Ibid.*: 1417.

84. Rothstein, 1983, 1987.

85. Rothstein, 1983: 1411.

86. *Ibid.*: 1412.

87. Labour Research Department, 1989, 1990.

88. Morrell, 1990: 8.

89. Britton, 1987.

90. (Alb) IRPA s 8(1); (Man) HRC ss 14(3) and (4) and 18; (NB) HRA s 3(4); (NS) HRA s 8(2) and (3); (Ont) HRC s 23(2) and (3); (PEI) HRA s 6(3); (Québ) CHR&F s 18.1; (Sask) HRC s 19.

91. 28 CFR s 41.55 and 28 CFR s 42.513. See also: 29 CFR s 32.15 and 45 CFR s 84.14. The regulations were held to be violated, for example, where an employer asked an applicant whether he had ever experienced a nervous breakdown: *Doe* v *Syracuse School District* (1981) 508 FSupp 333 (ND NY).

92. 41 CFR s 60-741.6. By connecting job-relatedness to business necessity, s 503 required medical examinations and screening procedures to have a scientifically valid basis and a high predictive value, and to be the most accurate and least onerous alternative.

93. 42 USC s 12112(d). See: Feldblum, 1991a; Rothstein, 1992a; Maselek, 1992. It is reported that two US states (Wisconsin and Iowa) have already moved to control genetic testing in the workplace as a condition of employment. See *HR Focus* (September 1992) at 9 and *Personnel Journal* (September 1992) at 118.

94. Johnstone (1988: 115) cites evidence that suggests that nearly four-fifths of Australian employers in manufacturing use pre-employment health assessments. His analysis points to tensions and contradictions between the contract of employment, health and safety law and equal opportunities legislation in the context of screening for disability. He argues for the legal regulation of health screening so as to permit its proper use while safeguarding individual rights.

95. *O'Brien* v *Prudential Assurance Co Ltd* [1979] IRLR 140 (EAT); *Walton* v *TAC Construction Materials Ltd* [1981] IRLR 357 (EAT).

96. 42 USC s 12112(c)(1) includes medical examinations and inquiries within the prohibition on disability discrimination. See also: 29 CFR ss 1630.13-14.

97. 42 USC s 12112(c)(3); 29 CFR s 1630.15(f).

98. 29 CFR s 1630.14(b). The business community objected to blanket controls on the administration of medical testing (as opposed to the limitations placed upon the use of examination results) and to the need to job-validate every medical examination: Feldblum, 1991a: 536. As a result, the legislative compromise in 42 USC s 12112(c)(2) and (3) was reached. As a result, employers are allowed in theory (although probably unwilling to do so in practice) 'to identify *all disabilities* of applicants, after conditional job offers had been made, including those disabilities carrying social stigma': Feldblum, 1991a: 539–40 (emphasis added).

99. Shaller and Rosen, 1991: 422.

100. Rothstein, 1983: 1445.

101. This is also apparent from the EEOC regulations: 29 CFR s 1630.14.

102. 42 USC s 12112(c)(4)(A). This allows employers to make fitness-for-duty decisions under federal, state or local laws: 29 CFR s 1630.14(c) and Appendix. Under s 504, there were no apparent restrictions placed upon medical examinations of disabled employees once in employment. In *Leckelt* v *Board of Commissioners of Hospital District No. 1* (1989) 714 FSupp 1377 (ED La), *affirmed* (1990) 909 F2d 820 (5th Cir), the court thought that the medical examination provisions might only protect disabled *applicants* from *pre-employment* invasions of privacy and might not extend to *employees*.

103. (1989) 490 US 642. See Mayerson, 1991b: 511–12 and Feldblum, 1991a: 546–7 for a fascinating account of the legislative negotiations and subsequent compromise represented by this phrase. The *Wards Cove* burden of proof upon the plaintiff in disparate impact cases has been modified, in any case, by s 105 of the Civil Rights Act 1991. Once it is shown that a practice has an indirectly discriminatory effect upon a protected class, the burden shifts to the employer to prove job-relatedness and consistency with business necessity: 42 USC s 2000e-2 as amended.

104. This gloss is derived from the legislative history of the provision. See: 29 CFR ss 1630.10(a) and 1630.13(b).

105. This is explained by interpretative guidance in the EEOC regulations expanding upon 29 CFR s 1630.13: 'The purpose of this provision is to prevent the administration to employees of medical tests or inquiries that do not serve a legitimate business purpose. For example, if an employee suddenly starts to use increased amounts of sick leave or starts to appear sickly, an employer could not require that employee to be tested for AIDS, HIV infection, or cancer unless the employer can demonstrate that such testing is job-related and consistent with business necessity.'

106. 42 USC s 12112(c)(4)(B).

107. Feldblum, 1991a: 540.

108. 42 USC s 12112(c)(3). See also: 29 CFR ss 1630.14(b) and 1630.15(f). These provisions are applied also to acceptable examinations and inquiries during employment: 42 USC s 12112(c)(4)(C).

109. This is a more common practice in Britain than in the USA.

110. 42 USC s 12112(c)(2); 29 CFR s 1630.14(a).

111. See Feldblum, 1991a: 537.

112. 45 CFR s 84.14(b).

113. Feldblum, 1991a: 543.

114. Interpretive guidance to 29 CFR ss 1630.1(b), 1630.1(c) and 1630.14(a).

115. Feldblum, 1991a: 545.

116. *Ibid.*: 533.

117. *Ibid.*: 538. Creasman and Butler (1991: 54) predict that restrictions on pre-employment screening will force employers to rethink their approach to screening or interviewing candidates and that this will increase the costs associated with the recruitment process.

7

Identifying the Protected Class

INTRODUCTION

With few exceptions, the identification of the protected class for the purposes of sex and race discrimination law has not been generally problematic. It is not possible to be as sanguine about disability discrimination legislation.[1] The definition of 'disability' must be both inclusive and exclusive: embracing individuals outside the limited popular perception of disability, yet excepting idiosyncrasies, human traits and transient illness. A distinction must be drawn between chronic or handicapping conditions and temporary or minor maladies. The boundaries between disabilities and handicaps which are the respective products of medical condition, social or environmental construction and educational disadvantage must be carefully drawn. If it were otherwise, disability discrimination law would be easily subverted, and diverted to provide a cause of action for any aggrieved or disadvantaged worker. The law would be brought into contempt and its objectives of promoting equal employment opportunities for disabled persons would be easily undermined. It is, however, easier to state the problem than to provide a solution.

LEGAL DEFINITIONS OF DISABILITY

As used in this study, disability denotes a physical or mental condition substantially modifying daily life functions without destroying the ability to work.[2] However, more legally familiar definitions of disability might be gleaned from social welfare or social security law. For the purposes of qualifying for the receipt of social welfare services, for example, a disabled person is someone who is blind, deaf or dumb, or who suffers from a mental disorder, or who is substantially handicapped by illness, injury or congenital deformity or other prescribed disability.[3] In social security law, disablement benefit has been payable to an employed earner who suffers, as a result of an accident, from a loss of physical or mental faculty, provided the disability is assessed at not less than 14 per cent.[4] The disabilities to be taken into account are all disabilities incurred (as a result of the relevant loss of faculty) and that present a disadvantage or handicap to which the claimant may be expected to be subject in comparison with a person of the same age and sex whose physical and mental condition is normal. The claimant's particular circumstances would be disregarded in making this assessment, and loss of earning power or incurring of additional expenses would not be relevant.

These definitions would not be appropriate in the context of disability discrimination laws. In the enquiry which preceded the enactment of the DP(E)A 1944, the Tomlinson Committee defined disability by reference to the handicap it created in obtaining suitable employment.[5] That definition covered disablements of all kinds and from all causes, excluding those of a minor or temporary character. A distinction between handicaps produced by disability and those resulting from other disadvantages was drawn. The definition was subjective, rather than dependent upon objective medical criteria, but recognized that disability is a changing social construct resulting from the interaction of person and environment. Accordingly, for the purposes of the 1944 Act, a disabled person is defined as

> a person who, on account of injury, disease, or congenital deformity, is substantially handicapped in obtaining or keeping employment, or in undertaking work on his own account, of a kind which apart from that injury, disease or deformity would be suited to his age, experience and qualifications.[6]

The status of a registered disabled person is the basis for certain, although not all, disabled employment rights in Britain.[7]

Although the definition of disability under the 1944 Act could be adopted and adapted for the purposes of disability discrimination law, the substance and framework of the definition is flawed and tainted. First, the definition is employment-specific, whereas discrimination law may need to address discrimination against disabled persons in a number of social fields. Second, the association of the definition with the process of registration is unfortunate. It is believed that the register 'encourages the view that disabled people are a separate and stereotyped category of human being rather than individuals with diverse and changing needs'.[8] Registration can stigmatize and highlight disabilities rather than abilities, while producing a risk of permanent categorization as disabled. While the individual should bear the burden of proving membership of a protected class, disabled persons ought not to be asked to register their status in order to enjoy basic human rights. If disability discrimination law is to be introduced in Britain, a legal redefinition of disability must precede the enfranchisement of disabled workers.[9]

Comparative Perspective

In the USA, disabled persons constitute a broadly defined protected class. In Canadian and Australian legislation the definition of disability is sufficiently precise to exclude negative judicial interpretation, but flexible enough to recognize disability as a product of self-definition and social construction. These comparative perspectives point a way forward. So, for example, under US law, 'disability' is defined as an actual or recorded or perceived physical or mental impairment that substantially limits one or more of an individual's major life activities.[10] The test is a two-stage one: (a) does the plaintiff have a recognized impairment and (b) if so, does it represent a substantial limitation upon major life activities? In contrast, the Canadian definitions of disability tend to involve a one-stage test that focuses upon the nature or cause of impairment, and illustrates the types of disability intended to be covered.[11] Australian law comports much more closely with the one-stage test approach of the Canadian jurisdictions, although New South Wales departs from this pattern and employs a two-stage test similar to the US model.[12]

In Britain, recent attempts to introduce disability discrimination legislation have been patently influenced by the (US) RA 1973 and ADA 1990. In the view of the present writer, although the two-stage approach of the US model may be implicit in the Canadian and Australian statutes, the two-stage test needs to be made explicit in any British law reform. To do so will ensure that disability discrimination law can operate with a judicious mixture of flexibility and predictability, while balancing the legitimate rights, expectations and interests of disabled persons and employers. Accordingly, the two-stage approach will be adopted for the present analysis.

WHO IS A DISABLED PERSON?

Present or Actual Disability

In the USA, the anti-discrimination provisions of the RA 1973 and the ADA 1990 address the employment rights of individuals with 'handicaps' or a 'disability'.[13] This means that the protected class embraces any person who has a physical or mental 'impairment'.[14] A physical impairment is defined as

> any physiological disorder or condition, cosmetic disfigurement, or anatomical loss affecting one or more of the following body systems: neurological; musculoskeletal; special sense organs; *respiratory, including speech organs*; cardiovascular; reproductive, digestive; genitourinary, hemic and lymphatic; skin; and endocrine,[15]

while a mental impairment constitutes

> any mental or psychological disorder, such as mental retardation, organic brain syndrome, emotional or mental illness, and specific learning disabilities . . .[16]

although there are slight differences between the different regulatory definitions.

Canadian federal human rights law addresses the rights of persons with a 'disability', but without amplification of the meaning of disability.[17] Provincial human rights laws variously protect persons with a 'disability' or a 'handicap'. All provincial jurisdictions now address the question of discrimination against persons with physical or mental disabilities. Four provinces fail to define what is meant by disability or handicap, but Alberta defines 'physical disability' as

> any degree of physical disability, infirmity, malformation or disfigurement that is caused by bodily injury, birth defect

> or illness and, without limiting the generality of the foregoing, includes epilepsy, paralysis, amputation, lack of physical co-ordination, blindness or visual impediment, deafness or hearing impediment, muteness or speech impediment, and physical reliance on a guide dog, wheelchair or other remedial appliance or device.[18]

Most other jurisdictions follow that model, except perhaps with the inclusion of illustrative disabilities. Nova Scotia's definition includes a 'loss or abnormality of psychological, physiological or anatomical structure or function' and any 'restriction or lack of ability to perform an activity',[19] while in Ontario 'an injury or disability for which benefits were claimed or received under the Workers' Compensation Act' is deemed a disability.[20] The term 'mental disability' is typically defined as:

> (a) any condition of mental retardation or impairment, (b) any learning disability, or dysfunction in one or more of the mental processes involved in the comprehension or use of symbols or spoken language, or (c) any mental disorder.[21]

Alberta expands upon the concept of 'mental disorder',[22] while in Yukon Territory a 'mental disability' includes any mental or psychological disorders such as mental retardation, organic brain syndrome, emotional or mental illness or learning disability.[23]

In Australia, discrimination is prohibited on the ground of 'impairment' or against a 'handicapped person'.[24] Victoria outlaws discrimination on the ground of 'status', but defines status as including 'impairment'.[25] The more recent Commonwealth legislation deals with 'disability' discrimination. Building upon the South Australian and Victorian definitions,[26] it contains the most extensive definition of 'disability' in relation to a person:

> (a) total or partial loss of the person's bodily or mental functions; or (b) total or partial loss of a part of the body; or (c) the presence in the body of organisms causing disease or illness; or (d) the presence in the body of organisms capable of causing disease or illness; or (e) the malfunction, malformation or disfigurement of a part of the person's body; or (f) a disorder or malfunction that results in the person learning differently from a person without the disorder or malfunction; or (g) a disorder, illness or disease that affects a person's

> thought processes, perception of reality, emotions or judgment or that results in disturbed behaviour.[27]

In New South Wales, a 'physical impairment' means

> any defect or disturbance in the normal structure and functioning of the person's body whether arising from a condition subsisting at birth or from illness or injury,

and an intellectual impairment is

> any defect or disturbance in the normal structure and functioning of the person's brain, whether arising from a condition subsisting at birth or from illness or injury.[28]

The Western Australian definitions are derived from this root.[29]

Four things are immediately noticeable about these various and diverse definitions. First, they are extremely incestuous and interbred, growing as they have out of the original 1973 definitions of the American legislation. The result is that it is possible to trace the genesis and subsequent evolution of each definition, and to see the influences which have produced slightly differentiated definitions at different stages in the development of disability discrimination theory. Second, the definitions are very much rooted in the medical model of disability and pay their respects to the World Health Organization's classification of impairment, disability and handicap, although many of the jurisdictions being compared do admit a social construction of disability. Third, in the twenty years of disability discrimination law, with few exceptions, there has been an increasing preference for the terminology of 'disability' or 'impairment', rather than the pejorative 'handicap'. The one remarkable exception, which appears in a number of instances, is the use of the term 'mental retardation' in the definition of mental disability. This is a term regarded as outdated by British disability rights activists. These differences reflect the growing awareness of the negative power of labels and the predilection of disabled persons for descriptive language which focuses upon the individual rather than the disability. In legal terms, however, the choice of nomenclature is not significant and these terms are interchangeable without affecting their legal import. Finally, and not surprisingly, the most sophisticated or extensive definitions are those to be found in the most recent examples of reformist laws: the (US) ADA 1990 and the Australian (Cth) DDA 1992.

Record of Disability

The protected class must admit to its membership those who are not presently disabled, but who have a previous history of disability (for example, a cancer rehabilitee or someone with a history of heart disease, depression or mental illness),[30] or who have been misclassified as disabled (for example, misclassification as learning disabled).[31] US legislation extends to individuals with a record of impairment or disability.[32] A person who has a record of impairment is someone who 'has a history of, or has been misclassified as having, a mental or physical impairment that substantially limits one or more major life activities'.[33] In Canada, the laws of Prince Edward Island and Ontario protect a person from discrimination based on a previous disability.[34] In Australia, provision in Western Australia includes past impairments,[35] while Australian Commonwealth legislation incorporates past and present disabilities and, somewhat unusually, a disability which may exist in the future.[36]

Perceived Disability

Many disability rights advocates argue that a definition of disability which focuses upon functional limitations produced by impairment does not go far enough. The argument is that many disabled persons do not consider themselves to be limited in life activities, yet are 'disabled' by the reaction of others. The rights of all persons with impairments should be protected, including those who are wrongly perceived as being disabled (for example, someone who has a cosmetic disfigurement, such as a facial birthmark). The law must also be broad enough to cover situations where employment decisions are made based upon the misconceptions of co-workers.[37] Illustratively, the dismissal of an HIV-infected employee (or one erroneously assumed to be HIV-infected), because co-workers feared transmission of the virus, should be remediable. The employee should not need to show that the perception is incorrect or that he or she is not actually disabled at all. It is the employer's perception which matters, not the employee's actual medical status.

The (US) RA 1973 and ADA 1990 formulae of 'regarded as disabled' would seem to go a long way towards meeting these arguments.[38] The legislation seeks to protect individuals who are regarded as having an impairment or disability.[39] A person regarded as having an impairment is one who:

> (A) has a physical or mental impairment that does not substantially limit major life activities but that is treated . . . as constituting such a limitation; (B) has a physical or mental impairment that substantially limits major life activities only as the result of the attitudes of others toward such impairment; or (C) has none of the impairments defined . . . but is treated . . . as having such an impairment.[40]

Thus, the protected class includes a person whose disability represents no handicap to employment but is treated by employers as if it did; or whose disability is a handicap to employment but only as a result of the attitudes of others towards it; or who has no disability at all but is erroneously treated by employers as disabled.[41] As the Supreme Court has explained,

> [an] impairment might not diminish a person's physical or mental capabilities, but could nevertheless substantially limit that person's ability to work as a result of the negative reactions of others to the impairment . . . Congress acknowledged that the society's accumulated fears about disability and disease are as handicapping as are the physical limitations that flow from actual impairment.[42]

Discrimination against disabled persons which is founded upon stereotypical attitudes and ignorance is caught, as well as that based upon prejudice. For example, an employer who, without any attempt at an individual medical assessment, inaccurately prejudges epileptic applicants for positions as being unable to perform the job, will have treated those applicants as disabled, even though in fact their impairments might not limit their major life activities at all or only to the extent that others react adversely to them.[43] A severely scarred burns victim has been cited as an example of an individual who would be regarded as a disabled person under this branch of the definition.[44]

In Australia, the New South Wales statute requires regard to be had to 'community attitudes' relating to a physical impairment and to the physical environment.[45] This would appear to recognize that disability is often a social construction rather than a medical condition. Victorian legislation embraces 'an impairment which is imputed to a person',[46] and Commonwealth law includes imputed disabilities.[47] In Canadian federal legislation, there is no express provision for perceived disabilities.[48] Perceived disabilities are protected in Nova Scotia and Ontario.[49] However, it would appear that, even in provinces where no explicit provision is made, there is scope for treating a person as discriminated against because of disability if an employer perceives a person's condition as a disability and acts upon that perception.[50]

SUBSTANTIAL LIMITATION ON MAJOR LIFE ACTIVITIES

In the USA it is not enough to show that the plaintiff is an individual with an actual or recorded or perceived disability. It must also be demonstrated that the disability substantially limits the major life activities of that individual.[51] This second stage of a two-stage test acts to filter out from the protected class individuals with minor, temporary or trivial medical conditions and illnesses which do not really affect the individual's role in life. It is necessary to show that impairment or disability produces some form of 'handicap'. This incorporates by implication the World Health Organization's conception of a handicap as being a

> disadvantage for a given individual, resulting from an impairment or a disability, that limits or prevents the fulfilment of a role that is normal (depending on age, sex, and social and cultural factors) for that individual.

In that regard, the US definition of an individual with disabilities is not far removed from the British definition of disabled person for the purposes of registration under the 1944 Act.

Major Life Activities

Major life activities are 'those basic activities that the average person in the general population can perform with little or no difficulty'.[52] They are illustrated, without exhaustion, as meaning 'functions such as caring for one's self, performing manual tasks, walking, seeing, hearing, speaking, breathing, learning, and working', and might also include sitting, standing, lifting and reaching.[53] It is clear from the US Department of Labor's section 504 regulations and the OFCCP's section 503 regulations that persons are 'substantially limited' in a major life activity if, because of their impairment or disability, they are likely to experience difficulty in securing, retaining or advancing in employment.[54] The inclusion of working as a major life activity is certain but controversial. When the EEOC's ADA regulations were being drafted, employers objected to this inclusion because its effect might be to cover persons who were merely unable to perform particular types of job and who were not really disabled at all.[55] To address this fear, the EEOC regulations state that limitation in the major life activity of working can only be relied upon when an individual is not disabled in any other life activity.[56] The regulations also explain that a disability must preclude an individual from working in a class or broad range of jobs for an employer in order to constitute a substantial limitation on working activity. Inability to work in a particular job or profession or for a particular employer is insufficient. This will be particularly the case where the disability merely prevents the individual pursuing a vocation in a specialized job or profession involving extraordinary skill, prowess or talent.

Substantial Limitation

Minor impairments or disabilities are not contemplated by the definition. This is because of the requirement that there must be a *substantial limitation* on major life activities. The ADA regulations state that 'limits' means for an individual that he or she would be:

> (i) Unable to perform a major life activity that the average person in the general population can perform; or (ii) Significantly restricted as to the condition, manner or duration under which an individual can perform a particular major life activity as compared to the condition, manner, or duration under which the average person in the general population can perform that same major life activity.[57]

A distinction is thus drawn between permanent, chronic conditions, on the one hand, and temporary, non-chronic impairments (such as broken bones, sprains, influenza etc.), on the other.[58] Some impairments will be inherently substantially limiting; other impairments will constitute a limitation for one person, but not for another, depending upon how far they are advanced, what degree of disability they produce and so on. A paraplegic, with paralysis of the legs, is undoubtedly substantially limited in the major life activity of walking, whereas an insulin-dependent diabetic is only substantially limited in a number of life activities *without* the aid of medication.[59] This means that some conditions (such as hypertension, diabetes, cancer or depression) will occupy a grey area. Even with some so-called traditional disabilities it may be difficult to demonstrate a limitation on a major life activity.[60] Such examples include medication-controlled epilepsy, insulin-regulated diabetes, multiple sclerosis or cancer in remission, cosmetic disfigurements and amputation with prosthesis. In particular, doubts about whether cancer in remission was a protected disability led many commentators to call for amendment of existing US civil rights laws and a number of Bills were introduced in Congress to attempt clarification.[61] It may be that these 'grey area' cases are best resolved by focusing upon the discriminator's perception of the discriminatee's medical condition or status, so arguing that it is the consequences of such negative attitudes that are disabling or that constitute a limitation on major life activities, rather than the physical (or mental) condition itself.

The nature, severity, duration and permanent or long-term impact of the impairment should be considered when determining whether an individual is substantially limited in a major life activity.[62] There must be a causal connection between a disability and the substantial limitation on a major life activity. A job applicant who is unable to read because of dyslexia is considered as disabled, but not where illiteracy is owing to lack of education.[63] In the case of the major life activity of working, a substantial limitation indicates a significant restriction (when compared to an average person with comparable skills, training and abilities) in a person's ability to perform a class of jobs or a broad range of jobs in various classes.[64] An inability to perform a single, particular job is not sufficient. For example, an individual with a minor vision impairment might be disqualified from being a commercial airline pilot, but might remain qualified for other flight crew positions.

The regulations also allow the consideration of a number of factors in the determination of whether an individual is substantially limited in the major life activity of working.[65] First, the geographical area to which the individual has reasonable access will be relevant. Second, consideration may be given to the job from which the individual has been excluded, and the number and types of jobs utilizing similar training, knowledge, skills or abilities (within the relevant geographical area) from which the individual is also disqualified. Third, a further or alternative factor is the job from which the individual has been disqualified, and the number and types of other jobs not utilizing similar training, knowledge, skills or abilities (within the geographical area) from which the individual is also excluded because of the impairment. The application of these factors is in turn illustrated by the regulations.[66] For example, an individual who suffers breathing difficulties as an allergic reaction to construction materials used in high-rise buildings would be substantially limited in the major life activity of working. He or she is prevented from working in a broad range of jobs of various descriptions that take place in high-rise office buildings within the geographical area to which he or she has reasonable access. Moreover, an individual with a back complaint might be substantially limited in the major life activity of working if the condition is a bar to any unskilled heavy labouring job (i.e. a class of jobs), even if jobs of another class, such as semi-skilled work, remained open to him or her.

Judicial View

The requirement that an impairment should substantially limit major life activities has been problematic. Under its section 503 regulations the Department of Labor defined substantial limitation by reference to the likelihood of a disabled person experiencing 'difficulty in securing, retaining or advancing in employment because of a handicap'.[67] In one case, a plaintiff with cerebral palsy whose condition could only be detected with sophisticated diagnostic medical equipment was not treated as a disabled individual, primarily because there was no evidence that any major life activities were substantially limited by the condition.[68] Mere character traits, diagnosed by a psychologist as including poor judgment, irresponsibility and impulsiveness, did not amount to a mental impairment substantially limiting major life activities.[69] In another case, the medical evidence suggested that the plaintiff suffered no substantial limitations resulting from knee and back injuries, where the only problem anticipated was the need to avoid walking for long periods while carrying heavy loads. The plaintiff was otherwise medically fit to perform the work in question.[70]

The fact that an impairment prevents individuals from carrying out a job in one particular way, or disqualifies them from one particular employment position only, or adversely affects one particular activity, is unlikely to convince a court that such individuals meet the substantial limitation condition. For example, in one case a knee injury prevented an employee from climbing telephone poles with spikes but not with ladders. He was able to undertake the duties of numerous other positions and the only activity that seemed to be affected was his ability to climb telephone poles.[71] In contrast, an employee with osteoarthritis of the hip was substantially limited in a way which disqualified him from any job involving manual labour or long periods of standing or walking.[72] Although mere back pain is not commonly recognized as a disability,[73] evidence that a severe lumbosacral sacroiliac sprain with radiculopathy caused the plaintiff severe pain and limited her ability to walk, sit, stand or drive convinced a court that the plaintiff was a disabled individual.[74] Clearly, plaintiffs need to establish that their impairment substantially limits the available choice of occupations or positions; but the fact that they might admit that an impairment does not prohibit the performance of a particular job is not fatal to establishing substantial limitation if they have not indicated that the present position held or applied for is the only one they are incapable of performing.[75] However, even if an individual's impairment does not *actually* substantially limit major life activities, the fact that a prospective employer *perceives* the individual to be suffering a condition that substantially limits major life activities may be enough to trigger the law's protection.[76]

The leading case under US federal law is *EE Black Ltd* v *Marshall* decided under section 503 of the RA 1973.[77] As a result of a pre-employment medical examination, an apprentice carpenter was refused employment. Although he had no symptoms, the examination revealed a congenital back abnormality (a partially sacralized transitional vertebra). At first instance, an administrative law judge found as a fact that the plaintiff was not impaired in his ability to perform all the elements of the job. The judge ruled that the plaintiff had an impairment but was not substantially limited in a major life activity because it only partially limited his access to employment. The test was whether the impairment impeded activities relevant to many or most jobs. On appeal to the Assistant Secretary of Labor for Employment Standards, the plaintiff was found to be a disabled individual. The Assistant Secretary's ruling derived from a reading of the Act as extending to any impairment that was a current bar to the employment of the individual's choice.

That reading was overturned by a district court which held that the statute envisaged a *substantial* handicap or limitation and not merely any impairment or limitation to any degree. If it were otherwise, said the court, an acrophobic applicant offered ten jobs by an employer, of which only one was on an upper storey, would be a disabled individual within the meaning of the Act, even though nine other jobs within that person's limitations were on offer. The district court also rejected the administrative law judge's formulation of the test as being too narrow. Persons whose impairments are a handicap to employment in their chosen field are substantially limited in a major life activity, even though more menial occupations, not employing their educational qualifications or training, might remain open to them. The district court ruled that the test to be applied was whether the perceived impairment of a rejected, but otherwise qualified, employee represented a substantial handicap to the employment of that individual. The focus was upon the individual job-seeker and not solely upon the impairment or perceived impairment. The court took account of the number and type of jobs from which the employee would be disqualified, the number of employees in the relevant area to which the criteria were applicable, the geographical area to which the employee had reasonable access, and the employee's job expectations and training. The court was prepared to assume that the disqualifying criterion would be used generally by employers. It would require the employer to show that the disqualifying criterion was not a general bar to employment. The court also assumed that an employer would attempt to place the applicant in a similar job at another location if the impairment had a bearing on employment in only one job location. The court concluded that the carpenter was a disabled individual because his medical status would substantially limit his opportunities for practising his trade in employment.

Flaccus comments that the *EE Black* decision made the definition of 'individual with handicaps' fairly easy to meet in most cases.[78] Although the requirement that the disability must substantially limit major life activities appears to restrict the scope of that definition, she anticipated that the court's reasoning, together with the amplification provided by the model regulations, in fact expands the definition of who is protected. Larson explains *EE Black* as establishing

> the rule that a specific physical or mental condition that has the exact same effect on different individuals may amount to a protected handicap for one person and not for the other. In other words, the definition of what is a protected handicap under the Rehabilitation Act is not limited to literal descriptions of disabilities . . . [and] most attempts to define protected handicaps solely on the basis of the nature of the disability will not be successful.[79]

That view is repeated in the ADA 1990 regulations, which draw on the *EE Black* jurisprudence.[80] Johnson believes that *EE Black* demonstrates the gap between the legal model of discrimination and the situation of disabled workers.[81] He points out that the courts are required to decide whether an impairment affects the plaintiff's ability to work, a task for which they have no prior expertise. If so, only then can the court proceed to consider whether the plaintiff has been discriminated against because of his or her disability, and only if the answer to that question is affirmative can the court judge whether the discrimination is unlawful (because the employer failed to consider or to make reasonable accommodation).

An example of the *EE Black* reasoning in practice may be seen in *Jasany* v *US Postal Service*.[82] The plaintiff suffered from mild strabismus or crossed-eyes. He had passed a vision examination and had satisfied other requirements to become a postal sorting machine operator. After three months, the plaintiff developed eye problems and headaches as a result of using the machine in question. He refused to operate the machine and, after a medical examination, was dismissed as unfit for postal sorting. In subsequent litigation, the fact of an impairment was not disputed, but the employer argued that it did not amount to a substantial limitation on major life activities. The appeals court adopted the *EE Black* reasoning, but asserted that the burden of proof fell on the plaintiff to show both the existence of an impairment and a resulting substantial limitation on a major life activity. There was no evidence that the strabismus had ever had any effect on the plaintiff's other activities, apart from his ability to operate this particular machine. The court also doubted whether the crossed-eye condition even amounted to an impairment itself.[83]

Subsequently, however, the courts applied *EE Black* narrowly and disallowed reliance upon the 'regarded as having such an impairment' test of disability where the plaintiff had merely been rejected from a single job because of a physical or mental criterion.[84] This caused much confusion and criticism.[85] The legislative history of the ADA 1990 seeks to resolve this, so that rejection from a particular job based upon a physical or mental criterion means that the plaintiff has been regarded or treated as disabled.[86] On the other hand, other courts have tended to ignore the *EE Black rationes* by assuming that the plaintiff is a disabled person without discussing whether there is an impairment substantially limiting major life activities. When faced with 'traditional' disabilities (such as epilepsy, cardiovascular disease or mental depression) it is easy to presume that the condition is substantially limiting in the manner required. It might also take little proof of some limitation in life activities for a court to conclude that the plaintiff is a member of the protected class. In many cases too, whatever the expected limitation created by an impairment, the attitude of others towards it might convert it into a substantially limiting condition.[87]

PARTICULAR DISABILITIES

What individual impairments constitute a recognizable disability (or handicap)? In the American legislation, no attempt is made to list specific diseases or conditions which would constitute impairments. It would be impossible to do so (although examples and illustrations are given in other jurisdictions). No comprehensive catalogue of diseases or conditions could be easily assembled, nor would it be possible to anticipate or predict what new impairments might emerge in the future, in the way that HIV and AIDS did during the 1980s.[88] Some assistance may be gleaned from the (US) RA 1973, which in another context (for the purposes of access to rehabilitation programmes and services) defines the term 'severe handicap' as a disability requiring multiple services over an extending period and resulting from:

> amputation, blindness, cancer, cerebral palsy, cystic fibrosis, deafness, heart disease, hemiplegia, mental retardation, mental illness, multiple sclerosis, muscular dystrophy, neurological disorders (including stroke and epilepsy), paraplegia, quadriplegia and other spinal cord conditions, renal failure, respiratory or pulmonary dysfunction.[89]

Regulations issued by the US Department of Justice illustrate impairments as including:

> such diseases and conditions as orthopedic, visual, speech and hearing impairments, cerebral palsy, epilepsy, muscular dystrophy, multiple sclerosis, cancer, heart disease, diabetes, mental retardation, emotional illness, and drug addiction and alcoholism.[90]

The congressional reports on the ADA 1990 also indicate that specific learning difficulties or infection with HIV should be regarded as examples of covered diseases and conditions.[91] However, none of these paradigms is really of assistance.

In the US courts, the substantive definition of 'individual with handicaps' has been held to apply to a variety of impairments and disabilities, including, for example, asbestosis, back injury, cardiovascular disease, epilepsy, severe depressive neurosis, schizophrenia and visual impairment.[92] Nevertheless, in developing disability discrimination laws, it is not the description of disability that matters, but rather its effect upon a person's major life activities. The existence of an impairment or disability must be demonstrated, but must also represent a substantial handicap to the individual's life. Most medical conditions will have some, if not a substantial, impact on life activities. For example, dyslexia will cause problems in learning and in education; paraplegia will create difficulties for mobility; and emphysema produces breathing problems which might reduce physical activity.[93] On the other hand, mere physical characteristics, such as left-handedness, are not normally classified as impairments.[94] However, between these two extremes lies a grey area which only judicial interpretation or legislative clarification can resolve.

For example, is a general status of ill health to be protected? In the USA, in *Stevens* v *Stubbs*,[95] an employee experienced health problems of uncertain diagnosis involving repeated absences from work. He unsuccessfully sought reassignment. During this period his work was unsatisfactory, although the employer's medical officer had passed the employee as fit for duty. The court refused to accept that the employee was a 'handicapped individual' because the term 'impairment' could not be said to encompass transitory illness which has no permanent effect on a person's health. In Canada, in *Ouimette* v *Lily Cups Ltd*,[96] a board of inquiry had no difficulty in finding that influenza did not constitute a protected disability, although asthma might have but for problems of evidence in the particular case. In contrast, chronic fatigue immune dysfunction syndrome has been held to be a protected disability,[97] while a combination of impairments might render an individual disabled.[98] In Canada, it has been accepted that hypertension is within the scope of the human rights codes' protection.[99] On the other hand, an intermittent eye inflammation did not constitute a disability where, despite inability to attend work predictably, constantly and on schedule, the applicant could meet all the physical criteria of the job description.[100] Equally, acrophobia has not been recognized as a disability,[101] although it might be better to say that such a condition might prevent an employee from fulfilling the 'otherwise qualified' condition.

The problem remains of where and how to draw the lines between marginal or unorthodox impairments and true disabling conditions. Difficulties also arise as to how to address the argument which seeks to exclude from protection disabilities that might be regarded as the product of voluntary actions. A number of problematic 'disabilities' are now examined to see whether and how they would fit the framework established by the discussion so far.

Alcoholism

Whether drug or alcohol abusers should be within the protected class of disabled individuals is a controversial issue.[102] In Larson's view,[103] there are two complicating factors. First, stimulant abuse is an elusive disability, because for much of the time, when not under the influence of drugs or alcohol, the abuser might appear to be perfectly capable of employment. Second, there is the perception that drug addiction or alcoholism is voluntary and, therefore, not meriting civil rights protection. However, it is undoubtedly the case that drug abuse and alcoholism attract social stigma. This has meant that few claims based upon this alleged 'handicap' have been litigated.

Prior to 1978, alcohol dependency was recognized as an implicit disability under the (US) RA 1973. However, an alcoholic employee might fail to show that he or she was 'otherwise qualified' for employment, particularly when the behavioural manifestations of alcoholism were taken into account.[104] In any event, in *Davis* v *Bucher*,[105] a US federal district court ruled that only individuals who had overcome or were attempting to overcome alcoholism were covered by section 504. Then in 1978, responding to employers' concerns about whether they could be forced to employ or retain alcoholic workers, Congress amended the legislation to make it clear that only rehabilitating or rehabilitated alcoholics were protected and not those who were simply in need of rehabilitation.[106] This distinction was followed by most courts,[107] although the appellate court in *Simpson* v *Reynolds Metal Co.*[108] took a contrary view that individuals with current problems or histories of alcoholism *were* members of the protected class unless their addiction or prior use prevented them from meeting the otherwise qualified standard.

The position now would appear to be that, under US law, a person who merely made casual use of alcohol short of dependency would not normally be treated as impaired, but an employer who acted as if such use were an impairment would be regarding that person as disabled and might be caught by the legislation. Employers may discriminate against alcoholics in need of rehabilitation, and against rehabilitating and rehabilitated alcoholics whose condition prevents them from performing the job or poses a threat to property or safety. The Supreme Court has insinuated that employers have a fairly wide discretion in deciding whether an alcoholic can perform the job effectively and safely.[109] Apart from these provisions, alcoholics are entitled to the same protection under the Act as individuals with other disabilities.[110]

Drug Abuse

The original definition of an 'individual with handicaps' did not address the question of whether an illegal drug user was a disabled person for the purpose of the (US) RA 1973. Despite that, trial courts had held persons with histories of drug use, including participants in methadone maintenance programmes, to be protected persons.[111] The 1978 amendments excluded from protection drug abusers whose current use of drugs prevented them from performing the job or caused them to be a risk to safety or property.[112] Now, individuals who are current illegal users of drugs are excluded from coverage under the ADA 1990 and that Act amends the earlier legislation accordingly.[113] So an employer may discriminate against a current drug user (if such discrimination is grounded in such use) even though that person is quite capable of fulfilling the requirements of the job. In contrast, rehabilitating or rehabilitated drug users are covered, provided they are no longer using drugs.[114] Discrimination against such individuals would be discrimination against a person with a record of disability. A person who is erroneously perceived as a current illegal drug user would also be protected from discriminatory actions. Psychoactive substance use disorders resulting from current illegal use of drugs are expressly excluded as protected disabilities.

Because the (US) ADA's protection does not extend to individuals whose disability is the product of current illegal drug use, the Act is consistent with federal policy on drug-free workplaces.[115] It permits, but does not necessarily encourage, drug-testing of applicants and employees, enabling employers to make discriminatory employment decisions based upon test results.[116] First, an employer may adopt and administer reasonable policies and procedures, including drug-testing, to ensure that allegedly rehabilitating or rehabilitated illegal drug users are not engaging in drug abuse.[117] Second, an employer may prohibit the use of alcohol or illegal drugs in the workplace, require that employees shall not be under the influence of alcohol or be engaging in the illegal use of drugs in the workplace, and require employees to conform with the Drug-Free Workplace Act 1988.[118] Third, an employer may hold an illegal drug user or alcoholic to the same qualification standards for employment, job performance and behaviour as other employees, and it is irrelevant whether or not any unsatisfactory performance or behaviour is related to drug use or alcoholism.[119] Fourth, employers in the defence and transport industries may require employees to comply with particular federal government regulations regarding illegal drug use and alcohol which apply to those industries.[120] Finally, employers in the transport sector may test employees and applicants for illegal drug use and on-duty alcohol impairment with regard to positions involving safety-sensitive duties and to remove from such positions anyone who tests positive.[121]

Contagious Diseases and Infections

In 1988, a further amendment was made to the RA 1973 to deal with the question of whether contagious diseases or infections are a covered disability:

> For the purposes of sections 793 and 794 of this title, as such sections relate to employment, such term does not include an individual who has a currently contagious disease or infection and who, by reason of such disease or infection, would constitute a direct threat to the health or safety of other individuals or who, by reason of the currently contagious disease or infection, is unable to perform the duties of the job.[122]

This provision clarifies the extent of the recognition by the Supreme Court in *School Board of Nassau County, Florida* v *Arline* that a person suffering from the contagious disease of tuberculosis could be a disabled person within the meaning of the statute.[123] This amendment survives the 1990 reforms.[124] The contagiousness of a disease is more likely to make an individual disabled than the disease itself, especially by how others react to or perceive him or her. On the other hand, the very contagiousness of the disease makes the disabled individual a risk to others and so he or she may be unable to surmount the 'otherwise qualified' hurdle. In *Arline* the plaintiff had contracted tuberculosis as a child, but had subsequently qualified and worked as a teacher for a number of years. She was dismissed after she suffered three relapses of the disease. The district court refused to accept that Congress intended contagious diseases to be within the mischief of the RA 1973. A federal appeals court found that tuberculosis was an impairment of the respiratory functions and fell within the definition of disability under the statute and regulations. That view was upheld by the Supreme Court, but it directed an inquiry as to whether the plaintiff could satisfy the 'otherwise qualified' standard, especially given the possibility of risks to the health of others or the plaintiff's ability to carry out the duties of a teacher.

HIV and AIDS

A treatise on the impact of HIV and AIDS upon the workplace and employment law is beyond the scope of the present study.[125] Under US legislation, a person with HIV would be regarded as someone with a physical or mental impairment substantially limiting major life activities. Any form of the illness would seem to suffice, ranging from asymptomatic infection through to AIDS.[126] Case law established as much under the RA 1973,[127] while the legislative history of the ADA 1990 indicates that Congress intended to continue these precedents.[128] Asymptomatic HIV-positive individuals are within the Act as persons 'regarded as having' a physical impairment[129] and AIDS sufferers are similarly able to establish a *prima facie* status as a disabled individual. The position would appear to be similar under Canadian and Australian legislation.[130] The remaining question, therefore, is whether a person with HIV or AIDS is otherwise qualified for employment and whether the condition represents a risk to health and safety.

Physical Appearance Disabilities

The boundaries of disability discrimination law have been frequently tested by its reaction to discrimination on the basis of physical appearance or characteristics, such as weight, height or disfigurement. Appearance discrimination has been defined by reference to the 'immutable aspects of bodily and facial appearance', in contrast with such mutable aspects as hair length, cleanliness and orthodoxy of dress.[131] There have been a number of studies of the incidence of discrimination on the basis of physical attractiveness,[132] while there is historical evidence of local legislation in the USA regulating the appearance in public of 'unsightly' diseased, deformed or mutilated persons.[133] Because disability discrimination laws are often applied beyond the circumference of 'traditional' disabilities, it would seem possible to extend the law to appearance discrimination (although there would be undoubted problems of proof and causation).

In the USA, the definition of impairment expressly includes 'cosmetic disfigurement', including 'disfiguring scars'.[134] In any event, if employers react adversely to facial or bodily appearance, it would be possible to argue that the object of such reaction has been treated or perceived as impaired, and the failure to be granted employment opportunity has interfered with a major life activity.[135] An employer might seek to justify such discrimination by reference to the 'otherwise qualified' standard, and this might be easier to sustain in respect of certain occupations – such as modelling, acting, cabin crew, retail selling etc. – where it might be argued that appearance is an aspect of the job. However, in the context of sex discrimination, appearance has been rejected as an essential job function, at least in the context of employer and customer preference for female flight attendants.[136] There seems no reason in principle why the same logic should not apply to disability discrimination.

The issue is sharply focused in respect of weight discrimination. In *Davison* v *St Paul Lutheran Home,*[137] a Canadian provincial decision, a complainant with a weight problem was not offered employment and successfully claimed disability-related discrimination at first instance. A board of inquiry concluded that obesity could be a disability if caused by bodily injury, birth defect or illness or if its origins were a mental disorder. The board concluded that the employer's perception of the complainant was that she suffered from a disability and she had been judged on the basis of the employer's poor experience of a former employee with a weight condition. However, this decision was overturned on appeal.[138] In *Horton* v *Regional Municipality of Niagara,*[139] a board of inquiry refused to find that obesity was a disability where no medical evidence was brought to show that the plaintiff's weight condition was caused by bodily injury, birth defect or illness. A similar approach has been taken in the USA.[140] The question is whether weight or obesity is a physical characteristic or the result of a recognizable physiological disorder. If the latter, and there is interference with a major life activity (such as walking or breathing), obesity should be a protected disability.[141] However, in *Tudyman* v *United Airlines*,[142] the plaintiff was refused employment as a cabin crew member because he exceeded the airline's weight requirements owing to his body-building activities. The court rejected his claim on the grounds, *inter alia*, that the applicant's weight problem was voluntary and not the result of a physiological disorder.

Smoking and Passive Smoking

Non-smokers with an allergic reaction to tobacco smoke or who otherwise alleged harm from passive smoking have not been automatically treated as individuals with disabilities.[143] Employers will be more willing to challenge the basis of the disability claim because, as tolerance to tobacco smoke is not an essential element of any job, the second line defence based upon the 'otherwise qualified' standard cannot be utilized. However, unusual sensitivity to tobacco smoke might constitute a disability, especially if that hypersensitivity produces a substantial limitation upon a major life activity of the individual, such as an inability to work in an environment that is not smoke-free.[144] It might be possible, therefore, that persons with particular pulmonary problems (such as emphysema) might be able to use disability discrimination law to require employers to make reasonable accommodation by ensuring a smoke-free working environment.

An interesting and topical question is whether *smokers* can be regarded as persons with disabilities protected from discrimination by the (US) ADA 1990? The Act does not prevent employers prohibiting or restricting smoking in the workplace and non-smokers are thus afforded a degree of protection from passive smoking.[145] This does not answer the question either way.[146] However, it is unclear whether or not a smoker is covered by the Act in the sense of whether he or she might be an individual with a disability. If so, an employee who smoked, and who was treated differently or unfavourably because of this, might have an action for employment discrimination under disability discrimination law.[147]

CONCLUSION

The identification of disabled persons for the purposes of delineating the protected class will always prove difficult for the drafters of disability discrimination laws. The British system of identifying the law's beneficiaries by registration of status appears fundamentally objectionable and, in any event, does not alleviate the problem of how to determine (and who is to determine) whether the individual is covered by the statute. An alternative approach might be suggested by the position under section 503 of the Rehabilitation Act 1973, where disabled plaintiffs alleging breach of a federal contractor's affirmative action obligations towards them must self-certify their status, specifying their impairment or disability.[148] Further documentation or evidence may be required of the complainant and the contractor may require an applicant or employee to submit medical documentation or undergo a medical examination to verify his or her status as a protected person. However, while self-certification might be useful as a device for identifying targeted minorities under equal opportunity planning or positive action programmes, it is unlikely to be acceptable in the litigious context of complaints of disability discrimination.

A further dilemma for British reformers will be whether to list or illustrate the types of impairment or disability that might be envisaged as protected by any newly introduced disability discrimination legislation. A court might refuse to treat as a disability any condition unlisted, while a failure to exemplify indicative impairments could be a hostage to fortune as courts will tend to construe the protected class narrowly. Public policy might also require the exclusion or exceptional treatment of certain 'disabilities', such as alcoholism, drug dependence and contagious diseases.[149]

It might be that few claimants will want to attract the social stigma which attaches to a characterization of a person as disabled. Relatively few cases are litigated in the USA unless the plaintiff is clearly a person with disabilities. Moreover, in marginal cases, the court will have to be convinced that a substantially limiting disability exists but that, as a result, the individual is not so disabled as to be unable to perform the job in question. This 'Catch-22' will affect a claimant's perception of the chances of winning a case. Employers can have it both ways. They may discriminate against someone because he or she is 'disabled', but then defend that discrimination by arguing that the disability is not serious enough to warrant the protection of the legislation. Yet it was presumably serious enough to warrant a denial of employment opportunity.[150] On the other hand, American employers seldom challenge a plaintiff's claim to be a disabled person, especially when there is a second line of defence – a challenge to the plaintiff's ability to work or qualification for employment – which is discussed next.

NOTES

1. There is evidence of appreciable variations in the assessment of whether an individual is a disabled person for the purposes of registration under the 1944 Act: Prescott-Clarke, 1990: 79.

2. Borrowing from Weiss, 1974 and the jurisprudence of US disability discrimination law.

3. National Assistance Act 1948 ss 29(1) and 64(1); Mental Health Act 1959 s 8(2); Chronically Sick and Disabled Persons Act 1970 s 2; Health and Social Services Adjudications Act 1983 Sch 4; Disabled Persons (Services, Consultation and Representation) Act 1986 ss 5, 9 and 16.

4. Social Security Contributions and Benefits Act 1992. Benefit would also be payable in respect of prescribed industrial diseases and injuries.

5. Tomlinson, 1943.

6. DP(E)A 1944 s 1(1).

7. See Chapter 2.

8. National Advisory Council on the Employment of Disabled People, 1986: para. 6.11.

9. Research carried out in the 1980s found that the 1944 definition of disability tended to match employers' perceptions of disability, but with a slight bias towards adopting an exclusive rather than inclusive definition: Morrell, 1990: 7.

10. 29 USC s 706(8)(B); 42 USC s 12102(2). See the discussion in Chapter 4. Originally, the 1973 definition defined a 'handicapped' individual as someone whose disability limited employability: (US) RA 1973 s 7(6).

11. See the discussion in Chapter 5.

12. (NSW) ADA 1977 s 4(1) and see the discussion in Chapter 5.

13. 29 USC ss 791(b), 793(a) and 794(a); 42 USC s 12112(a). The burden of proof is on the plaintiff to show that he or she is a disabled person: *Prewitt* v *US Postal Service* (1981) 662 F2d 292 at 309 (5th Cir); *Pushkin* v *Regents of the University of Colorado* (1981) 658 F2d 1372 at 1385 (10th Cir); *Walders* v *Garrett* (1991) 765 FSupp 303 (ED Va).

14. 29 USC s 706(B); 42 USC s 12102(2). See generally: Bogaards, 1982; Simon, 1984; Larson, 1986, 1988; Feldblum, 1991b.

15. 29 CFR s 1613.702(b)(1); 28 CFR s 41.31((b)(1)(i); 29 CFR s 1630.2(h)(1). The words in italics did not appear in the RA 1973 definition. The s 503 regulations do not define physical impairment.

16. 29 CFR s 1613.702(b)(2); 28 CFR s 41.31((b)(1)(ii); 29 CFR s 1630.2(h)(2). The section 503 regulations do not define mental impairment.

17. (Can) HRA s 3(1). For this purpose, 'disability' denotes 'any previous or existing mental or physical disability': (Can) HRA s 25.

18. (Alb) IRPA s 38(i).

19. (NS) HRA s 3(1).

20. (Ont) HRC s 10(1).

21. (NB) HRA s 2;(New) HRC s 2(h); (NS) HRA s 3(1); (Ont) HRC s 10(1); (Sask) HRC s 2(d.1)(ii); (YT) HRA s 34.

22. (Alb) IRPA s 38(e. 1): 'a disorder of thought, mood, perception, orientation or

memory that impairs (A) judgment, (B) behaviour, (C) capacity to recognize reality, or (D) ability to meet the ordinary demands of life'. See also, to like effect: (Sask) HRC s 2(i.1).

23. (YT) HRA s 34.
24. (NSW) ADA 1977 ss 49A and 49P; (SA) EOA 1984 s 67; (WA) EOA 1984 s 66A.
25. (Vic) EOA 1984 s 21.
26. (SA) EOA 1984 s 5; (Vic) EOA 1984 s 4(1)
27. (Cth) DDA 1992 s 4(1).
28. (NSW) ADA 1977 s 4(1).
29. (WA) EOA 1984 s 4(1).
30. See, for example: *Davis* v *Bucher* (1978) 451 FSupp 791 (ED Pa) (rehabilitated drug user); 45 CFR Part 84 Appendix.
31. 29 CFR Part 1630 Appendix.
32. 29 USC s 706(8)(B)(ii); 42 USC s 12102(2)(B).
33. 28 CFR s 41.31(b)(3); 29 CFR s 1613.702(d); 29 CFR s 1630.2(k); 45 CFR s 84.3(j)(2)(iii). The record might be contained in educational, medical, employment or other records. A record as disabled for another purpose (for example, social security) would not necessarily bring an individual under the cover of this prong of the definition.
34. (PEI) HRA s 1(1)(l); (Ont) HRC s 10(1).
35. (WA) EOA 1984 s 4(1).
36. (Cth) DDA 1992 s 4(1).
37. Shaller and Rosen, 1991: 412. The OFCCP s 503 regulations indicate that this situation might be caught under the 'record of impairment' provision: 41 CFR Part 60-741 Appendix.
38. LaPlante, 1991: 63.
39. 29 USC s 706(8)(B)(iii); 42 USC s 12102(2)(C).
40. 28 CFR s 41.31(b)(4); 29 CFR s 1613.702(e); 29 CFR s 1630.2(l); 45 CFR s 84.3(j)(2)(iv).
41. 29 CFR Part 1630 Appendix.
42. *School Board of Nassau County, Florida* v *Arline* (1987) 480 US 273 at 283–4. In *Arline*, a plaintiff with tuberculosis was held to be disabled because the condition had required hospitalization and thus the plaintiff had a 'record of impairment', but the case is equally explicable as one where the plaintiff had been discriminated against because of the perception of tuberculosis as a contagious disease. See Mayerson, 1991b: 504.
43. *Duran* v *City of Tampa* (1977) 430 FSupp 75 (MD Fla).
44. Jones, 1991a: 490; 29 CFR Part 1630 Appendix.
45. (NSW) ADA 1977 s 4(1).
46. (Vic) EOA 1984 s 4(1).
47. (Cth) DDA 1992 s 4(1). Disability status is also found where a person possesses bodily organisms capable of causing disease or illness, thus possibly addressing discrimination against carriers or persons with benign or stable viral infections.
48. (Can) HRA s 25.
49. (NS) HRA s 3(1); (Ont) HRC s 10(1).
50. See for example, *Davison* v *St Paul Lutheran Home* (1991) 91 CLLC para. 17,017 (Sask HRC) discussed further below.
51. 29 USC s 706(8)(B); 42 USC s 12102(2). See also: (NSW) ADA 1977 s 4(1).
52. 29 CFR Part 1630 Appendix.
53. 28 CFR s 41.31; 29 CFR s 1613.702(c); 29 CFR s 1630.2(i) and Appendix; 45 CFR s 84.3.
54. 29 CFR s 32.3; 41 CFR s 60-741.2 and Appendix A. The Department of Labor regulations and the OFCCP regulations focus upon life activities including communication, ambulation, self-care, socialization, education, vocational training, employment, transportation, adapting to housing etc., but primary attention is given to life activities affecting employability.
55. Shaller and Rosen, 1991: 410.
56. 29 CFR Part 1630 Appendix.
57. 29 CFR s 1630.2(j)(1). The RA 1973 regulations did not attempt such an explication.
58. 29 CFR Part 1630 Appendix.
59. Bayler, 1992.

60. Burgdorf, 1991: 448. He doubts whether the need for the legal ingredient of a limitation on a major life activity is self-evident.

61. Sigel, 1984; Bazemore, 1986; Hoffman, 1986; Canfield, 1987; Streicher, 1987; McEvoy, 1990.

62. 29 CFR s 1630.2(j)(2).

63. 29 CFR Part 1630 Appendix.

64. 29 CFR s 1630.2(j)(3)(i).

65. 29 CFR s 1630.2(3)(ii).

66. 29 CFR Part 1630 Appendix.

67. 41 CFR s 60-741.2.

68. *Pridemore* v *Legal Aid Society of Dayton* (1985) 625 FSupp 1171 (SD Ohio); *Pridemore* v *Rural Legal Aid Society of West Central Ohio* (1985) 625 FSupp 1180 (SD Ohio).

69. *Daley* v *Koch* (1989) 892 F2d 212 (2nd Cir).

70. *Taylor* v *US Postal Service* (1990) 771 FSupp 882 (SD Ohio).

71. *Elstner* v *Southwestern Bell Telephone Co.* (1987) 659 FSupp 1328 (SD Tex). See also to like effect: *de la Torres* v *Bolger* (1985) 610 FSupp 593 (DC Tex).

72. *Coley* v *Secretary of Army* (1987) 689 FSupp 519 (D Md).

73. *Diaz* v *US Postal Service* (1987) 658 FSupp 484 (ED Cal) where an employee with chronic lumbar or low back pain was otherwise able to perform all the arduous duties of a postal delivery worker.

74. *Perez* v *Philadelphia Housing Authority* (1987) 677 FSupp 357 (ED Pa).

75. *Carty* v *Carlin* (1985) 623 FSupp 1181 (DC Md).

76. *Pridemore* v *Rural Legal Aid Society of West Central Ohio* (1985) 625 FSupp 1180 (SD Ohio).

77. (1980) 497 FSupp 1088 (D Haw). See: Haines, 1983.

78. Flaccus, 1986b: 276.

79. Larson, 1986: 764.

80. 29 CFR Part 1630 Appendix.

81. Johnson, 1986b: 258–9.

82. (1985) 755 F2d 1249 (6th Cir).

83. See for example: *Oesterling* v *Walters* (1985) 760 F2d 859 (8th Cir) (plaintiff's varicose veins were an impairment and limited major life activities by affecting her ability to sit and stand, but no evidence that this limitation was substantial).

84. *Forrisi* v *Bowen* (1986) 794 F2d 931 (4th Cir); *de la Torres* v *Bolger* (1985) 610 FSupp 593 (ND Tex), affirmed (1986) 781 F2d 1134 (5th Cir); *Tudyman* v *United Airlines* (1984) 608 FSupp 739 (CD Cal) cited by Mayerson, 1991b: 506. But cf. *Thornhill* v *Marsh* (1989) 866 F2d 1182 (9th Cir).

85. Bogaards, 1982.

86. Mayerson, 1991b: 507–8.

87. Richards, 1985: 7–8.

88. Feldblum, 1991c: 84.

89. 29 USC s 706(13).

90. 28 CFR s 41.31.

91. US Senate, 1989: 22; US House of Representatives, 1990a: 51; 1990b: 28.

92. *Fynes* v *Weinberger* (1985) 677 FSupp 315 (ED Pa); *Schuett Investment Co* v *Anderson* (1986) 386 NW2d 249; *Bey* v *Bolger* (1982) 540 FSupp 910 (DC Pa); *Reynolds* v *Brock* (1987) 815 F2d 571 (9th Cir); *Doe* v *Region 13 Mental Health-Mental Retardation Commission* (1983) 704 F2d 1402 (CA Miss); *Halberman* v *Pennhurst School and Hospital* (1977) 446 FSupp 1295 (DC Penn); *Gladys* v *Pearland Independent School District* (1981) 520 FSupp 869 (DC Tex); *Norcross* v *Sneed* (1983) 573 FSupp 533 (DC Ark).

93. Feldblum, 1991c: 85.

94. *de la Torres* v *Bolger* (1986) 781 F2d 1134 (5th Cir). See: McEvoy, 1988.

95. (1983) 576 FSupp 1409 (DC Ga).

96. (1990) 12 CHRR D/19, 90 CLLC para. 17,109 (Ont HRC).

97. *Walders* v *Garrett* (1991) 765 FSupp 303 (ED Va).

98. *Fitzgerald* v *Green Valley Area Education Agency* (1984) 589 FSupp 1130 (DC Iowa) (nocturnal epilepsy, dyslexia and cerebral palsy with left side hemiplegia); *Carty* v *Carlin*

(1985) 623 FSupp 1181 (DC Md) (manic depression and myocardial infarction with probable coronary artery disease); *Harrison* v *Marsh* (1988) 691 FSupp 1223 (WD Mo) (typist less able to type continuously because of mastectomy involving removal of upper arm and shoulder muscle); *Johnson* v *Sullivan* (1991) 764 FSupp 1053 (D Md) (heart condition, narcolepsy and stress disorder).

99. *Horton* v *Regional Municipality of Niagara* (1988) 88 CLLC para. 17,004 (Ont HRC).

100. *Santiago* v *Temple University* (1990) 739 FSupp 974 (ED Pa).

101. *Forrisi* v *Heckler* (1985) 626 FSupp 629 (MD NC); *Forrisi* v *Bowen* (1986) 794 F2d 931 (4th Cir). This plaintiff might have succeeded by arguing that he was a person 'regarded as having a disability': Jones, 1991b: 43.

102. Canadian federal legislation expressly includes previous or existing dependence on alcohol or a drug: (Can) HRA s 25. Nova Scotia law includes persons with previous dependency on drugs and alcohol: (NS) HRA s 3(1).

103. Larson, 1986: 757.

104. 45 CFR Part 84 Appendix; *Simpson* v *Reynolds Metals Co* (1980) 629 F2d 1226 (7th Cir); *Crew* v *Office of Personnel Management* (1987) 834 F2d 140 (8th Cir).

105. (1978) 451 FSupp 791 (ED Pa).

106. See now: 29 USC s 706(8)(C)(v).

107. See, for example: *Tinch* v *Walters* (1985) 765 F2d 599 (6th Cir); *Anderson* v *University of Wisconsin* (1988) 841 F2d 737 (7th Cir); *Railway Executives' Association* v *Burnley* (1988) 839 F2d 575 (9th Cir); *Whitlock* v *Brock* (1984) 790 F2d 964 (DC Cir).

108. (1980) 629 F2d 1226 (7th Cir).

109. *New York City Transport Authority* v *Beazer* (1979) 440 US 568.

110. See further: 29 CFR ss 1630.10 and 1630.16; Sullivan, 1985; Fitzpatrick, 1991; William and Mary Law Review, 1992.

111. *Davis* v *Bucher* (1978) 451 FSupp 791 (DC Pa). See generally: Columbia Human Rights Law Review, 1973; New York University Law Review, 1974.

112. 42 USC s 706(7)(B); *American Federation of Government Employees, AFL-CIO* v *Skinner* (1989) 885 F2d 884 (DC Cir); *Heron* v *McGuire* (1986) 803 F2d 67 (2nd Cir); *Burka* v *New York City Transit Authority* (1988) 680 FSupp 590 (SD NY).

113. 42 USC ss 12114(a) and 12111(6); 29 CFR s 1630.3(a).

114. 42 USC s 12114(b); 29 CFR s 1630.3(b). See: Rand, 1988; Robbins, 1991.

115. Drug-free Workplace Act 1988: Pub L No. 100-690 ss 5151–60; 102 Stat 4181, 4304–8; codified at 41 USC ss 701–7. This Act requires federal contractors and federally funded employers to formulate and publish policies to restrict the use of alcohol and illegal drugs in the workplace. These exclusions only apply to a user of controlled substances and not to prescribed drugs or patent medicines. Thus a valium-addicted individual would be a disabled person for the purposes of the law.

116. 42 USC s 12114(d)(2); 29 CFR s 1630.3(c). A drug test is not a medical examination for the purposes of the Act: 42 USC s 12114(d)(1); 29 CFR s 1630.16(c)(1).

117. 42 USC s 12114(b); 29 CFR s 1630.3(c). The interaction of drug-testing policies and disability discrimination law has exercised many American employers. See generally: Black, 1988; Heshizer and Muczyk, 1988; Lips and Lueder, 1988; Bible, 1990; Crow, 1992.

118. 42 USC s 12114(c)(1)–(3); 29 CFR s 1630.16(b)(1)–(3).

119. 42 USC s 12114(c)(4); 29 CFR s 1630.16(b)(4).

120. 42 USC s 12114(c)(5); 29 CFR s 1630.16(b)(5) and (6).

121. 42 USC s 12114(e); 29 CFR s 1630.16(c)(2).

122. 42 USC s 706(8)(D).

123. (1987) 107 SCt 1123, 480 US 273.

124. Subject to the food handling exception: 42 USC s 12112(d); 29 CFR s 1630.16(e).

125. See generally: Harvard Law Review, 1986; Leonard, 1987a; Rothstein, 1987; Wasson, 1987; Fagot-Diaz, 1988; Kushen, 1988; Sherman, 1989; Alexander, 1990; Cohen, 1992.

126. Feldblum, 1991c: 86.

127. *Chalk* v *US District Court* (1988) 840 F2d 701 (9th Cir).

128. US Senate, 1989: 22; US House of Representatives, 1990a: 52; 1990b: 28 n. 18.

129. *Harris* v *Thigpen* (1991) 941 F2d 1495 (11th Cir).

130. See: Kenney, 1988; Kussner, 1989; Smith, 1989; Roussos, 1990; Waters, 1990. For the

position under British law, see: Southam and Howard, 1987; Napier, 1989, 1991; Watt, 1992. For a comparison between the legal positions in the USA and the EC see: Dworkin and Stegger, 1989.

131. *Harvard Law Review*, 1987: 2035. Physical appearance discrimination might also affect persons with restricted or stunted growth or abnormal height: Miller, 1987.

132. *Ibid.*: 2037–42.

133. Burgdorf and Burgdorf, 1975: 863.

134. Canadian federal law also includes disfigurement as a disability: (Can) HRA s 25.

135. *Harvard Law Review*, 1987: 2044–5.

136. *Diaz* v *Pan American World Airways* (1971) 442 F2d 385 (5th Cir). It has been suggested that the employment selection process could be altered to eliminate unnecessary judgements made on appearance: e.g. by using telephone interviewing rather than face-to-face interviews, by interviewing behind screens, or by separating the interviewing function from the selection function: *Harvard Law Review*, 1987: 2049–51.

137. (1991) 91 CLLC para. 17,017 (Sask) HRC.

138. (1992) 92 CLLC para. 17,007 (Sask QB); (1993) 94 CLLC para. 17,001 (Sask) CA. Subsequently, the complaint was dismissed: (1992) 92 CLLC para. 17,026 (Sask HRC).

139. (1987) 9 CHRR D/4611, 88 CLLC para. 17,004 (Ont) HRC.

140. See generally: Baker, 1982; Mason, 1982; Bierman, 1990; Shapiro, 1991; McEvoy, 1992; Stolker, 1992. The ADA regulations do not appear to regard obesity as an impairment: 29 CFR Part 1630 Appendix.

141. Feldblum, 1991b: 19.

142. (1984) 608 FSupp 739 (DC Cal). See also: *Russell* v *Salve Regina College* (1986) 649 FSupp 391 (D RI). Cf. *Cook* v *State of Rhode Island* (1992) 783 FSupp 1569 (D RI); (1993) 10 F3d 17 (1st Cir).

143. *GASP* v *Mecklenburg County* (1979) 256 SE2d 477 (CA NC). Ironically, this is one alleged disability to which social stigma does not attach; quite the opposite, in fact, for such a plaintiff often becomes the focus of public support (Larson, 1986: 759).

144. *Vickers* v *Veterans Administration* (1982) 549 FSupp 85 (DC Wash).

145. 42 USC s 12201(b).

146. Jones, 1991b: 43.

147. This conjecture has given rise to a lively debate in the legal literature in the USA. See, for example: Vaughn, 1988; Fox and Davison, 1989; Goh, 1991; Sculco, 1992; Garner, 1993; Grasso, 1993.

148. 41 CFR s 60-741.7.

149. Special rules have also been developed under US law to address the exclusionary treatment of homosexuality, bisexuality, so-called 'sexual behaviour disorders' and anti-social behaviour (such as kleptomania): 42 USC ss 12208 and 12211.

150. Burgdorf, 1991: 448–9. See, for example, two cases cited earlier in this chapter: *Forrisi* v *Bowen* (1986) 794 F2d 931 (4th Cir) (the dismissal of an acrophobic not protected); *Jasany* v *US Postal Service* (1985) 755 F2d 1244 (6th Cir) (dismissal of individual with mild strabismus not unlawful).

8

Fitness for Work

INTRODUCTION

Anti-discrimination and equal opportunity legislation is often said to promote reverse discrimination or preferential treatment in favour of the minority or group the law was designed to protect. It is sometimes argued that the law results in employers unwillingly or unwittingly engaging or promoting members of minorities, regardless of their abilities or qualifications, and whether or not they are the best persons for the job. Disability discrimination law is remarkably sensitive to this argument. The contention that employers will be forced to employ or retain disabled persons incapable of doing the job must be refuted. There are a number of legal formulae by which any suggestion of reverse discrimination is ruled out.

The (US) RA 1973 only prohibits discrimination against 'otherwise qualified' individuals with handicaps.[1] Although the Act embraces all individuals with an impairment that limits major life activities, whether or not the impairment is related to ability, only 'otherwise qualified' persons may seek the protection of the statute's anti-discrimination directive. The (US) ADA 1990 also contains a similar 'otherwise qualified' condition,[2] and state disability laws frequently contain an 'ability to work' specification.[3] In Canadian federal legislation, the same effect is achieved by allowing employers to discriminate against disabled workers who cannot satisfy a '*bona fide* occupational requirement' or 'qualification'.[4] This formula is also to be found in Canadian provincial laws, although in various shapes and guises.[5] State and Commonwealth legislation in Australia also expects that, as a pre-condition to alleging disability-based discrimination, the disabled plaintiff is able to carry out the work in question.[6] It is thus a defence to show that the reason for the alleged act of discrimination was not the plaintiff's disability but rather an inability to perform the work in question.

As was noted in Chapter 7, American employers seldom challenge a plaintiff's claim to be a disabled individual.[7] Conceding this question allows the employer's defence to concentrate on establishing that the employee is not 'otherwise qualified' for the employment.[8] Few claimants will want to attract the social stigma which attaches to a characterization of a person as disabled, so few cases are litigated unless the plaintiff is clearly a person with disabilities. Furthermore, in marginal cases, a plaintiff will have to convince the court that a substantially limiting disability exists but that as a result the individual is not so 'handicapped' as to be unable to perform the job in question. Such a contradictory task may affect a claimant's perception of the chances of winning a case.[9] Defendant employers will also not wish to lose the sympathy of the court by aggressively attacking the plaintiff's disability status, especially when there is a second line of defence presented by the 'otherwise qualified' standard. One might also add that, as the experience of personal injury litigation suggests, the need to marshall expert medical evidence to undermine a claimant's contentions will cause an employer to measure the costs against the benefits of doing so. Given the uncertainties of psychology and psychiatric medicine, there will also be additional problems in challenging a plaintiff who seeks to rely upon mental disability to qualify for the protected class.[10]

An 'ability to work' or 'otherwise qualified' or '*bona fide* occupational requirement' standard will inevitably reduce eligibility for membership of the protected class. Applied literally or strictly, such a standard would exclude from discrimination protection large numbers of disabled persons who can meet the employer's educational and vocational criteria, but who cannot satisfy the employer's physical or occupational or environmental requirements. For example, a wheelchair user applying for the post of assistant solicitor with a law firm might have the necessary academic and professional qualifications for the position, but might fail to meet the firm's demands for mobility or might be unable to negotiate the architectural barriers and inaccessibility of the firm's office building. A visually impaired individual applying for a skilled craft job might have completed an apprenticeship and have the necessary vocational qualifications, but might fail the employer's pre-employment eyesight requirements. As Flaccus comments,

> When statutes are restrictive both in the definition of 'handi-

> cap' and the ability to work requirement, they tend to eliminate from coverage both people whose handicap is sufficiently mild that it does not interfere with their ability to work and people whose handicap is sufficiently severe that it necessitates some change in the work place or job duties in order for them to be able to do the job. A statute with both a narrow definition of 'handicap' and a strict ability to work requirement places the plaintiff in a dilemma.[11]

The dilemma is: do disabled persons argue that their disabilities are serious, thereby attracting the defence that they are unable to carry out the essential elements of the job, or do they contend that their disabilities are not so severe as to affect employability, thereby risking a finding that they are not sufficiently disabled to attract the law's protection?

If disability discrimination law is to achieve real change in the attitude to disabled workers, it must find a solution to this impasse. One way might be to subject the employer's requirements to the strict scrutiny of a business necessity test or essential job functions approach. Another might be to require the employer to adjust or modify working practices or environment. Aspects of both solutions are to be found in the substance of legislative 'fitness for work' standards. This topic is now examined by looking at the North American models adopted in the USA and in Canada, and subsequently by comparing the Australian approach.

OTHERWISE QUALIFIED IN THE UNITED STATES[12]

Business Necessity Test

Subjecting employers' actions that have an adverse impact upon minority groups (or that discriminate indirectly against them) to the strict scrutiny to a business necessity or justification test is a familiar feature of the anti-discrimination laws of the major common law countries. In the race discrimination case of *Griggs* v *Duke Power Co.*, a landmark for discrimination law in general, the US Supreme Court stressed that the law required

> the removal of artificial, arbitrary, unnecessary barriers to

> employment when the barriers operate invidiously to discriminate on the basis of racial or other impermissible classification . . . The touchstone is business necessity. If an employment practice which operates to exclude Negroes cannot be shown to be related to job performance the practice is prohibited.[13]

In various degrees, this business necessity test survives to inform anti-discrimination law beyond race-based prejudice and beyond the jurisdiction of the USA.[14]

Regulations promulgated under section 503 of the RA 1973 require a disabled plaintiff to be capable of performing the particular job, but at the same time insist that any qualifications should be job-related and consistent with business necessity and safety.[15] Federal contractors who are subject to section 503 must review and apply physical or mental job qualification requirements ensuring that, to the extent that they screen out qualified disabled persons, they are job-related and consistent with business necessity and safe job performance. Under the ADA 1990, employers may not use qualification standards, employment tests or other selection criteria that screen out disabled persons unless they are shown to be job-related and consistent with business necessity.[16] Furthermore, medical examinations and inquiries as to disability must satisfy the job-relatedness and business necessity tests.[17]

Essential Functions Approach

In the USA, an alternative approach to the identification of a disabled individual, who is 'otherwise qualified' for the employment in question, begins with the question: can he or she satisfy the requisite skills, experience, education and other job-related requirements of the position? If so, is he or she a person who 'can perform the essential functions of the job in question'.[18] The 'essential functions' approach has been described as

> a further mediating principle between the equal treatment and equal impact paradigms. It retains a core notion of functional competence and efficiency but at the same time indicates a zone of marginal incapacity that an employer must either tolerate or accommodate.[19]

Accordingly, if a disability only prevents a person from discharging non-essential tasks or job duties, he or she is 'otherwise qualified'. In determining who is an otherwise qualified disabled person, the US Supreme Court envisioned a two-stage inquiry.[20] First, without reference to disability, it is necessary to decide whether the individual satisfies the prerequisites for the job and then, second, to determine whether he or she can perform the essential functions of the position, with or without reasonable accommodation. This two-step process is also reflected in the EEOC's ADA 1990 regulations.[21] The problem inherent in this approach, however, is how to differentiate between essential and non-essential functions of a job.

Significantly, the RA 1973 regulations did not attempt to identify any test for essential job functions. This was left to the courts on a case-by-case basis. In *Simon* v *St Louis County*,[22] for example, the plaintiff police officer had been dismissed after being shot while on duty. The defendant employer argued that his resulting paraplegia prevented him from performing the role of a police officer. Although some tasks were marginal to his present duties, the police authority insisted that he should be multi-capable in accordance with its job flexibility practices. The federal appeal court remitted the case for an inquiry as to whether an ability to perform all the tasks of a police officer was a reasonable, necessary and legitimate qualification.[23] In contrast, the EEOC's ADA 1990 regulations assay a definition of 'essential functions' of a job. At first, this is rather circular and reiterative in stressing that essential functions are 'fundamental job duties' excluding 'marginal functions'.[24] However, more helpfully the regulations proceed to explain that

> A job function may be considered essential for any of several reasons, including but not limited to the following: (i) The function may be essential because the reason the position exists is to perform that function; (ii) The function may be essential because of the limited number of employees available among whom the performance of that job function can be distributed; and/or (iii) The function may be highly specialized so that the incumbent in the position is hired for his or her expertise or ability to perform the particular function.[25]

The EEOC's interpretative guidance to and commentary upon the regulations is more expansive.[26] There is a two-stage inquiry. First, does the employer actually require employees in the relevant position to perform that function as a matter of practice? Second, if so, would removing that function fundamentally alter the job position? This second stage will involve a consideration of one or more of the factors quoted above.

The application of the essential functions test under the ADA 1990 is illustrated by the EEOC interpretative guidance. An ability to proof-read documents is clearly an essential function of the position of proof-reader in a publishing house and is the very reason the position exists at all. Furthermore, in a small employer's undertaking, the possibilities for reallocating marginal functions will be fewer and farther between. The EEOC's example is based upon *Treadwell* v *Alexander* where the employer lawfully refused to employ an applicant with a heart condition as a park technician.[27] His disability prevented him from walking more than one mile per day and the ability to walk substantial distances was an essential function of a job which involved patrolling a 150,000 acre park. There were only up to four other employees available and it was not realistic to 'double up' patrolling duties. Such problems might even arise in a larger undertaking with a fluctuating work flow cycle and labour intensity. In one case,[28] an individual with a growth disorder was denied employment as a postal distribution clerk. He could not perform the essential functions of the job because of his less than average height and reach. Because the employer's operations required multi-skilled employees to cope with heavy demand for labour-intensive work during peak periods, it was not feasible to allocate task-specific duties to the plaintiff within his capabilities. Furthermore, in the case of highly skilled or professional occupations, many tasks will be central to the position and not capable of delegation.

Each case must be decided on its merits as a question of fact. The EEOC regulations list various kinds of evidence that will be crucial to this exercise.[29] In deciding what functions are 'essential', due consideration is given to the employer's judgment, but the employer's view is not determinative of the issue. The existence of a written job description prepared in advance of recruitment and selection is considered evidence of the job's essential functions, but would not be accepted uncritically. However, in practice, it may inhibit a court from substituting its judgment for that of the employer. The plaintiff might also need to overcome a rebuttable presumption that a task contained in a job description is 'essential'. On the other hand, an incomplete job description might be used to counter an employer's claim that a task is an essential function of the job.[30] Evidence might also be brought of the amount of time spent performing the function, the consequences of it not being performed by the job-holder, the relevant terms of any collective agreements, the work experience of past holders of the position, and the current work experience of co-workers in similar jobs. For example, in *Hall* v *US Postal Service*,[31] the postal service failed to defend its job criteria, which included a requirement that workers should be able to lift up to 70 pounds weight. The evidence was that the plaintiff had never been asked to meet this criterion previously, nor did any of her co-workers perform such heavy lifting.

Best practice suggests that to comply with the law employers must identify and document the requirements for a position in terms of skills, experience and education, and should apply job analysis techniques to catalogue the essential functions of the post.[32] The legislation does not attempt to second guess the employer's choice of standards or criteria. Provided these standards and criteria are uniformly and actually imposed and required, a court will not question the reasoning behind them. However, if it is suspected that such standards and criteria were intentionally selected to exclude disabled persons from employment opportunities, then the employer might be called upon to offer a rational and non-discriminatory reason for their selection.[33] Nevertheless, despite the best efforts of the EEOC to produce a litmus test for essential job functions,

> The distinction between essential and non-essential functions . . . is ultimately artificial and is unable to provide a consistent or articulable standard for distinguishing cases. The dichotomy implies that different job functions may be rationally separated according to a pre-existing standard of evaluation . . . A non-controversial standard of differentiation simply does not exist.[34]

The regulations are probably no more than instructive and much will depend upon the lessons to be learned from cases under the RA and future litigation.[35] A recent, post-ADA 1990 example of the application of the 'otherwise qualified' standard under the RA 1973 is *Walders* v *Garrett*,[36] a case where a civilian naval employee suffering from a chronic fatigue syndrome was dismissed without being offered reasonable accommodation. The employer's evidence was accepted as showing that the essential requirements of the employment included regular and predictable work attendance, so that substantial, irregular absenteeism would undermine the employee's contention that she was otherwise qualified for the employment in question.

BONA FIDE OCCUPATIONAL REQUIREMENT IN CANADA

Under Canadian federal legislation, an employer might defend an employment decision based on disability if it can be shown to have been informed by the need for a '*bona fide* occupational requirement'.[37] A defence of *bona fide* occupational qualification or requirement is available in all Canadian provinces, with the exception of the Northwest Territories.[38] In Saskatchewan, implementing regulations provide that a reasonable occupational qualification is one:

> (i) that renders it necessary to hire members . . . of a certain physical ability exclusively in order that the essence of the business operation is not undermined; or (ii) that is essential or an overriding, legitimate business purpose; or (iii) that renders it necessary to hire members . . . of a certain physical ability exclusively in order that the duties of the job involved can be performed safely.[39]

However, this does not include an occupational qualification which is 'based on assumptions of the comparative employment characteristics' of physically disabled persons in general, or which is based on 'stereotyped characterizations' of physical disability,[40] or which is based on 'the preferences of co-workers, the employer, clients or customers'.[41]

Canadian case law is rich in examples of the *bona fide* occupational requirement exception being applied or denied. In *Ward* v *Canadian National Express*,[42] on the evidence there was no *bona fide* occupational requirement where a physically fit plaintiff with a good work record and relevant experience was refused employment as a warehouseman because he had no fingers on one hand. In contrast, in *Husband* v *Canadian Armed Forces*,[43] the armed forces minimum standards for uncorrected vision were held to be a *bona fide* occupational requirement for a military musician because even a musician could be required to carry out military tasks and the use of corrective lenses under military conditions was not practicable. In *Bicknell* v *Air Canada*,[44] the defence was made out where an airline refused to employ a licensed commercial pilot with colour vision impairment. Although he had passed federal vision standards, he could not meet Air Canada's higher standards, which had been established in good faith and had been adopted in order to maintain the highest standards of air safety. In *Gaetz* v *Canadian Armed Forces*,[45] the dismissal of a supply technician in the armed forces, who was an insulin-dependent diabetic, was successfully defended on the grounds that, for the performance of his duties, he could be required to work shifts and be stationed away from medical or food supplies. He needed to counteract his condition by an ingestion of sugar and could lapse into a diabetic coma without warning. His ability to work as required had not been demonstrated. In *Seguin* v *Royal Canadian Mounted Police*,[46] the setting of minimum uncorrected visual acuity standards for police positions involving guard duties and day-to-day police work was held to constitute a *bona fide* occupational requirement, especially where the same standards were adopted by other police forces and had previously been investigated by the Human Rights Commission without action being taken. In *Lee* v *British Columbia Maritime Employers Association*,[47] a longshoreman with complications from a childhood brain injury was dismissed without discrimination. He had a speech impediment and left-side lack of co-ordination, which the employer successfully argued prevented the employee from performing various loading tasks, from walking across the uneven surfaces of the workplace, from understanding instructions and from responding quickly to emergency situations.

An example of the *bona fide* occupational requirement defence being operated under Canadian provincial law is provided by *Cook* v *Noble, Prysianziuk, Ministry of Human Resources, and Tranquille Hospital*.[48] The plaintiff had been born with cerebral palsy, resulting in under-development of the limbs of the body's left side and some curvature of the spine. This imposed few limitations on the plaintiff's life activities. He had a previous work history involving physical activity and had recently completed a course to qualify as a community health care worker. He was refused employment in such a role in an institution for the mentally disabled. His complaint of disability-based discrimination was dismissed. The essential functions of the job included emergency lifting of patients which, based upon medical opinion, the employer concluded the plaintiff would not be able to perform. The refusal to hire was held to be fair and based upon reasonable cause. In *Cameron* v *Nel-Gor Castle Nursing Home*,[49] a plaintiff with abnormally short middle digits of her left hand was refused employment as a nursing aide after revealing the disability in a pre-employment medical questionnaire. The employer had formed the honest opinion that the plaintiff would be unable to perform gripping and lifting tasks which were components of the job, but this opinion had been reached without testing the plaintiff's abilities and without reference to any previous medical or employment records. Furthermore, the employer could not establish objectively that the disability prevented performance of the essential functions of the job. The complaint was upheld. In *Sandiford* v *Base Communications Ltd*,[50] an employee suffered an epileptic fit at work and was dismissed. The employer refused to reinstate her, despite a letter from her doctor stating that she was capable of performing the duties of a switchboard operator (the position she had held) and the evidence from her newly commenced employment elsewhere that she was rated as an above-average employee. Her complaint of disability-based employment discrimination succeeded, and she recovered lost wages and damages for humiliation. The employer could not demonstrate objectively that a requirement that a switchboard operator should not be an epileptic was a reasonable occupational qualification.

QUALIFICATION FOR EMPLOYMENT IN AUSTRALIA

Australian Commonwealth legislation expects that the disabled person must be able to carry out the 'inherent requirements' of the job in order to be protected from discrimination.[51] In New South Wales and Western Australia, discrimination informed by a person's disability is permitted if the employer has taken a reasonable view that the disabled person would be unable to carry out the work 'required to be performed', or could do so only with *unreasonable* accommodation.[52] An employer may also allow a disability, or the limitations and requirements of a disabled person, to be a factor in making employment decisions and extending employment opportunities.[53] South Australia allows employers to discriminate if a disabled person is not able adequately to perform the work 'genuinely and reasonably required' for the job in question.[54] The employer's main defence under Victorian disability discrimination law arises where a plaintiff has been shown to be unable adequately to perform the 'reasonable requirements' of the job.[55] In deciding this question, the plaintiff's past training, qualifications and relevant experience (and, where appropriate, employment performance) must be taken into account.[56]

The leading case on employment qualification or fitness for work in the Australian jurisdictions is *Jamal* v *Secretary, Department of Health*.[57] Dr Jamal had been refused employment by a hospital because bilateral cataracts had impaired his vision. This prevented him from doing fine suturing work and driving at night between different parts of the hospital. The hospital's defence was that his capacity to fulfil the requirements of the position was not the same as or similar to that of an able-bodied applicant who had been appointed to the disputed post. In short, it was contended that Dr Jamal was unable to carry out the full range of functions or duties of a hospital doctor. Suturing was part of the routine work of a medical officer while, because the hospital occupied twelve acres of grounds, it was accepted practice that doctors had to be able to drive between wards.

Although the case revolved around the question of whether the hospital should have made reasonable accommodation for Dr Jamal's impairment, an Equal Opportunity Tribunal found that the hospital had failed to demonstrate that the plaintiff could not do the work. In particular, the Tribunal decided that the hospital should have considered whether Dr Jamal could satisfy the 'essential nature' of the position and, on the evidence, the Tribunal was not satisfied that it was essential to be able to do the suturing or night driving. On appeal to the Supreme Court, Hunt J ruled that it was not the Tribunal's view of whether the plaintiff could perform the work required that mattered, but rather whether it appeared to the employer that Dr Jamal would be unable to carry out the work. Hunt J criticized the Tribunal's formulation (or introduction) of a test of the essential nature of the job and ruled that what had to be assessed was the plaintiff's ability to do the actual job applied for (and not some approximation of that job). The Court of Appeal agreed with the criticisms made by the Supreme Court:

> The clearest mistake on the part of the Tribunal was its reference to what it described as 'the *essential nature* of the job'. There is no warrant in the Act for differentiating between 'essential' and 'non-essential' aspects of the job. The Act requires a global approach to be taken . . . [It] requires consideration to be given 'with respect to *the work* required to be performed'. It is only if it appears to the employer, on grounds upon which it is reasonable to rely, that the physically handicapped person because of physical impairment would be

> unable to carry out *that* work . . . that the discrimination escapes categorization as unlawful.[58]

Hence the appellate court was of the view that, subject only to any question of reasonable accommodation, a disabled worker has to be able to satisfy all the requirements of the job. The Court of Appeal also confirmed that the test is a subjective one (in the sense of whether it appeared to the employer that the applicant was unable to perform the required work) rather than an objective one.

Although the legal reasoning in *Jamal* may be faultless in its literality, it reinforces what Astor has called the 'inflexible definition of work' in the New South Wales statute.[59] Thornton comments that

> This focus on the physically impaired person's ability to perform all aspects of the job, conceived in terms of physical normalcy, constitutes further evidence of a desire to impose an overly narrow construction on . . . [disability discrimination legislation]. It would seem that the practical effect of this interpretation is that a . . . [disabled person] would simply never be able to meet the insuperable nature of the burden, for there would necessarily always be some aspect of the job, however minor, which the applicant could not perform if a strict comparability test were to be applied, but which could constitute the subject of reasonable accommodation negotiations.[60]

It may even encourage employers to draft job descriptions with a view to excluding otherwise well-qualified disabled candidates from proper consideration. Thornton opines that

> The deference to managerial prerogative in assessing an applicant's ability to perform all aspects of the job clinches the elusiveness of the legislation as a remedial tool for people with impairments.[61]

The Victorian and South Australian legislation (but not the Western Australian statute) appears to avoid this possibility by focusing upon the work which is genuinely or reasonably required for the position in question. Astor believes that such a focus might 'persuade or require unimaginative or intransigent employers to make adjustments in job design where such adjustments are reasonable'.[62] The present writer is not so convinced. The latter formulation certainly allows a tribunal or court to scrutinize what actually happens in practice and would prevent employers deliberately designing jobs on paper to exclude disabled workers. However, it stops short of permitting scrutiny of the essential functions of a job, leading to the possibility that the employer must tolerate or accommodate the disabled employee's inability to perform marginal or non-essential functions. The requirement in Australian federal legislation that the disabled person should be able to carry out the 'inherent requirements' of the job would seem to be a beacon for reform. It would also seem to promote an objective test and demote the employer's view of what should be the necessary constituents of employment.

FUTURE SAFETY RISK

An aspect of fitness for work and qualification for employment which is worthy of separate treatment is the question of whether demonstrability that a disabled person does not represent a future safety risk is an aspect of the otherwise qualified standard or a *bona fide* occupational requirement. The importance of this issue derives from the fact that employers' obligations under health and safety laws are often used to justify employment discrimination against disabled persons. Utilization of safety-related arguments as the basis for compromising disabled employment rights reflects an often baseless fear that the nature of an employee's disabilities makes him or her an unusual safety risk. The safety risk alleged might appertain to the disabled person himself or herself, or to fellow workers, or to third parties. It might even embrace concern for a risk to property.

This is undoubtedly one area where the potentially conflicting objectives of disability discrimination legislation and health and safety laws need to be reconciled. At common law, employers owe a duty of reasonable care to provide for the occupational health and safety of their employees. In exercising that duty of care towards a disabled employee, the employer must take into account the greater risk and degree of injury faced by employees with particular disabilities. This may lead to the employer needing to take additional steps or precautions to ensure the safety of disabled workers to those that might otherwise apply to their able-bodied colleagues. For example, the need for enhanced training or closer supervision of some disabled employees might be called for. This analysis is underlined in Britain by the Health and Safety at Work etc. Act 1974, which indicates that the employer has a duty to the workforce to provide safe fellow employees, and a duty to third parties not to expose their health and safety to risk through the activities of the employer's business.

Safety Risk and Occupational Qualification in the United States

Somewhat controversially, US employers are permitted to adopt as a qualification standard a requirement that an individual shall not pose a direct threat to the health and safety of other individuals in the workplace.[63] Because this provision is offered as a defence, the burden of proof of safety risk is clearly placed upon the employer. However, the threat must involve a significant risk to health and safety which cannot be eliminated by reasonable accommodation. Avoidance of safety risk might be implied as part of the essential functions of a job under the 'otherwise qualified' standard in any event. The origin of the safety risk defence (or, at least, its authoritative judicial treatment) is the Supreme Court's decision in *School Board of Nassau County* v *Arline.*[64] The plaintiff in *Arline* had a history of tuberculosis and the court was of the view that, in order to satisfy the 'otherwise qualified' test of ability to work, the plaintiff would have to show that she did not pose a significant risk to the health and safety of others. In order to

> achieve the goal of protecting handicapped individuals from deprivations based on prejudice, stereotypes, or unfounded fear, while giving appropriate weight to such legitimate concerns of [employers] as avoiding exposing others to significant health and safety risks,[65]

the inquiry as to whether the plaintiff did pose a safety risk must be individualized and based upon objective medical evidence about the nature, duration and severity of the risk.

The EEOC ADA 1990 regulations take the premise presented by *Arline* and the Act itself, and expand it into a full-blown safety risk defence.[66] An employer may set a qualification standard that an individual shall not pose a direct threat to the health or safety of the *individual* or others in the workplace. There must be a significant risk of substantial harm to health or safety that cannot be eliminated or reduced by reasonable accommodation. This is to be determined by an assessment (based upon a reasonable medical judgment relying on current medical knowledge or the best available objective evidence) of the individual's present ability to perform the essential job functions safely. The assessment should take account of various factors, including the duration of the risk, the nature and severity of potential harm, the likelihood of such harm occurring and the imminence of potential harm. It is clear from the legislative history of the ADA 1990, as codified by the EEOC regulations, that employment opportunities should not be denied to disabled persons simply because there is a slight increase in safety risk.[67] There must be a high probability of substantial harm, rather than speculative or remote risk. The employer may only act having identified the specific risk posed by an individual, and this must be done on a case-by-case basis, avoiding stereotypes, subjective perceptions, irrational fears and patronizing attitudes. Account should be taken of all the evidence, including the view of the disabled individual, his or her prior experience in similar positions and the expert opinion of doctors, counsellors or therapists with direct knowledge of the individual or the disability.

The safety risk defence was not explicit in the RA 1973 or its regulations,[68] but it was implicit in the 'otherwise qualified' standard. The pre-1990 case law is replete with useful illustrations of the safety risk controversy.[69] For example, in *Strathie* v *US Department of Transportation*,[70] a hearing-impaired individual was rejected as a school bus driver. The federal appellate court held that it was not necessary to eliminate all possible safety risks, but only those risks which were appreciable (and this could be done with reasonable accommodation). In *Doe* v *Region 13 Mental Health–Mental Retardation Commission*,[71] in contrast, the defendant's dismissal of a staff psychologist was permitted where the defendant had substantial, rational grounds for concluding that the plaintiff's psychological condition could pose a risk to her patients. In *Mantolete* v *Bolger*,[72] an epileptic with twelve years' accident-free experience in a mechanized working environment was rejected for employment as a machine distribution clerk on safety grounds. The appellate court held that the refusal was discriminatory because an elevated risk of injury on the job was not enough; there must be a reasonable possibility of substantial harm. The case law clearly establishes that a remote chance of future safety risk is not sufficient to deny a disabled person the status of an 'otherwise qualified' individual.[73] If a remote risk or elevated risk to safety were to permit a compromising of disabled employment opportunities, almost any disabled person could be excluded from the workplace because many disabilities are capable of being characterized as presenting an increased risk of injury.[74]

It is noteworthy that the safety risk defence allows employers to discriminate where an individual with disabilities poses a heightened safety risk to himself or herself. The EEOC illustrates this point by saying that an employer could refuse to hire as a carpenter a narcoleptic who frequently and unexpectedly loses consciousness, where the essential functions of the job involve the use of power saws or other dangerous equipment.[75] However, the employer may not act upon generalized fears. For example, a job applicant with a history of mental illness should not be refused employment on the general ground that the work is stressful and this might cause a recurrence of emotional disturbance. Similarly, employers should not make assumptions (for example, about wheelchair users) concerning a disabled person's safety in evacuation of the workplace or other emergency procedures. The risk to the disabled person must be assessed on the basis of individualized and objective evidence. Despite this guidance, objection can be taken to the inclusion of a 'safety risk to self' defence in the EEOC regulations, as it goes beyond the wording of the Act.[76] This would seem to allow paternalism in through the back door and give employers additional or stronger grounds for raising the safety issue. It ignores the right of disabled persons to make judgments about their own lives and the risks that they are prepared to undertake. Disability rights advocates were unsuccessful in their attempt to get the EEOC to erase this reference to safety risk for self. It can be expected that this will be an early battleground in litigation under the ADA 1990. Under the RA 1973, moreover, a federal court had already held that a qualification for employment based on a future risk of injury to the disabled person would be subjected to special scrutiny.[77]

Safety Risk and Occupational Qualification in Canada

In Canadian federal human rights law, a *bona fide* occupational requirement will include a need to avoid posing a significant safety risk to the disabled individual, fellow employees and others.[78] Employers must rely upon medical evidence rather than uninformed assumptions,[79] but it is the employer's judgment which ultimately seems to count.[80] Health and safety requirements may also be taken into consideration in provincial law, either implicitly as a *bona fide* occupational requirement, or explicitly as a statutory concession.[81] The case law is instructive.

In *De Jager* v *Department of National Defence*,[82] there was discrimination where an asthmatic was dismissed because of a blanket policy with respect to asthmatics which was based upon stereotypical assumptions rather than medical fact and where there was no evidence that asthmatics posed a significantly greater safety risk than other employees. In contrast, in *Canadian Pacific Ltd* v *Canadian Humans Rights Commission*,[83] there was no discrimination where a diabetic was refused employment as a trackman, despite evidence that he was a stable diabetic with low odds of having a severe hypoglycaemic reaction, because there was nevertheless a real safety risk. Sufficiency of risk refers to the reality, not the degree, of risk, said the court. Similarly, in *Rodger* v *Canadian National Railways*,[84] no discrimination was found where a railwayman, diagnosed as an epileptic, was reassigned to restricted duties because the original position involved physically demanding work with heavy machinery and, if a seizure were to occur at work, there was a risk to the safety of the employee, co-workers and the general public. However, after a seizure-free period of sufficient length, a refusal to reassign to the old position might no longer be supported by reference to a *bona fide* occupational requirement, it was suggested.

In *Galbraith* v *Canadian Armed Forces*,[85] a plaintiff with a catheter as a result of colostomies failed in a challenge to the armed forces' refusal to engage him in the reserve militia because he could not meet minimum enrolment standards which screened out such applicants as being a safety risk in the field. In *Erickson* v *Canadian Pacific Express & Transport Ltd*,[86] a heavy truck driver whose hearing loss required the use of a hearing aid was dismissed because of his employer's blanket policy of not employing hearing aid users. A finding of discrimination was made because the employee met federal standards and licensing requirements and there was no evidence that the employer had tested the employee on an individual basis for evidence of work inability or increased safety risk. In *Forseille* v *United Grain Growers Ltd*,[87] the employee was a diabetic hired as a grain handler. He was dismissed when medical evidence commissioned by the employer suggested that the diabetes was unstable, although this was contradicted by the employee's medical evidence. The assessment of risk therefore had to be made by the employer, who concluded in good faith that there was a safety risk in continuing to employ the employee. The *bona fide* occupational requirement defence was made out. In contrast, in *Cinq-Mars* v

Les Transports Provost Inc.,[88] a truck driver with a congenital spine deformation was held to have been unlawfully dismissed where the medical evidence was conflicting and merely suggested a possibility of a safety risk, while the employer had re-engaged the plaintiff without restricting or limiting his driving duties.

Safety Risk and Occupational Qualification in Australia

The Victorian EOA 1984 permits disability-informed discrimination if the nature of an impairment, the working environment or the nature of the work gives rise to a likely and unreasonable risk that the disabled person will injure others or there is a substantial risk that the person will injure himself or herself.[89] In *MacLeod* v *State of Victoria*,[90] the EOB rejected a complaint of discrimination brought by a diabetic police driver where the police authority had refused to reissue his driving permit on the grounds of a poor driving record and a substantial risk of injury to himself or others. However, employers may not generalize about who or what condition represents a risk to safety. Medical evidence and other relevant factors must be accounted for.[91] It has been suggested that the safety risk exception should be restricted to cases where the employer cannot reduce the risk to a level similar to that of other employees by reasonable accommodation, but should be extended to allow for a significant risk to a person's health, safety *or property* to inform employment decisions.[92] In New South Wales, an employer's defence to disability-based discrimination arises if a person with an impairment would not be able to perform the work without endangering himself or herself or other persons or to respond adequately to reasonably anticipated situations of emergency in connection with the employment.[93]

CONCLUSION

Proposals for reform in Britain retain the concept of the qualified individual with disabilities. This will ensure that to some extent British employers will be able to predetermine which disabled persons qualify for membership of the protected class. Although the emphasis will be upon the individual's ability to carry out the essential functions of a job, with or without reasonable accommodation, there is much scope for employers to define or redefine job parameters. The prognosis is not good. In a survey of British employers, employers' perceptions of job requirements were tested.[94] The respondents were asked to identify the abilities they considered to be vital for various types of job, in the sense of whether loss of a particular ability would result in inability to carry on in the job without substantial assistance. The findings emphasize 'the extent of barriers to the employment of disabled people which still have to be surmounted'.[95] It is clear from the results that employers' perceptions of job requirements are very narrowly drawn and that this can act only to the disadvantage of disabled persons and their frequent exclusion from the scope of any new emancipatory legislation.

The need for disabled persons to prove their fitness for work and qualification for employment is inherently part of the requirement of proving membership of the protected class. As has been seen, it is an additional hurdle that must be leapt in order to have one's basic civil rights entertained. This might not seem unreasonable at first blush. However, as Burgdorf argues,

> the notion of otherwise qualified should be subsumed in the question of discrimination on the basis of disability: if an individual is denied an opportunity because of a failure to meet qualification standards, then the individual is not being disadvantaged on the basis of disability, but rather because of a failure to meet applicable job standards. In contrast, other types of civil rights laws do not require establishing membership in a protected class. These statutes focus on the discriminatory acts that occur, not the qualities of the person discriminated against.[96]

It seems incomprehensible that a person's ability to do the job or be qualified for employment should go to the question of whether or not the court or tribunal has jurisdiction, rather than to the issue of whether or not there has been discrimination on a prohibited ground.

The disappointing irony of this situation will not be lost upon disabled persons themselves. Having spent much of their lives under disability stressing their abilities rather than their limitations, they are forced in the arena of litigation to prove that they are disabled or handicapped by their impairment or medical condition. Then, having established their deviation from the 'norm', they must show that they are not so disabled that they are incapable of working. In sex and race discrimination cases, no one suggests that female or black plaintiffs should re-establish in the eyes of the tribunal their right to a hearing of the substantive issues. The legislature has established that right and it is not for the judiciary to second guess that right. Similarly, it should be sufficient in disability discrimination law to show that the plaintiff has a recognizable impairment or medical condition (or a record of one) or is perceived as disabled. The question of whether the disability predetermined the outcome of employment opportunities or whether he or she was simply not the best person for the job would then be the sole issue for the court.

A fitness for work condition or a qualification for employment requirement or an absence of safety risk proviso in any disability discrimination legislation may be neutralized or at least ameliorated if the law also requires employers to afford reasonable accommodation to the disabilities of a disabled worker. If the requirements of the job are in essence unchallengeable, then the efficacy of disability discrimination law will depend upon whether those requirements are capable of being met by other means, and whether disabled persons are allowed and enabled to demonstrate ability on their terms. We next turn to consider the role of reasonable accommodation in permitting disabled workers to compete in the labour market on an equivalent, if not equal, footing with their 'able-bodied' peers.

NOTES

1. 29 USC ss 793(a) and 794(a); 41 CFR s 60-741.1 and 28 CFR s 41.51. Although the 'otherwise qualified' requirement is not explicit in the language of 29 USC 791(b), it is assumed to be implicit by the implementing regulations: 29 CFR s 1613.703.

2. 42 USC s 12112(a); 29 CFR s 1630.4. The ADA 1990 applies to 'qualified' individuals with disabilities.

3. Flaccus, 1986b: 299–303.

4. (Can) HRA s 15(a).

5. (Alb) IRPA ss 7 and 8; (BC) ss 6 and 8; (Man) HRC s 14; (NB) HRA ss 3 and 6; (New) HRC s 9; (NS) HRA s 6; (Ont) HRC ss 11, 17 and 25; (PEI) HRA ss 6 and 14; (Québ) CHR& F s 20; (Sask) HRC s 16; (YT) HRA s 9.

6. For example: (Cth) HR&EOCA 1986 s 3; (Cth) DDA 1992 s 15; (NSW) ADA 1977 ss 49I and 49X; (SA) EOA 1984 s 71; (Vic) EOA 1984 s 21; (WA) EOA 1984 s 66Q.

7. Larson, 1986; 755.

8. See, for example, the cases cited in Larson, 1986: 754–5.

9. Nevertheless, such marginal disability cases are litigated on occasion. See, for example: *de la Torres* v *Bolger* (1983) 610 FSupp 593 (DC Tex) (left-handedness not a handicap, although it caused the dismissal of a postal worker who was unable to work quickly with his

right hand: the plaintiff was healthy and the court would not accept left-handedness as an impairment). See: McEvoy, 1988.

10. Larson, 1986: 759. See, in particular: Larson, 1988.

11. Flaccus, 1986b: 272.

12. See generally: Maffeo; Snyder, 1993 (reviewing the position under the RA 1973 and the ADA 1990).

13. (1971) 401 US 424 at 430–1.

14. See, for example, its reincarnation as the objective justification test in British race and gender discrimination law: SDA 1975 s 1(1)(b)(ii); RRA 1976 s 1(1)(b)(ii).

15. 41 CFR ss 60-741.2 and 60-741.6(c).

16. 42 USC ss 12112(b)(6) and 12113(a).

17. 42 USC s 12112(d)(4)(A).

18. 28 CFR s 41.32 (Department of Justice s 504 regulations); 29 CFR s 1613.702(f) (EEOC s 501 regulations); 42 USC s 12111(8) (ADA 1990); and 29 CFR s 1630.2(m) (EEOC ADA regulations).

19. *Harvard Law Review*, 1984: 1011. Cf. Gray, 1992.

20. *Southeastern Community College* v *Davis* (1979) 442 US 397.

21. 29 CFR s 1630.2(m).

22. (1981) 656 F2d 316 (8th Cir), *certiorari denied* (1982) 455 US 976. See also: *Bentivegna* v *Department of Labor* (1982) 694 F2d 619 (9th Cir); *Stutts* v *Freeman* (1983) 694 F2d 666 (11th Cir); *Jasany* v *US Postal Service* (1985) 755 F2d 1244 (6th Cir).

23. The trial court subsequently found that the police authority's requirements were reasonable, necessary and legitimate: (1983) 563 FSupp 76 (DC Mo). This was upheld on appeal: (1984) 735 F2d 1082 (CA Mo).

24. 29 CFR s 1630.2(n)(1) based on the legislative history of the statute: US Senate, 1989: 26. An example of a marginal job function might be a requirement of a driving licence where driving is not a major or frequent component of the actual work done or where any driving duties could be allocated to co-workers.

25. 29 CFR s 1630.2(n)(2).

26. 29 CFR Part 1630 Appendix.

27. (1983) 707 F2d 473 (11th Cir).

28. *Dexler* v *Tisch* (1987) 660 FSupp 1418 (D Conn).

29. 29 CFR s 1630.2(n)(3).

30. *Guinn* v *Bolger* (1984) 598 FSupp 196 (D DC).

31. (1988) 857 F2d 1073 (6th Cir).

32. Barlow and Hane, 1992; Phelan, 1992.

33. 29 CFR Part 1630 Appendix.

34. *Harvard Law Review*, 1984: 1011–12, written in the context of the RA 1973.

35. Holtzman *et al.*, 1992: 282.

36. (1991) 765 FSupp 303 (ED Va).

37. (Can) HRA s 15(a). See generally: Barrett, 1989 and *Attorney General of Canada* v *Robinson and Canadian Human Rights Commission* (1994) 94 CLLC para. 17,029 (Can) FCA.

38. (Alb) IRPA ss 7(3) and 8(2); (BC) HRA ss 6 and 8; (Man) HRC s 14; (NB) HRA ss 3(5) and 6; (New) HRC s 9(1); (NS) HRA s 6(e) and (f); (Ont) HRC ss 11 and 17; (PEI) HRA ss 6(4)(a) and (b) and 14(1)(d); (Québ) CHR&F s 20; (Sask) HRC s 16(7); (YT) HRA s 9(a),(d).

39. Section 1(b)(i)–(iii) of the 1979 Regulations under the Saskatchewan Human Rights Code: Sask Reg 216/79 as amended by Sask Reg 258/79 and Sask Reg 144/91.

40. (Sask) HRC Reg s 1(b)(iv) and (v).

41. (Sask) HRC Reg s 1(b)(vi).

42. (1982) 82 CLLC para. 17,012 (Can HRT).

43. (1991) 91 CLLC para. 17,030 (Can HRT); (1994) 94 CLLC para. 17,014 (Can) FCA.

44. (1984) 84 CLLC para. 17,006 (Can HRT).

45. (1989) 89 CLLC para. 17,014 and para. 17,023 (Can HRT).

46. (1989) 89 CLLC para. 17,018 (Can HRT).

47. (1989) 89 CLLC para. 17,025 (Can HRT). This is a case where a safety risk was also made out.

48. (1983) 83 CLLC para. 17,020 (BC HRC). See also: *British Columbia Forest Products Ltd* v *Foster* (1980) 80 CLLC para. 14,023 (BC SC); *Matlock* v *Canora Holdings Ltd* (1983) 83 CLLC para. 17,022 (BC HRC); *Isaac* v *Tahsis Co Ltd* (1984) 84 CLLC para. 17,007 (BC HRC).

49. (1984) 84 CLLC para. 17,008 (Ont HRC).

50. (1984) 84 CLLC para. 17,024 (Sask HRC). See also: *Anderson* v *Woloschuk & Saskatchewan Economic Development Corporation* (1986) 86 CLLC para. 17,011 (Sask HRC); *McDougall* v *Saskatchewan Transportation Company* (1989) 89 CLLC para. 17,009 (Sask QB) and (1991) 91 CLLC para. 17,006 (Sask HRC).

51. (Cth) DDA 1992 s 15(4)(a). The employer is permitted to take into account the individual's record of relevant training, qualifications, experience and employment performance, together with any other reasonably relevant factors.

52. (NSW) ADA 1977 ss 49I(1) and 49X(1); (WA) EOA 1984 s 66Q(1).

53. (NSW) ADA 1977 ss 49I(2) and 49X(2); (WA) EOA 1984 s 66Q(2).

54. (SA) EOA 1984 s 71(2).

55. (Vic) EOA 1984 s 21(4)(g). For a criticism of this aspect of the Victorian legislation, see: Johnstone, 1989.

56. Discrimination in employment terms or conditions is also permitted to take account of any limitations in working capacity or any accommodations made to enable a disabled employee to work, as well as to accord with collective bargaining arrangements: (Vic) EOA 1984 s 21(4)(i).

57. (1986) EOC 92-162 (NSW EOT); (1986) EOC 92-183 (NSW SC); (1988) 14 NSWLR 252 (NSW CA).

58. (1988) 14 NSWLR 252 at 260 (Kirby P), emphasis in the original. See, to like effect, Samuels JA at 264 and Mahoney JA at 267–9.

59. Astor, 1990: 122.

60. Thornton, 1990: 113.

61. *Ibid.*: 114.

62. Astor, 1990: 122.

63. 42 USC ss 12113(b) and 12111(3). See: Frierson, 1992a.

64. (1987) 480 US 273.

65. (1987) 480 US 273 at 288.

66. 29 CFR ss 1630.15(b)(2) and 1630.2(r).

67. 29 CFR Part 1630 Appendix.

68. With the exception of the s 501 regulations which defined 'qualified handicapped person' by reference to ability to perform the essential functions of a job 'without endangering the health and safety of the individual or others': 29 CFR s 1613.702(f).

69. See: Perras and Hunter, 1986.

70. (1983) 716 F2d 1227 (3rd Cir).

71. (1983) 704 F2d 1402 (5th Cir).

72. (1985) 767 F2d 1416 (9th Cir). See Berns, 1986.

73. See also: *Prewitt* v *US Postal Service* (1981) 662 F2d 292 (5th Cir); *Bentivegna* v *US Department of Labor* (1982) 694 F2d 610 (9th Cir); EE *Black Ltd* v *Marshall* (1980) 497 FSupp 1088 (D Haw).

74. Adelman, 1986: 157. But contrast *Leckelt* v *Board of Commissioners* (1990) 909 F2d 820 (5th Cir) where the court suggests that an HIV-positive health care worker might not be 'otherwise qualified' because of the threat posed to patients' health, even though the transmission of HIV was extremely unlikely. This would appear to be a case where the nature, severity and duration of the risk was allowed to outweigh the probability or imminence of the risk.

75. 29 CFR Part 1630 Appendix, subject to reasonable accommodation.

76. Neal, 1992.

77. *Bentivegna* v *US Department of Labor* (1982) 694 F2d 610 (9th Cir).

78. *De Jager* v *Department of National Defence* (1986) 86 CLLC para. 17,017 (Can HRT); cf. *Canadian Pacific Ltd* v *Canadian Human Rights Commission* (1985) 85 CLLC para. 17,025 (Can HRC), (1987) 40 DLR (4th) 586 (Can FCA); *Rodger* v *Canadian National Railways* (1985) 85 CLLC para. 17,019 (Can HRT); *Canadian Human Rights Commission and Husband* v *Canadian Armed Forces* (1994) 94 CLLC 17,014 (Can FCA). See the further discussion in Barrett, 1989.

79. *Erikson* v *Canadian Pacific Express & Transport Ltd* (1987) 87 CLLC para. 17,005 (Can HRT).

80. *Forseille* v *United Grain Growers Ltd* (1985) 85 CLLC para. 17,024 (Can HRT); cf. *Cinq-Mars* v *Les Transports Provost Inc* (1987) 88 CLLC para. 17,002 (Can HRT).

81. See, for example: (Ont) HRC s 11(1)(a) and (2); also s 1(b)(i)–(iii) of the 1979 Regulations under the Saskatchewan Human Rights Code.

82. (1986) 86 CLLC para. 17,017 (Can HRT).

83. (1985) 85 CLLC para. 17,025 (Can HRC), (1987) 87 CLLC para. 17,023 and (1987) 40 DLR (4th) 586 and (1987) 76 NR 385 (Can FCA).

84. (1985) 85 CLLC para. 17,019 (Can HRT).

85. (1989) 89 CLLC para. 17,021 (Can HRT).

86. (1987) 87 CLLC para. 17,005 (Can HRC).

87. (1985) 85 CLLC para. 17,024 (Can HRT).

88. (1987) 88 CLLC para. 17,002 (Can HRT).

89. (Vic) EOA 1984 s 21(4)(h).

90. (1987) AILR para. 285 (Vic EOB).

91. *Urie* v *Cadbury Schweppes P/L* (1987) AILR para. 283 (Vic EOB).

92. Law Reform Commission of Victoria, 1989 and 1990a.

93. (NSW) ADA 1977 s 71(2).

94. Morrell, 1990: 10 and Table 12.

95. *Ibid.*: 9–10.

96. Burgdorf, 1991: 442. See also the earlier analysis of Lang (1978). The burden of proof would appear to be upon the disabled plaintiff, but whether that should be so is questionable (see Schau, 1986).

9

Accommodating Difference

INTRODUCTION

Anti-discrimination legislation is based on the concept of comparability. Employers are required to treat individuals of one group in society in the same way that any other group would be treated. The comparability approach does not work well in respect of disabled people where disability creates a difference in the way in which a job can be done, so that disabled applicants are often not directly comparable with able-bodied applicants.[1] This point is well made by West:

> Often a stated goal of non-discrimination policy for persons in other stigmatized groups is to be treated in a neutral fashion, or just like everyone else; this may not be the case for persons with disabilities. The goal may be to 'forget' that the individual is a woman, or an African-American, as standards are applied. It is often said that the law should be administered in a 'color blind' fashion. While this may be the case in some situations for persons with disabilities, in other situations the goal, in fact, may be the opposite: a recognition of the functional impairment and an effort to adapt an environment or situation to enhance functioning and/or discover alternatives that will yield meaningful involvement.[2]

Accordingly, equality of opportunity requires anti-discrimination legislation to take account of the needs of disabled persons to have accommodations made for disability, save where this would cause an employer undue hardship. This necessitates a balancing act between the needs of the employer to conduct a profitable business and the aspirations of disabled people to enjoy employment opportunities.[3]

It follows that the concept of reasonable accommodation is the keystone of disability discrimination laws. Reasonable accommodation involves the making of modifications or adjustments to the employment process and to the workplace environment so as to ensure that disabled persons are not discriminated against, but may enjoy equal employment opportunities with others.[4] It has been described as:

> providing or modifying devices, services, or facilities or changing practices or procedures in order to match a particular person with a particular program or activity. Its essence is making opportunities available to handicapped persons on an individualized basis.[5]

Reasonable accommodation has also been portrayed as:

> the extent of an employer's duty to make a job amenable to a current or prospective employee who has a special requirement that imposes extra cost or inconvenience upon the employer.[6]

More simply and succinctly, Hearne has defined reasonable accommodation as 'any intervention that facilitates a person's ability to perform a job'.[7]

Although it can be argued that the principles underlying the notion of reasonable accommodation are pervasive in anti-discrimination law at large,[8] it is in the context of disability discrimination legislation that the concept is both explicit and fundamental. The philosophy of reasonable accommodation informs disabled employment policies and practices in all Western industrialized democracies but, most pertinently for present purposes, is enshrined in the language of many, but not all, equal opportunity statutes that embrace disabled persons within their protection. A requirement to make reasonable accommodation in respect of disability is a feature of the RA 1973 in the USA,[9] although that terminology does not appear in the substantive provisions of the Act. Rather, in a remarkable example of legislating via administrative rule-making,[10] the reasonable accommodation mandate emerged from the implementing regulations of the Department of Labor under section 503 in 1976, from where it proceeded to influence the content of the section 501 and section 504 ordinances. Reasonable accommodation is also central to the control of discrimination under the (US) ADA 1990. In Canada and Australia, however, the importation of a statutory directive of reasonable accommodation is not a universal feature of national or sub-national disability laws,[11] and, even in those jurisdictions where provision is made, its effect is often less than complete.

LEGAL FRAMEWORK OF REASONABLE ACCOMMODATION

The legal concept of reasonable accommodation plays four possible roles. First, it might determine whether a disabled person is within the protected class for the purposes of protection from discrimination. Reasonable accommodation is thus often an aspect of the decision whether disabled persons are 'qualified' or not, in the sense of whether they can perform the essential functions of the job. If they can do the job, with or without reasonable accommodation, then they are 'qualified'.[12] This aspect of the term has been seen in the preceding chapter and need not be explored in detail here. Second, a failure to make reasonable accommodation might be a primary act of discrimination, as might be a refusal to employ disabled applicants because the employer would have to accommodate their disabilities. Again, this has been referred to in a previous chapter. Third, reasonable accommodation might form part of the positive remedies available to a tribunal or court redressing an individual act of discrimination or fashioning a remedy to prevent future incidents of disability discrimination. This will be returned to in a later chapter. Fourth, where legislation permits, encourages or requires affirmative action, reasonable accommodation will almost invariably be a feature of such action, as will be seen subsequently. In the present chapter, however, it will be useful to examine how far, if at all, reasonable accommodation is recognized in the three countries that have specific anti-discrimination measures covering disabled persons. Moreover, the judicial reaction to reasonable accommodation must be assessed here.

United States

Federal disability discrimination laws in the USA protect qualified individuals with a disability. For this purpose, a qualified disabled individual is someone who can perform the essential functions of the job, *with or without reasonable accommodation.*[13] Furthermore, a refusal to make reasonable accommodations to the limitations of an otherwise qualified disabled person is a discriminatory act, as would be a denial of employment opportunities to such a person because the employer would have to make reasonable accommodations for him or her.[14] In addition, an employer might seek to justify the use of indirectly discriminatory qualification standards, tests or selection criteria (which are job-related and consistent with business necessity) provided that even the provision of reasonable accommodation would not equip a disabled applicant to satisfy the standard, test or criterion in question.[15]

Despite the seeming clarity of these provisions today, judicial reaction to them in the early days of the RA 1973 now appears antediluvian. The seminal case was *Southeastern Community College* v *Davis.*[16] The plaintiff, who had a serious hearing disability, wished to train as a registered nurse but was denied admission to the defendant's training programme. It was believed that she could not participate in the programme or subsequently practise as a nurse because her disability raised safety questions. Any modifications to the programme to accommodate her disability would radically alter her training as a nurse. Her complaint of disability discrimination under section 504 of the RA 1973 was dismissed by the federal district court on the ground that her disability prevented her from safely performing the role of a nurse in both training and employment, so that she was not a qualified individual protected under the statute. The federal appellate court overturned that decision, arguing that section 504 required the college to appraise the plaintiff solely on her academic and technical qualifications, without regard to her disability, and that section 504 required the defendant to modify its programme to accommodate applicants with disabilities.

The Supreme Court restored the first instance decision. Powell J, giving the opinion of the court, noted that

> Section 504 by its terms does not compel educational institutions to disregard the disabilities of handicapped individuals or to make substantial modifications in their programs to allow disabled persons to participate. Instead, it requires only that

> an 'otherwise qualified handicapped individual' not be excluded from participation in a federally funded program 'solely by reason of his handicap', indicating only that mere possession of a handicap is not a permissible ground for assuming an inability to function in a particular context.[17]

Accordingly, an 'otherwise qualified person is one who is able to meet all of a program's requirements *in spite* of his handicap'.[18] Addressing the plaintiff's argument that the college should be compelled to undertake 'affirmative action' by dispensing with parts of the training programme and providing her with individual supervision, Powell J concluded that section 504 could not be interpreted as requiring such particular accommodations. What was being proposed went beyond mere modifications in the programme and, even if the section 504 regulations required such extensive accommodations, it 'would constitute an unauthorized extension of the obligations imposed by' the Act.[19]

The decision in *Davis* was a definite setback for the proponents of reasonable accommodation and was widely criticized.[20] What is especially noticeable is the Supreme Court's interpretation of section 504 as requiring only 'evenhanded treatment of qualified handicapped persons' and excluding any mandate of affirmative action.[21] The decision is probably correct on its facts, but its *ratio decidendi* narrowed the scope of reasonable accommodation by regarding it as some form of 'affirmative action' (and, therefore, suspect as preferential treatment) rather than as properly part of the non-discrimination standard. The confusion in the mind of the court itself is evident in the following passage:

> We do not suggest that the line between a lawful refusal to extend affirmative action and illegal discrimination against handicapped persons always will be clear. It is possible to envision situations where an insistence on continuing past requirements and practices might arbitrarily deprive genuinely qualified handicapped persons of the opportunity to participate in a covered program. Technological advances can be expected to enhance opportunities to rehabilitate the handicapped or otherwise qualify them for some useful employment. Such advances also may enable attainment of these goals without imposing undue financial and administrative burdens ... *Thus situations may arise where a refusal to modify an existing program might become unreasonable and discriminatory.*[22]

The italicized portion suggests that the court could have disposed of *Davis* on its facts without muddying the waters of reasonable accommodation.

Subsequently, *Davis* was frequently distinguished by the lower courts and confined to its narrowest *ratio* to the effect that employers cannot be required to make accommodations, however reasonable, which would not assist the disabled person in any event. In *Simon* v *St Louis County*,[23] for example, a police officer was dismissed after becoming paraplegic, the employer arguing that he could not perform all the elements of police work, despite the fact that not all police positions required performance of all those elements. The contention was that he could be required to transfer from one job to another and, therefore, must be multi-capable. The court appeared unconvinced that this requirement was reasonable and of business necessity. Such a case was ripe for reasonable accommodation to be made. In *Strathie* v *Department of Transportation*,[24] a hearing-impaired bus driver was dismissed because he wore a hearing aid. The employer argued that passengers' safety could be endangered by the plaintiff losing his hearing aid, by the device suffering mechanical failure, by the driver choosing to turn down its volume to block out background noise, or by the driver being unable to localize sounds. The court, in remitting the case for a re-examination of the evidence, doubted whether reasonable accommodation had been made. The employer's fears could be met by the assurance that the driver would use a hearing aid built into his glasses, that he would carry spare batteries or submit the aid to periodic testing, that the device should be used at a preset volume, and that the driver's stereo-aided hearing be tested to determine his ability to locate sounds. In *Stutts* v *Freeman*,[25] the employer had refused to promote a dyslexic person to the position of heavy equipment operator because a low score on a general aptitude test suggested that he would be unable to complete successfully a pre-promotion training course. The employer argued that it had attempted to make reasonable accommodation by trying to get access to earlier independent tests of the employee, which he said showed him to be of above average intelligence, and by attempting to have the aptitude test administered orally. The court held that these unsuccessful efforts did not amount to reasonable accommodation.

The Supreme Court did not get an opportunity to indulge in revisionism for almost six years. That chance came in *Alexander* v *Choate*.[26] The case concerned a challenge to Tennessee's proposed reduction in the number of days in a fiscal year that the state would pay hospitals on behalf of a Medicaid recipient. It was alleged that this would have a disproportionate impact upon disabled individuals and thus was discriminatory contrary to section 504. The district court had dismissed the class action on the ground that section 504 did not address disparate impact discrimination. The federal appeal court rejected that view. The Supreme Court overruled the appellate court, assuming that section 504 did reach some forms of indirect discrimination but not the species of disproportionate effect alleged in Tennessee's budgetary prudence.

The first question before the court was whether proof of discriminatory *animus* or intent is a necessary ingredient of section 504 or whether the provision also attacks discrimination against disabled people by effect rather than by design.[27] Marshall J for the court recognized that disability discrimination

> was perceived by Congress to be most often the product, not of invidious animus, but rather of thoughtlessness and indifference – of benign neglect . . . In addition, much of the conduct that Congress sought to alter in passing the Rehabilitation Act would be difficult if not impossible to reach were the Act construed to proscribe only conduct fuelled by a discriminatory intent.[28]

However, the court could not accept that it followed that section 504 reached all actions having a disparate impact upon disabled people:

> Because the handicapped typically are not similarly situated to the nonhandicapped, respondents' position would in essence require each recipient of federal funds first to evaluate the effect on the handicapped of every proposed action that might touch the interests of the handicapped, and then consider alternatives for achieving the same objectives with less severe disadvantage to the handicapped. The formalization and policing of this process could lead to a wholly unwieldy administrative and adjudicative burden.[29]

The court was minded to balance the need to give effect to the objectives of section 504 and a desire to keep it within manageable bounds. So, having assumed that section 504 did capture some instances of indirect discrimination, what instances were within 'manageable bounds'? This would require the revisiting of *Davis* and led the court in *Choate* to explain *Davis* as striking a balance between the legal rights of disabled people to social integration and the legitimate interests of businesses and institutions to preserve the integrity of their activities. Thus:

> while a grantee need not be required to make 'fundamental' or 'substantial' modifications to accommodate the handicapped, it may be required to make 'reasonable' ones.[30]

Disabled persons are entitled to be given meaningful access to a benefit, such as training or employment, and reasonable accommodation may be necessary to assure such access. The benefit cannot be defined in a way that effectively blocks access to it for disabled persons.

Although the disabled class action in *Choate* did not succeed on its facts, it did much to restore the standing of reasonable accommodation. This process was continued in *School Board of Nassau County, Florida* v *Arline*.[31] The plaintiff school teacher had suffered relapses of tuberculosis contracted some years previously. She was dismissed on the grounds of her susceptibility to the disease. Her claim that this violated section 504 was rejected by the district court, which ruled that infection with a contagious disease did not bring her within the definition of the protected class and, even if it did, she was no longer 'qualified' to teach because of her condition. The appellate court rejected the first finding and remitted the case for a rehearing as to whether the plaintiff was 'otherwise qualified', with or without reasonable accommodation. On further appeal by the school board, however, the Supreme Court held by a majority that a person with a record of contagious disease was covered by section 504 and that tuberculosis was a protected disability (the minority held that the dismissal was by reason of contagiousness rather than impairment and that contagiousness in itself was not a disability). The case was remanded for further findings as to whether the risk of infection, if any, rendered the plaintiff not 'otherwise qualified' as a teacher. Brennan J, speaking for the majority, noted that

> Employers have an affirmative obligation to make a reasonable accommodation for a handicapped employee. Although they are not required to find another job for an employee who is not qualified for the job he or she was doing, they cannot deny an employee alternative employment opportunities reasonably available under the employer's existing policies.[32]

The rehabilitation of reasonable accommodation in the USA was complete.

Canada

The position of reasonable accommodation under federal Canadian law is not so secure.[33] Although employers are permitted to take special action to prevent, eliminate or reduce disadvantage faced by disabled individuals in employment opportunities,[34] this provides blessing only to voluntarily conceded reasonable accommodation. The federal legislation does not contain an express reasonable accommodation requirement and, furthermore, an employer might defend an employment decision based on disability if it can be shown to have been informed by the need for a '*bona fide* occupational requirement'.[35] This combination was interpreted in *Bhinder*, a case of religious discrimination, as excluding any duty of reasonable accommodation and any requirement of an individualized assessment of the impact of an employer's policy or practices upon an identifiable group of workers.[36] The decision was attacked in many quarters, not least by the Canadian Human Rights Commission, which declared:

> The effect of the *Bhinder* decision is to . . . put the Commission's ability to achieve its legislatively-defined objectives in doubt. This can mean, for example, that workplaces may not have to be modified to enable disabled individuals to earn a livelihood.[37]

Some commentators argued that this interpretation would not be applied in disability discrimination cases because, unlike religious or racial groups, disabled persons were not a homogenous class and so as a matter of necessity had to be treated on an individual basis.[38] In *O'Malley*,[39] another religious discrimination suit, the Supreme Court had ruled that in cases of adverse effects discrimination employers *are* required to attempt reasonable accommodation of an individual discriminated against by the effects of a *bona fide* occupational requirement or rule. Although a duty to accommodate was not part of human rights law, 'it was introduced by the Supreme Court as part of the baggage of the concept of "adverse effect" discrimination borrowed from the United States'.[40]

The apparent contradiction between the positions of the Canadian Supreme Court in *Bhinder* and *O'Malley* was resolved in *Alberta*

Human Rights Commission v *Central Alberta Dairy Pool*, a third religious observance case.[41] The Court ruled that in cases of direct discrimination, a work rule or condition that is a *bona fide* occupational requirement gives rise to no duty to accommodate the employee; if it is not a *bona fide* occupational requirement, then the question of accommodation does not even arise because the rule will be struck down as discriminatory. In contrast, in cases where a work rule has indirectly discriminatory effects, but is shown by the employer to be a *bona fide* occupational requirement, in order to be able to defend its use the employer has to show that there was a reasonable attempt to accommodate the plaintiff short of undue hardship.[42] The compromise achieved in *Central Alberta Dairy Pool* is still less than satisfactory, however, and McKenna, for example, has proposed that Canadian legislation should be amended to impose a positive duty of accommodation upon employers in all cases of discriminatory treatment or impact (subject to an undue hardship defence).[43]

The tensions inherent in the trilogy of Canadian Supreme Court decisions are likely to be replicated in provincial human rights statutes that contain an express *bona fide* occupational requirement exception without a countervailing reasonable accommodation duty. Nevertheless, *Central Alberta Dairy Pool* arose under Alberta's Individual Rights Protection Act and the Supreme Court's resolution of that litigation should go some way towards plugging the gap in provincial laws. A better approach, however, is that adopted in those provinces that spell out the clear distinction between direct and indirect discrimination and that require employers to make reasonable accommodation.[44] In spite of this, many argue that employment equity laws provide a more proactive solution by providing a framework in which institutionalized discrimination can be removed by collective positive action.[45] Canada's Employment Equity Act 1985 and Ontario's Pay Equity Act 1987 are often cited as model measures in this regard, and will be discussed below.

Australia

The incongruities witnessed in Canadian jurisprudence on reasonable accommodation are also evident in the Australian case law. The leading decision in Australia is the disability discrimination case of *Jamal* v *Secretary, Department of Health* under the (NSW) ADA 1977.[46] The plaintiff was a doctor with a visual disability caused by bilateral cataracts. This resulted in an inability to perform work tasks such as fine suturing and night driving, which were both job-related requirements. He had been refused employment at a hospital because of his inability to carry out the full range of tasks required to be performed. A tribunal found unlawful discrimination and held that the respondent employer had failed to prove that the plaintiff was unable to fulfil the *essential* requirements of the job or that the provision of any services or facilities required was not reasonable in the circumstances. The plaintiff could have walked or might have been driven by another colleague, while the fine suturing was an infrequent element of the work in question and could be undertaken by another doctor if it did arise.

That decision was overturned on appeal. Hunt J in the NSW Supreme Court held that section 49I of the NSW ADA 1977 did not require the employer to redefine the work to be performed. That section states that, in determining who should be offered employment, an employer is permitted to discriminate on the ground of disability if,

> with respect to the work required to be performed in the course of the employment or engagement concerned, it appeared to the employer, ... on such grounds as, having regard to the circumstances of the case, it was reasonable to rely, that the ... handicapped person, because of his ... impairment – (a) would be unable to carry out that work; or (b) would, in order to carry out that work, require services or facilities which are not required by persons who are not ... handicapped persons and which, having regard to the circumstances of the case, cannot reasonably be provided or accommodated by the employer.[47]

In Hunt J's view, this entitled an employer to reject an application if it appeared that the applicant's physical impairment would result in an inability to carry out the work or would require the provision of special facilities which would be unreasonable in the circumstances. It was for the employer to decide whether services or facilities could be reasonably provided. Section 49I was not a charter for affirmative action. Thus Hunt J falls into the same trap as the US Supreme Court in *Davis* by assuming that reasonable accommodation is some form of preferential treatment.

Astor comments that the decision of Hunt J in *Jamal* created 'significant problems for the employment prospects of people with disabilities' and demonstrated 'how a well intentioned and much needed piece of legislation can rapidly become almost useless to help those it was designed to protect'.[48] The result of *Jamal* would be to require disabled applicants for employment to demonstrate at the first hurdle that they are able to perform all the elements of the job in comparison with their able-bodied competitors. If they cannot perform all the elements of the position as *described by the employer*, or can do so only by adjustments to the manner or extent of performance, then the employer will not have treated them less favourably than in similar circumstances non-disabled persons would have been treated. They would have been treated differently because their inability to do the work without accommodation was a material difference in the circumstances. Section 49I would not need to be considered because it merely provides an employer with a defence and does not import any, or even the most minimal, requirement of reasonable accommodation. The Act would then only protect a disabled applicant who is automatically rejected for employment by an employer whose prejudice against disabled applicants is intentional and manifest. Section 49I(b) would be rarely relevant, if at all, as a disabled person who surmounts the hurdle in section 49I(a) must have been capable of doing the job without any accommodation. Where section 49I was relevant, it would be the employer's judgment of what accommodation was reasonable that would matter.

Fortunately, some of the reasoning, but not the decision, of Hunt J was subsequently overturned by the NSW Court of Appeal, having first reviewed the background to and purposes of the legislation prohibiting employment discrimination on the ground of physical disability. Kirby P, the presiding appellate judge and giving the leading judgment, relied upon the reasoning of the US Supreme Court in *Alexander* v *Choate*,[49] together with the report upon which the law reform was based and the parliamentary debates which preceded the legislation.[50] He ruled that, unless section 49I is construed as part of the provisions prohibiting disability discrimination, the effectiveness of the legislation would be nullified and section 49I would be virtually redundant. However, Kirby P then agreed with Hunt J that the statute required a global approach to the consideration of what was the work which the job required to be performed, as defined by the employer. There was no mandate in the Act which called for the employer to consider only whether an applicant could perform the *essential* elements of the job: an applicant's ability to perform the job as a whole was a relevant criterion upon which to base an employment decision. If the applicant could not perform all the elements of the job then, and only then, was the inquiry to be directed to whether the job could be carried out with reasonable accommodation. Finally, the judge agreed that the consideration of whether an accommodation was reasonable or not was a matter for the subjective judgment of the employer.

Thornton, commenting upon the Court of Appeal decision in *Jamal*, concludes that

> The deference to managerial prerogative in assessing an applicant's ability to perform all aspects of the job clinches the elusiveness of the legislation as a remedial tool for people with impairments . . . [There] is no attempt to read the section [section 49I] either in the light of the overall intention of the legislation or in the light of the employment problems arising from the ground of impairment . . . Strict literalism will always operate to legitimate the employer's decision and thereby retain the status quo.[51]

Waters observes that the net result is that the legislation

> may be of limited assistance to individuals whose handicaps have some moderate impact on their work capacities, but it is unlikely to be of much assistance to the more significantly impaired.[52]

He points out that *Jamal* is likely to influence the course of reasonable accommodation in those Australian jurisdictions, such as Western Australia,[53] whose comparable statutes are modelled upon the NSW template. Waters is more optimistic that the more objective language of the Victoria and South Australia legislation will produce a more flexible approach to reasonable accommodation in line with developments in the USA.[54] However, the Victorian legislation, like that of NSW and Western Australia, fails to express reasonable accommodation as a positive obligation, but rather incorporates reference to it as part of the excusatory language of the exception clauses where discrimination is *permitted*; a flaw that is carried forward into recent Commonwealth legislation.[55] This is hardly calculated to raise reasonable accommodation as a priority in the minds of employers.[56] The error of drafting is perpetuated solely because disability is treated as merely one of a number of prohibited grounds of discrimination in a statutory context where the paradigm is one of equal treatment. The concept of reasonable accommodation of disabled persons fits uneasily into such a model.[57]

LIMITS OF REASONABLE ACCOMMODATION

As we have seen, the mandating of reasonable accommodation of disabled persons in the workplace has been capricious in the jurisdictions that have moulded the anti-discrimination principle to fit the experience of disability. The combination of political reticence, poor legal draftmanship and antipathetic judicial reasoning has placed unnecessary limitations upon what should be the most incisive weapon in the fight against disability discrimination. The honourable exception, of course, is recent federal enactments in the USA (and the remaining discussion in this chapter will focus upon the US model), but even here some boundaries have necessarily been placed upon the concept of *reasonable* accommodation. Employers are not expected (nor should they be) to accommodate without regard for their own self-interest; but how is legitimate self-interest to be recognized?

Undue Hardship Defence

In the USA, a failure to make reasonable accommodation is subject to the defence of 'undue hardship'.[58] If the employer can demonstrate that the proposed accommodation would cause undue hardship to the operation of the business, a failure to provide accommodation is not discriminatory. In considering what would amount to undue hardship, the nature and cost of the accommodation should be looked at.[59] The availability of grants from public funds to meet the expense of the accommodation will thus be significant. The effect of the accommodation on the workplace should be examined in the context of its financial resources, its workforce, its expenses and the impact upon the operation of the site. Nevertheless, in many cases, especially where the employer is part of a corporate group, it may be necessary to widen the inquiry so as to consider the employer's overall financial resources, the overall size of the business, the type of operation and the overall composition, structure and functions of the workforce. Otherwise, there is a danger that a parent company might prefer to close a small or isolated branch or site rather than incur investment costs in making reasonable accommodation or, alternatively, might argue that compliance with reasonable accommodation will result in job losses. On the other hand, the EEOC regulations certainly contemplate that the question of undue hardship may be site-specific in certain circumstances. For example, a franchisee operating an independently owned fast-food unit, and receiving no financial assistance from the franchiser, will not be judged by the resources of the overall franchise venture.[60]

The burden of proof should be upon the employer to demonstrate undue hardship. The employer is simply in a better position to know what the job involves, to assess the options for accommodation, to apply the experience of other employers in like circumstances or to seek the advice of specialist agencies. What amounts to 'undue hardship' is a question of fact to be decided on the individual merits of the case; but the American legislation defines undue hardship as an action requiring significant difficulty or expense. What is a significant difficulty or expense is relative to the employer in question. The issue of how far accommodations should go, or what accommodations it is reasonable to make, was tackled in the leading case of *Nelson* v *Thornburgh.*[61] This was a decision cited with approval by Congress during the ADA debates.[62] A number of blind employees were held entitled to be accommodated by the provision of readers, braille forms and a braille-compatible computer. The cost of these accommodations was not insubstantial. However, in the context of the size of the programme, the employer's operation and the composition of the workforce, the cost was a mere fraction of the employer's personnel budget and, therefore, quite reasonable and not an undue hardship. The decision would clearly have been otherwise if the employer in question had been a small business with limited resources. The ADA regulations give the additional example of a visually impaired person applying for a position as a waiter in a dimly lit nightclub. The request that the club should be brightly lit as a reasonable accommodation to assist the applicant to perform the essential elements of the job will not involve the employer in any great expense. However, the accommodation is not reasonable if as a result the ambience of the nightclub is radically changed.[63]

A Costs Ceiling or Efficiency Defence?

Despite, or perhaps because of, the flexible approach in *Nelson*, subsequent cases, although demonstrating consistency of approach, do not always reveal consistency of outcome.[64] In addition, the flexibility of the undue hardship standard caused concern to many American employers. As Feldblum recognizes:

> Understandably, businesses want certainty; it is hard for an employer to imagine providing reasonable accommodation if the employer can never be sure whether a particular accommodation would ultimately be required under the law or not.[65]

Furthermore, the right to reasonable accommodations for disabled persons inevitably entails expense for employers. Thornburgh points to the need for employers to offset such costs against the benefits that can accrue at large.[66] Not only does the employer gain access to an enlarged pool of labour, but many accommodations in the workplace benefit existing employees as well. Besides, the ADA 1990 mandates the provision of technical assistance by the state for employers willing to employ disabled workers. In any case, there is no reason why the costs of accommodating disabled persons in the workplace should be onerous or cannot be subsumed within existing budgets supporting the needs of other workers.[67]

In the USA, 75 per cent of employers said that the average cost of hiring a disabled person was about the same as that for a non-disabled person.[68] Nevertheless, American businesses argued that a cost ceiling should be placed on any accommodation. Ten per cent of the annual salary of the job in question was suggested. This was rejected as tending to focus insufficiently on the employer's resources and producing a low threshold of accommodation for jobs attracting low pay.[69] A cap of 10 per cent of the employer's gross income would take no account of whether the employer's other expenses had been particularly burdensome or not that year, while a limit of 10 per cent of net income would allow employers too much discretion to allocate income to other expenses, whether or not these had a social utility. The cost of an accommodation should not be relevant to the employer's defence, in any case, where external funding or assistance is available.[70] In any event, if outside funding is unavailable and the cost of an accommodation would otherwise be an undue hardship, the disabled individual might be allowed – although never required – to contribute to the net cost of the accommodation. That means that the disabled person may be allowed to pay the proportion of the cost that is attributable to undue hardship and has not been recoverable through an alternative funding source.[71]

The costs and efficiency argument remains at the heart of the debate about reasonable accommodation requirements. Writing from an economist's perspective, Collignon comments:

> Unlike other provisions that focus on the fact that disabled

> persons may be just as productive as other potential workers, the accommodation provision recognizes that some disabled persons will *not* be as productive as other workers *unless* the accommodation occurs.[72]

This means that an accommodated disabled worker will potentially cost the accommodating employer more to employ than a non-disabled worker (or a disabled worker who does not require accommodation). It would be tempting to reflect this extra cost by depressing the wage received by the accommodated worker or to demand higher productivity from him or her to offset the cost. Moreover, that in turn would produce a separate act of discrimination informed by the worker's disabled status. However, society undoubtedly receives some benefit from the accommodation – a reduction in the social security burden, an additional contributor to the gross national product, a further source of income tax revenue etc. – but it is the individual employer who bears the cost of producing these social gains. In theory, an employer cannot seek to pass on these costs in higher prices because the competitive product market militates against such a solution. Accordingly, an employer who is committed to making reasonable accommodation will do so at the expense of profit margins. This will act as a disincentive to employers at large adopting positive policies towards disabled workers and will give an incentive to a minority of employers to look for loopholes or ways around any duty to make reasonable accommodation.[73] That argument becomes less convincing, however, if there is a general duty to accommodate placed upon all employers. Then the costs of accommodation can be passed on to the consumer in increased prices, or to the taxpayer if the costs of accommodation would qualify for tax credits or favourable tax treatment.[74]

Collignon himself rebuts these arguments.[75] First, he points out that an accommodation can improve general production efficiency by improving the working environment and practices of all workers in the workplace. As a result, the true cost of an accommodation should be calculated across all the employer's workers and should be discounted to reflect any marginal benefits which accrue to all. Second, the cost of accommodating the disabled individual will be quickly written off by evidence which supports the view that disabled workers experience lower turnover, less absenteeism and greater loyalty to employers than non-disabled workers. There might even be gains in higher productivity. Third, accommodation of a disabled worker with special skills in short supply will be self-justifying. Many highly skilled jobs are often designed around the person best qualified for the position, in any case, without such designs being labelled 'accommodations'. Fourth, for the employee who becomes disabled on the job, and for whose disabilities the employer would be liable, there are compelling reasons to accommodate the employee in order to maintain employment and reduce compensation costs.

REASONABLE ACCOMMODATION IN ACTION

The reasonable accommodation provisions of the ADA 1990, although welcomed, have also attracted predictions of practical problems and litigious issues.[76] It is less the broad scope of the Act and more the generality of its requirements that informs such concerns. It would seem that many of these problems and issues will have to be resolved by case law, which in turn will undoubtedly produce uncertainty and inconsistency.[77]

Examples of Reasonable Accommodation

In the US legislation, reasonable accommodation includes:

> making existing facilities used by employees readily accessible to and useable by individuals with disabilities; and . . . job restructuring, part-time or modified work schedules, reassignment to a vacant position, acquisition or modification of equipment or devices, appropriate adjustment or modifications of examinations, training materials or policies, the provision of qualified readers or interpreters, and other similar accommodations for individuals with disabilities.[78]

The ADA 1990 regulations categorize reasonable accommodations in three ways. First, modifications or adjustments to the job application process may be necessary to enable a qualified disabled applicant to be considered for the position.[79] Second, reasonable accommodation may need to be made to the working environment, or to the manner and circumstances in which the job is customarily performed, in order to allow a qualified disabled employee to perform the job's essential functions.[80] Third, so as to enable a disabled employee to enjoy employment benefits and privileges in equal opportunity with other similarly placed (but non-disabled) employees, it may be necessary to make further modifications or adjustments.[81]

Job restructuring entails the reallocation or redistribution of non-essential or marginal functions, or the alteration of the performance of an essential function. It should not involve a fundamental alteration of the position's particular requirements.[82] The regulations cite with approval the example of *Coleman* v *Darden*,[83] a case where an employer refused to hire a visually impaired applicant for the position of research analyst, having concluded that the possible accommodation of appointing a reader to assist the applicant would not be reasonable as it would result in the duties of employment being largely performed by the reader and not by the applicant. Despite this, it is clear that the EEOC otherwise considers that the hiring of a personal assistant might be a reasonable accommodation in some circumstances.[84]

Unlike the RA 1973 and its regulations, the ADA 1990 explicitly includes reassignment to a vacant position as an example of reasonable accommodation.[85] As the original section 504 model regulations defined 'qualified handicapped person' as a 'handicapped person who, with reasonable accommodation, can perform the essential functions of the job in question',[86] judicial interpretation was against job reassignment as reasonable accommodation. In *Carter* v *Tisch*,[87] the court held that a duty of reassignment, if any, could not be a reasonable accommodation if it flew in the face of a collective bargaining agreement. The plaintiff was thus denied reassignment to permanent light duties where such positions were reserved under the collective agreement according to seniority, a condition which the plaintiff did not satisfy. The same result was reached even in the absence of a collective bargaining agreement in *Carty* v *Carlin*,[88] where the court thought that the absence of reassignment among the enumerated forms of reasonable accommodation in the relevant regulations was significant. Furthermore, another court held that 'job restructuring', an explicit form of reasonable accommodation under the regulations, did not connote reassignment to a different job.[89] However, according to the Supreme Court decision in *School Board of Nassau County, Florida* v *Arline*,[90] if other employees were given the option of reassignment under the employer's existing personnel policies then, as a matter of equal treatment or non-discrimination (rather than as a matter of reasonable accommodation or affirmative action), a disabled person should also be offered reassignment.

These difficulties should be avoided under the ADA 1990, which not only expressly includes reassignment as a means of reasonable accommodation, but also defines 'qualified person with a disability' in a way which makes it clear that it is not only the person's current job which must be considered.[91] Mayerson adds that the legislative history of the ADA 1990 makes it clear that employers cannot use collective bargaining agreements to circumvent the objectives of the legislation,[92] although whether such agreements could be used for determining whether the accommodation was reasonable or not (for example, by articulating job-related standards for the position subject to the reassignment question) remains to be seen. The EEOC regulations under the ADA merely state that collective agreements may be relevant for determining whether an otherwise reasonable accommodation would constitute an undue hardship.[93] In any event, reassignment need only be considered in respect of positions for which the disabled person is qualified. If a vacant position is not immediately available, reassignment should only be considered if the employer knows of a position which will become vacant within a reasonable time (say, a period of a few weeks). It is also permissible to reassign to a job at a lower grade if the employee cannot be accommodated in the present job and there are no equivalent vacant positions. Ideally, the salary of the disabled employee should be 'red-circled' or maintained at its present level, but only if red-circling would also occur upon reassignment for other reasons.[94] Reassignment should not be in itself a cause of disability discrimination. Reassignment of disabled employees to segregated or undesirable work militates against the general principles of the Act.[95]

Alongside job restructuring or reassignment, the ADA 1990 also contemplates the acquisition or modification of equipment or devices as a reasonable accommodation. Reasonable accommodation could be made in the form of adaptive equipment or software to enable a disabled employee to undertake the work, albeit in a different manner.[96] The regulations further provide that disabled employees must be allowed to use their own equipment, aids or services, even if the employer would not be required to provide them as a reasonable accommodation. It is unlikely, for example, that an employer would be required to provide a visually impaired employee with a guide dog, but it should be prepared to allow such an employee to use his or her own guide dog in the workplace.[97]

Implementing Reasonable Accommodation

What will amount to appropriate accommodation will be an individualized question. The interpretation of what amounts to reasonable accommodation will be a question of fact and will necessarily vary from individual case to case.[98] In West's view,

> Unlike race and gender, . . . disability is often a dynamic and changing characteristic. A disability that may require no accommodation in one situation may demand complex technological intervention in another. Furthermore, some disabilities change in their intensity from day to day or week to week and may require different accommodation at various times. The same impairment often affects individuals differently. A critical aspect of accommodations is flexibility.[99]

Feldblum argues that

> The basic characteristic of a reasonable accommodation is that it is designed to address the unique needs of a person with a particular disability . . . The underlying goal is to identify aspects of the disability that make it difficult or impossible for the person with a disability to perform certain aspects of a job, and then to determine if there are any modifications or adjustments to the job environment or structure that will enable the person to perform the job.[100]

The legislative history of the ADA 1990 makes it clear that the search for reasonable accommodation should result from a dialogue or consultation between employee and employer.[101] Congress suggested a four-step procedure and this is now reflected in regulations.[102]

First, in order to identify the barriers to equal opportunity, the essential and non-essential elements of the job and the abilities and limitations of the worker must be determined. Second, by consulting the employee and then external sources of expertise, the employer should identify possible accommodations. Third, the employer must assess the 'reasonableness' of the possible accommodations, weighing both how effective the accommodation might be and whether it will promote equality of employment opportunity for the individual. Fourth, the employer must select and implement the most appropriate accommodation, subject to the 'undue hardship' considerations. Mayerson writes:

> In the light of this structure, the governing principle in determining an appropriate reasonable accommodation is whether it provides the person with the disability an opportunity to attain the same level of achievement as a person with comparable ability and without a disability.[103]

Of course, disabled persons can refuse a proffered reasonable accommodation, but might thereby disqualify themselves from protection under the Act.[104] Equally, an employer cannot be expected to make reasonable accommodation for disabilities of which the employer is unaware. If an accommodation is necessary, the disabled person must draw this to the employer's attention; alternatively, the employer may ask whether reasonable accommodation is required.[105] In this latter situation, the employer walks a tightrope because such an inquiry needs to be framed without reference to disability in order not to fall foul of the general prohibitions on disability-related questions.[106]

Extent and Experience of Reasonable Accommodation

Undoubtedly, employers' willingness to make reasonable accommodations increases a disabled person's chances of working.[107] In the USA, the evidence suggests that 35 per cent of disabled workers with employment experience had encountered employers who were prepared to make some accommodation in the workplace. LaPlante projects that some 23 per cent of disabled persons who report being unable to work would be able to work if employers were amenable to accommodating them in the workplace environment.[108] He also forecasts that up to 44 per cent of disabled persons limited in the kind or amount of work that they can do would enjoy increased employment opportunity if the working environment was to be more adaptable. However, research points to a clear correlation between size of employer, propensity to recruit disabled employees and likelihood of undertaking expensive accommodations. One survey found that the participation of disabled workers in the respondents' labour forces was 2.5 per cent, but for larger firms this participation rate was 3.5 per cent.[109] This leads Collignon to observe that

> efforts to expand the employment of disabled individuals, especially those requiring accommodation, might wisely be

> focused on larger firms, rather than on the small business sector.[110]

That observation is borne out by a survey of accommodations in the small business sector. It found few examples of expensive accommodations and that employers made appeals to constraints on management time as an explanation for lack of action.[111]

American employers' fears that reasonable accommodation requirements would entail frequent and costly actions is not borne out by the evidence.[112] In one US study of the placement of severely disabled persons in federal government employment, fewer than 16 per cent of such persons required accommodation and, in the main, such accommodations as were required were incidental.[113] This finding was also corroborated by an investigation into compliance with section 504 of the RA 1973 by public agencies.[114] A further large scale study was undertaken of private sector employers contracting with the US federal government and, therefore, subject to section 503 of the RA 1973.[115] About 55 per cent of respondent employers had experienced the need to make reasonable accommodation for disabled workers, 17 per cent employed disabled workers without accommodation and 28 per cent had no record of employing disabled persons. As to costliness, the consistent finding of detailed surveys of employers has been that expensive job modification or accommodation is rarely needed by disabled workers.[116] In one survey, just over half of reported accommodations cost nothing, a further fifth cost less than $100 (at 1982 prices), while four-fifths of accommodations cost less than $500.[117] A 1987 study found that 50 per cent of accommodations cost less than $50 and 69 per cent cost less than $500.[118]

The types of accommodations reported by federal contractors were manifold and no particular example emerged as commonplace. Most workers required more than one accommodation, and there was a tendency for the more expensive accommodations to be targeted at the more skilled workers and at those whose disability was particularly handicapping (blind workers and wheelchair users). Provision of special equipment or adaptations to the workplace tended not to be aimed at less skilled workers, for whom job redesign, retraining and selective placement were more usual accommodations.[119] The chance of a worker being accommodated for disability would be greater if the worker became disabled on the job or while in employment rather than being disabled already at the time of recruitment. Interestingly, one-fifth of disabled employees in firms covered by the survey reported unmet needs for accommodation. The same percentage (although not necessarily the same respondents) reported that accommodations made had improved their career potential. Thirty per cent of employers thought that accommodations had improved disabled workers' career mobility and advancement. Exactly one half of respondent employers concluded that making accommodations had increased productivity, while 39 per cent felt that the costs of accommodation had been more than covered by the benefits of accommodation.[120]

A limitation of many of these surveys is the difficulty in judging how accurate the data responses are. Information about the costs of accommodations may not be stored or collated methodically. Respondents may be unaware of many inexpensive or marginal adjustments made to working practices or the workplace.[121] This under-reporting can be exacerbated by the fact that many workers do not identify themselves as disabled and thus the making of accommodations cannot be linked with them. Furthermore, management respondents tend to measure the costs of accommodations only in terms of direct expense. Little, if any, account is taken of indirect costs (or opportunity costs), such as management time, internal labour costs involved in constructing or adapting accommodations, or materials costs where these are subsumed within existing maintenance budgets. The true costs of reasonable accommodations must account for these items.

BRITISH EMPLOYERS AND REASONABLE ACCOMMODATION

Reasonable accommodation of disabled applicants and employees is not a legal requirement in Britain. If law reform were to make it so, one might expect an outcry from employers, arguing that it imposes upon them undue regulation and a further burden on business. The arguments that greet disability rights legislation elsewhere would be rehearsed. None the less, the evidence suggests that many British employers already practise elective reasonable accommodation and that compulsion would cause many businesses little concern.

For example, in research carried out in the late 1980s, about 30 per cent of British employers had experienced an employee becoming disabled while in their employment in the previous two years.

In about two-fifths of cases, the newly disabled employee had been retained in employment, with or without retraining or accommodation, via shorter hours or modified workload. However, about one-fifth were absent on long-term sick leave and, in the remaining two-fifths of cases, the employee had left or retired or could not be accounted for.[122] Among employers who were employing disabled workers generally, approximately 20 per cent of establishments reported undertaking job restructuring to accommodate disability. Special training or retraining was mentioned by about 15 per cent of establishments, and the same percentage of employers made changes to existing equipment or furniture. Superficial adaptations of premises were necessary in 16 per cent of cases, and structural adaptations to premises were attempted in about 12 per cent of cases. Granting extra time off or instituting a shorter working day for the disabled worker was mentioned in about 11 per cent of instances, with flexible working hours being a feature of about 10 per cent of examples of accommodations.[123]

The SCPR survey found that 10 per cent of economically active, occupationally handicapped respondents had a need for special equipment or aids. Such need was greatest among those in professional and related occupational groups, and for those respondents with sight disabilities, hearing impairment or mental handicaps.[124] Some 8 per cent of respondents presently in work indicated that there was special equipment that they did not possess, but that would help in their job. Again, this report was highest among those in the professional and related occupational groups, and among those with the disabilities involving sight, hearing or mental handicaps (including, on this occasion, mental illness or nervous disorder).[125] Prescott-Clarke remarks:

> the range of items mentioned was wide, and this, coupled with the fact that the number naming *any* of them was small, makes it not very useful to break the results down very far.[126]

Such evidence shows the type of needs that disabled workers might ask employers to accommodate and demonstrates that such needs are not overwhelming. In fact, it was calculated recently that the average cost of equipment supplied under the Department of Employment's Special Aids to Employment Scheme was £906 at 1993 prices.[127] The SCPR survey demonstrates that about 10 per cent of disabled workers would require accommodation in respect of access to and accommodation within the workplace, and that the most commonly mentioned accommodations were lifts and hand rails, followed by access ramps and special washroom facilities.[128]

What percentage of disabled workers reported any accommodation of their disabilities by their employers? Using evidence from the OPCS surveys,[129] only slightly more than one quarter of disabled workers reported any accommodation of their disabilities by their employers, although 15 per cent thought that no provisions were necessary in any event. The most frequently reported accommodation was to allow a disabled worker time off or to keep the job open. Other examples of accommodation cited included job modification, provision of specially designed jobs, allowance of different hours, provision of special aids or equipment, arrangement of adaptations, modification of conditions and provision of special training. Interestingly, among disabled workers reporting that their disability did not affect their current job, only 8 per cent replied that their employer had made provision for their disability and 24 per cent that no provisions were necessary.[130] Of those who said that their disability did affect the current job, 42 per cent said that their employer had made provisions for them and 8 per cent that provisions were unnecessary. The nature of the research data, however, means that it is impossible to explore the underlying causes of this finding or to draw broad conclusions from it.

CONCLUSION

A mandate of reasonable accommodation is an essential feature of any effective disability discrimination law. Without a condition that employers should be required to recognize difference and accommodate it within workplace policies and practices, many (but by no means all or even a majority of) disabled persons will be denied true equality of opportunity. The idea of reasonable accommodation has often been misunderstood and mistaken as a form of preferential treatment or positive action. This has coloured the reaction of both legislators and judiciary to the original inclusion and subsequent interpretation of the reasonable accommodation ingredient in disability discrimination measures. The compromising of reasonable accommodation in Australian statute law and its misinterpretation and misapplication in Canadian case law demonstrates this point. Instead, as in the US legislation, reasonable accommodation must be seen as an integral part of the non-discrimination standard. It should not be regarded as a species of affirmative action, thereby attracting heightened scrutiny, judicial suspicion and narrow application. Although any future introduction of mandatory reasonable accommodation for disabled workers in Britain will undoubtedly cause practical problems for some employers, the evidence suggests that for many employers such a development will merely formalize existing voluntary practices. Reasonable accommodation as an explicit legal concept may even influence the advancement of sex and race discrimination norms, as employers come to recognize the need to acknowledge and to entertain difference.

The erroneous association of reasonable accommodation with forms of preferential treatment, however, will be a difficult perception to erase in the minds of many employers. Nevertheless, a degree of preferential treatment, in the true sense of that expression, has been tolerated for disabled workers in Britain for much of the twentieth century, and without any serious suggestion that this offends any fundamental principles of justice or equality. In the next chapter we turn to consider the role of preference and the use of quotas as a response to disability discrimination and disadvantage in the workplace.

NOTES

1. Astor, 1988: 79–80.
2. West, 1991b: 8.
3. Astor, 1988: 80.
4. 29 CFR s 1630.2(o).
5. US Commission on Civil Rights, 1983: 139. See also: US Department of Labor, 1982.
6. Dolatly, 1993: 524.
7. Hearne, 1991: 124. In its legal sense, the term 'reasonable accommodation' originated under US law requiring employers to accommodate employees' religious practices. See: 42 USC s 2000e(j) and *Trans World Airlines* v *Hardison* (1977) 432 US 63.
8. For example, in gender discrimination, an employer might be said to have a duty to 'accommodate' pregnancy and maternity or, in race discrimination, cultural differences (as in dress codes).
9. See generally: Martin, 1980; Kelly, 1986; Sklar, 1986. For a comparison of the position under federal and state disability discrimination laws, see: Kaufman, 1987; Flaccus, 1986b.
10. Scotch, 1984; Percy, 1989.
11. See, for example: (Can) EEA 1985 ss 2 and 4; (Man) HRC ss 9(1)(d), 11 and 12; (NSW) ADA 1977 ss 49I(1) and 49X(1); (WA) EOA 1984 s 66Q(1); (Cth) DDA 1992 s 15(4)(b).
12. The reasonable accommodation question is thus treated as part of the 'otherwise qualified' inquiry: *Brennan* v *Stewart* (1988) 834 F2d 1248 (5th Cir). This ensures that

'employers may not summarily determine what qualifications they wish to impose and then hold individuals with disabilities to them': Burgdorf, 1991: 458, citing 42 USC s 12111(8).

13. 42 USC s 12111(8) (ADA 1990); 29 CFR s 1613.702(f) (RA 1973 s 501 regulations); 41 CFR s 60-741.2 (RA 1973 s 503 regulations); 28 CFR s 41.32 (RA 1973 s 504 regulations).

14. 42 USC s 12112(b)(5) (ADA 1990); 29 CFR s 1613.704 (RA 1973 s 501 regulations); 41 CFR s 60-741.6(d) (RA 1973 s 503 regulations); 28 CFR s 41.53 (RA 1973 s 504 regulations).

15. 42 USC s 12113(a). This is implicit in the RA 1973 s 501 and 503 regulations: 29 CFR s 1613.705(a) and 41 CFR s 60-741.6(c). See also: 28 CFR s 41.54 (RA 1973 s 504 regulations).

16. (1976) 424 FSupp 1341 (ED NC); (1978) 574 F2d 1158 (4th Cir); (1979) 442 US 397 (US SC). For a critique of the impact of this case upon the reasonable accommodation requirement, see: Olenick, 1980.

17. (1979) 442 US 397 at 405 (footnote omitted).

18. *Ibid.* at 406 (emphasis added).

19. *Ibid.* at 410.

20. See, for example: Egan, 1979; Butler, 1980; Forsyth, 1981.

21. (1979) 442 US 397 at 410–11.

22. *Ibid.* at 412–13 (emphasis supplied).

23. (1981) 656 F2d 316 (8th Cir), *certiorari denied* (1982) 455 US 976.

24. (1983) 716 F2d 227 (3rd Cir).

25. (1983) 694 F2d 666 (11th Cir).

26. (1985) 469 US 287; *sub nom Jennings* v *Alexander* (1981) 518 FSupp 877 (MD Tenn); (1983) 715 F2d 1036 (6th Cir).

27. (1985) 469 US 287 at 292.

28. *Ibid.* at 295 and 296–7 (footnoted omitted).

29. *Ibid.* at 298, citing *Harvard Law Review,* 1984: 1008 in support of this analysis of the problems of applying indirect discrimination theory in the context of employment discrimination against disabled persons.

30. *Ibid.* at 301.

31. (1985) 772 F2d 759 (11th Cir); (1987) 480 US 273. The first instance decision is unreported.

32. (1987) 480 US 273 at 289.

33. See generally: Ratushny, 1986; Barrett, 1989; Taras, 1992.

34. (Can) HRA s 16(1).

35. (Can) HRA section 15(a). This section also includes exceptions based on the age of an individual (e.g. in respect of retirement or pensions). Federal Bill C-108, introduced in December 1992, would have amended the (Can) HRA so as to require employers to make reasonable accommodation for the needs of protected minorities, including disabled persons.

36. *Bhinder* v *Canadian National Railway Co* (1985) 23 DLR (4th) 481 (Can) SC.

37. Canadian Human Rights Commission, 1986: 4. See also: Berlin, 1985.

38. See, for example: Barrett, 1989: 167–9, relying upon the earlier arguments of Gittler, 1978: 979.

39. *O'Malley* v *Simpson Sears* (1985) 23 DLR (4th) 321 (Can SC). The case originates under Ontario's Human Rights Code.

40. McKenna, 1992: 330.

41. (1990) 72 DLR (4th) 417 (Can SC), a decision under Alberta's Individual Rights Protection Act. For a commentary on the case see: Vizkelety, 1991; Taras, 1992.

42. For a discussion of this decision and the different approaches of the majority and the minority in the court, see: McKenna, 1992: 334. The minority (concurring in the result) argued that reasonable accommodation was a necessary part of establishing that an occupational requirement was *bona fide* in the first place in both direct and indirect discrimination.

43. McKenna, 1992: 336–7.

44. See, for example: (Man) HRC s 9(1)(d) in combination with s 9(3); (Ont) HRC s 11 in combination with s 17. Ontario's HRC requirements are supplemented by guidelines to employers for the assessment of reasonable accommodations for disabled workers: Ontario Ministry of Citizenship, 1989.

45. McKenna, 1992: 338.

46. (1986) AILR para. 433 and (1986) EOC 92-162 (NSW EOT); (1987) AILR para. 280 (NSW SC); (1988) 14 NSWLR 252 (NSW CA).
47. (NSW) ADA 1977 ss 49I(1) and 49X(1).
48. Astor, 1988: 79.
49. (1985) 469 US 287, discussed above.
50. Anti-Discrimination Board (NSW), 1979 and 1981.
51. Thornton, 1990: 114.
52. Waters, 1990: 404.
53. (WA) EOA 1984 s 66Q which is based on s 49I of the NSW Act.
54. (SA) EOA 1984 ss 66(d) and 71(2), as amended in 1989; (Vic) EOA 1984 s 21(4)(g). See the concurring view of Astor, 1990: 122.
55. (Cth) DDA 1992 15(4).
56. This criticism of weak draftsmanship is echoed by Johnstone, 1989: 729.
57. This criticism is made more cogently by Nothdurft and Astor, 1986: 340–1 and by Astor, 1990: 119. The NSW ADB has recommended in its annual reports that the NSW ADA 1977 should be amended to include a positive obligation to make reasonable accommodation, subject to undue hardship, along American lines.
58. See, for example, under the (US) ADA 1990: 42 USC s 12112(b)(5). See: Crespi, 1990; Gardner and Campanella, 1991.
59. 42 USC s 12111(10).
60. 29 CFR s 1630.2(p) Appendix. See also: Shaller and Rosen, 1991: 419.
61. (1983) 567 FSupp 369 (ED Pa), *affirmed* (1984) 732 F2d 146 (3rd Cir), *certiorari denied* (1985) 469 US 1188. See Schreiber, 1984; Janis, 1986. See also: *Gardner* v *Morris* (1985) 752 F2d 1271 (8th Cir).
62. US House of Representatives, 1990b: 41. See Mayerson, 1991b: 519.
63. 29 CFR s 1630.2(p) Appendix.
64. Dolatly, 1993: 537.
65. Feldblum, 1991c: 95.
66. Thornburgh, 1991.
67. Job Accommodation Network, 1987; Du Pont and Company, 1990.
68. Louis Harris and Associates, 1987: 9. See also: US Commission on Civil Rights, 1983: 106–8; National Council on the Handicapped, 1988: 15.
69. Jones, 1991a: 484; Mayerson, 1991b: 518.
70. 29 CFR s 1630.2(p) and Appendix (for example, in the form of tax credits or a vocational rehabilitation agency grant). To support employer efforts of compliance with the ADA 1990, the US Congress also fine-tuned the tax code so as to allow businesses some relief for ADA-related expenditure: Schaffer, 1991. Note also the provisions for financial support and technical assistance from federal agencies authorized under the ADA to assist employers to better comprehend and comply with their obligations under the Act: ADA s 506; 42 USC s 12206 (and see also: 29 CFR s 1630.9(c)).
71. 29 CFR s 1630.2(p)(2)(i) and Appendix.
72. Collignon, 1986: 206 (emphasis in the original).
73. *Ibid.*: 207.
74. See Schaffer, 1991.
75. Collignon, 1986: 207–11. At least one health economist takes a diametrically opposed set of views. Chirikos (1991) argues that the ADA 1990 will lead to more severely disabled persons entering employment and that they will require expensive accommodations.
76. See for example: Barnard, 1990; Cooper, 1991; Lavelle, 1991; Murphy, 1991; Shaller, 1991; Stuhlbarg, 1991; Weirich, 1991; Stine, 1992; Schiff and Miller, 1993; Dolatly, 1993. Some commentators have been hostile to the reasonable accommodation requirement: Holtzman *et al.*, 1992.
77. Dolatly, 1993: 544.
78. 42 USC s 12111(9). See further: Cooper, 1991; Weirich, 1991.
79. 29 CFR s 1630.2(o)(i).
80. 29 CFR s 1630.2(o)(ii).
81. 29 CFR s 1630.2(o)(iii).
82. 20 CFR ss 1630.2(o)(2) Appendix and 1630.2(n) Appendix.

83. (1979) 595 F2d 533 (10th Cir).
84. 29 CFR s 1630.2(o) Appendix (page turner for manually disabled employee or sight guide to assist blind employee during occasional business trips) but without further guidance.
85. 42 USC s 12111(9). See 29 CFR s 1630.2(o)(2)(iii); cf., for example, 45 CFR s 84.12 under the RA 1973. The doubts about whether reassignment was a required form of reasonable accommodation under the pre-1990 law are explored by Tate (1989). See now: *Fedrov Reno* (1994) 21 F3d 1391 (7th Cir).
86. 45 CFR s 84.3(k)(1).
87. (1987) 822 F2d 465 (4th Cir).
88. (1985) 623 FSupp 1181 (D Md).
89. *Alderson* v *Postmaster General* (1984) 598 FSupp 49 (WD Okla).
90. (1987) 480 US 283.
91. 42 USC s 12111(8) defining a qualified disabled person as an 'individual with a disability who, with or without reasonable accommodation, can perform the essential functions of the employment position that such individual holds or desires'. Cf. 45 CFR s 84.3(k)(1) defining a qualified handicapped person as a 'handicapped person who, with reasonable accommodation, can perform the essential functions of the job in question'.
92. Mayerson, 1991b: 515.
93. See further on this point Shaller and Rosen, 1991: 419. The interaction of the reasonable accommodation mandate and collective bargaining agreements is expected to cause much confusion and scope for litigation. See generally: Ervin, 1991; J. Smith, 1992; Mello, 1993; Stahlhut, 1993.
94. 29 CFR s 1630.2(o) Appendix.
95. 29 CFR s 1630.5.
96. Jones, 1991a: 483; Mayerson, 1991b: 510.
97. 29 CFR s 1630.2(o) and Appendix.
98. This is the view taken under the comparable provisions of s 504 of the RA 1973: *Alexander* v *Choate* (1985) 469 US 287; *Southeastern Community College* v *Davis* (1979) 442 US 397. Reasonable accommodation of individuals with certain types of disabilities (such as mental disabilities, alcoholism, drug dependence or substance abuse) will challenge the imagination of employers, but does not necessarily present insuperable difficulties: Haggard, 1993. The focus upon an individualized inquiry means that employers must not make assumptions about the possibilities (or impossibilities) of reasonable accommodation.
99. West, 1991b: 8–9.
100. Feldblum, 1991c: 93–4.
101. US Senate, 1989: 34–5; US House of Representatives, 1990a: 66; 1990b. See the EEOC regulations to the same effect: 29 CFR s 1630.2(o)(3).
102. 29 CFR s 1630.9 Appendix.
103. Mayerson, 1991b: 516.
104. 29 CFR s 1630.2(o) Appendix.
105. 29 CFR s 1630.9. An employer might request documentary evidence of the need for the accommodation.
106. Frierson, 1992b.
107. Nagi, 1975.
108. LaPlante, 1991: 71.
109. US Department of Labor, 1982.
110. Collignon, 1986: 217.
111. Premus and Carnes, 1982.
112. See generally: Combs and Omvig, 1986.
113. O'Neill, 1976.
114. Johnson and Associates, 1980.
115. US Department of Labor, 1982.
116. Collignon, 1986: 211. Burkhauser (1990), however, has argued that the costs of reasonable accommodation will be sizeable, but he argues in this way because he believes that the ADA 1990 cannot be made to work unless the federal government is willing to finance the implementation of the legislation from public expenditure. His position can be expected to be bolstered by the arguments of Chirikos, 1991.

117. US Department of Labor, 1982: Vol. 1, 29; Collignon, 1986: Table 8.1.
118. Job Accommodation Network, 1987. Fewer than 1 per cent of accommodations cost over $5,000. See Hearne, 1991: 126.
119. US Department of Labor, 1982: Vol. 1, 56–7 and 66; Collignon, 1986: 217–27.
120. Collignon, 1986: 228–9.
121. Collignon, 1986: 214.
122. Morrell, 1990: Table 22.
123. *Ibid.*: Table 23.
124. Prescott-Clarke, 1990: Tables 12.1 and 12.2.
125. *Ibid.*: Tables 12.3 and 12.4.
126. *Ibid.*: 139 (emphasis in original) and see *idem*: Table 12.5.
127. *Employment Gazette* Vol. 101 No. 8 at 434 (September 1993).
128. Prescott-Clarke, 1990: Table 12.6.
129. Martin *et al.*, 1989: Table 7.30.
130. *Ibid.*: 84.

10

Quotas and Preferential Treatment

INTRODUCTION

In Britain, the orthodox position in discrimination law holds that all sex-conscious or race-conscious discrimination is unlawful. Formal justice requires that like cases should be treated alike and that the characteristics of gender or race are irrelevant factors in employment decisions. This orthodoxy militates against the use of the law to permit preferential treatment in favour of women and racial minorities. Thus 'reverse' or 'benign' or 'inclusive' discrimination is prohibited. Preferential treatment (or reverse discrimination) describes the process by which applicants or employees are given priority over equally qualified or better qualified candidates for employment opportunities, and where the preference is informed by the distinguishing characteristics of a disadvantaged group.

The application of the anti-discrimination principle to disability would seem to produce a similar conclusion to that obtaining in discrimination law at large. Disability-conscious employment decisions in favour of disabled persons would be proscribed, even though such decisions might be said to be 'benign' rather than 'malign'. Yet, for the best part of fifty years in Britain, the primary legal strategy for protecting disabled workers in the labour market has been a statutory quota scheme, supported by reserved occupations, in which, in theory at least, disabled persons have been accorded some preferential treatment in employment competition. The continued role of the quota scheme, if any, is a central feature of the analysis in this chapter. We commence that analysis by looking at how employment quotas fit into discrimination theory.

Quotas, Preferences and Discrimination Theory

The arguments in favour of preferential treatment or reverse discrimination have been recently reviewed by Pitt.[1] Pitt's concerns are with women and ethnic minorities, but her analysis is recruited to the present discussion of disabled persons. She points out that reverse discrimination is often justified by appealing to the argument that 'it is intended to make up for past systemic discrimination against' disadvantaged groups or minorities, and 'is a kind of remedy for past deprivation of opportunity'.[2] Appeals to the compensation argument to justify preferential treatment of disabled persons in the labour market are ill-founded. Borrowing from Pitt's analysis, the present writer believes that reverse discrimination in favour of disabled persons must be viewed as 'a counterbalancing measure, attempting to compensate for the inherent bias in the system'.[3]

An alternative approach is to seek comfort in arguments based upon social utility. Increasing the representation of disadvantaged and minority groups in employment brings a number of potential benefits in its wake. The removal of disabled claimants from unemployment and social security benefit programmes will result in savings in public expenditure. Their employment in turn leads to increased revenues from direct taxes, increased consumer spending and consequent additional revenues from indirect taxation. In addition, the employment of a previously marginalized group will add to productivity and to the gross national product. Furthermore, disabled employees would gain access to promotion opportunities and would provide role models for other disabled individuals to emulate. The social and vocational integration of preferred disabled persons would break down the barriers of misunderstanding between the disabled and non-disabled worlds, which in turn would reduce the prospects of continuing disability-based discrimination. In short, immeasurable social benefits might accrue from reverse discrimination in favour of persons with disabilities.

The social utility argument is one based upon expediency rather than principle, and is not without flaws. Without necessarily associating herself with the counter-arguments, Pitt puts the opposing view in the following terms:

> The policy might reinforce feelings of inferiority in those who benefit from it, and cause others to assume that they must be second rate . . . There might be an increase in social tension

> because the dominant group would feel a strong sense of grievance if they were themselves victims of discrimination. And far from healing divisions in society, reverse discrimination would actually make people more aware of [disability] ... In a similar vein, it is suggested that not to choose the best person for the job regardless of [disability] would lead to overall inefficiency.[4]

In the original, Pitt is referring to race and gender where the term 'disability' appears in square brackets, but the quotation has been adapted to fit the present context. While there might be some merit in the counter-argument based on reinforcement of the perception of inferiority, the risk of increased social tension were reverse discrimination to be applied to disability seems unlikely. It has not been suggested that existing disabled quota schemes, for example, have been anything but accepted or welcomed by the 'able-bodied' community. Making society more aware of disability might cause discomfiture, uneasiness or embarrassment for some, but would be an attractive by-product of preferential treatment.

Finally, the contention that abandoning the merit principle would produce greater inefficiency misstates the preferential treatment argument. It is not suggested that disabled persons preferred for employment should not be 'otherwise qualified' for the work in question. In any event, any loss of efficiency could be outweighed by gains in other dimensions, as was noted during the discussion of reasonable accommodation in the previous chapter. In short, discrimination theory could easily withstand the concession of preferential treatment based upon disability status. In the following section, the operation of disability preferences in practice is discussed.

DISABILITY AND EMPLOYMENT PREFERENCES

Reserved Occupations

As described in Chapter 2, certain classes of employment are reserved for registered disabled persons on the grounds that they afford especially suitable disabled employment opportunities. The employment of passenger electric lift attendant and car park attendant have been singled out as designated occupations. Any employer, whether or not otherwise subject to the quota scheme, who engages or employs a person other than a registered disabled person in such reserved occupations commits an offence, subject to parallel exceptions to those in the quota scheme. Registered disabled persons employed in reserved occupations do not count towards the fulfilment of the employer's statutory quota.

The Tomlinson Committee did not intend that the scheduled occupations should become regarded as the proper employment objective of disabled persons without regard to individual intelligence or capacity.[5] In spite of that, the reserved occupations do tend to reinforce the prejudice that disabled workers are only capable of low-grade, low-paid employment, and such provision 'should not form part of any policy which is seriously attempting to improve the lot of workers with disabilities'.[6] Furthermore, when the quota scheme was reviewed in the 1970s, the Department of Employment opined that designated employment or reserved occupations had 'never made any very substantial contribution' to disabled employment opportunities.[7] With the increasing use of automatic passenger lifts and barrier-operated car parks, such opportunities must have declined even further. The evidence suggests nevertheless that nearly 90 per cent of disabled persons supported the principle of designated occupations, although this figure dropped to 70 per cent when the reservation of the jobs of car park or lift attendant was specifically mentioned.[8]

The Piercy Committee considered whether further reserved occupations might be designated, but decided that

> in practice, designation can be applied only to low-grade employment, and any extension of the scheme might encourage the mistaken and undesirable belief that disabled persons are only capable of that type of work.[9]

In 1979, the Manpower Services Commission expressly rejected any attempt to extend the range of designated occupations to include more popular and higher status jobs, although such an idea appeared to attract support from disabled people.[10] Sixty-five per cent of disabled respondents surveyed supported this idea.[11] The most frequently mentioned occupations to which designation might be extended were telephonist or telex/switchboard operator, clerical work, receptionist, security jobs, gardener, cloakroom/toilet attendant, 'doorman' or commissionaire, cleaning work, assembling and sorting. Other occupations receiving particular mention included typing work, traffic warden or meter attendant, porter, cashier or check-out operator, shop assistant, road sweeping, messenger, packer, storekeeper, stock-taker and machinist.[12] Almost needless to say, increasing the numbers of reserved occupations would be an unpopular proposal among employers.[13] It is equally unlikely to attract governmental support. Accordingly, the future of the reserved occupations would seem to be inextricably bound up with the future of the quota scheme.[14] In 1981, the logical step was taken to recommend the abolition of reserved occupations.[15] However, it was thought that 'practical realities, rather than philosophical arguments, point to the need to continue the scheme' during a period of high unemployment.[16]

Background to the Disabled Quota Scheme[17]

The problem of how to provide open employment opportunities for disabled workers was first addressed in Britain in the peculiar labour market conditions of the First World War. Government was reluctant to plan for the future problem of how to reabsorb disabled ex-servicemen into employment after the war. Not for the first time, this reluctance was partly explicable by a desire not to alienate employers or trade unions. Nevertheless, proposals arose in other quarters for a Royal Appeal to employers which would take the form of a voluntary commitment by employers to employ what would be effectively a 5 per cent quota of disabled workers in their workforces. These suggestions played upon employers' sense of patriotism, which would be rewarded and acknowledged in a published roll of honour.

Not surprisingly, these proposals were not met with universal approbation. The trade unions and the Labour Party, for example, feared the exploitation of disabled workers. The Ministry of Labour simply refused to recognize that there was a dearth of employment opportunities for disabled war pensioners. The official view was that the existing machinery worked quite well enough, that employers would only reserve menial jobs (such as gatekeeper or doorman) for disabled persons and that employers could not be expected to commit themselves to a quota of any percentage until they had reinstated their own returning ex-employees. Despite that unpromising background, there soon emerged a voluntary scheme of the very type proposed. In the face of growing unrest among ex-servicemen experiencing a worsening financial situation amid worsening employment opportunities, clamour for reform brought suggestions of a 4 per cent quota of disabled workers to be compulsory for employers.[18] Instead, the Government's response was to adopt a national scheme for the employment of disabled war veterans. The scheme began in September 1919 and, instigated by Royal Proclamation, was known as the King's National Roll. Employers were asked to engage disabled war pensioners up to at least 5 per cent of their workforce, that being the approximate percentage of war pensioners among the total working population. Employers who met this obligation would be entered in a Roll of Honour and be entitled to use a dye on their documentation to show their compliance with the aims and objectives of the scheme.

The King's National Roll did not have an auspicious start. Not for the first time in these matters, employers found ways around the scheme. Local government employers were apathetic to it and many employers preferred to prioritize the re-engagement of industrially injured workers. Key trade unions were also ill-disposed towards it. Furthermore, government departments were outside the scheme and fewer than 20 per cent of employers had entered the Roll.[19] Bolderson records the view, apparently prevalent in government circles at the time, that state compensation and pension provisions were an adequate substitute for disabled employment opportunities.[20] This was not a view shared by disabled war veterans themselves, and the call for employment openings and training provision was loudly heard. Interest was being expressed in the experience of other European countries, which had established compulsory employment schemes to assist disabled ex-service personnel.[21] Particular interest was shown in the French model, which incorporated a 10 per cent quota obligation and extended to war pensioners, but only as and when vacancies arose. The Select Committee on Training and Employment of Disabled Ex-Servicemen nevertheless rejected a compulsory scheme.[22] Instead, the Select Committee recommended that the King's National Roll should continue for at least another year. As Bolderson comments,

> The King's Roll with minor adjustments and a slightly improved system of grants to undertakings employing severely disabled ex-servicemen staggered on until 1971 . . . [having] gained a little more substance by arrangements made in 1921 and subsequently in 1926 to restrict government contracts to firms on the Roll.[23]

Modified compulsion was seen as a solution of last resort. However, the solution of last resort soon became the solution of choice.

Bolderson records that the inter-war years had seen pressures from the trade union movement and the medical profession for reform of workmen's compensation.[24] This had led to calls for comprehensive rehabilitation services. With the outbreak of the Second World War, these pressures became irresistible and the influence of Ernest Bevin, the Minister of Labour, began to exercise itself upon the problem. The Tomlinson Committee was appointed with terms of reference to consider and make recommendations for a comprehensive scheme for the rehabilitation and training of disabled persons of all categories, and for securing satisfactory employment for them.[25] The Committee was especially anxious to take account of the views of the trade union movement, which could be expected to oppose any proposals that led to disabled workers struggling to retain jobs beyond their capacities or being forced into light work with inadequate wages. The possibility of a legally sanctioned pool of cheap labour, undercutting the position of the able-bodied worker, was one that trade unionists would not countenance.[26] It was against that background that there emerged the Tomlinson proposals for a disabled quota, backed by a register of disabled persons handicapped in employment, plus reserved occupations and employment protection for disabled workers.

Most employers accepted the Tomlinson proposals on the basis that there would be a moral obligation towards employing disabled individuals after the war and that the quota was an expression of that obligation.[27] However, not all employers were well-disposed to the recommendations, and arguments were fashioned against them based upon fears of bureaucratic controls, skills shortages and prejudices about the capacities and production efficiency of disabled persons. Particular concern was voiced about penalties for non-compliance and the limitation upon the employer's prerogative of dismissal. Employers were largely mollified by assurances from the Government that prosecutions for non-compliance would not be lightly embarked upon, assurances that have influenced the subsequent enforcement and destiny of the quota scheme. Although the passage of the Bill giving effect to the Tomlinson Report was not entirely without event,[28] the Tomlinson recommendations finally received the Royal Assent on 1 March 1944 in the guise of the Disabled Persons (Employment) Act 1944 and were brought into force in stages over the next two years.

Ingredients of the Quota Scheme

As described in Chapter 2, the DP(E)A 1944 obliges employers of at least twenty workers to employ registered disabled persons up to a standard quota currently fixed at 3 per cent. It is estimated that the scheme covers 59 per cent of the employed population and applies to some 34,000 employers.[29] Although it is not binding upon the Crown, government departments have accepted that the principle of the quota applies equally to them.

If an employer is not employing the quota of registered disabled persons at times when vacancies occur, vacancies must be allocated for this purpose. An employer shall not employ, or offer to employ, any person other than a registered disabled person if, immediately after employing such other person, the employer is below quota.[30] The legality of the employment of a person resulting in breach of the statutory quota scheme is unaffected, but contravention of this duty is a criminal offence. The statutory quota does not apply to the filling of vacancies by an employer with an exemption permit. An exemption permit will be issued, if expedient, in the light of the nature of the employment vacancies, and the qualifications and suitability for that work of available registered disabled persons. Permits will also be granted if there are no (or insufficient numbers of) registered disabled persons available for that work. A permit may authorize the employment in identified occupations of named individuals or a specified number of non-registered individuals. Alternatively, a bulk permit may allow the employment of a specified number of workers during the following six months, although the employer is still notionally (although not legally) bound to notify vacancies and consider sympathetically registered disabled persons available during the permit's currency.

CRITICISM OF THE QUOTA

Despite the apparent advantage that disabled persons are given in the labour market by the statutory quota, the scheme has been a manifest disappointment. The quota scheme has been characterized as 'ineffective, unenforceable and incapable of achieving its aim'.[31] The scheme has been the subject of much dissatisfaction within the disability rights movement, and has been under almost continuous review within and outside government since the early

1970s. During 1994, the quota was once again under review: this time in the hands of the House of Commons Employment Committee. In this section we examine the various practical criticisms that have been made of the quota scheme.

Awareness of the Quota Legislation

Research reported in 1978 found that only 20 per cent of disabled respondents had knowledge of the quota scheme although, with prompting, this figure rose to 70 per cent.[32] Research undertaken in 1987 by IFF Research Ltd, and reported by Morrell in 1990, tested employers' awareness and understanding of the quota scheme. Morrell found that approximately 40 per cent of employers employing under 100 employees (but twenty or more employees, and thus in principle subject to the quota) were unaware of the quota scheme or its requirements. In contrast, over four-fifths of head offices of multi-site employers were aware of the scheme, although only three-quarters of branch sites of such firms had heard of the legislation.[33] These findings suggest that the quota scheme suffered from widespread ignorance of its existence among employers but that, in larger enterprises and at the centre of multi-branch organizations, awareness was greater than in small or single unit undertakings.

Nearly half the respondents were unaware that it was a criminal offence not to comply with the quota without a permit, while just over one-third could not identify the level at which the quota was set. On the other hand, only one-fifth of employers did not know that the scheme applied to workforces of twenty or more employees, and one-tenth were not aware that the quota only applied to registered disabled persons.[34] The quota scheme does not appear to exercise any great influence over employers in making personnel decisions. Just over three-quarters of employers reported that the scheme had never influenced a decision to recruit or retain a disabled worker and only one-fifth of respondents thought that the scheme generally encouraged the employment of disabled people. It was thought that the lack of enforcement of the scheme had produced this ambivalence towards it. There would appear to have been little contact with the enforcement authorities among the employers surveyed.[35]

Compliance with the Legislation

There are two ways in which the efficacy of the quota scheme may be measured: the average rate of compliance and the proportion of firms who comply. Taking the first measure, official statistics indicate that the 3 per cent quota has not been achieved since 1961.[36] By 1965, the average rate of quota compliance had fallen to 2.7 per cent and by 1970 to 2.3 per cent. The compliance rate continued to fall in the following decade, reaching 1.9 per cent by 1975 and 1.5 per cent by 1980. By 1985 the rate of compliance had dropped to 0.9 per cent and by 1993 to 0.7 per cent. Quota compliance in the public sector has been habitually poor. Between 1986 and 1990, the Government estimates that the percentage of registered disabled persons employed in the public sector has been constant at 0.8 per cent. The 1993 figures, for example, show that the average rate of quota compliance in county councils, London boroughs and district councils varied from 0.7 to 1.2 per cent of their workforces.[37] In the National Health Service, the compliance rate does not exceed 0.6 per cent (although two health trusts are believed to be up to quota). Nationalized industries and public authorities manage to employ registered disabled persons as only 0.6 per cent of their workforce. The leaders in the field are government departments, with an average quota rate of 1.5 per cent, but even here compliance is variable. A recent report from the TUC estimates that if public sector employers were to reach the quota level, some 92,000 disabled persons would cease to be unemployed.[38]

These figures of non-compliance do not necessarily buck a trend observable under comparative quota systems. Under the German disabled quota system, for example, a 6 per cent quota has been set. The evidence suggests that among public employers the quota is being broadly met (5.9 per cent), whereas among private employers the quota is being under-achieved (4.7 per cent).[39] About one-fifth of German employers met or exceeded their quota obligations, a further two-fifths were in partial compliance, but as many as 30 per cent of employers employed no disabled workers at all. French employers are similarly failing to meet their quota obligations under the 1987 quota law. On 1989 statistics, at a time when the quota level was set at 4 per cent, an average of 3.6 per cent of posts were filled by disabled workers and this appeared to represent a ceiling upon disabled employment opportunities.[40] The following year, when the quota had graduated to 5 per cent, the quota actually achieved was only 3.8 per cent, although the number of disabled persons being recruited had increased substantially from 5,600 in 1987 to 9,600 in 1990.[41]

The second measure of quota compliance – the proportion of employers meeting their obligations – is no more edifying. Research undertaken by the Department of Employment in a London district in 1970 revealed that, of 222 firms covered by the quota scheme, 35 per cent were at or above quota and 65 per cent were below quota. Of the 144 firms below quota, 53 per cent were below 2.5 per cent and 31 per cent were below 1.5 per cent.[42] At that time, this could be partly explained by the fact that the numbers of registered disabled persons had declined while the national labour force had increased, thus causing the average rate of quota compliance naturally to deteriorate. More recently, the Department of Employment has estimated that only about 19 per cent of employers currently meet their quota obligations.[43]

Registration as Disabled

It has often been contended, with little room for dispute, that the 3 per cent quota is statistically unattainable by employers subject to the scheme, as long as the number of registrations remains so low. In 1973, for example, it was calculated that if all unemployed registered disabled persons were to be recruited by employers subject to the quota obligation, the average level of compliance would still only be 2.75 per cent.[44] Furthermore, in 1979, when quota compliance was 1.7 per cent, if all unemployed registered disabled persons were to have been recruited, the national rate of quota compliance would have risen only to 2.1 per cent.[45] On 1982 calculations, if employers subject to the quota employed all unemployed registered disabled persons, the total number of registered disabled workers in their employment (including those already employed by them) would not have exceeded 1.9 per cent of their workforce.[46] More recently still, the Department of Employment has estimated that it is arithmetically impossible for all employers to meet a quota of 3 per cent since registered disabled people make up only about 1 per cent of the workforce.[47]

Registration as disabled under the DP(E)A 1944 is therefore crucial to the success of the statutory quota scheme. Only registered disabled persons are eligible to be counted towards employers' general obligation to maintain a 3 per cent quota of disabled employees. Registration as a disabled person under the 1944 Act has declined throughout the post-war years, although simultaneously the number of disabled persons registered for social welfare purposes was rising. In 1946, some 482,221 persons registered and by 1950 there were 936,196 registered disabled persons. During the 1960s, the register remained pretty static, although the period 1960–70 saw a drop from 691,724 to 634,336 persons on the register. In the following decade, the number of registrants fell more quickly to 557,217 in 1975 and to 470,588 in 1980. Since then, the decline has been uniform. In 1985, the register stood at 404,170 and by 1990 had fallen still further to 355,591. At April 1993, the number of registered disabled persons was computed as 371,734 and, although it is the case that during the 1990s the number of registrations has risen, the shortfall since 1988 has not yet been made good.[48]

Research reported in 1978 found that only 19 per cent of disabled persons surveyed were registered. Of disabled persons in employment, only 15 per cent had registered, as opposed to 27 per cent of unemployed disabled persons.[49] A decade later, the OPCS surveys sought to discover the extent to which disabled adults under pension age registered their status as disabled persons under the 1944 Act. Only 14 per cent of disabled adults under pension age had registered: an estimated 300,000 registrations.[50] Martin, White and Meltzer narrate that of those disabled adults who had reported being in work, 16 per cent had registered under the 1944 Act, whereas of those looking for work or intending to look for work (but temporarily ill), or available for work but not looking, the proportions for registration were 21, 12 and 17 per cent respectively.[51] Significantly, 16 per cent of those who regarded themselves as permanently unable to work and 13 per cent of those assessing themselves as retired (but under pension age) had registered under the legislation. In a separate survey for the SCPR, Prescott-Clarke found that only 13 per cent had a valid 'Green Card' (i.e. had registered under the Act).[52] Extrapolation from these data suggests that there should be a total of 175,000 registered disabled persons who are economically active or anticipate being so in the next twelve months. In contrast, at the time of the survey, the Department of Employment had approximately 367,000 registrations.[53] Therefore, both the OPCS and the SCPR surveys imply a much lower figure of registrations under the Act than is actually recorded. Prescott-Clarke suggests that the discrepancy might be partly explained by registrants who were no longer economically active or who were simply confused about the terminology of registration. It is also interesting to note that 84 per cent of the disabled respondents to the SCPR survey were separately assessed by officials as *registrable* under the 1944 legislation.[54] Of these, 80 per cent were in work, suggesting an estimated population of 854,000 persons registrable as disabled and in employment.

These data call for some explanation of disabled persons' attitudes towards registration. There are various possible reasons for the reluctance of disabled people to register under the 1944 Act, although the relative importance of each is difficult to judge.[55] First, many disabled persons may not have heard of the scheme. Second, many disabled persons may not require the forms of protection and assistance that are a by-product of registration. Third, once in employment, a disabled employee may see little purpose in registering or in renewing registration, especially as, after minimum periods of service, employees enjoy greater protection under the general provisions of employment law as opposed to the 1944 Act. Fourth, there is a perceived stigma of inferiority in the status of 'registered disabled person'. Fifth, many individuals with less visible disabilities are unwilling to declare their disability. Sixth, some medical advisers may counsel against registration as disabled if a person's self-esteem were to be devalued and his or her rehabilitation thereby hampered by this action. Seventh, many disabled people do not recognize or regard themselves as disabled. Eighth, registration is not seen as being essential, either because the quota scheme is regarded as ineffectual or because disabled employment services are open to all regardless of registration. Ninth, many disabled persons do not wish to be separately identified in a way which might hamper their social acceptance and integration into the workforce. Tenth, disabled people may simply see no advantage in registration.

Many of these possible reasons for non-registration are borne out by the evidence. Many 'disabled persons' simply do not regard themselves as 'disabled', regardless of medical or legal classification.[56] In research among disabled persons who had not registered under the 1944 Act, 36 per cent did not consider themselves disabled, 19 per cent said registration was not necessary, 16 per cent reported that their disability was only minor and 11 per cent did not know about registration.[57] Prescott-Clarke found that most economically active disabled persons had not heard of the register. Only 59 per cent of disabled respondents had heard of the disabled persons' register.[58] Awareness of the register was highest among disabled employees and lowest among disabled persons who anticipated wanting to work in the near future. Overall, men were more likely than women to be registered as disabled. For example, Prescott-Clarke found that 64 per cent of economically active disabled males and 53 per cent of economically active disabled females had heard of the register, while 18 and 7 per cent respectively had a valid 'Green Card'.[59]

These latter figures are comparable with the OPCS survey findings. The proportion of disabled adults registered as disabled also appears to increase with the severity of disability, except in the highest severity categories where severely disabled persons are less likely to be economically active. Disabled men were also more likely to register as disabled where their occupational status fell in the lower reaches of the socio-economic hierarchy (junior non-manual, semi-skilled manual and unskilled), but no pattern emerged in respect of disabled women.[60] Overall, it is gender, disability severity and employment status that seem to influence registration. Age is an uncertain variable, as Prescott-Clarke found that knowledge of the register increased with age, but actual registration was more likely in the 25–34 and 35–44 years age groups than for younger or older disabled workers.[61]

The SCPR survey demonstrates that, of those who had registered as disabled, 29 per cent did so in order to assist themselves in getting a job, but a surprising 18 per cent had no conscious motive in deciding to register.[62] Some 37 per cent had registered upon the advice of third parties and a further 8 per cent had registered on the advice of an employer. Among disabled persons who had not registered (but who were aware of the scheme), nearly half regarded registration as inapplicable to them, a quarter had never thought about registration and a fifth averred that they had never needed a 'Green Card'.[63] In fact, registration was thought of as a disadvantage by 5 per cent of this group. Prescott-Clarke's analysis makes the following points:

> Not surprisingly, those having a card were more likely to see advantages than those without a card, particularly in respect of getting work. Two-thirds of those without a card who were economically active thought that there were no advantages, or could not think of any. Around two-thirds of those with a card could think of no disadvantage to being on the Register – the majority saying positively there were no disadvantages. Similar proportions of those not on the Register knew of no disadvantages.[64]

Nevertheless, about a quarter of all respondents believed that registration as disabled was a positive handicap to entering employment and about 10 per cent felt that registration compounded the process of being labelled as 'disabled' and 'abnormal'.[65] Indeed, the evidence suggests that registered disabled persons fare no better, and often worse, than unregistered disabled persons in the incidence and duration of unemployment or in successful placement into employment.[66]

Enforcement of the Quota

The enforcement of the quota scheme is perhaps most controversial. Employers must keep records, open to inspection, relating to the employment of registered disabled persons and quota compliance, and ought to make annual returns to Job Centres, whose staff regularly draw the quota obligation to employers' attention. Some 2,000 inspections per year have been carried out and infringing employers could expect follow-up visits.[67] Up to half of these inspections reveal infringements and an identifiable number of infringements remain uncorrected even after a follow-up visit. However, only ten prosecutions (eight successful) have been brought during the history of the scheme.[68] The two unsuccessful prosecutions concerned a failure to keep records and a dismissal of a registered disabled person while below quota. Six of the successful prosecutions concerned engagements without permit while below quota and resulted in an admonishment, a £20 fine, a £4 fine, a £10 fine, a £50 fine (two charges) and a £200 fine (two charges) respectively. Two cases concerned dismissals without reasonable cause and resulted in a £50 fine plus costs and a £100 fine plus costs.[69]

The authorities are believed to receive legal advice that counsels against prosecution in cases where employers are already employing *unregistered* disabled employees.[70] In any event, the penalties for breach of the quota may be of little deterrence to employers ignoring their statutory obligations, as was recognized by an unsuccessful attempt to raise them in the Companies (Disabled Employees Quota) Bill 1986. Undoubtedly, the inability of employers to meet the quota in principle, consequent upon the decline in the numbers of registered disabled persons, makes enforcement academic. Previous attempts to enforce the quota more rigorously only resulted in employers putting pressure on *existing* employees to register rather than leading to new engagements.[71] In 1975, for example, a campaign of strict enforcement of the quota scheme was conducted as a six-month experiment in six towns. This resulted in an increased number of applications from disabled persons to be placed upon the register, some increases in the number of applications for exemption permits and a small increase in the number of notified vacancies for disabled workers.[72] Two prosecutions also resulted, producing fines of £25 and £200 respectively. However, there was no noticeable change in the employment position of disabled persons as a consequence. Zealous enforcement of the law is thus seen to be counterproductive to the coterminous strategies for placement of disabled persons into employment. Emphasis is upon education, advice and encouragement rather than prosecution. The existence of the quota scheme appears to have had little impact upon the outlook or actions of employers who are below quota. Where employers are reminded that they are below quotas, it is often the case that their first response will be to persuade existing employees with disabilities to register under the 1944 Act.[73] The majority of employers in compliance with the scheme comply primarily out of a sense of social responsibility.[74]

It is highly unlikely that the approach to enforcing the disabled workers' quota will change in the near future. In 1992, judicial review proceedings were brought by a disabled individual against the Department of Employment, challenging the Government's apparent policy of not enforcing the 1944 legislation.[75] The plaintiff, a registered disabled person with multiple sclerosis, was concerned that the Department had failed to prosecute her former employer following her dismissal as a secretary 'without reasonable cause' contrary to section 9 of the Act. The Department's defence was that it had no such policy of non-enforcement, but that it attempted to resolve cases of statutory breach by negotiation and advice before consideration would be given to prosecution. In practice, however, the prosecuting authorities are unlikely to recommend a decision to prosecute unless there is a high probability of success on the evidence. It is also suggested that prosecutions may not be in the interests of disabled persons and would thus not be in keeping with public policy generally. The case was withdrawn before the matter came to trial.

Abuse of Exemption Permits

While the proportion of employers fulfilling quota has been in free fall, the number of employers below quota but holding permits has risen inexorably. Nearly 60 per cent of all employers subject to the scheme have been issued with exemption permits.[76] Bulk permits now represent 98 per cent of all permits issued.[77] The issuing of bulk permits is designed to reduce the amount of time spent upon routine administration of the scheme. Consequently, the Department of Employment has previously admitted that it is difficult to ensure that the issue of a permit is justified by an employer's individual circumstances.[78] The Department suspects that many below-quota employers recruit non-disabled persons without first obtaining a permit and that many employers issued with bulk permits do not notify vacancies as they are supposed to do. In view of the fact that the Department of Employment cannot withhold permission for an employer to recruit an able-bodied worker unless it is satisfied that a suitable registered disabled person is available for the position, and that the employer's view of suitability is likely to be decisive, the issuing of permits is often a formality. There was also evidence that

> the process of permit application has become a matter of routine for many below quota firms – a twice yearly exercise which has only a minimal impact on their policies and practices.[79]

Research carried out in 1978 showed that many employers regard the provision of permits as a right rather than a discretionary concession, enhancing their view that permits provided automatic exemption from the law.[80]

REFORM OF THE QUOTA SCHEME

Fifty-six per cent of disabled persons strongly favoured special legislation to help disabled people to find and keep work and a further 38 per cent favoured such laws.[81] About nine in every ten disabled persons favoured or strongly favoured quota legislation.[82] On the other side of the fence, there is strong evidence that employers would favour changes being made to the quota scheme. Research in 1979 indicated that employers were generally happy with the quota scheme. They believed that special statutory protection was essential, but opposed strict enforcement or extra legislative obligations.[83] However, just over half the employers interviewed in the IFF Research survey thought that the scheme should be changed, with this opinion being the strongest held among large employers.[84] Less than one-third of employers would vote for the status quo. At least half of the employers interviewed thought that the quota scheme could be usefully amended by increasing awareness of the scheme, having different levels of quota for different employers, including all disabled persons within its scope, or providing incentives to disabled people to register. There was little support for making registration compulsory. Fewer than one-third of employers favoured changing the 3 per cent level, altering the definition of disability, making different permit arrangements or altering enforcement procedures.[85]

It may be that any reform of the quota will be doomed from the start, as any successor scheme would be tainted by the failure of its predecessor.[86] Nevertheless, the arguments for retaining a statutory system imposing obligations upon employers were summarized by the Manpower Services Commission in its 1979 review of the quota scheme:

> [a] Clearly expresses society's concern for the protected group; [b] Can set minimum standards which, if achieved, will offer some real protection to the group; [c] Can keep the issue before employers and the public by requiring procedures, submission of records or accountability to an enforcing authority; [d] Can be used, if appropriate, to force people to take action.[87]

The Commission considered five possible arguments for doing away with statutory protection.[88] First, the minimal impact of existing statutory measures suggests that non-statutory methods might achieve equally adequate protection for disabled workers. Second, the bureaucracy associated with a flawed scheme diverts resources and staff time that might be better employed in helping persons with disabilities in other ways. Third, a statutory scheme that lacks credibility can be counterproductive. In order to make the scheme work, more rigorous enforcement would be necessary. This might antagonize employers and undermine efforts to encourage disabled employment opportunities through voluntary action. Fourth, the decline in registration might suggest that some disabled persons no longer require the protection of a statutory scheme. Fifth, the statutory scheme singles out disabled persons for special treatment. This conflicts with the merit principle and the right of disabled persons to full integration. To these arguments can be added a sixth objection. The quota scheme is an unambitious way of helping disabled workers, for it extends its influence only marginally beyond recruitment and says little about the quality of disabled employment opportunities once in work.[89] However, before we examine the possible abolition of the quota legislation, we shall first assess various proposals for its root and branch reform.

Disabled Persons Covered by the Quota

Whether the quota scheme is retained and amended or whether it is replaced, for example, by anti-discrimination legislation, some means of identifying disabled persons for statutory purposes will need to be devised.[90] One possibility would be to devise a multi-purpose system of identification, so that recognition as disabled for one purpose would count as recognition for all purposes. So, for example, receipt of certain social security benefits or assistance from social welfare services would also designate the individual as being a disabled person for the purpose of employment law. Another possibility would be to insist upon registration under the 1944 Act as a precondition to access to other rehabilitation, training and employment services. A third suggestion would be to provide inducements to register. Giving disabled persons incentives to register has been considered and rejected on more than one occasion.[91] In its 1981 review of the quota scheme, the Manpower Services Commission considered whether disabled people might be given incentives to register in the form of tax relief.[92] The Commission doubted whether any additional incentives would overcome disabled persons' existing reluctance to register and feared that it might simply lead to disabled *employees* moving on to the register, with a consequent artificial boost to quota compliance. Incentives based upon tax relief were also seen as costly options, as well as placing disabled people in a preferential position *vis-à-vis* other disadvantaged individuals.[93]

Allowing employers to count *unregistered* disabled persons towards quota compliance would seem superficially to be a more attractive option. It might be regarded as more equitable, might encourage a greater willingness to comply with the law, could improve the chances of pursuing employers in breach, and would result in a more easily administered permit system.[94] This solution, however, also brings its own difficulties. First, it would be difficult to identify those employees who would count as disabled for this purpose. Registration resolves that problem. It might be that this reform would still require some degree of certification, but this presents problems for uniformity in treatment.[95] Second, why should employees who have not voluntarily chosen to identify themselves as disabled be labelled in this way, perhaps against their will and in contravention of medical confidentiality? Third, such a reform hardly improves the employment position of disabled people, but merely makes life easier for employers (although identifying disabled employees would create new problems for employers too). Fourth, logically an increase in the percentage of the labour force that is recognized as disabled should lead to an increase in the level of the quota; but to what level and with what further consequences for attainment and compliance? This latter difficulty, however, might be illusory now that there are better statistics on the numbers of disabled persons who are or seek to be economically active.

Despite these problems, survey evidence suggests that nearly six out of ten disabled people would favour the inclusion of unregistered disabled persons in the quota count, and the large majority of these held to their opinion even when it was pointed out that this would mean that employers would need to know who was disabled.[96] Fewer than half the respondents could suggest alternatives to the voluntary registration system. Of these, 51 per cent suggested that disabled individuals could be identified from medical records, 13 per cent through hospitals, 11 per cent through social welfare services and 13 per cent through other public agencies holding such information.[97] These suggestions do not appear very appealing. In any case, and by whatever means, the inclusion of unregistered disabled people within the scope of the quota system would obviously create problems for enforcement and verification. Employers suggest that these problems could be overcome by keeping records for inspection, instituting check-ups on employers or requiring medical evidence of disability.[98] Employers were confident that they could correctly identify those members of their workforces who would be counted for this purpose, although there was recognition that some workers might conceal disability or that disabilities that did not affect working ability might be overlooked.

Stricter Enforcement

Could the statutory scheme be more strictly enforced? A number of stricter enforcement strategies might be contemplated, including tighter permit procedures, more rigorous inspection and prosecution of employers below quota.[99] It can be argued that stricter enforcement of the quota scheme would lead to more registered disabled persons obtaining a foothold in employment. In turn, this would encourage more disabled people to register and thus employers would find it easier to fulfil the quota obligation. A further consequence might be that more employers would be encouraged to attempt to meet the quota and this would create a virtuous circle of registration, employment and quota compliance.[100]

On the other hand, a number of objections have been raised to stricter enforcement.[101] First, it would be a futile exercise where the quota is not mathematically achievable because of the insufficient numbers of registered disabled persons. Second, it has been suggested that a lack of skills and experience among unemployed disabled persons means that there is a mismatch between disabled workers in the labour market and available vacancies.[102] Third, stricter enforcement would ensure that the scheme is compulsory, but this would be viewed as incompatible with a system of registration that is voluntary. Fourth, stricter enforcement might only lead to disabled employees being cajoled by employers into registration and this could undermine the employment security and prospects of unregistered disabled persons, whether employed or unemployed. Fifth, it follows that stricter enforcement of the scheme would not necessarily lead to any improvement in the employment position of disabled persons. Sixth, given the numbers of *registrable* disabled persons already in employment, it is probable that some employers are already in compliance with the spirit of the scheme and yet could be penalized by stricter enforcement of it. Seventh, stricter enforcement might overlook the need to resettle disabled workers in the right job and lead to unsuitable workers being forced upon unwilling employers. Eighth, stricter enforcement would challenge the goodwill of employers and thus represent a diminishing of disabled employment prospects. Ninth, there are opportunity costs in stricter enforcement. Stricter enforcement would be bureaucratic and would lead to a diversion of administrative resources in a way that might not prove to be the best use of time and staff.

Reduced Quota

Reduction of the quota has been frequently advocated, especially in tandem with stricter enforcement of the scheme.[103] If a more realistic target were to be set, compliance would be more easily achieved and enforcement strategies would be more readily accepted by employers. The level of the quota might be set to take a more accurate account of the size of the target population.[104] In 1973, by way of illustration, the Department of Employment considered that a realistic quota would be of the order of 2.0 to 2.5 per cent, at a time when average quota compliance was at a maximum possible level of 2.75 per cent.[105] Although this is a superficially attractive reform, it would mean that government had sanctioned a lower target by which employers were to measure their commitment to disabled employment opportunity. This might force quota compliance down even further and represent 'retrospective approval of an unsatisfactory situation'.[106] An alternative proposal might be to calculate the quota as a percentage of new hirings each year rather than as a percentage of the employer's workforce. This addresses the anomalous position that disabled employees who are settled in employment continue to count towards the quota. However, this proposal has been rejected in the past on the grounds that it would bear unevenly upon employers with a large staff turnover and consequent greater number of new engagements, as well as being administratively difficult to enforce.[107] A further alternative would be to count *severely* disabled persons with more weighting for quota purposes. Again, this has been considered and rejected, on the ground of difficulty in classifying and identifying such persons.[108]

The views of disabled persons on the level of the quota are quite instructive. In a 1978 survey, 14 per cent favoured keeping the current percentage level. Only 5 per cent favoured reducing it. Not surprisingly, just over half the respondents championed a raised quota level, with a level of 5 or 10 per cent commanding observable support.[109] About eight in ten respondents would accept a proposal to vary the quota size between different firms or different industries.[110] This idea was also supported by an influential parliamentary committee.[111]

Abolition of the Permit System

It has been suggested that the issuing of bulk permits should be restricted.[112] About one in five disabled persons are opposed to the permit system.[113] Given the abuses of the permit system, a worthwhile reform might be to introduce an unqualified obligation on employers to fulfil the quota and achieve that by abolishing permits.[114] One problem with this suggestion is that it takes no account of the geographical distribution of disabled persons or the distribution of employment skills in the disabled population. Some employers would always have difficulties in meeting the quota because of insufficient or unsuitable disabled workers in a local labour market. The abolition of permits could only be made to work if regional or local variations in the quota percentage were to be permitted and that does not seem to be a practicable proposal.[115] An alternative solution might be to provide employers with a defence of reasonable cause where they are below quota.[116] This would switch the emphasis away from permits and on to enforcement and inspection. It does not, however, deal with the existing problem of how to challenge an employer's contention that certain jobs are unsuitable for disabled persons or that an available disabled person is not suitable for the vacancy in question. The Department of Employment is unlikely to be any more willing to second guess employers' judgments than it is in respect of permit applications. The only alternative would be to leave the issue to arbitration or to an industrial tribunal.

Financial Sanctions

More radically, the enforcement of the quota via levies against recalcitrant employers has been urged, an approach favoured in a number of European models.[117] The Department of Employment's view that prosecution of firms for quota non-compliance is counter-productive leads to suggestions that there should be instead financial sanctions available against recalcitrant employers.[118] Employers would effectively be given a choice of fulfilling the quota or making a payment to a special fund for each unfilled quota place. Such a levy system could have a number of potential advantages.[119] First, it would be administratively convenient. Second, it would produce revenue that could be used in pursuit of other disabled employment strategies. Third, it would ensure a degree of equity in employers' contributions to disabled employment opportunities, either directly, by fulfilling quota, or indirectly, by contributing to the financing of other policies. Fourth, it would retain a compulsory, but flexible, system and would take account of the different circumstances of different employers.

However, opponents of a levy scheme point out that, given the maldistribution of disabled persons geographically and in terms of skills and qualifications, financial sanctions would bear unevenly on some employers who would be penalized for local labour market conditions beyond their control.[120] The ability of employers to buy out their obligations to disabled workers is also hardly calculated to lead to an increase in disabled employment opportunities.[121] The Manpower Services Commission cited evidence that many German employers opt to pay the levy as a way out of their obligations to disabled people and then pass the costs on to their customers,[122] and there is equivalent evidence that French employers prefer to pay a contribution into a national development fund rather than attempt to attain quota.[123] Thus, the level at which the levy is fixed becomes crucial. Too low a level of levy will encourage employers to pay to avoid recruiting disabled individuals; too high a levy could lead to employers recruiting unsuitable disabled persons into unsuitable positions or bringing pressure to bear on unregistered disabled persons in the workforce to register. A levy system also over-emphasizes the burdensome aspects of employing disabled persons and could retrench the negative attitudes of employers.[124] Furthermore, it is another form of preferential treatment of disabled persons and could not be defended on the ground that it targeted protection upon a small group of *severely* disabled persons.[125]

Nevertheless, just over half (52 per cent) of disabled persons indicated support for the idea of making employers pay a levy while they remain below quota.[126] In contrast, support for the idea of placing a levy on employers who failed to engage sufficient numbers of disabled employees was not strong among employers. About two-thirds believed such reform to be inappropriate and only about one-fifth supported the idea.[127]

Abolition of the Quota

It may be that the political and legislative rationale for the statutory scheme has been irredeemably undermined,[128] leaving abolition inevitable. A further argument is that retention of a quota for disabled workers is unjustifiable as long as similar special treatment of other disadvantaged or minority groups does not exist.[129] However, the idea that the quota should be extended to cover other individuals facing difficulties or 'handicaps' in obtaining employment has never seriously been considered.[130] As far as a disabled quota is concerned, a Gallup Poll commissioned by *New Society* and the BBC in 1980 tested the attitude of the electorate to the quota scheme.[131] Sixty-nine per cent of voters supported the strengthening of the quota scheme to make it work, while only 4 per cent would have abolished the scheme. There appeared to be little variation between supporters of the three main political parties on this point.

None the less, there are some who see the abolition of the quota scheme as desirable or inevitable. Of these, a number would not replace the quota scheme, no doubt viewing it as an example of burdens upon business or unnecessary regulation of a free labour market. A second group would replace the quota by concentrating on improved employment and training services for disabled persons, as well as greater efforts in persuading and educating employers to employ disabled people.[132] A third view is that employers should be given temporary or permanent subsidies to encourage the recruitment and retention of workers with disabilities.[133] An alternative version of this proposal would be to provide incentives to employers who fulfil their quota but continue to recruit disabled workers.[134] One person's subsidy is usually another person's levy. Both Tomlinson and Piercy rejected the subsidization of disabled employment as objectionable in principle.[135] Subsidies would validate the erroneous view that disabled workers are less capable than non-disabled workers, and would reinforce the prejudice that disabled employees are a burden on business.[136] Wage subsidization is unlikely to meet the approval of the trade union movement, which in the past has objected to the use of disabled workers as a form of cheap labour.[137] The Piercy Committee also feared that subsidies would be an expensive way of promoting disabled employment and would be difficult to administer, and that difficulties in determining who should be subsidized could lead to such a scheme growing out of control.[138]

CONCLUSION

Despite the catalogue of weaknesses that has been exposed in this chapter, the quota has shown remarkable durability and has survived largely because of the symbolic significance attached to it.[139] The quota has even been shown to be an attainable goal, albeit not without difficulties, given requisite political and managerial will.[140] Moreover, the SCPR survey concluded that there were an estimated 844,000 occupationally handicapped persons in employment. It further estimated that the proportion of all employees in employment who might be assessed as registrable under the 1944 Act would be approximately 4 per cent.[141] This suggests that the quota scheme could be made to work. It is remarkable too that the British and other European disabled quota systems continue to excite the interest of other countries and, in particular, the USA,[142] although the advent of comprehensive disability discrimination laws elsewhere might stifle that interest for the foreseeable future.

Nevertheless, Britain's official attitude towards the quota has always been at best ambivalent. At the time of the 1973 review, the Department of Employment commented:

> It cannot be gainsaid that the existence of the quota scheme may act as a constant suggestion that the employment of disabled people constitutes a burden which needs to be shared and that they are not as productive as able-bodied workers.[143]

On the other hand, the Piercy Committee regarded the quota scheme as providing a 'sound basis for publicity' and as demonstrating the 'industrial value of disabled persons'.[144] The Department of Employment once thought that there was some merit in that view.[145] The scheme was seen as emphasizing employers' responsibilities towards disabled persons, encouraging and reinforcing the good employer. Furthermore, the quota could act as a spur to employers who might be tempted to ignore the problems of disabled employment and could furnish officials with vital opportunities to visit employers to discuss ways of improving employment opportunities for disabled workers. However, the bureaucratic and compulsory nature of the scheme is increasingly seen as objectionable, while policing the quota has not been easily accommodated alongside the public sector agencies' role in advising employers on placing and resettling disabled employees.

More recently, the Department of Employment's 1990 consultative document contains the results of the latest in a series of government reviews of disabled employment policy and legislation.[146] Of central importance is the Government's view that the statutory quota scheme of the 1944 Act has become unsatisfactory in operation and that the arrangements for registering the status of disabled persons have encouraged stereotyping. Although the document considers a number of legislative alternatives to the statutory quota scheme, it appears to signal that in the future there may be less reliance upon statutory regulation of disabled employment.[147] More emphasis is likely to be placed upon education of employers, together with improved training and employment services to disabled persons. This is evidenced by the introduction of a new disability symbol that employers may use on their letterheads, documents and recruitment literature to indicate their commitment to good practice in the employment of disabled persons.

The voluntary approach will be returned to in the penultimate chapter. As this chapter has sought to demonstrate, the prognosis for the future of statutory regulation of disabled employment rights is not good, and even the long-standing commitment to a limited form of preferential treatment is under threat, if not from repeal then at least from decay by neglect. If the disabled workers' quota were to replaced or supplemented by anti-discrimination legislation, would the record of enforcement and the armoury of remedies be any more satisfactory than at present? This is the issue addressed in the next chapter.

NOTES

1. Pitt, 1992.
2. *Ibid.*: 284.
3. *Ibid.*: 286. Of course, Pitt did not have disabled people in mind in the context of this quotation.
4. *Ibid.*: 289. Pitt also points out that the utility argument could be used to justify malign discrimination: ibid.: 290.
5. Tomlinson, 1943: para. 80.
6. Lonsdale and Walker, 1984: 26.
7. Department of Employment, 1973: para. 102.
8. Research Surveys of Great Britain, 1978: Tables 8.5.1. and 8.5.2.
9. Piercy, 1956: para. 177.
10. Manpower Services Commission, 1979: para. 76.3.
11. Research Surveys of Great Britain, 1978: Table 9.7.1.
12. *Ibid.*: 64–7.
13. Morrell, 1990: Table 9.
14. Department of Employment, 1973: para. 104.
15. Manpower Services Commission, 1981: para. 8.18.
16. House of Commons Employment Committee, 1981: para. 27.
17. See generally: Bolderson, 1980, 1991, upon which this account draws.
18. Wages subsidization of disabled employees, whose real economic value to an employer was less than the standard wage for the job, was also proposed, as were national factories for disabled workers.
19. *Report from the Select Committee on Pensions* 1920, HC 185 (1920. London: HMSO) paras 2, 3 and 11.
20. Bolderson, 1991: 42–3.
21. 'ILO Report on Compulsory Employment of Disabled Men in Private Undertakings

in Certain Foreign Countries' in *Report from the Select Committee on Training and Employment of Disabled Ex-Servicemen*, HC 170 (1922. London: HMSO) Appendix II.

22. Bolderson (1991: 43–4) gives an interesting insight into the Committee's reasons for rejecting compulsion and refusing to draw comparisons with the continental European experience.

23. *Ibid.*: 45.

24. *Idem*, 1980: 174–7.

25. Tomlinson, 1943: para. 1. On the deliberations of the Committee, see: Bolderson, 1980: 177–80.

26. Bolderson, 1991: 109.

27. *Ibid.*: 112.

28. *Ibid.*: 113–17.

29. National Audit Office, 1987: 19.

30. Unless, for example, where complying with an unfair dismissal re-employment order.

31. National Audit Office, 1987: para. 16. See also: House of Commons Committee of Public Accounts, 1988: para. 16; Department of Employment, 1990: 8. It is estimated that the quota scheme costs £1–2 million per year at 1987 prices to administer: National Audit Office, 1987: para. 5.2. This is relatively small in comparison with the Department's estimated expenditure of £400 million at 1989–90 prices on assisting disabled people through its general and specialist services: Department of Employment, 1990: 7.

32. Research Surveys of Great Britain, 1978: Tables 6.1 and 6.2. Some 40 per cent, when prompted, knew of the designated occupations and 20 per cent about registration.

33. It would seem that communication about the quota between head offices and branch sites is poor: Morrell, 1990: Table 2.

34. *Ibid.*: 5 and Table 1.

35. *Ibid.*: 6.

36. House of Commons Employment Committee, 1994: 21.

37. *Employment Gazette* (April 1993) Vol. 101 No. 4, 134–8. Research by the TUC (1993), however, suggests that seventeen district councils are complying with the quota.

38. TUC, 1993.

39. Commission of the European Communities, 1988: 5; Lunt and Thornton, 1993: 152.

40. Reported in *European Industrial Relations Review* No. 207 (April 1991) at 5.

41. *European Industrial Relations Review* No. 221 (June 1992) at 6; Lunt and Thornton, 1993: 128–31.

42. Department of Employment, 1973: para. 44.

43. House of Commons Employment Committee, 1994: 21.

44. Department of Employment, 1973: para. 46. The Department believed that, if only half the registrable disabled persons in employment were to register, the true average compliance rate would be approximately 4 per cent.

45. Manpower Services Commission, 1979: para. 30.

46. *Idem*, 1985: 12.

47. Department of Employment, 1990: 36–7; House of Commons Employment Committee, 1994: 7.

48. House of Commons Employment Committee, 1994: 20.

49. Research Surveys of Great Britain, 1978: Table 1.1.1.

50. Martin *et al.*, 1989: Table 7.32. They note that the comparable Department of Employment statistics at the time suggested that there were about 404,000 registered disabled persons. The discrepancy might be explained by the threshold definition of disability necessary to be included in the OPCS survey, together with uncertainty or forgetfulness among respondents about whether or not they had registered.

51. *Ibid.*: Table 7.33.

52. Prescott-Clarke, 1990: 74 and Table 8.1.

53. *Ibid.*: 74.

54. *Ibid.*: 79.

55. Manpower Services Commission, 1979: para. 58; 1981: para. 4.4; 1985: para. 2.4.

56. Research in 1979 suggests that, in a sample of disabled people, only 28 per cent of

non-registered disabled persons regarded themselves as 'disabled' compared with 72 per cent of registered disabled persons: Manpower Services Commission, 1979: para. 59.

57. Research Surveys of Great Britain, 1978: Table 1.2.1. The remainder either were uncertain whether they were entitled to register (4 per cent), did not like being classified as disabled (3 per cent), had never thought about registration (6 per cent) or saw no advantages in it (4 per cent). Significantly, 72 per cent of this sample of 'disabled persons' did not consider themselves disabled: Table 2.1.

58. Prescott-Clarke, 1990: 74 and Table 8.1.

59. *Ibid.*: 75 and Table 8.2.

60. Martin *et al.*, 1989: Table 7.36.

61. Prescott-Clarke, 1990: 75 and Table 8.2.

62. *Ibid.*: 75–6 and Table 8.3.

63. *Ibid.*: Table 8.4.

64. *Ibid.*: 78.

65. In a survey of employers' attitudes towards the quota scheme, Morrell found that 50 per cent of respondents thought that disabled persons did not register because they did not want to be labelled as 'disabled': Morrell, 1990: Table 4.

66. Department of Employment, 1973: para. 55 and Table 4.

67. Manpower Services Commission, 1985: 15–16; National Audit Office, 1987: para. 5.8. More recently, Mr M. Forsyth (Minister of State, Department of Employment) has revealed that the 1944 Act is currently 'monitored' by a rolling programme of inspections of employers' quota records, an annual postal survey into the quota position of employers, reminders to employers of their duties and obligations, and local monitoring of the records of employers who are subject to quota and their quota position: HC Deb Vol. 217 col 839.

68. House of Commons Employment Committee, 1994: 24.

69. A small number of s 9(5) dismissal complaints are received by the Department of Employment each year, but precise figures are not available and since 1975 none have led to prosecution: HC Deb Vol. 217 col 839 (28 January 1993) Mr M. Forsyth, Minister of State, Department of Employment.

70. Manpower Services Commission, 1985: para. 2.11.

71. National Audit Office, 1987: para. 5.11.

72. Manpower Services Commission, 1979: para. 34; 1981: para. 4.9. The exercise is explained in more detail by Mr B. Swindell (Head of Resettlement, Manpower Services Commission) in evidence to a parliamentary committee: House of Commons Employment Committee, 1981: Q2.

73. Department of Employment, 1973: para. 54.

74. Manpower Services Commission, 1981: para. 4.6.

75. *R* v *Secretary of State for Employment, ex parte Pirie* reported in brief in *Equal Opportunities Review* No. 45 (September/October 1992) at 9–10.

76. House of Commons Employment Committee, 1994: 21.

77. National Audit Office, 1987: 20. There are no centralized records of the number of permits issued, but the number of employers to whom permits are issued is known. Between 1987 and 1991, for example, about 18,000 employers were issued with permits each year: HC Deb Vol. 214 cols 706–8.

78. Department of Employment, 1973: para. 54.

79. Manpower Services Commission, 1979: para. 32.

80. Manpower Services Commission, 1981: para. 4.6.

81. Research Surveys of Great Britain, 1978: Table 7.1.

82. *Ibid.*: Tables 8.1.1. and 8.2.1. Sixty-five per cent favoured the use of criminal sanctions against employers who did not comply with their quota obligations, but about 80 per cent opposed imprisonment (as opposed to a fine) as the appropriate sanction: Table 8.3.1 and 8.4.1.

83. Manpower Services Commission, 1979: para. 68.

84. Morrell, 1990: Table 10.

85. *Ibid.*: Table 3.

86. Manpower Services Commission, 1979: para. 73.4

87. *Ibid.*: para. 65 (sub-paragraph numbering in the original omitted).

88. *Ibid.*: para. 67.
89. *Idem*, 1981: para. 8.19.
90. *Idem*, 1979: para. 60; 1981: para. 73.1.
91. See, for example: *Idem*, 1985: 28.
92. *Idem*, 1981: para. 8.2.
93. *Ibid.*: para. 8.3.
94. Department of Employment, 1973: para. 68; Manpower Services Commission, 1979: para. 77.1; 1981: para. 8.10.
95. Manpower Services Commission, 1979: para. 77.1(i). The Manpower Services Commission reported that few employers spontaneously suggested extending the scheme to unregistered disabled persons and that most could see difficulties in the identification process. However, a small majority of disabled persons in 1979 supported this reform.
96. Research Surveys of Great Britain, 1978: Tables 9.1.1 and 9.1.2.
97. *Ibid.*: Table 9.2.1.
98. Morrell, 1990: 7.
99. Department of Employment, 1973: para. 62.
100. Manpower Services Commission, 1985: para. 3:4.
101. Department of Employment, 1973: para. 62; Manpower Services Commission, 1981: para. 4.8. See also: Manpower Services Commission, 1979: para. 73.2.
102. Manpower Services Commission, 1985: paras 2:6 and 2:7.
103. Department of Employment, 1973: para. 63; Manpower Services Commission, 1979: para. 76; 1981: para. 8.5.
104. Manpower Services Commission, 1979: para. 76.1; 1981: para. 5.5. Bolderson (1991: 117) records that the quota percentage was originally set at 2 per cent in 1946 and raised to 3 per cent in 1947. She indicates that the quota was fixed at a level which it was hoped would obviate the need for large scale applications for exemption permits.
105. Department of Employment, 1973: para. 64.
106. *Ibid.*: para. 65; Manpower Services Commission, 1981: para. 8.8. See also Manpower Services Commission, 1979: para. 76.1 (extolling the virtue of setting a target that is difficult to achieve).
107. Manpower Services Commission, 1979: para. 77.1(iii).
108. *Ibid.*: para. 77.1(iv).
109. Research Surveys of Great Britain, 1978: Table 9.3.1.
110. *Ibid.*: Tables 9.4.1 and 9.4.2.
111. House of Commons Employment Committee, 1981: para. 8.
112. Manpower Services Commission, 1985: paras 3:9 and 3:10.
113. Research Surveys of Great Britain, 1978: Tables 8.1.1. and 8.2.1.
114. Department of Employment, 1973: para. 70; Manpower Services Commission, 1981: para. 8.16.
115. Manpower Services Commission, 1985: 49–51. Although this idea was supported by disabled respondents in a 1979 survey, it was rejected as being too difficult and costly to administer: *Idem*, 1979: para. 76.2.
116. Department of Employment, 1973: para. 72.
117. Brooke-Ross, 1984; Floyd and North, 1986.
118. Department of Employment, 1973: para. 74; Manpower Services Commission, 1979: para. 77.2(ii); 1981: para. 8.14.
119. Department of Employment, 1973: para. 75.
120. *Ibid.*: para. 76.
121. House of Commons Employment Committee, 1981: para. 11.
122. Manpower Services Commission, 1981: para. 8.15.
123. Reported in *European Industrial Relations Review* No. 207 (April 1991) at 5.
124. Department of Employment, 1973: para. 77.
125. Manpower Services Commission, 1981: para. 8.15
126. Research Surveys of Great Britain, 1978: Table 9.5.1.
127. Morrell, 1990: Table 9.
128. McDonnell and Weale, 1984; Jones and Cullis, 1988.
129. Manpower Services Commission, 1979: para. 73.3.

130. *Ibid.*: para. 77.1(ii).
131. Cited in *Idem*, 1985: 32.
132. Department of Employment, 1973: paras 88–95.
133. Manpower Services Commission, 1985: 38–9.
134. *Idem*, 1979: para. 77.2(ii). The Manpower Services Commission found, in an employer survey, that employers opposed levies as leading to greater interference and administrative burdens, as well as providing some firms with an excuse to ignore their social responsibilities. Levies also appeared to meet with little support among disabled people.
135. See in particular: Piercy, 1956: para. 197.
136. Department of Employment, 1973: para. 83.
137. *Ibid.*: para. 84.
138. Piercy, 1956: para. 197; Department of Employment, 1973: paras 85–6.
139. Bolderson, 1980.
140. *Equal Opportunities Review*, 1989.
141. Prescott-Clarke, 1990: 115.
142. See, for example: Stubbins, 1982; Kulkarni, 1983. A number of respected disability scholars take a positive view of quota systems, despite their flaws, and regard them as part and parcel of any disability rights regime. See, for example: Cornes, 1984; Hahn, 1984. However, the introduction of disabled quotas into a country such as the USA would require major changes in disability policy and civil rights thinking: Bordieri and Comninel, 1987: 55.
143. Department of Employment, 1973: para. 39.
144. Piercy, 1956: para. 154.
145. Department of Employment, 1973: para. 38.
146. Department of Employment, 1990.
147. The official position is that no change in the quota scheme is contemplated but the legislation will be kept under review (House of Commons Employment Committee, 1994: 9).

11

Enforcement and Remedies

INTRODUCTION

The reputation and authority of disability discrimination laws will rest very much upon how the law is enforced and what effective remedies are available for transgressions of its letter. The ultimate failure of the British disabled quota scheme might be largely explained by the inability of the authorities adequately to police and enforce the legislation, and the paltriness of such penalties as have been exacted from employers in breach. The failure to provide disabled persons with an individual right of action to enforce their rights under the existing law, and the choice of the criminal justice system as the forum for executing the law, have both contributed to the resulting futility of the legislation. The setting of a new agenda for disability employment rights in Britain must also address the manner in which and the means by which any new discrimination or equal opportunity legislation is to be enforced. This will in turn raise questions concerning institutional and individual enforcement strategies, the role of judicial enforcement and the appropriateness of remedies. In this chapter we look at the possibility of the establishment of a Disablement Commission with institutional powers to enforce, administer and implement new legal objectives. We also look at what lessons might be learned from existing laws in Britain and comparable laws elsewhere in respect of the justiciability of disability-related employment issues and the remedying of individual acts or broader patterns of disability discrimination.

INSTITUTIONAL ENFORCEMENT

From time to time, it has been suggested that the Equal Opportunities Commission (EOC) and Commission for Racial Equality (CRE) should be merged to produce one body responsible for the overview and enforcement of equal opportunities legislation.[1] The obvious parallels are with the Equal Employment Opportunities Commission (EEOC) in the USA, or the human rights commissions and councils in Canada, or the anti-discrimination or equal opportunity boards, commissions and commissioners in Australia. Merger has been rightly resisted on the suspicion that it is merely a pretext for public expenditure cuts in the financing of anti-discrimination initiatives. Furthermore, both the EOC and CRE have been lukewarm to any proposals that disability discrimination law, if enacted in Britain, would become part of their individual portfolios.[2] Subsequently, disability rights activists themselves have seen the dangers that such recommendations would hold and that, in particular, disability would have to compete for attention and resources with other prohibited grounds in any grand anti-discrimination enforcement agency.[3] Attention has thus switched to the establishment of a Disablement Commission.

Proposed Disablement Commission

A central feature of proposals in Britain for disability discrimination legislation has been the mooted establishment of a Disablement Commission. This has been an essential part of many of the private members' Bills alluded to in Chapter 2 and, in particular, of the recent Civil Rights (Disabled Persons) Bills. Such a Commission would be charged with a number of functions. First, it would work towards the elimination of disability-informed discrimination. Second, it would have powers to carry out general investigations to ensure that the new law was being complied with. Third, the Disablement Commission would investigate individual complaints of non-compliance with the law and provide a conciliation service in respect of such complaints. Fourth, it could provide assistance, including legal and financial assistance, to disabled persons seeking to enforce their new rights under the legislation. Fifth, the operation of the legislation would be kept under review and the Commission would be responsible for submitting proposals for statutory amendments. Sixth, the Disablement Commission would be responsible for publishing codes of practice directed at the requirements of the legislation.

The Disablement Commission, if established, would be made up of a number of Commissioners (eight to fifteen has been suggested as the appropriate number) under a full-time chairman, who would be a person with disabilities. It is proposed that 75 per cent of the seats on the Commission should be filled by disabled persons or their authorized representatives, and that Commissioners should hold office for up to five years, subject to reappointment. The Commission would be founded as a body corporate but would not be an emanation of the Crown. It would not be subject to Crown immunity nor would its staff be civil servants. However, the Commission would rely upon public funding for its activities, expenses and payroll. Furthermore, the Secretary of State would have to promulgate regulations to address the powers and procedures of the Commission when carrying out individual or general investigations, including the power to issue non-discrimination notices or to take cases of discrimination to the tribunals or courts. The Commission would be expected to report annually to the Secretary of State and to Parliament.

It will be readily recognized that the template for the suggested Disablement Commission is that provided by the EOC and the CRE. However, there are two noticeable differences between the proposed model and its progenitors. First, unlike the CRE and EOC, the proposed Disablement Commission would not be given express research and education functions. This omission might be more than purely accidental. The 1980s have seen calls for disability discrimination law met with the political response that more research is required to identify the incidence and experience of disability, while the preferred governmental approach to disability discrimination is a policy of education and persuasion. Disability rights activists would be understandably suspicious of enshrining this strategy in law and could be rightly concerned that the justiciability of these issues might be down-graded. It is worth recalling that in the original 1976 Anti-Discrimination Bill in New South Wales, physical disability and condition were included as 'other grounds' of discrimination. However, disability was subsequently relegated within the statute that emerged as an issue solely for research (rather than regulation) by the newly-formed Anti-Discrimination Board. However, not to give any new Commission here a research and education mandate appears short-sighted, whatever the tactical reasons for not so doing.

Second, and more significantly, there is no explicit legal requirement that the CRE and EOC should be constituted so as to represent an appropriate racial or gender mix of Commissioners, whereas disabled Commissioners are to be in the majority on a Disablement Commission.[4] Given the symmetry of race and sex discrimination legislation, it would obviously send an undesired signal to employers if the EOC and CRE were to practise racial or sexual quotas or set-asides in their own constitutions. Disability discrimination law, on the other hand, would be asymmetrical and the same objection in principle could not be taken to the reservation of commissionerships for a predetermined proportion of disabled persons. Furthermore, disabled persons, perhaps more keenly than women and ethnic minorities, have felt themselves to be commandeered by others (primarily the disability professions, charities and organizations *for*, rather than *of*, disabled people) who have purported to speak on their behalf, and they would now seek a clear voice of their own. Moreover, it can be argued that first-hand knowledge and experience of disability and disability discrimination are important qualifications for those who would shape the destiny of any new disability discrimination law.[5]

Role of Institutional Enforcement

Whatever body is charged with responsibility for disability discrimination law, one of its central functions will involve it in investigations of compliance and non-compliance with the legislation. The power to conduct formal investigations into suspected discriminatory activities of individuals or enterprises has been, at least on paper, an important weapon in the armoury of institutional enforcement.[6] However, in practice, both the EOC and CRE have been hidebound in the pursuit of formal investigations and subjected to judicial control that has blunted the edge of this weapon.[7] In turn, this has diminished the role of non-discrimination notices, issued as a result of formal investigation, addressed to named parties and requiring them to discontinue identified discriminatory acts or practices.[8] Moreover, little (if any) use has been made of the Commissions' powers to seek injunctive relief against persistent discrimination.[9] Consequently, the burden of the EOC and CRE's main efforts in the enforcement area has been limited to assisting individual complainants (although, importantly, including advice and legal representation).[10] When empowering a new Disablement Commission, account must be taken of the experience of the CRE and EOC and of the limitations placed upon their authority by judicial control.

COMPARATIVE PERSPECTIVES ON ENFORCEMENT

Canada

Under the Canadian federal jurisdiction, where it is believed that an employer is discriminating on the grounds of disability, an individual or group of individuals may complain to the Canadian Human Rights Commission under Part III of the Human Rights Act.[11] The Commission may deal with the complaint provided that there are reasonable grounds for suspecting discriminatory practices and it is within the Commission's jurisdiction. The Commission might take the view that internal grievance or review procedures should be exhausted first, but otherwise the Commission will designate a person to investigate the complaint.[12] The investigator is vested with powers of entry and inspection while carrying out the investigation. At the conclusion of the investigation, a report is made to the Commission, which may request the appointment of a Human Rights Tribunal if an inquiry into the complaint is warranted.[13] Conciliation of the complaint may be attempted at this point if it has not already been so.[14] The Canadian Human Rights Tribunal, acting as a superior court of record, will inquire into the complaint and give the parties a hearing.[15] If a complaint has been heard by the Canadian Human Rights Tribunal consisting of fewer than three members, an appeal on a question of law or fact may be made to a Review Tribunal of three members established from the Human Rights Tribunal Panel.[16]

The administration, enforcement and overview of human rights laws in the Canadian provinces is placed in the hands of Human Rights Commissions or, in the case of British Columbia, a Human Rights Council, and, in the case of Québec, the Commission des Droits de la Personne.[17] The Commissions are usually charged with advancing the principle of equality and non-discrimination, promoting an understanding of and compliance with the legislation, researching and developing educational programmes designed to eliminate discriminatory practices, and encouraging and co-ordinating human rights programmes and activities.[18]

Although the procedure for handling discrimination complaints varies from province to province only in respect of fine detail, the Alberta practice is not untypical. An individual complaint of discrimination is made to the Alberta Human Rights Commission, which will investigate the complaint and attempt to effect a settlement.[19] If a settlement is not reached, and if the complaint is not without merit, a board of inquiry is appointed with plenipotentiary authority.[20] The complainant has the initial burden of proving a *prima facie* case, but then the evidentiary burden moves to the employer to show a legitimate, non-discriminatory reason for the actions which form the basis of the complaint. An appeal from a decision of the board of inquiry is heard by the Court of Queen's Bench and may involve a question of law or of fact.[21]

The procedure in the other provinces is very similar.[22] In Manitoba, for example, mediation is employed to attempt a settlement between the parties,[23] and any subsequent inquiry into the complaint is conducted by an adjudicator rather than a board of inquiry.[24] At the request of any person, the Manitoba Human Rights Commission is empowered to give an 'advisory opinion' as to whether the Code has been contravened. Unless this opinion is revised or revoked, the person to whom it is issued is entitled to rely upon it as conclusive of the issue of whether he or she was acting in accordance with the Code.[25]

United States

Under the (US) RA 1973, sections 501 and 503 were largely enforced through administrative mechanisms overseen by the EEOC and the OFCCP. Individual complaints of discrimination would only be heard in the federal courts via a challenge for judicial review of an administrative law decision. The potential lack of a private right of action for disabled plaintiffs also dogged the early years of section 504, although the right of the federal courts to entertain individual complaints was subsequently established.[26] The same problems are not anticipated under the (US) ADA 1990. The enforcement of the ADA 1990 is ultimately in the hands of the EEOC and is discharged primarily by the investigation of individual claims of discrimination. The ADA 1990 adopts the administrative and judicial enforcement mechanisms and remedies available under Title VII of the Civil Rights Act 1964. Accordingly, disabled litigants in employment discrimination cases have the same rights and remedies as ethnic and racial minorities, women and religious adherents. The first stage is to submit the discrimination complaint to the administrative processes of the EEOC.[27] This will include attempts to resolve the complaint by conciliated agreement. The second stage, if the complaint is not disposed of at the first stage, is to bring a private action in court.[28] The primary remedy available in a successful case will be injunctive relief, including an order for reinstatement and/or an order that the plaintiff be employed in a specific job and/or an order for monetary compensation for lost wages.[29] Compensatory or punitive damages would not normally have been available.[30] However, section 102 of the Civil Rights Act 1991 now allows compensatory damages to be awarded in Title VII or ADA 1990 or RA 1973 litigation where *intentional* discrimination is found, and punitive damages in cases of malicious or reckless discrimination.[31] Nevertheless, claims for compensatory damages in disability discrimination cases might now be met with a defence that the employer has made 'good faith' attempts, in consultation with the plaintiff, to make reasonable accommodation for disability.

It has been estimated that the EEOC will need an annual budget of $15 million in order to carry out its enforcement functions under the ADA 1990.[32] Furthermore, the EEOC anticipated a caseload under the ADA 1990 of approximately 12,000 complaints per year. By the end of April 1993, nine months after the Act first came into force, some 8,505 complaints had been received, comprising 15 per cent of the EEOC's caseload.[33] The EEOC data reveal that 48 per cent of complaints concerned disability-related dismissals, 21 per cent related to a failure to accommodate disability and 14 per cent went to alleged discriminatory recruitment and selection decisions. Nearly 10 per cent of filed complaints alleged harassment, 7 per cent were derived from disciplinary decisions, 5 per cent were about lay-offs and nearly 4 per cent were related to employee benefits (the ADA's impact upon occupational health insurance and benefits, in particular, appears to be exercising employers). In what is believed to be the first case to be tried under the ADA regime, an executive director, dismissed by his employer when it was learnt that he had developed terminal brain cancer, was awarded $577,000.[34] The award was made up of $22,000 back pay, $55,000 compensatory damages and $500,000 punitive damages. The case is an early example of the EEOC's reinvigorated approach to discrimination damages after the reforms under the Civil Rights Act 1991 and prefaced in a policy statement issued by the EEOC in July 1992.[35]

Australia

In New South Wales, complaints and allegations of discrimination are initially put to the Anti-Discrimination Board for investigation.[36] If the complaint is not dismissed at this early stage, an attempt will be made to resolve the issue by conciliation,[37] failing which the complaint will be referred to the Equal Opportunity Tribunal (EOT).[38] After an inquiry by the EOT, the complaint may be dismissed or upheld and, if upheld, the EOT may declare the parties' rights, award damages, order that discriminatory conduct should not be repeated, require that the plaintiff be employed, reinstated or promoted (as befits the nature of the complaint) and/or declare void any contract or agreement made in contravention of the legislation.[39] An order of the EOT is enforceable in the ordinary courts, while its decisions are appealable to the NSW Supreme Court on a question of law.

The position in Queensland is little different, except that original complaints are handled by the Anti-Discrimination Commission and adjudicated upon by the Anti-Discrimination Tribunal.[40] In South Australia and Western Australia, the roles of investigation and adjudication are filled respectively by the Equal Opportunity Commission and the Equal Opportunity Tribunal,[41] while in Victoria the relevant bodies are the Equal Opportunity Commission and the Equal Opportunity Board.[42] The recently enacted Commonwealth disability discrimination law provides for complaints of disability discrimination to be referred to the Human Rights and Equal Opportunity Commission.[43] At the first stage, an inquiry will be held by the Disability Discrimination Commissioner, who will endeavour to settle the matter by conciliation, before referring the matter back to the Commission.[44] The Commission will hold a formal inquiry into the complaint and the parties will enjoy rights of appearance and legal representation.[45] Again, conciliation plays a role in the inquiry and the Commission must take all reasonable steps to attempt an amicable settlement.[46] If the complaint is not dismissed by the Commission, it may make a declaration of the parties' rights and may make positive orders and/or award compensation.[47]

JUDICIAL ENFORCEMENT

It will be clear from the foregoing account that disability discrimination is a justiciable issue, but that in Canada and Australia disability discrimination complaints tend to be handled within the machinery of institutional enforcement, albeit with quasi-judicial overtones. The emphasis upon inquiry and alternative dispute resolution, particularly the use of conciliation, is noteworthy. The issue is also dealt with in an environment, exemplified by the use of special boards of inquiry or anti-discrimination and equal opportunity tribunals, that allows expertise in discrimination questions to come to the fore in adjudication. In contrast, in the USA, disability-related litigation takes place in the mainstream federal courts or administrative law courts and is treated as just another example of litigious matter. This raises the question of the appropriate forum for disposing of disability discrimination complaints if discrimination law in Britain were to be extended to cover this forbidden ground.

Earlier proposals for disability discrimination legislation envisaged that the county courts would hear assertions that the law had been breached. However, the Civil Rights (Disabled Persons) Bills of recent parliamentary sessions have pointed to the industrial tribunals as the appropriate arena for disputes concerning disability in employment. This follows the pattern adopted for sex and race discrimination applications. Clearly, the industrial tribunals are a more fitting medium for the resolution of disability-related actions for *employment* discrimination, and certainly preferable to the ordinary courts, on the one hand, or the other specialist administrative tribunals, on the other hand. It might be argued, for instance, that bodies such as the Medical Appeal Tribunal or Social Security Appeal Tribunal already have 'expertise' in disability issues. However, these bodies might be expected to take a welfarism approach to disability discrimination law, would have little experience of discrimination or employment concepts and would be associated with the medical model of disability which new rights would set out to challenge. Nevertheless, the industrial tribunal system might not be the perfect solution to the problem of adjudication.

The evidence suggests that the industrial tribunals and those involved in their jurisdictions lack understanding of discrimination and of the law that attempts to confront it.[48] It has been suggested that discrimination cases should be assigned to a specialist division of the industrial tribunal system,[49] allowing tribunal members to establish expertise by continuous contact with a discrimination caseload. Furthermore, the importance of ensuring that at least one member of the tribunal has experience of disability, whether personal or otherwise acquired, is essential if disabled plaintiffs are to have confidence in the system. It is suggested that, assuming employment-related disability discrimination complaints will be assigned to industrial tribunals, a special panel of disabled persons or persons with knowledge of disability may need to be established by regulation and that one member of the tribunal should be drawn from that panel to hear such complaints. Whether or not a specialist division of tribunals is established to deal with disability discrimination cases, the training of tribunal members will have to take on board comprehension of the nature and experience of disability and the subtle forms in which disabled people encounter discrimination.

Although, in the view of the present writer, the industrial tribunals are, in the absence of a practical alternative, the best forum for hearing disability-related complaints, the system as a whole remains flawed. It is not intended to rehearse here the arguments in the debate about the efficacy of industrial tribunals, but a few summary points should be made. There is the problem of access to the tribunal system. For disabled litigants that means *physical* access to and within the buildings housing the industrial tribunals, but it also refers to the difficulties of enforcing rights in an adversarial system. Access to legal advice and representation will be a crucial aspect of any meaningful rights to be protected from prohibited actions in the workplace. Given complex questions about the definition of disability, fitness or qualification for work and the requirements of reasonable accommodation, disabled plaintiffs will require not only legal expert assistance, but also access to sources of information and expert witnesses who can attest to those issues. The potential cost of pursuing these new rights may also be prohibitive, especially in the early cases where fundamental principles will need to be established. The role of the proposed Disablement Commission will be pivotal here. Once before the tribunal, questions concerning the burden of proof, discovery of documents and legal procedure generally will determine the chances of success, just as they do in discrimination and employment protection cases generally. Disability rights activists should not be seduced into believing that the enactment of a disability discrimination statute will produce readily enforceable rights and remedies.

REMEDIES

In the nature of things, concern to establish the shape and scope of the principle that discrimination is unlawful has often led to the question of available remedies being overlooked or given second order priority. However, as Morris and Nott observe in the context of gender discrimination,

> The remedies available to a successful complainant should not only be aimed at compensating the victim in a way commensurate with the injury suffered but should also deter a repetition of the unlawful act. One way to achieve deterrence is to ensure a level of compensation which is more than nominal and a system of enforcement which provides for further significant sanctions against non-compliance.[50]

Unfortunately, in British discrimination law, the available remedies have neither compensated adequately nor deterred sufficiently.[51] Recent developments in the USA under the Civil Rights Act 1991 suggest that disability discrimination litigation in that jurisdiction will begin to produce effective and compensatory remedies. In this section, we look at the availability of remedies under existing British legislation and compare and contrast it with the position in Canada.

Compensatory Damages

In Britain, discrimination compensation is calculated as if it were an award of damages for a statutory tort.[52] In principle, this means that in employment cases a successful plaintiff should be entitled to lost wages, both up to the date of the hearing and as to the future. However, in complaints of discrimination in appointment or promotion (as opposed to dismissal), the essence of the case is one of lost opportunity rather than denied benefits. Accordingly, the British courts have been reluctant to allow the recovery of such financial loss predicated upon a speculation as to the outcome of a non-discriminatory process. In practice, therefore, the plaintiff's redress will usually be limited to compensation for out-of-pocket expenses and injury to feelings.[53] Nevertheless, even then, damages for injury to feelings have been comparatively small (usually of the order of £100), although in isolated cases a court has been minded to make a more generous award,[54] and more recently it has been suggested that £500 is now the more appropriate figure.[55] But even when pecuniary damages are accounted for, discrimination awards are not generous. In a study of sex discrimination cases in the early 1980s, it was found that the average award in recruitment complaints was just under £300.[56] Although over the past decade this benchmark has improved, the most recent tribunal statistics covering the period 1990–1 show that the average award in race discrimination cases is £1,749, while in sex discrimination cases the median award is £1,142. It is only in rare cases that a plaintiff manages to breast the £2,000 mark.[57]

The picture is probably coloured by the fact that the British legislation previously placed a ceiling upon the amount of compensation that can be awarded in an individual case. The maximum limit was £11,000 at 1 June 1993.[58] This was bound to force down the average level of awards as the tribunals were naturally unwilling to make awards at the upper end of the scale for discrimination claims that they might regard as run-of-the-mill. However, it did seem at best ambivalent towards the objectives of the law to design a discrimination remedy akin to a statutory tort, but then to put a cap upon the amount of compensation that might be recovered. Placing an upper limit upon compensation (inclusive of *pecuniary* damages) is not a feature of the discrimination laws of the three common law jurisdictions that have been used as the basis of this comparative study. Pecuniary damages are at large and the only ceiling placed upon awards might be that element relating to non-pecuniary compensation. For example, Canadian federal legislation sets out to compensate the plaintiff for lost wages and expenses without limitation but, in the case of wilful or reckless discrimination or discrimination resulting in injury to feelings or self-respect, the payment of special compensation may be made only up to $5,000.[59] British Columbia allows an award of special additional compensation of up to $2,000.[60] In cases of wilful or reckless discrimination contrary to Ontario human rights law, a defendant may be ordered to pay damages for mental anguish of up to $10,000.[61] In cases of wilful contravention of the Saskatchewan Code involving injury to feelings or self-esteem, an award of additional compensation of up to $5,000 may result.[62] Strictly speaking, these provisions establish an unassailable right to this head of damages, where such a right might not otherwise exist at common law, rather than represent an artificial restraint upon the calculation of the award.

By pointing to the analogue of sex and race discrimination

statutes as the basis of proposals for disability discrimination law, British disability rights activists might have risked inviting a similarly imposed ceiling of £11,000 (or its uprated equivalent) on compensation. However, the European Court of Justice decision in *Marshall* v *Southampton and South-West Hampshire Area Health Authority (No. 2)* is likely to prove pivotal.[63] The Court ruled that the British SDA 1975 was contrary to Article 6 of the EC Equal Treatment Directive 76/207 in setting an upper limit to recoverable compensation in sex discrimination complaints. European Community law required that a plaintiff be made whole where true equality of opportunity has been denied. If monetary compensation is the instrument of remedial action, then damages must be adequate and the loss sustained by the plaintiff must be made good in full. No distinction is made between pecuniary and non-pecuniary losses. As a result of *Marshall*, British sex and race discrimination law has been amended so as to allow all employees to enjoy a remedy without constraint.[64] Although this does not naturally follow from these amendments, it is probable that any new disability discrimination law would also contain uncapped monetary remedies.

Exemplary Damages

While compensatory damages, if used imaginatively, can make a plaintiff whole, such an award might not act as a sufficient punishment of the discriminator or as an adequate deterrent to other employers. Exemplary or punitive damages may be more appropriate.[65] At common law, exemplary damages may be awarded where there has been oppressive, arbitrary or unconstitutional action by government servants or where the defendant's conduct has been calculated to accrue a profit that exceeds any compensation paid to the defendant. The leading case in discrimination law relies upon the first of these grounds. In *Bradford Metropolitan City Council* v *Arora*,[66] a race discrimination case, exemplary damages were awarded against a local authority for the actions of its senior officers. The tribunal awarded the sum of £1,000 in this respect and this was upheld by the Court of Appeal. Nevertheless, in Britain the award of compensation under this head has and will continue to be rare, possibly because a claim for exemplary damages should be specifically pleaded. By way of comparison, discrimination contrary to the Québec Charter entitles the victim to obtain 'the cessation of [such discrimination] and compensation for the moral or material prejudice resulting therefrom'.[67] In the case of intentional interference, exemplary damages may be awarded. In a case of a malicious contravention of the Yukon Territory Act, exemplary damages may be awarded. Unusually, if the complainant has acted frivolously or vexatiously, the board of adjudication can award the defendant party its costs against the complainant and order the complainant to pay damages for injury to reputation.[68] In Manitoba, where there is evidence of malice or recklessness, an employer might be ordered to pay a penalty or exemplary damages of up to $2,000 in an individual case and up to $10,000 in any other case.[69]

Positive Remedies

There has been a tendency in discrimination law, as in employment law generally, to regard monetary compensation as being the primary remedy. This is undoubtedly owing to the reluctance of the tribunals and courts to fashion a remedy that has the effect of creating specific performance of a contract for personal services. This must also be especially so in cases where no contract has yet been formed because of the intervening discrimination. However, both the SDA 1975 and the RRA 1976 contemplate that a tribunal or court might grant positive remedies to a successful plaintiff. First, an order may be made declaring the rights of the parties in relation to the complained of act.[70] Second, the judicial body may make a recommendation that the employer take action to obviate or reduce the adverse effect upon the plaintiff of the discrimination in question. A failure to comply with such a recommendation without reasonable justification entitles the plaintiff to original or increased compensation.[71] The British tribunals and courts have resiled from an interpretation of these positive remedies that would lead to judicial approval of positive discrimination. So, for example, the tribunal cannot recommend that the successful plaintiff be appointed to the next available suitable vacancy.[72] Similarly, a recommendation may not be made that the plaintiff should be promoted forthwith, for such an action may transgress the merit principle and cause counter-discrimination affecting other employees.[73] Such timidity is not to be found in other jurisdictions.

In Canada, the Canadian Human Rights Tribunal may order a defendant to cease a discriminatory practice, to take measures to prevent future discrimination (including adopting an affirmative action plan) or to provide the plaintiff with the rights, opportunities or privileges which have been denied (such as engagement or reinstatement).[74] In addition, if the Tribunal finds the complaint to be substantiated,

> but that the premises or facilities of the person found to be engaging or to have engaged in the discriminatory practice require adaptation to meet the needs of a person arising from such disability, the Tribunal shall (a) make such order . . . for that adaptation as it considers appropriate and as it is satisfied will not occasion costs or business inconvenience constituting undue hardship, or (b) if the Tribunal considers that no such order can be made, make such recommendations as it considers appropriate.[75]

Thus the Tribunal may also order an employer to adapt its premises or facilities to accommodate a disabled plaintiff, subject to avoiding costs or business inconvenience constituting undue hardship.

In the Canadian provinces, a board of inquiry may order that the discrimination should cease, that future contraventions should be avoided, that the complainant be extended the rights which have been violated by the discriminatory act, or that lost income and expenses for up to two years prior to the complaint be compensated for by the defendant. Alternatively, a board of inquiry may order any other action which it deems proper, so as to put the complainant in the position that would have prevailed but for the discrimination.[76] In cases of disability-based discrimination in Saskatchewan, a board of inquiry may order additionally that facilities be arranged to ensure that physical access is not impeded and that proper amenities are provided for disabled persons. However, this is subject to the defendant showing that the cost and business inconvenience involved in meeting such an order would cause undue hardship. This presently means:

> intolerable financial cost or disruption to business occasioning such costs in the circumstances, but does not include, *inter alia*, the cost or business inconvenience of providing washroom facilities, living quarters or other facilities for physically disabled persons of a kind that must be provided by law for persons of both sexes.[77]

However, an amendment, which is not yet in force, would allow regard to be had to the effect of the order upon the financial stability and profitability of the business, the value of existing amenities, structures and premises in comparison with the cost of providing proper amenities or physical access, the essence or purpose of the business and (disregarding personal preferences) its workforce, clients and customers.[78]

In Manitoba, an unsuccessful defendant may be required to adopt and implement an affirmative action programme or other special programme, if there has been a pattern or practice of contravention.[79] In a case of disability-based discrimination where the contravention of the Code involves the impeding of access of physically disabled persons or the failing to provide them with proper amenities in a building or facility, the adjudicator may *recommend* that this state of affairs be remedied. The adjudicator shall not make such an order if it is established that cost or business inconvenience would result and undue hardship would be caused.[80] Once a complaint has been lodged and remains to be disposed of, the Commission can seek an interlocutory order of the court to restrain conduct which is alleged to contravene the Code.[81]

The Canadian approach is illustrated by the sex discrimination case of *Canadian National Railway Company* v *Canadian Human Rights Commission.*[82] The Human Rights Tribunal ordered the employer to cease discriminatory recruitment practices on terms that would require the employer to hire a quota of women until their participation in blue collar jobs in the employer's undertaking was equal to the proportion of women in blue collar jobs in Canada as a whole. It was argued that the Tribunal had exceeded its jurisdiction in attempting to remedy past discrimination rather than preventing future recurrence of discriminatory practices. However, that argument was rejected on the ground that, to prevent discrimination against the identified groups protected by the Act, the statute must be given a fair, large and liberal interpretation. The Tribunal's order had been designed to tackle systematic discrimination and to prevent similar discriminatory practices reoccurring, rather than to compensate past victims of discrimination or to provide fresh opportunities for individuals previously refused employment. It was permissible to seek out and to destroy past patterns of discrimination in order to ensure that future applicants did not face the same discriminatory barriers which had blocked the employment opportunities of earlier generations.

The application of this philosophy is demonstrated in a disability discrimination case as well. In *Cameron* v *Nel-Gor Castle Nursing Home,*[83] a successful plaintiff was awarded compensation for lost wages and damages for injured feelings. Moreover, the employer was also directed to cease and desist discriminatory hiring practices, and ordered to offer the disabled plaintiff the next available vacancy. Furthermore, in a number of provincial decisions at first instance, boards of inquiry have ordered employers to adopt an affirmative action programme to prevent future contraventions of human rights codes.

Criminal Sanctions

The use of criminal sanctions as a means of enforcing special legislation on behalf of disabled persons is, of course, a particular feature of the law in Britain and in continental Europe. The quota provisions of the DP(E)A 1944 are in principle enforceable within the criminal justice system. The use of the criminal law and criminal penalties might also be a limited feature of anti-discrimination laws in general: for example, in respect of discriminatory advertisements or persistent discriminatory practices.[84]

In the Canadian provinces, however, more extensive use (or potential for use) of the criminal process exists. For example, a failure to comply with a provision of the New Brunswick Human Rights Act is also a criminal offence and a fine of $100–5,000 may be levied.[85] Breach of the Nova Scotia legislation is also a criminal offence for which a fine of up to $1,000 is payable.[86] In Ontario, with the consent of the Attorney-General, a criminal prosecution may also be pursued, as an infringement of any right under the Code is a criminal offence punishable by a fine of up to $25,000.[87] In Prince Edward Island, an infringement of the Act or a non-compliance with a ministerial order is a criminal offence punishable with a fine of $100–500 or thirty days' imprisonment, in the case of an individual, and a fine of $200–2,000 in any other case. The burden of proof in this instance is the civil one. The appropriate Minister may also seek a court order to injunct a convicted party from further offences.[88] Failure to comply with a recommendation of the Québec Commission can result in an injunction being sought and, moreover, employment discrimination is a criminal offence under this province's Charter.[89]

In Saskatchewan, a failure to comply with an order of a board of inquiry or interference with the rights of a person under the Code is a criminal offence. In the case of an individual, this may result in a fine of $500–2,000; in any other case, the fine is $2,000–3,000.[90] Where an employer has been convicted of suspending, transferring, laying off or dismissing an employee contrary to the Code, the court may order reinstatement with compensation.[91] A prosecution may be instituted by a trade union, occupational association or employers' organization.[92] In addition, the Commission may seek a court injunction to prevent a person convicted of an offence under the Code from continuing or repeating the offence, and the court may also issue such an injunction in private proceedings under the Code.[93] In limited circumstances, infringement of the Yukon Territory Act is a criminal offence punishable by a fine of up to $2,000.[94] Following the commencement of either civil or criminal proceedings, the Supreme Court may grant a temporary injunction to restrain allegedly discriminatory conduct or to require compliance with the Act, pending the completion of the proceedings. Finally, in Manitoba, in a serious case of the Code being contravened, the Minister may consent to a criminal prosecution.[95] A fine of up to $10,000 may be imposed. Despite these many examples of the use of criminal law to address disability discrimination, however, little is known or understood about the impact of the criminal justice process upon employers and disabled persons.

CONCLUSION

In the final analysis, carefully drafted discrimination statutes are often only as good as their procedural and remedial frameworks allow them to be, however far-sighted their substantive provisions might be. The ability of disabled persons to challenge incidents and patterns of disability-informed discrimination rests entirely upon those parts of discrimination legislation that provide a cause of action, a route to litigation and an array of enforceable responses to identified unlawful actions, policies or practices. The law's emphasis upon the individual-based complaint process of the British SDA 1975 and RRA 1976 is often blamed for the alleged failure of the legislation to root out systematic and institutionalized discrimination. The want of formal class action procedures in this country also leads to a failure to learn the lessons of discriminatory episodes beyond the confines of the individual case. The treatment of discrimination complaints in isolation, and as being limited to their peculiar circumstances, frequently results in the repetition of unlawful behaviour and the consolidation, rather than demolition, of discriminatory policies and practices. With these limitations of the traditional anti-discrimination legal model in mind, we turn in the penultimate chapter to look at legal strategies that go beyond enforcement and that seek to provide lasting solutions to disability disadvantage.

NOTES

1. See, for example: House of Commons Employment Committee, 1991: Q627.

2. See, for example: House of Commons Employment Committee, 1990b: QQ87–92.

3. See in particular oral evidence given to the House of Commons Employment Committee (1990a: 57–8). Prior to the enactment of the (Northern Ireland) Fair Employment Act 1989, it was suggested that omnibus discrimination legislation, encompassing race, sex, religious conviction and disability, might be adopted in the province, necessitating a merged enforcement agency: Department of Economic Development, 1986. This did not meet with universal approval and did not subsequently feature in the pre-legislative proposals: EOC for Northern Ireland, 1986; Fair Employment Agency, 1987. See the slightly more sympathetic response of the Standing Advisory Commission on Human Rights (1990: 74–5).

4. This proposal does not appear to be modelled upon any similar provision in comparative disability discrimination laws elsewhere.

5. This argument, as applicable to race and sex, is implicitly recognized in the actual make-up of the CRE and EOC.

6. SDA 1975 ss 57–61; RRA 1976 ss 48–52.

7. See, in particular: *R* v *CRE, ex parte Cottrell and Rothon* [1980] IRLR 279 Div Crt (CRE is discharging a quasi-judicial function and must observe natural justice and fair process); *Hillingdon London Borough Council* v *CRE* [1982] AC 779 HL (CRE may not carry out a formal investigation unless it has genuine belief, and not mere suspicion, that the party subject to investigation has committed discriminatory acts); *CRE* v *Prestige Group plc* [1983] IRLR 408 QBD (CRE must inform the party to be investigated so that representations can be made before any investigation commences). See also: *Science Research Council* v *Nass* [1979] 3 All ER 673 HL.

8. SDA 1975 ss 67–70; RRA 1976 ss 58–61.

9. SDA 1975 ss 71–3; RRA 1976 ss 62–4.

10. SDA 1975 ss 74 and 75; RRA 1976 ss 65 and 66.

11. (Can) HRA s 40. Disability discrimination complaints make up about one-third of the Commission's caseload: Bhatia, 1990: 108. A member of the Commission's staff, Bhatia acknowledges that these complaints only scratch the surface of disability-related discrimination and that many more complaints would be forthcoming if the complaints procedure were more widely known about and more efficient.

12. *Ibid.*: ss 41 and 43.

13. *Ibid.*: s 44.

14. *Ibid.*: s 47. The Commission must approve the terms of any settlement of the complaint: s 48. Failure to comply with the terms of an approved settlement is a criminal offence: s 60.

15. *Ibid.*: ss 49 and 50. The Tribunal is appointed from a panel established under ss 48.1–48.5. The Commission is a party to the action and may appear and be represented before the Tribunal: s 51.

16. *Ibid.*: ss 55 and 56.

17. (Alb) IRPA ss 14 and 15; (BC) HRA s 10; (Man) HRC ss 2–8; (NB) HRA ss 10–19; (NS) HRA ss 22–6A; (Ont) HRC ss 27–31; (PEI) HRA ss 16–19; (Québ) CHR&F ss 58–68; (Sask) HRC ss 21–5 (and the Human Rights Commission Act 1972); (YT) HRA ss 15–18.

18. (Alb) IRPA s 16. See also: Alberta Human Rights Commission Procedure Regulations 1980 (Alb Reg 263/80); Commission Procedure Regulation 1990 (Alb Reg 150/90).

19. *Ibid.*: ss 19 and 20. Protection is afforded against complainants being victimized: s 11. The Commission has powers of investigation, entry and inspection: ss 21–6.

20. *Ibid.*: ss 27–30.
21. *Ibid.*: s 33.
22. (BC) HRA ss 11–16 (and the Human Rights Code Board of Inquiry Regulations 1975 BC Reg 151/75, as amended by 137/82); (Man) HRC ss 22–7; (NB) HRA s 20; (NS) HRA ss 27–37; (Ont) HRC s 32–42; (PEI) HRA ss 21–8; (Québ) CHR&F ss 69–80; (Sask) HRC ss 27–30; (YT) HRA ss 19–23.
23. (Man) HRC ss 28–31.
24. *Ibid.*: ss 32–42.
25. *Ibid.*: s 21.
26. *Consolidated Rail Corporation* v *Darrone* (1984) 465 US 624. See generally: Paolicelli, 1979; Schoon, 1979; Boller, 1982.
27. 42 USC s 2000e-5.
28. 42 USC s 2000e-5(f). Actions might also be brought by the EEOC or the Attorney General.
29. 42 USC s 2000e-5(g); *Shah* v *Mount Zion Hospital & Medical Center* (1981) 642 F2d 268 at 272 (9th Cir).
30. Because of restrictions under Title VII of the Civil Rights Act 1964: *Mosley* v *Clarksville Memorial Hospital* (1983) 574 FSupp 224 (MD Tenn); *DeGrace* v *Rumsfeld* (1980) 614 F2d 796 (1st Cir). Cf. the opposite position under 42 USC s 1981 (Civil Rights Act 1866), although see *Patterson* v *McLean Credit Union* (1989) 491 US 164 (restricting s 1981 compensatory and punitive damages to recruitment and selection discrimination). See now s 101 Civil Rights Act 1991. Compensatory or punitive damages might have been available under state fair employment laws.
31. 42 USC s 1977A. However, a cap is put upon compensatory and punitive damages (not including back pay or past pecuniary losses or possibly future loss of earnings) in sex, religion and disability suits depending upon the size of the employer: 15–100 employees ($50,000), 101–200 employees ($100,000), 201–500 employees ($200,000) and over 500 employees ($300,000).
32. US Senate, 1989: 90–1; Yelin, 1991: 141.
33. *HR Focus* (July 1993) at 3. See also Dolatly, 1993: 544.
34. *EEOC* v *AIC Security Investigations Ltd* (1993) 823 FSupp 571 and 820 FSupp 1060 (ND Ill).
35. *Enforcement Guidance: Compensation and Punitive Damages Available Under Section 102 of the Civil Rights Act of 1991* (reprinted in *Daily Labor Reporter* No. 131, E-1, 7 August 1992).
36. (NSW) ADA 1977 s 89.
37. *Ibid.*: s 92.
38. *Ibid.*: s 94.
39. *Ibid.*: s 113.
40. See generally: (Qld) ADA 1991 ss 134 *et seq.*
41. See generally: (SA) EOA 1984 ss 93 *et seq*; (WA) EOA 1984 ss 75 *et seq.*
42. (Vic) EOA 1984 ss 44 *et seq.*
43. (Cth) DDA 1992 s 69.
44. *Ibid.*: ss 71–6.
45. *Ibid.*: ss 77–102.
46. *Ibid.*: s 93.
47. *Ibid.*: s 103. The declarations or orders are enforceable in the federal courts.
48. Leonard, 1987c.
49. Justice, 1987.
50. Morris and Nott, 1991: 161.
51. Leonard, 1987b.
52. SDA 1975 s 65(1)(b); RRA 1976 s 56(1)(b). The award of compensation must be regarded as just and equitable in the first place, although thereafter the award is calculated upon common law principles: *Hurley* v *Mustoe* (No. 2) [1983] ICR 422 (EAT).
53. SDA 1975 s 66(4); RRA 1976 s 57(4). For the principles of assessment of general damages in discrimination cases see: *Alexander* v *Home Office* [1988] ICR 685 CA.
54. See, for example: *Noone* v *North West Thames Regional Health Authority* [1988] ICR 813

CA (3,000 for severe injury to feelings in a race discrimination case); cf. *Coleman* v *Skyrail Oceanic Ltd (t/a Goodmos Tours)* [1981] ICR 864 CA.

55. *Sharifi* v *Strathclyde Regional Council* [1992] IRLR 259 EAT.

56. Leonard, 1987b: 14.

57. *Employment Gazette* Vol. 99 No. 12 (December 1991).

58. SDA 1975 s 65(2) and RRA 1976 s 56(2) by reference to EP(C)A 1978 s 75 and Unfair Dismissal (Increase of Compensation Limit) Order 1993 SI 1993/1348.

59. (Can) HRA s 53. It is within the Commission's jurisdiction to award interest upon any compensation to be paid: *Attorney-General of Canada* v *Rosin* (1991) 91 CLLC para. 17,011 (Can) FCA.

60. (BC) HRA s 17. The (BC) Human Rights Amendment Act 1992 (SBC 1992 c 43) has subsequently lifted this limit on damages and provides a general power to award compensation for injury to dignity, feelings and self-respect.

61. (Ont) HRC s 41.

62. (Sask) HRC ss 29–31.

63. [1993] IRLR 445 (ECJ).

64. Sex Discrimination and Equal Pay (Remedies) Regulations 1993; Race Relations (Remedies) Act 1994.

65. The general principles for the award of exemplary damages are set out in *Rookes* v *Barnard* [1964] AC 1129 (HL); *Cassell & Co. Ltd* v *Broome* [1972] AC 1027 (HL); and *AB* v *South West Water Services Ltd* [1993] 1 All ER 609 (CA).

66. [1991] ICR 226 (CA).

67. (Québ) CHR&F s 49.

68. (YT) HRA ss 24–24.1.

69. (Man) HRC s 43. An order may not have the effect of removing a person from an employment position accepted in good faith: s 44. The parties usually bear their own costs, unless either party has acted frivolously or vexatiously: s 45. An order is enforceable as a court judgment: s 48.

70. SDA 1975 s 65(1)(a); RRA 1976 s 56(1)(a).

71. SDA 1975 s 65(1)(c),(3); RRA s 56(1)(c),(3).

72. *Noone* v *North West Thames Regional Health Authority* (No. 2) [1988] IRLR 530 CA.

73. *British Gas plc* v *Sharma* [1991] ICR 19 EAT.

74. (Can) HRA s 53. It is within the Commission's jurisdiction to award interest upon any compensation to be paid: *Attorney-General of Canada* v *Rosin* (1991) 91 CLLC para. 17,011 (Can) FCA.

75. *Ibid.*: s 53(4).

76. See for example the Alberta model: (Alb) IRPA ss 31–31.1. An order for costs may also be made. An order of the board of inquiry is enforceable as an order of the court: s 32.

77. (Sask) HRCReg s 1(d).

78. (Sask) Reg 144/91 s 3.

79. (Man) HRC s 47 (the adjudicator has jurisdiction to supervise or vary such an order, with the Commission's assistance, until there is full compliance).

80. *Ibid.*: s 43(4). Such a decision of an adjudicator is subject to judicial review: s 50.

81. *Ibid.*: s 54. See also s 55.

82. (1985) 20 DLR (4th) 668 (Can) FCA; (1987) 40 DLR (4th) 193 (Can) SC.

83. (1984) 84 CLLC para. 17,008 (Ont) HRC.

84. See generally: SDA 1975 Part IV; RRA 1976 Part IV.

85. (NB) HRA s 23. A prosecution requires ministerial consent: s 24. In such criminal proceedings arising from employment discrimination, the court may order reinstatement and/or lost wages up to the date of conviction: s 25. An order enjoining further violations may be issued and enforced as an order of the Supreme Court: s 27.

86. (NS) HRA s 29. A prosecution requires ministerial consent: s 30. An order may also be made to injunct further offences: s 32.

87. (Ont) HRC s 44.

88. (PEI) HRA ss 29–32.

89. (Québ) CHR&F ss 81–3 and 87–9.

90. (Sask) HRC s 35.

91. *Ibid.*: s 40.
92. *Ibid.*: s 36.
93. *Ibid.*: s 38.
94. (YT) HRA ss 27–9.
95. (Man) HRC s 51.

12

Beyond Enforcement

INTRODUCTION

The weaknesses of the individual complaint-based anti-discrimination law and the alleged failure of institutional enforcement in the field of gender and race discrimination have led many commentators to argue for a fresh approach. It is noteworthy, for example, that at the same time as US disability rights activists were pressing for comprehensive disability discrimination laws, in Canada – where such laws had been in place under human rights legislation for some time – Canadian disability advocates were looking to employment equity principles (involving the use of statistics, goals and timetables) to replace or supplement the reduced momentum of the non-discrimination principle as applicable to disabled persons. In Britain, too, the past decade or so has seen increasing interest in ideas of fair participation and equality of opportunity, employing methodologies that go beyond a simple proscription of direct or indirect discrimination on prohibited grounds. In this final substantive chapter, we examine some of these trends as they might apply to disabled employment rights and, in particular, we look at the role of positive action, contract compliance and equal opportunity policy-making.

POSITIVE ACTION

Meaning of Positive Action

As understanding of discrimination has deepened, concern over the efficacy of the individual complaint-based model of legal enforcement of anti-discrimination norms has led to consideration being given to alternative strategies of 'positive action' or 'affirmative action'.[1] As McCrudden explains, 'affirmative action' is the term used in the USA

> to refer to actions taken to identify and replace discriminatory employment practices, and to develop practices which result in the greater inclusion and participation in the work force of women and minorities.[2]

In Britain, the term 'positive action' is usually preferred. Positive action can play a role in the range of judicial remedies available to courts and tribunals to address findings of discrimination. For example, an order might be made that the successful plaintiff in a discrimination action should be promoted or that the unsuccessful employer-defendant should dismantle a discriminatory recruitment practice. In the present context, however, concern is with *voluntary* positive action or with positive action that is encouraged or required by the legal framework itself. McCrudden identifies five types of possible (although not necessarily permissible) positive action.[3]

First, employers might take steps to eradicate discrimination by identifying and replacing unjustifiably discriminatory practices bearing upon one group rather than another. Close scrutiny of selection tests for inherent bias would illustrate this approach. This not only is permitted in existing discrimination law, but is an implicit legal duty. Second, enterprises might adopt 'facially neutral but purposefully inclusionary policies' in order to increase the representation in the workforce of minority group members without directly using a prohibited ground to do so. McCrudden gives the example of recruiting from among the unemployed or within a certain local catchment area to demonstrate this point. The problem with this form of positive action is that it will usually amount to direct or indirect reverse discrimination.[4] Third, employers might institute an outreach programme to ensure that groups that have suffered discrimination in the past are made aware of employment opportunities and encouraged to apply for them. If necessary, minority group members might be extended the assistance of training programmes designed to qualify or re-skill these groups to compete for those opportunities. Outreach, however, does not extend into the selection or promotion process itself, and there the minority group members must compete on merit. With that limitation in mind, outreach appears to be permitted by existing discrimination legislation.

Fourth, positive action might involve a degree of reverse discrimination, where employers address the under-representation of a disadvantaged group by according group members preferential treatment in recruitment, selection, promotion or employment security. The adoption of a quota of jobs for particular minorities is the manifest example of this type of positive action. This transgresses existing sex and race discrimination law. Fifth, and finally, employers might redefine 'merit' by including membership of a group or group characteristics as a relevant qualification for a job. The classic example is the recruitment of Afro-Caribbean applicants for positions as social workers providing welfare services to the Afro-Caribbean community. This form of positive action is permitted within narrow terms by the 'genuine occupational qualification' exceptions under the Sex Discrimination and Race Relations Acts.

Positive Action and Disability

In Britain, the absence of a symmetrical (or even an asymmetrical) disability discrimination law has permitted (although not required) employers to utilize any or all of the above five forms of positive action in respect of disabled workers. The use of outreach techniques is in fact recommended by the Code of Good Practice on the Employment of Disabled People.[5] Employers are also encouraged there to review job descriptions and requirements, and application and selection procedures, to ensure that disabled applicants are not inadvertently excluded from employment opportunities.[6] Disabled workers may also have benefited through some local authorities' policies that direct new job opportunities towards applicants on the unemployment register or within a narrowly defined local labour market. The use of 'reverse discrimination' is mandated, of course, by the quota scheme under the 1944 Act, and some public sector employers have used the quota, in tandem with a redefinition of merit, so as to increase the representation of disabled people in their workforce.[7]

Nevertheless, positive action, in general, and towards disabled workers in particular, remains in the realms of voluntarism in Britain. While the enactment of a disability discrimination statute would undoubtedly encourage some employers to take positive action towards disabled persons, the experience of other countries suggests that a positive action mandate, to be effective and universal, has to be enshrined in law. One way in which this might be done is through statutory contract compliance techniques.

A ROLE FOR CONTRACT COMPLIANCE?

In the USA during the 1970s and 1980s, the message that hiring disabled workers was good for business was often heard.[8] Appeals to the commercial instincts of employers as a tactic for promoting the employment opportunities of minorities are frequently seen as a signal of weak or non-existent legislation regulating social discrimination in the labour market. Indeed, market forces have recently been recruited to demonstrate the futility of anti-discrimination laws in the first place and to argue the case for allowing a micro-economic solution to the problem of employment discrimination.[9] However, harnessing commercial energy to the cause of equal opportunity and the anti-discrimination principle is not necessarily incompatible with the role of legal regulation. Contract compliance techniques have been a feature in ensuring fair labour standards for many decades.

Meaning and Use of Contract Compliance

Contract compliance has been described in the following terms:

> With contract compliance the public sector insists that the firms from which it buys goods or services meet certain minimum employment standards. Rather than leaving it to other agencies to ensure that those standards are honoured, the purchasing body itself, or an agency acting directly on its behalf, seeks to ensure that they are met or that they will be met within a reasonable time. If the purchasing body cannot satisfy itself, at least on this latter point, then the firm forfeits the right to tender for public sector contracts.[10]

In other words, unless contractors meet specified employment standards for their workforce, they will lose the right to compete for or retain business contracts with the public sector. Contract compliance ensures that the purchasing power of the public sector is employed in the pursuit of social policy. In principle, there is nothing to prevent the private sector using contract compliance but, altruism apart, there are few motives for doing so. In practice, therefore, contract compliance techniques are almost invariably used by central and local government or by organs of the state.

Although contract compliance is often thought of as a fairly modern phenomenon, a form of contract compliance was practised in government contracting in Britain after 1891 by virtue of the House of Commons Fair Wages Resolutions.[11] In essence, a fair wages clause in government contracts insisted that contractors should observe minimum wage and labour standards, enforceable through compulsory arbitration, and subject to the ultimate sanctions of contract termination and removal from the lists of approved tenderers.[12] However, central government fair wages clauses did not address discrimination other than anti-union policies and practices, although government contracts after 1969 required contractors to conform with the race relations legislation. Furthermore, the last Fair Wages Resolution was rescinded by the Government with effect from 1983 and, with the advent of compulsory competitive tendering, other public sector employers resiled from including non-commercial considerations in their contractual arrangements.[13]

The use of contract compliance as a tool of equal opportunity policy developed in the USA during the early 1940s to combat racial discrimination in the defence industries.[14] Since 1965, moreover, with the signing of Executive Order No. 11246 and the establishment of the Office of Federal Contract Compliance (OFCCP), contract compliance and affirmative action were placed upon a firmer footing and extended to embrace discrimination on the grounds of race, colour, religion, gender and national origin.[15] In Britain, nevertheless, fair wages resolutions aside, *statutory* contract compliance has not been a feature of the anti-discrimination and equal opportunity battery. Instead, such experiments with contract compliance as there were occurred in local government on a *voluntary* basis, although undoubtedly inspired by the specific duty of local authorities under race discrimination law to promote equality of opportunity.[16] This encouraged a small number of councils to utilize their tendering procedures and commercial contracts to attempt to project the effects of their commitment to equal employment opportunity to third parties with whom they did business.[17] The brave new world of contract compliance was short-lived, however, as the Local Government Act 1988 effectively outlawed the inclusion of non-commercial conditions in local authority contracts and restricted the ability of local government entities to vet contractors during the tendering stage.[18]

Contract Compliance and Disabled Persons

In Britain, the primary emphasis in the use of contract compliance methods has been in fostering improved employment opportunities and conditions for ethnic minority workers. Women and other disadvantaged social groups have tended to take second place in the order of priorities. Nevertheless, disability has featured as an issue in voluntary contract compliance programmes. For example, the Greater London Council's pre-contract procedures took account of the percentage of disabled employees engaged by any firm tendering for a contract. Successful tenderers would be expected to liaise with the appropriate authorities to attempt the fulfilment of statutory and extra-statutory obligations towards this group.[19] In spite of this, there is little, if any, evidence of the effect of such programmes upon disabled employment. Now the Local Government Act 1988 surely prevents any further use of local authorities' purchasing power to advantage disabled workers.[20]

If a comparative perspective is adopted, it is clear that disabled persons in other countries do enjoy the formal protection of *statutory* contract compliance programmes. In Canada, the Federal Contractors Programme applies to employers with over 100 employees bidding for federal contracts for the supply of goods and services valued at at least $200,000.[21] Such employers must observe the principle of employment equity in their workforce and this extends to disabled persons. The sanctions available where the principle is being ignored include the eventual exclusion of employers from tendering for federal contracts. The federal government has the right to review employers' records in order to assess efforts being made, levels of compliance and results achieved. Among the Canadian provinces, Ontario also uses contract compliance to address employment discrimination by providing that it is an implied term of every Ontario government contract and sub-contract that the right to equal treatment in employment without discrimination on the ground of disability shall not be infringed during the performance of that contract.[22] A similar provision applies in respect of government grants and loans.[23] Breach of the implied term shall be grounds for the cancellation of the contract (or grant or loan) and may justify a refusal to enter into further contracts with the discriminator (or make further grants or loans thereto).[24]

In the USA, a form of contract compliance is implicit in section 504 of the RA 1973, which insists that disabled persons shall not be excluded from participation in any programme or activity receiving federal financial assistance or conducted by an arm of the federal government. This mandates equal employment opportunity and prohibits disability-based discrimination where employers are the beneficiaries of federal funding. However, as this gives the individual directly enforceable rights against the employer and does not strictly involve the medium of *commercial* contracting, it is not a true example of contract compliance techniques in practice. Such an example is provided by section 503 of the Act, which makes separate provision for disabled persons to benefit from contract compliance theory. This is such an important illustration of the genre that it deserves separate treatment.

DISABILITY AND CONTRACT COMPLIANCE IN THE UNITED STATES

Section 503 of the Rehabilitation Act 1973

In the USA, section 503 of the federal RA 1973 introduced statutory contract compliance as a means of promoting equal employment opportunities for disabled workers.[25] Any employer contracting with the federal government is required to take affirmative action to employ and advance disabled persons if the value of the contract exceeds $10,000. This provision covers procurement contracts for goods or services and construction contracts. It also applies to any similar sub-contracts which exceed $10,000 and which are entered into by a federal contractor in order to carry out the main contract.[26] Every relevant contract with the federal government must incorporate a model provision requiring the federal contractor, when employing persons to carry out the contract, to take affirmative action to employ and advance in employment qualified disabled persons.[27]

Federal contractors holding contracts in excess of $50,000 and employing over fifty employees are subject to additional obligations. Within 120 days of the relevant contract commencing, such employers must prepare and maintain an affirmative action programme at each of their establishments.[28] The programme must set out the employer-contractor's policies, practices and procedures regarding affirmative action in respect of all employment practices and in respect of all levels of employment.[29] It must be available for inspection upon request by any employee or applicant and, for this purpose, information about the availability and accessibility of the programme has to be posted at each workplace.[30] The programme must be kept under review and updated annually, provided that any significant changes that result are communicated to employees and would-be employees.[31] The contractor-employer must invite individuals who may be covered by the legislation to come forward if they wish to take advantage of the affirmative action programme. A model form of invitation is found in the regulations.[32] Such action on the part of a disabled person has to be voluntary and treated as confidential and in accordance with the legislation. A refusal by disabled persons to identify themselves as potential beneficiaries of an employer-contractor's affirmative action programme is not to be the subject of adverse treatment.[33] Compliance with the particular requirement to develop an affirmative action programme does not relieve the employer of any obligation to take affirmative action in respect of a person of whose disability the employer already has knowledge, but equally the employer is not obliged to search its medical files to identify disabled persons who are not otherwise known or who have not come forward voluntarily.[34]

Affirmative Action Programmes

Whether or not a government contractor is required to devise a *formal* affirmative action *programme*, all employers subject to section 503 must consider the effect of the affirmative action mandate upon their policies, practices and procedures. Personnel processes call for review to decide whether

> present procedures assure careful, thorough and systematic consideration of the job qualifications of known handicapped applicants for job vacancies filled either by hiring or promotion, and for all training opportunities offered or available.[35]

If necessary, the personnel procedures must be modified and, in any event, must be designed so as to allow compliance with the affirmative action obligation to be monitored. The OFCCP suggests, but does not require, that employers adopt model procedures contained in the section 503 regulations.[36] Application or personnel forms might be annotated so as to identify vacancies for which a known disabled applicant was considered. Such forms should be easily retrievable for internal and external review in investigations and compliance activities. Disabled employees' personnel or application records might identify each promotion and training programme for which the individual was considered. Where a disabled employee or applicant is turned down for any employment opportunity, the form should contain a statement of the reason for that outcome, including a comparison with the qualifications of the successful and unsuccessful candidates, and a description of any accommodations considered.[37] The application form or personnel record should also describe any accommodation undertaken by the employer to place a disabled individual in a job where the individual was successful in being hired, promoted or trained for that position.

As part of an affirmative action programme, contractors must provide and adhere to a schedule for the review of job qualification requirements.[38] Insofar as such requirements tend to screen out qualified disabled persons, the employer must ensure that they are job-related, consistent with business necessity and essential for the safe performance of the job. Affirmative action generally dictates that the application of job qualification requirements in the employment process should accord with these principles and the burden of so proving is upon the contractor.[39] However, the section 503 regulations allow federal contractors to conduct pre-employment medical examinations of applicants 'provided that the results of such an examination shall be used only in accordance with the requirements of' these provisions.[40] Any inquiry or medical examination relating to an individual's physical or mental condition must lead to the information thus gleaned being treated as confidential.[41] Naturally, section 503 requires federal contractors to make reasonable accommodation to the limitations of a disabled applicant or employee.[42] If applicants or employees identify themselves as disabled persons desirous of benefiting under the contractor's affirmative action programme, where the contractor is obliged to invite such identification, the contractor must seek the advice of the applicants or employees in question regarding their proper placement and appropriate accommodation.[43] The extent of the obligation to accommodate can take account of business necessity and financial cost and expenses, and reasonable accommodation need not be made if it can be shown that it would impose an undue hardship on the conduct of the business.

Affirmative Action in Practice

By requiring federal contractors to review their employment policies and practices, the OFCCP causes these employers to question whether their personnel procedures provide the required affirmative action necessary for the proper employment and advancement of disabled workers. The law requires that contractors must act upon the findings of such internal review. Accordingly, if the evidence shows that affirmative action is absent or deficient, contractors

> shall undertake appropriate outreach and positive recruitment activities . . . [and] the scope of a contractor's efforts shall depend upon all the circumstances, including the contractor's size and resources and the extent to which existing employment practices are adequate.[44]

The OFCCP regulations suggest a number of types of activities which might be undertaken, but the list is merely illustrative and not designed to be prescriptive or exhaustive.

The OFCCP suggests that contractors might develop effective internal communication of its affirmative action obligations.[45] The intention is to foster understanding, acceptance and support among all levels of management and the workforce, and to encourage the taking of necessary steps to aid the contractor in complying with the affirmative action obligation. In the OFCCP's words,

> A strong outreach program will be ineffective without internal support from supervisory and management personnel and other employees, who may have had limited contact with handicapped persons in the past.[46]

This policy dissemination within the workplace is crucial. This might be achieved via inclusion in the contractor's policy manual or by publication in any in-house media (such as company newspapers and annual reports).[47] The policy statement should be posted on bulletin boards. Alternatively or in addition, special meetings with managers and supervisors could be conducted to explain the policy's intent and the individual responsibility for implementing it. Similar meetings could be arranged for other employees, but in both cases the commitment and positive attitude of senior management towards the policy must be manifest. Affirmative action policy can also be the subject of employee orientation or induction programmes and management training sessions. Trade union officials should be made aware of the policy, their co-operation secured and non-discrimination clauses written into collective agreements.[48] Existing contractual provisions should be tested to ensure that they are non-discriminatory. It should be made clear that disabled workers will not face harassment or victimization for seeking to exercise their rights to equal opportunity.

It is further recommended by the OFCCP that internal procedures need to be in place to ensure that the policy is being implemented and is made operational.[49] The employer's commitment to increase disabled employment opportunities should be reiterated and reinforced periodically.[50] The assistance and support of recruiting sources might be enlisted as an additional means of underpinning that commitment.[51] Recruitment through disabled educational and training institutions might be attempted and contacts could be forged with social services agencies, disability organizations and so on, as a conduit for advice, technical assistance and referral of potential employees.[52] A further approach to policy implementation is to review employment records to discover whether the employment skills of existing disabled employees in the organization are being fully utilized and developed, and whether such employees are available for promotion and transfer.[53] Written dissemination of the company's policy on disabled employment opportunities should be made to sub-contractors, customers and suppliers, requesting appropriate action on their part.[54] A supplementary course of action, and the clearest example of outreach, is the taking of positive steps to attract qualified disabled workers outside the workforce who have the required skills and who could be recruited with affirmative action. Such workers can be located through local branches of disabled organizations and organizations of disabled people.[55] Finally, to repeat a point already made above in another context, employers might include disabled workers when employees are pictured in consumer, promotional and recruitment advertising.[56]

The responsibility for implementing an affirmative action policy is a matter which should be identified at all stages of espousing a policy and attempting to make it operational. The OFCCP recommends that an executive manager should be designated to manage the employer's affirmative action activities.[57] He or she should be clearly identified with the policy and associated programmes, and must be given the necessary support and staff to implement the policy. The section 503 regulations pinpoint seven key implementation activities for the responsible director or manager of an employer's affirmative action policy:

1 Development of policy statements, affirmative action programmes and internal and external communication techniques.
2 Identification of problem areas in the implementation of the affirmative action programme, in conjunction with line management and disabled employees, and development of solutions.
3 Design and implementation of auditing and reporting systems.
4 Liaison between the contractor and the OFCCP.
5 Liaison between the contractor and disability organizations, and arrangement of active corporate involvement in community service programmes for disabled people.
6 Informing management of latest developments in affirmative action.
7 Arranging career counselling for disabled employees.

The last four activities do not require further explication for the purpose of this study, but the first three points warrant expansion.

First, the responsibility for implementing an affirmative action policy requires the development of techniques of policy communication. The OFCCP advocates including regular discussions with managers, supervisors and employees in order to check policy compliance.[58] Supervisors should be made aware that, among the criteria by which their performance is being judged, their efforts and achievements in affirmative action are being evaluated. Second, identifying problems and developing solutions is particularly important in respect of the employer's reasonable accommodation obligations.[59] Third, the design and implementation of audit and reporting systems should ensure that the effectiveness of the programme is being measured and that the need for any remedial action is being indicated. The degree to which the company's affirmative action objectives are being attained should be determinable, while whether each workplace or location under the employer's control is complying with the relevant law must be confirmed.[60] Such systems should also ascertain whether disabled employees have had the opportunity to participate in all the employer's educational, training, recreational and social activities.

Once affirmative action policies and procedures are in place, contractors might be careful to ensure that good practice is being observed in the development and execution of their programmes. The OFCCP lists a number of *desiderata*.[61] Job qualification requirements, once reviewed to eliminate adverse impact upon disabled workers, should be made available to all employees and managers involved in recruitment, screening, selection and promotion. The selection process should be free of stereotyping disabled persons in a way which limits their employment opportunities. Personnel involved in employment processes (including the disciplinary process) should be carefully selected and trained in order to safeguard the integrity of the affirmative action policy or programme. Employers should ensure that representatives from recruiting sources are formally briefed so that the effects of the company's affirmative action policy are not dissipated beyond its boundaries.[62] Ideally, disabled employees should be part of the personnel staff or team and should be generally available as role models in community activities, such as career days. Recruitment in schools should incorporate special efforts to make contact with disabled pupils, while companies should consider work placement and work study connections with rehabilitation facilities and specialist schools so as to encourage disabled persons to enter the workplace. The OFCCP encourages contractors to 'use all available resources to continue or establish on the job training programs'.[63] Contractors should request state employment security agencies to refer disabled workers for consideration under an affirmative action programme.[64]

Breach of Contract Compliance Obligations

Two practices which could run counter to the spirit of affirmative action are given special consideration in the section 503 regulations. First, in employing or promoting a disabled individual, a federal contractor may not offer a reduced rate of pay to take account of any disability income, pension or benefit received from another source.[65] Second, contracts between the contractor-employer and a sheltered workshop do not count as affirmative action as a substitute for the employment and advancement of disabled individuals within the employer's direct workforce.[66] However, such contracts might be part of an affirmative action policy where the sheltered workshop undertakes training of disabled persons and the contractor has undertaken to place the newly qualified trainees in its workforce at full rates of pay.

A disabled person who contends that a federal contractor is in breach of the affirmative action clause of a contract covered by section 503 may complain to the federal Department of Labor:

> If any individual with handicaps believes any contractor has failed or refused to comply with the provisions of a contract with the United States, relating to employment of individuals with handicaps, such individual may file a complaint with the Department of Labor. The Department shall promptly investigate such complaint and shall take such action thereon as the facts and circumstances warrant, consistent with the terms of such contract and the laws and regulations applicable thereto.[67]

This leads to an investigation of the complaint by the OFCCP.[68] First, however, it is envisaged that normally the complaint will be pursued through the contractor's internal review procedures. If the complaint is not resolved within 60 days, the matter must be resolved by the OFCCP, if necessary using alternative dispute resolution methods. Compliance with section 503 obligations does not necessarily determine that the contractor is in compliance with other disability discrimination laws, and the reverse proposition is also true.[69] However, where there is a clear breach of section 503, and the matter cannot be resolved by informal means, the section 503 regulations allow for judicial enforcement proceedings to enforce the contractor's affirmative action obligations.[70] Furthermore, the Department of Labor, through the OFCCP, may then take such action as the facts and circumstances warrant,[71] consistent with the terms of such contract and the applicable laws and regulations.[72] In particular, the federal government contracting party may withhold progress payments under the contract, or cancel or terminate the contract, or debar the contractor from future federal contracting opportunities. In such cases, the contractor is entitled to a formal hearing before an administrative law judge.[73]

A Future Role for Contract Compliance?

At first blush, the US model of affirmative action for disabled persons under contract compliance appears quite an attractive option for advocates of disability rights legislation. However, some points and limitations should be borne in mind. Although the section 503 regulations require contractors to keep records appertaining to compliance with the statutory provisions, and these are available for inspection by OFCCP compliance officers, in reality scrutiny of contractors' policies and practices is random and thinly spread. Testimony suggests that only about 10 per cent of contractors subject to section 503 are troubled by compliance reviews.[74] An earlier audit of the OFCCP in 1977 had been critical of the OFCCP's implementation of section 503 and had pointed up the lack of a procedure for conducting comprehensive compliance reviews.[75] The agency had adopted a reactive response, triggered by complaints, rather than a proactive approach to compliance. The result was that a survey of federal contractors conducted in 1978 found that 90 per cent were not complying with the regulations in some way, 25 per cent had not adopted an affirmative action plan, 44 per cent had no outreach programme and 17 per cent did not practise reasonable accommodation.[76] Legal commentators were justly critical of the OFCCP's lack of aggressiveness and patent weakness in enforcing section 503 and protecting disabled employment expectations.[77] However, less than a decade later, these same criticisms were once again being voiced.[78]

Moreover, although there is evidence that contract compliance techniques have had a positive effect upon the employment chances of women and racial minorities,[79] there is little or no comparable evidence assessing the impact of section 503 upon disabled persons.[80] Intuition suggests that there must be some effect, but the measure of that effect and its quality is unknown.[81] Furthermore, notwithstanding the fact that section 503 has been interpreted judicially as importing a non-discrimination requirement, there has been much confusion and doubt about whether the section affords a disabled complainant a private right of action in the federal courts or whether enforcement is limited to proceedings before and by the OFCCP.[82] Federal appellate authority determines that section 503 does not create a private cause of action and that complainants are limited to the invocation of the OFCCP enforcement mechanisms.[83] Attempts to argue that disabled individuals have *locus standi* to sue a contractor on the basis that it is in general breach of its duty to take affirmative action towards disabled people, or that a disabled employee is a third party beneficiary of the commercial contract in question, have also failed.[84] The only other course of action available to a disabled plaintiff is to seek judicial review of an OFCCP decision with which he or she disagrees.[85]

In spite of these reservations, contract compliance undoubtedly has a role to play in the enfranchisement of disabled persons' employment rights. By going beyond the simple anti-discrimination principle and by mandating a degree of positive action on behalf of disabled workers, contract compliance provides a detailed framework within which employers can develop policies and practices with the prior approval of the state. Businesses contracting with the public sector will know that their commitment to good practice and fair employment standards will not disadvantage them in the tendering process and will even give them an edge over competitors who compete on the basis of low labour costs resulting from poor labour standards. On the other hand, governments subscribing to neo-classical economic theory will view contract compliance schemes as an unwarranted interference with the free play of the market and as an undue burden upon business, although a libertarian view might suggest that the elimination of morally abhorrent discrimination through the use of commercial pressures is more desirable than direct interference in business via social regulations such as anti-discrimination laws.[86]

EQUAL OPPORTUNITY POLICIES AND PLANNING

Statutory contract compliance lies at the crossroads between positive or affirmative action in one direction and equal opportunity plans and policies in the other direction. While contract compliance legislation is neither a necessary nor a sufficient condition for equal opportunity planning, it is clear that there must be some form of legal imperative if employers are to be encouraged to include disabled persons in corporate personnel policy.

Legal Spurs to Policy Formulation: the View from Abroad

In the USA, section 503 of the RA 1973 has encouraged and required the development of equal opportunity policy-making. Without equal opportunity plans and policies, employers lack the foundations upon which to build such positive action practices as the law permits or demands. Section 501 also requires the executive branch of the federal government – in its role as an employer – to develop and implement affirmative action plans for the hiring, placement and advancement of disabled persons.[87] This section has been much neglected in the literature on disability rights in the USA.[88] Although subsequently disability rights activists would be critical of the RA 1973 for its failure to address disability discrimination in the private sector, section 501 was crucial in the establishment of the credentials of the non-discrimination principle as it applies to disability. In remarkable contrast to the position in Britain, where such law as applies to disabled employment is directed at the private sector and is adopted in the public sector only by concession, section 501 required the federal government and its agencies to become model employers and to show the way towards disabled employment opportunities.

Percy notes that in the early years of section 501, visible change was generated in the employment practices of federal agencies, which began to devise and implement affirmative action plans covering disabled workers.[89] The US Civil Service Commission, upon whom responsibility for section 501 was originally bestowed, recorded that,

> Overall, we have observed a considerable increase in the interest and commitment to the program among agencies. One major accomplishment has been the development of an awareness by non-handicapped persons toward the capabilities, employment problems, and needs of handicapped individuals . . . [However], we found a wide range of quality in the plans. Some agencies displayed a keen interest in developing and implementing strong programs with ideas and methods that went beyond the suggested model. Other agencies submitted plans that can be classified as barely meeting minimum requirements.[90]

Despite this initial success, 'The evidence to date suggests mixed ratings for the federal government in implementing affirmative action in federal employment of persons with disabilities'.[91] The overview of section 501 was transferred to the EEOC in 1978 and in its 1986 annual report, for example, the Commission estimated that while 6 per cent of the US labour force were classifiable by reference to 'targeted' disabilities (including blindness, deafness, paralysis and mental disabilities), fewer than 1 per cent of federal government employees represented this group. The EEOC also reported that, as a result of on-site reviews of federal agency affirmative action programmes covering disabled persons, 93 per cent had appointed a disabled programme co-ordinator of seniority,[92] 37 per cent of sites were found to be accessible to disabled persons to some degree and 55 per cent of the reviewed installations had clearly defined disabled recruitment goals.[93]

Equal Opportunity Planning and the Role of Statistics

McCrudden observes that the role of statistics in discrimination and equal opportunity laws has been a controversial one.[94] He notes that statistics might be used in any of three ways. First, statistical information is an important ingredient of monitoring by employers for indirect discrimination resulting from their policies and practices. In this sense, statistics are used as a 'diagnostic tool'. Second, such information might be used as a 'benchmark of success'. Employers need to take a periodic snapshot of the workforce in order to be able to judge whether discrimination is being eliminated and whether minority members are being properly represented in the numbers of job applicants, interviewees, appointments, promotions and so on. In this sense, statistics might inform the setting of goals and timetables; that is, the employer sets a target by which the success of equal opportunity policies or positive action programmes will be assessed. For example, there might be an expectation (but no more than an expectation) that a certain percentage of a disadvantaged group will be encouraged to apply for jobs and/or be engaged in the next twelve months. Third, statistics could be used 'as ends in themselves'.[95] In this case, an employer decides to achieve as an objective the hiring or promotion of a specified percentage of minority group members, either absolutely or as a proportion of the existing workforce. This third use of statistics draws a distinction between goals or targets and timetables, on the one hand, and quotas, on the other hand. Confusion over this distinction and the means by which it is maintained is at the heart of the controversy about the use of statistics in equal opportunity policy and practice. McCrudden recommends that, for the avoidance of doubt about the legitimacy of using statistics in the first and second senses outlined here, statutory authority for statistics collection and analysis should be provided.[96]

Affirmative action planning in the USA under section 503 deliberately eschewed the setting of numerical goals because of the difficulties in determining disabled characteristics and numbers.[97] The setting of goals and timetables, and the collection of data to analyse disabled employment levels, is nevertheless encouraged under section 501.[98] In Canada, however, the use of statistics, goals and timetables is more overtly favoured. The federal Employment Equity Act 1985 requires federal employers of size to set annual goals for the implementation of employment equity. A timetable within which these goals are to be achieved must be laid down.[99] The law requires employers to publish annual statistics showing the total workforce and the number of disabled persons employed. Furthermore, a statistical breakdown must be provided, showing what occupational groups the employer has and the degree of representation of disabled persons in each occupational group. Information about salary ranges in the employer's workforce and the degree of representation of disabled persons in each range must also be highlighted. The statistical report must detail the number of employees hired or engaged, promoted and terminated (whether retired, resigned or dismissed, but not including temporarily laid off or absent by reason of illness, injury or labour dispute), with the degree of representation of disabled persons in those numbers.[100]

The use of statistics is also a feature in selected provincial legislation in Canada[101] and in the Australian Commonwealth in respect of public sector employment.[102] In the final analysis, however, there is still little evidence that the use of statistics, goals and timetables has radically improved the employment position of disabled persons in those sectors of the economy to which these examples apply. By way of illustration, in Canada it has been estimated that disabled persons constitute 9–17 per cent of the population, but that on 1990 figures approximately 19 per cent of employers subject to the (Can) EEA 1985 did not employ any disabled persons at all. The same source reveals that, whereas Canadians with disabilities make up 5.4 per cent of the Canadian workforce, only 2.4 per cent of the workforce is covered by the EEA regime.[103]

VIEW FROM BRITAIN

The agenda set by this study has been to learn the lessons from abroad for the development of a new legal model of disabled employment rights in Britain. The Conservative Government since 1979 (and, indeed, previous governments by default) has argued that the case for legislation to combat disability discrimination can be countered with a more effective case for a policy of education and persuasion. The evidence of the labour market status of disabled persons and the continued incidence of discrimination might be sufficient to suggest that this non-interventionist tactic has failed. However, such evidence is necessarily historic, and it might be said that employers are learning to put their own house in order. What proof is there that the voluntarist approach is working?

Disability and Equal Opportunity Policies

The enactment of sex and race discrimination laws has undoubtedly fostered the development of equal opportunity policies among employers. There are few hard data to suggest how widespread such policies are or what percentage of the labour market is covered by them. Neither the SDA 1975 nor the RRA 1976 requires employers to devise, adopt and implement such policies,[104] although undoubtedly employers who wish to avoid or alleviate challenges of discrimination would be well advised to do so. Many large, well-known employers have put such policies in place, but for most small and medium-sized British businesses an equal opportunity policy is a luxury or a matter of no concern and priority. Even among those enterprises that designate themselves as 'equal opportunity employers', the suspicion remains that this is a cosmetic title, without the underpinning of a written policy or the back-up of detailed practices and procedures.

When it comes to the issue of disability and employment, the absence of an anti-discrimination command in law deprives employers of any real incentive to make policy in this area. On its own, the 1944 Act contains little that would cause employers voluntarily to regulate their internal procedures. Although companies legislation requires employment policy in respect of disabled people to be recorded in the directors' annual report, this applies only to larger, incorporated businesses and hardly sets a challenging agenda.[105] The statement must describe *any* policy applied by the company for giving full and fair consideration to job applications from disabled people (having regard to their particular aptitudes and abilities), for continuing the employment of (and arranging appropriate training for) employees who become disabled during employment with the company, and for training, career development and promotion of disabled persons employed by the company. Unless the directors have taken all reasonable steps to ensure that such a statement is included in the annual report, a failure to publish a corporate disability employment policy is an offence. While formal compliance with this provision is widely observed, the measure has produced some pretty anodyne statements and little proof that the policy, once adopted, is either acted upon or periodically reviewed.[106]

It is suspected that many, but not all, equal opportunity employers tend to add additional disadvantaged groups to policies dealing with women and ethnic minorities, despite the lack of legal compulsion to do so. Cursory examination of recruitment advertisements, for example, indicates that disability is frequently added to the catalogue of grounds upon which employers disdain to discriminate. None the less, research indicates that only 21 per cent of employers have a formal written policy regarding the employment of disabled persons, but a large proportion were unable to say how such policy was implemented.[107] Of those able to identify their policy implementation methods, about a quarter employed regular monitoring methodology. Some 14 per cent of employers implement policy through management and employee involvement, but about the same number allocate responsibility to an executive manager. Setting recruitment targets was used by 7 per cent of employers who implemented policies and 5 per cent insisted on regular reports to senior management.[108] Among employers with no formal disabled employment policy, the most commonly encountered attitude was that disabled persons would be considered on merit. Three-quarters of such employers stated that they would not discriminate against disabled workers and 4 per cent claimed that they would positively encourage applications from disabled job-seekers.[109] Nevertheless, 13 per cent of employers said that they would only employ disabled persons for certain types of job and 6 per cent stated that they would not employ disabled workers under any circumstances.[110]

In spite of this, or maybe because of it, there is a groundswell of opinion that employers should be obliged to develop disabled employment policies. A large majority (80 per cent) of disabled respondents to a survey question – about attitudes to employers being obliged to publish what they have done and plan to do about employing disabled people – supported the imposition of such an obligation.[111] As to where such plans should be published, the most frequently mentioned places were the national press or newspapers, local press, and job centres, employment offices or careers offices. There was little support for the existing, limited practice of publishing disabled employment policies in company annual reports, although there was measurable support for the use of in-house company publications, noticeboards and posters.[112]

Code of Good Practice

The stimulus, such as it is, for the development of disabled equal opportunity policies is provided by the Employment Service's *Code of Good Practice on the Employment of Disabled People*, first issued in 1984 and updated in March 1993.[113] It suggests that companies should adopt sound and effective policy objectives in the employment of persons with disabilities.[114] The Code suggests seven objectives that employers might take up. First, the company should seek to be recognized in the community as a provider of disabled employment opportunities. Second, disabled applicants should know that they will be treated fairly and on their merits. Third, it would normally be expected that the employer will retain employees who become disabled while in service. Fourth, the employer should plan the integration of disabled workers, with any necessary accommodations in the work or working environment. Fifth, disabled employees are entitled to expect that the employer will develop their skills and potential, offering them training and promotion opportunities on ability. Sixth, non-disabled co-workers should readily accept their disabled colleagues without distinction. Seventh, the company should ensure that it is meeting its legal obligations towards disabled persons.

This list of *desiderata* can only be achieved by drawing up a written policy that fits the circumstances of the individual firm, involves all staff and management, sets objectives for managers, and identifies the means by which the policy will be achieved. To be effective, policy values must be shared, so the Code stresses the importance of developing a policy by consultation with staff and communicating the resultant policy to them.[115] Coordination of policy should be placed in the hands of an executive.[116] Regular assessment or monitoring of policy is desirable and,

> Although numbers alone cannot give the whole picture, one of the best indications of the success of a policy is whether the company offers people with disabilities their full share of opportunities.[117]

Significantly, the Code makes direct reference to the statutory 3 per cent quota of registered disabled persons as a measure of achievement and states that the quota 'should be regarded as a minimum for people with disabilities as a whole in any company's workforce'.

Part Two of the Code deals with detailed advice on how to put policy into practice. It addresses existing legal obligations as a prelude to an account of the identification of disabled people, the range of disabilities and the effectiveness of disabled employees. The Code provides detailed guidance on recruitment of disabled persons, including dealing with questions of safety, attendance, health, pension scheme eligibility, alterations to premises or equipment, communications, manual dexterity and physical effort. It advises employers on how to draw up job descriptions and job requirements without inadvertently excluding disabled applicants. Recommendations on outreach and recruitment methods are furnished. Selection procedures, the Code suggests, should be examined to ensure that disabled candidates are treated on merit and that practical advice is offered on the design of application forms, on the arrangements and procedures for interviewing disabled candidates, and on the pitfalls of health screening. Part Two of the Code counsels employers to give particular attention to the needs of disabled employees in respect of induction, health and safety, workplace integration, training and promotion, and redundancy. For employees who become disabled while in employment, firm and useful guidance is given to employers on taking decisions that will affect the newly disabled employee. A strong steer is given towards consideration of positive options that include retention in the same job or in alternative work, removal to part-time work or job-sharing, delayed return to work, other flexible working arrangements (including trial periods or working from home) and the knock-on effects of disability (for example, impact upon salary). Advice on employment termination as a last resort is also proffered.

The Code is undoubtedly a mine of information, advice and assistance, and should not easily be dismissed. However, unlike the EOC and CRE codes of practice, the Code wants for legislative underpinning and depends upon the good sense and goodwill of employers for its implementation. Nevertheless, the penetration of the Code in both the public and private sectors appears to be less than complete. Morrell found that by 1987 only 19 per cent of employers had had contact with the Code, although the chances of having knowingly received the Code increased with the size of the firm.[118] More encouragingly, however, her research shows that, where the Code has infiltrated the enterprise, it was reaching the senior decision-makers, such as managing directors, senior managers, department heads and personnel officers.[119] Among those who had read the Code, 35 per cent were of the opinion that it was very good, and a further 51 per cent that it was fairly good, as a point of reference. There were few criticisms of its content, style or readability, although its layout was not altogether welcomed.[120] Morrell comments that

> The major benefit of the Code of Good Practice appeared to be its usefulness in increasing awareness and highlighting the issue of employing people with disabilities. It would appear

> that the booklet had encouraged employers to stop and think about their current employment practices and consider the opportunities for people with disabilities in the workplace and the help that is available for employers.[121]

About two-fifths of employer respondents who had received a copy of the Code indicated that they had used or planned to use it.

It is interesting to note Morrell's finding that 80 per cent of employers purported not to have received a copy of the Code. This is surprising given the widespread publicity that the Code received at launch and subsequently, and the government agencies' perceptions that the Code had been widely disseminated. A possible explanation, apart from sheer forgetfulness, is that the Code may have reached the enterprise but had failed to filter into the different levels of management. A quarter of the employers who had not received the Code were at least aware of it, and a majority expressed an interest in obtaining a copy.[122] This group found that the sections of the Code dealing with assistance for newly disabled employees, the recruitment of disabled persons, employers' pertinent legal obligations and the position of disabled employees at work were potentially useful.[123] Significantly, however, only 3 per cent of employers who had not received the Code were interested in its provisions on drawing up a disabled employment policy. The message seems to be that there is a long way to go before voluntarism can produce a commitment to equal opportunity planning.

Voluntarism, Education and Persuasion

The voluntary approach nevertheless holds sway. In 1977, the Government launched a major programme to encourage and to educate employers about the employment of disabled persons ('Positive Policies'). Following a review of disabled employment services in 1982, the Disablement Advisory Service was established to promote progressive personnel policies and practices in respect of disabled people, a role now discharged by the Employment Service's Placing, Assessment and Counselling Teams. In addition, under the 'Fit for Work' award scheme, commenced in 1979, annual awards were made to employers who, by their record and performance, have promoted equal opportunities for disabled people at work.[124] That scheme has since been replaced from 1991 by the so-called 'Two Ticks' initiative. This allows employers to use a disability symbol, redesigned in 1992, to show commitment to good practice in the employment of disabled persons and to identify themselves to disabled workers as being positive about those workers' abilities. This scheme is the ultimate in voluntarism because, unlike the 'Fit for Work' awards, the Employment Service does not assess or judge whether an employer is meeting the criteria for the use of the symbol. Employers themselves decide whether to award themselves 'two ticks'. All that the Employment Service asks is that employers who award themselves this distinction should make five commitments to action:[125] first, to interview all minimally qualified disabled applicants and consider them on ability; second, to ask disabled employees on an annual basis what steps the employer might take to ensure that they develop and use their abilities in employment; third, to make every effort to retain in employment newly disabled staff; fourth, to develop disability awareness among key employees in order to make the firm's commitments to disabled employment operational; fifth, to review those commitments on an annual basis, monitor achievements, plan improvements and communicate the results to the workforce.

The voluntary principle has been adopted by employers as well as by government. The Employers' Forum on Disability is a group of organizations that have signed an Agenda for Action. The Forum is concerned with the training and employment of disabled persons and provides help and information to other employers on good practice, specialist services, legislation and other issues. The Agenda contains ten points for action to which subscribers are committed. Most significantly in the context of the present discussion, these action points include a commitment that the employment of disabled persons will form an integral part of equal opportunity policies and practices. The Agenda also deals with staff training and disability awareness, reasonable accommodations in the work environment, outreach initiatives in the recruitment process and equality of opportunity in career development, training and work experience. Forum members pledge to give the fullest support to newly disabled employees with a view to retaining their services in some way. A novel commitment is the promised recognition and response to disabled people as customers, suppliers, shareholders and members of the community, as well as a commitment to the participation of disabled employees in employment policy-making. Finally, a company that subscribes to the Agenda undertakes to monitor its progress in implementing these action points, audit performance annually, review progress at board level, and publish achievements and objectives to employees and in the directors' annual report. Quite apart from the Employer's Forum on Disability, undoubtedly a number of employers have given attention to disabled employment policies and their numerous published examples of good practice.[126] Employing disabled people has been seen as being 'good for business'. However, the effect of these various initiatives to educate and encourage employers to extend equal opportunities to disabled workers is hard to gauge.

CONCLUSION

Despite the evidence that points to the contrary, governments have resisted the pressures for legislative action to address disability discrimination in the labour market, while at the same time implicitly recognizing that there might be a problem that is at least worthy of resolution by education and persuasion. The comparative evidence suggests that positive action, contract compliance and equal opportunity planning might have some role to play in any new legal regime of disabled employment rights in Britain. Indeed, a by-product of the received wisdom that disabled disadvantage can be addressed by voluntary action is that many of the ideas explored here are already part and parcel of the official political reaction to disabled persons and their employment. The only missing ingredient is legal compulsion. Contract compliance and employment equity principles, with appropriate use of statistics, goals and timetables, would require employers to develop positive attitudes, policies and practices towards disabled job-seekers and employees. However, such legal strategies must be seen as complementary to and not a substitute for effective anti-discrimination laws.

NOTES

1. McCrudden, 1986: 219.
2. *Ibid.*: 220–1.
3. *Ibid.*: 223–5.
4. *Ibid.*: 230–2. Despite McCrudden's arguments, this form of positive action is fraught with difficulty and unlikely to meet with the approval of the British legal system.
5. Para. 5.3. See also paras 5.4 and 5.5.
6. Paras 5.2 and 5.6–5.19.

7. For an account of the efforts of the London Borough of Lambeth in this respect, see: *Equal Opportunities Review*, 1989. See also the experience of Manchester City Council recounted in *Equal Opportunities Review*, 1992: 15–18.

8. See, for example: Williams, 1972; Pati and Adkins, 1980.

9. Epstein, 1992: *passim*.

10. Carr, 1987: 2. See also: Institute of Personnel Management, 1987.

11. The use of fair wages clauses in local government pre-dates this development by two years: Carr, 1987: 9.

12. See Bercusson, 1978.

13. Fredman and Morris, 1989: 460–1.

14. See Carr, 1987: 3 for an account of this initiative.

15. 3 CFR s 339 and 42 USC s 2000e.

16. RRA 1976 s 71. There is no parallel provision in the SDA 1975. The use of s 71 as a plank for the pursuit of socio-political activity by local authorities has been fraught with difficulty. See, for example: *Wheeler* v *Leicester City Council* [1985] AC 1054 HL and *R* v *Lewisham London Borough Council, ex parte Shell UK Ltd* [1988] 1 All ER 938 Div Crt.

17. The leading proponent of this strategy was the now defunct Greater London Council. See: *Industrial Relations Review and Report*, 1986: 3–5; Carr, 1987: 10–16. Other examples of contract compliance practitioners are detailed in Institute of Personnel Management, 1987: *passim*. For an analysis of the legal basis, if any, upon which contract compliance has been practised in the public sector, see: Fredman and Morris, 1989: Chapter 12.

18. Local Government Act 1988 ss 17, 18 and 25 and see subsequently *R* v *London Borough of Islington, ex parte Building Employers' Confederation* [1989] IRLR 382 Div Crt. For an account of the impact of the 1988 legislation upon contract compliance, see Fredman and Morris, 1989: 464–9.

19. *Industrial Relations Review and Report*, 1986: 5; Carr, 1987: 15.

20. By virtue of s 17(5)(a). An attempt was made during the passage of the draft legislation to include a clause that would allow local authorities to ask tenderers and contractors questions relevant to the Code of Good Practice on the Employment of Disabled People. See, for example: HC Bill 54 (1987–8) cl 19 (as amended on Report). This clause did not survive the further scrutiny of the Bill.

21. See Chapter 5.

22. (Ont) HRC s 26(1). See also Manitoba's contract compliance measures: (Man) HRC s 56(1).

23. *Ibid*.: s 26(2).

24. *Ibid*.: s 26(3).

25. 29 USC s 793(a); 41 CFR Part 60-741. See Chapter 4.

26. 41 CFR s 60-741.2. The prime contractor and sub-contractor must include an affirmative action clause in the sub-contract either expressly or by reference: 41 CFR s 60-741.20.

27. 41 CFR s 60-741.4. The language of the clause may be adapted if necessary to identify properly the parties and their undertakings: 41 CFR s 60-741.21. The clause may be incorporated by reference: 41 CFR s 60-741.22; but, in any event, is deemed to be part of the contract whether or not it is an express term and whether or not the contract is in writing: 41 CFR s 60-741.23.

28. 41 CFR s 60-741.5(a). This may be integrated with any other affirmative action programmes. Originally, affirmative action plans had to be filed with the Department of Labor, but the evidence suggested that the Department found it impracticable to process and review the submitted plans, so this requirement was dropped in 1976: Percy, 1989: 204.

29. 41 CFR s 60-741.6(a). The policies, practices and procedures must accord with the standards set in 41 CFR s 60-741.6, which are discussed below.

30. 41 CFR s 60-741.5(d).

31. 41 CFR s 60-741.5(b).

32. 41 CFR Part 60-741 Appendix B.

33. 41 CFR s 60-741.5(c)(1). An employee is not precluded from coming forward under the affirmative action programme on some later occasion: 41 CFR s 60-741.5(c)(2).

34. 41 CFR s 60-741.5(c)(3). It follows also that compliance with this requirement does

not absolve the employer from disability-based discrimination under the legislation at large: 41 CFR s 60-741.5(c)(4).

35. 41 CFR s 60-741.6(b).

36. Appendix C to Part 60-741. For an insider's view of the role of the OFCCP under s 503 see: DeLury, 1975.

37. The statement should be available to the disabled person on request.

38. 41 CFR s 60-741.6(c)(1).

39. 41 CFR s 60-741.6(c)(2).

40. 41 CFR s 60-741.6(c)(3); cf. 45 CFR s 84.14.

41. 41 CFR s 60-741.6(c)(3). Supervisors and managers may be informed of any work or duty restrictions and of any accommodations necessary. First aid and safety personnel may be informed (where and to the extent appropriate) if the disabled person might require emergency treatment. Government officials investigating compliance with the law must also be informed. Confidentiality is thus subject to practical exceptions.

42. 41 CFR s 60-741.6(d).

43. 41 CFR s 60-741.5(c)(1).

44. 41 CFR s 60-741.6(f).

45. 41 CFR s 60-741.6(f)(1).

46. 41 CFR s 60-741.6(g).

47. Company publications might also assist the establishment of disabled role models: for example, by including articles on the achievements of disabled employees or by ensuring the proper visual representation of disabled persons in employee handbooks and recruitment literature.

48. See also 41 CFR s 60-741.9 as to the OFCCP's role in facilitating the co-operation of trade unions, recruitment agencies and training organizations in furthering the affirmative action goal.

49. 41 CFR s 60-741.6(f)(2).

50. 41 CFR s 60-741.6(f)(3).

51. 41 CFR s 60-741.6(f)(4): e.g. employment and rehabilitation agencies, sheltered workshops, trade unions, organizations of and for disabled people, colleges and educational agencies.

52. 41 CFR s 60-741.6(f)(5) and (6).

53. 41 CFR s 60-741.6(f)(7).

54. 41 CFR s 60-741.6(f)(9).

55. 41 CFR s 60-741.6(f)(10).

56. 41 CFR s 60-741.6(f)(8).

57. 41 CFR s 60-741.6(h).

58. 41 CFR s 60-741.6(h)(1).

59. 41 CFR s 60-741.6(h)(2).

60. 41 CFR s 60-741.6(h)(3).

61. 41 CFR s 60-741.6(i).

62. The OFCCP recommends plant tours, explanations of current and future vacancies, job descriptions and worker specifications. Explanations of selection processes and recruitment literature should be an integral part of these briefings, and formal arrangements should be made for referral of applicants, follow-up with sources and feedback on disposition of applicants: 41 CFR s 60-741.6(i)(4).

63. 41 CFR s 60-741.6(i)(9).

64. 41 CFR s 60-741.8.

65. 41 CFR s 60-741.6(e).

66. 41 CFR s 60-741.6(j).

67. 29 USC s 793(b). The s 503 regulations lay down procedures for handling complaints: 41 CFR ss 60-741.24–.26.

68. 41 CFR s 60-741.26.

69. 41 CFR s 60-741.1.

70. 41 CFR s 60-741.28.

71. 41 CFR s 60-741.27.

72. Note the national interest defence in 29 USC s 793(c).

73. 41 CFR s 60-741.29.
74. Brigham, 1985: 118–19.
75. Percy, 1989: 205–6.
76. *Ibid.*: 206.
77. See, for example: O'Dea, 1980.
78. Percy, 1989: 209.
79. Leonard, 1984.
80. In contrast, there is research into the economic impact of s 503 on businesses and, in particular, the ability of small firms to compete for government contracts in the face of contract compliance regulations: Premus and Carnes, 1982.
81. Some evidence of positive effects can be gleaned from a report of the US Department of Labor (1982). This source demonstrated that federal contractors had begun to change their attitudes and policies towards disabled workers, especially in respect of making reasonable accommodation.
82. This question has dominated the legal literature on s 503. See, for example: Paolicelli, 1979; Schoon, 1979; *Michigan Law Review*, 1981; Boller, 1982.
83. See, for example: *Beam* v *Sun Shipbuilding & Dry Dock Co.* (1982) 679 F2d 1077 (3rd Cir); *Davis* v *United Airlines* (1981) 662 F2d 120 (2nd Cir), *certiorari denied* (1982) 456 US 965; *Simpson* v *Reynolds Metals Co.* (1980) 629 F2d 1226 (7th Cir); *Simon* v *St Louis County* (1981) 656 F2d 316 (8th Cir), *certiorari denied* (1982) 455 US 976; *Fisher* v *City of Tucson* (1981) 663 F2d 861 (9th Cir), *certiorari denied* (1982) 459 US 881; *Rogers* v *Frito-Lay* (1979) 611 F2d 1074 (5th Cir), *certiorari denied* (1980) 449 US 889; *Hoopes* v *Equifax Inc* (1979) 611 F2d 134 (6th Cir).
84. See, for example: *Simpson* v *Reynolds Metals Co* (1980) 629 F2d 1226 (7th Cir); *Hodges* v *Atchison, Topeka and Santa Fe Railway* (1984) 728 F2d 414 (10th Cir), *certiorari denied* (1984) 104 SCt 97. These limitations in s 503 will be of no surprise to British employment lawyers familiar with the similar drawbacks to individual enforcement of fair wages clauses: *Simpson* v *Kodak Ltd* [1948] 2 KB 184.
85. See, for example: *Moon* v *US Department of Labor* (1984) 747 F2d 599 (11th Cir), *certiorari denied* (1985) 105 SCt 2117.
86. Epstein, 1992.
87. 29 USC s 791(b).
88. An honourable exception is Percy (1989: 196–202), on whom this portion of the chapter draws.
89. Percy, 1989: 196–7.
90. US Civil Service Commission, 1975: 13 and 27, cited by Percy, 1989: 197.
91. Percy, 1989: 201.
92. Although most spent only 10 per cent of their time on disability issues, only 14 per cent had been adequately trained and only 25 per cent had their disabled employment responsibilities written into their job descriptions.
93. US Equal Employment Opportunity Commission, 1986: 148–51, cited in Percy, 1989: 201–2.
94. McCrudden, 1986: 225.
95. *Ibid.*: 226.
96. *Ibid.*: 236. He also opines that there should be a legal requirement on employers to monitor the composition of their workforce. The model of the (Northern Ireland) Fair Employment Act 1989 might prove an interesting exemplar for disability discrimination law. In particular, the statute's requirement that employers should monitor the workforce for its religious composition might be usefully studied by disability rights reformers.
97. Percy, 1989: 207.
98. *Ibid.*: 199 referring to EEOC instructions to federal agencies for the implementation of s 501.
99. EEA 1985 s 5. See Chapter 5.
100. *Ibid.*: s 6; and the Employment Equity Regulations 1986. A failure to comply with this reporting requirement is a criminal offence punishable under s 7 by a fine of up to $50,000. See further: Employment and Immigration Canada, 1986 (containing the detailed guidance to Canadian employers on their obligations under the EEA 1985).

101. See, for example, the use of statistics under Québec's Charter of Human Rights and Freedoms and its Affirmative Action Programme Regulations. The (BC) Human Rights Amendment Act 1992 (SBC c 43) now also provides for affirmative action and employment equity programmes. See also Ontario's Employment Equity Act 1993.

102. Under the (Cth) Equal Employment Opportunity (Commonwealth Authorities) Act 1987. See also the mandating of equal opportunity management plans in the Australian states.

103. Employment and Immigration Canada, 1991a. This source also reveals that disabled persons' share of public sector employment opportunities has barely improved since the introduction of the EEA 1985 requirements. The latest statistics show that disabled persons have increased their representation with EEA employers from 2.4 to 2.5 per cent over the space of twelve months: Employment and Immigration Canada, 1992. This is an increase from 1.6 per cent in 1987 just before the EEA came into force. The Act is currently under review: Employment and Immigration Canada, 1991b.

104. Both the EOC and the CRE recommend that employers should adopt, implement and monitor an equal opportunity policy to obviate unlawful discrimination and promote equality of opportunity. See: *Code of Practice for the Elimination of Discrimination on the Grounds of Sex and Marriage and the Promotion of Equality of Opportunity in Employment* (1985) paras 33–40; *Code of Practice for the Elimination of Racial Discrimination and the Promotion of Equality of Opportunity in Employment* (1984) paras 1.1–1.4 and 1.33–1.43.

105. CA 1985 s 234 and Sch 7 para. 9. It should be noted that company law merely requires a statement of policy to be disclosed; it does not require there to be a written or detailed policy, let alone one that is made operational.

106. Doyle, 1987a.

107. Morrell, 1990: 12.

108. *Ibid.*: Table 17.

109. *Ibid.*: 13.

110. See further: Honey *et al.*, 1993.

111. Research Surveys of Great Britain, 1978: Table 9.6.1.

112. *Ibid.*: Table 9.6.2.

113. Doyle, 1987a.

114. Part One of the *Code of Good Practice on the Employment of Disabled People* addressed to directors and senior managers.

115. *Ibid.*: para. 10.3.

116. This is amplified in paras 9.1–9.3 of the Code, which provide a form of job description for such a role.

117. *Ibid.*: Part One.

118. Morrell, 1990: Table 30.

119. *Ibid.*: 20–1 and Table 32.

120. *Ibid.*: 21.

121. *Ibid.*: 21.

122. *Ibid.*: 22.

123. *Ibid.*: Table 34.

124. Recipients of the award numbered about 100 each year and were bestowed a presentation plaque, desk ornament and citation, as well as the right to use the award's emblem on company documents: Berthoud *et al.*, 1993: 41.

125. The symbol is designed to be used on letterheads and company literature, but should not be used in connection with the provision or promotion of commercial products or services.

126. See, for example, the case studies and other accounts in: Incomes Data Services Ltd, 1981; Doyle, 1987a; Birkett and Worman, 1988; Leach, 1989; Incomes Data Services Ltd, 1992.

13

Conclusion

Disability produces vulnerability and marginality in all aspects of the daily tableau of persons with disabilities often resulting in multiple 'handicaps', as the effects of disability are felt directly in the medical and health dimensions, and then indirectly in the spheres of education, transport, physical access and the built environment, social and welfare services, income and wealth, housing, health services, leisure activities and social interaction, and, above all in the present context, in competitive employment. *Disability* does not equal *inability* to work. Yet the statistical evidence shows that disabled people suffer a rate and length of unemployment that is far in excess of that visited upon any other minority group. While there are many studies that tend to confirm the employability of disabled workers, it is disappointing to note the continued expression of negative attitudes by employers towards disabled people.

Despite assertions to the contrary, the poverty and disadvantage of many disabled individuals is the product of prejudice, ignorance and sheer thoughtlessness. The research points to the crucial influence upon disabled employment opportunities of a form of social discrimination that is akin to that experienced by racial and ethnic minorities and women. If social and employment discrimination informed by gender and race has been treated as a subject fit for regulation and proscription, then the arguments for similar responses to disability discrimination are equally compelling. Moreover, the passage of legislation to prohibit discrimination against disabled persons would represent a fundamental change in society's attitudes towards disability and the disabled community. In short, it would constitute a shift from charity and welfarism to civil rights and integration.

If this argument is accepted, which of course hitherto has not been the case in government circles, then it is tempting to see disability as being a new prohibited ground of discrimination within the framework already erected by sex and race discrimination laws. However, the experience of the US disability rights legislation (and comparable experience in Canada and Australia) suggests that existing equal opportunities laws are not necessarily the most appropriate or efficacious means of addressing disability discrimination. Disability discrimination throws up unique problems and issues that cannot be readily resolved within a framework erected to redress other forms of social discrimination. As a US federal district court in New Hampshire observes, 'attempting to fit the problem of discrimination against the handicapped into the model remedy for race discrimination is akin to fitting a square peg into a round hole'.[1] In particular, it will be clear that the disability discrimination legal model must include the ingredients of reasonable accommodation and must provide means for removing structural and environmental barriers to integration and participation.

In Britain, however, the case for disability discrimination legislation is often made without being heard. It is still the case that our legislators adhere to the view that the plight of disabled workers is the result of the limitations of disability and of disabled persons themselves, and the notion that disability is often a social construct and the subject of negative social forces is implicitly rejected. Even when the counter-analysis is accepted, the current political orthodoxy insists that legislation is not the best means to assist disabled persons to compete in the labour market. The present Government, in particular, subscribes to the view that regulation of disabled employment rights would be a burden upon business and damaging to the employment prospects of disabled people because it risks the withdrawal of employers' goodwill. Instead, the strategy for assisting disabled persons into work is based upon voluntarism and focuses upon the role of education and persuasion. Nevertheless, as Daunt asserts,

> The notion that government must make a choice between *compelling employers and persuading them* is simplistic. The point sometimes made by employers' organizations that if they are effectively compelled by legislation to employ disabled people, their goodwill is going to be lost and they will no longer co-operate should be seen as a negotiating position.[2]

In fact, the evidence suggests that employer goodwill towards disabled workers is quite mythical and nothing more than a talisman against the perceived evils of regulation and compulsion. Trust in the voluntary approach and the willingness of employers to see the equation of their own self-interests with the rights and expectations of the disabled community is sorely misplaced. The case for special legislation to enfranchise disabled workers remains a strong and persuasive one.

However, before we consider the introduction of anti-discrimination legislation on behalf of disabled Britons, the failure of existing legal formulae to provide a real menu of employment rights for persons with disabilities must be accounted for. It has been rightly said that

> the positive effects of legislation, and in particular measures which impose quotas of disabled workers on employers, have been somewhat disappointing. Except in Germany, quota systems, introduced at a time of universal economic growth, have proved difficult to operate and have up till now failed as guarantees of equal opportunity in times of relative restraint.[3]

It is indeed ironic that quotas should at present hold such a fascination for those who advocate a new legal strategy for sex and race discrimination – one that would concentrate upon results rather than process – given the patent failure of disabled workers' quota schemes in many countries. Nevertheless, quota legislation should continue to play a part in special disability legislation in the short to medium term, but with emphasis and resources placed upon enforcement. The experience of the German, and to a lesser extent the French, quota models might be revisited with profit, and the linking of quota obligations with levies and subsidies is worth detailed reconsideration in the context of disabled employment. Strong laws require strong remedies and enforcement. In Britain, the failure of half a century of quota obligations can largely, albeit not entirely, be explained by a lack of commitment to and weakness in the policing of such special legislation as already existed.

It is clear, however, that even a renewed commitment to quota legislation will not adequately address the employment problems of disabled workers. We return again to the conviction that the anti-discrimination principle needs to be harnessed to the task of ensuring the equal treatment and fair participation of disabled people in the labour market. It is contended that individual and institutional disability discrimination demands a cause of action and an individual remedy. Increasingly disability rights advocates are looking to the USA for inspiration in the campaign for achieving equal opportunity rights. Research in the USA during the 1980s found that 70 per cent of disabled Americans believed that their lives had improved in the previous decade and two-thirds opined that federal legislation had provided better opportunities for disabled persons and had assisted them a great deal or somewhat.[4] Three-quarters of respondents wished to see anti-discrimination laws strengthened further. Disabled Britons too are optimistic that such laws would greatly enhance their lives and status.

This would seem to suggest that the Americans with Disabilities Act 1990, and its progenitor, the Rehabilitation Act 1973, provide a ready-made model for legislation that could be adopted in Britain. In fact, such statutes do provide a very important exemplar of how to enact new rights for a recognized minority and, in the particular context of disability, illustrate the importance of ensuring that such laws are comprehensive in their scope. Thus disability discrimination legislation must apply in both the public and the private spheres, and above all must extend beyond the control of discrimination in the labour market by addressing the hopes of disabled people in education, housing, transport, communications and public accommodations. As has been noted in earlier chapters, the recent Civil Rights (Disabled Persons) Bills are clearly patterned after the ADA 1990 and it is to the USA that disability rights activists are now looking for further instruction. In spite of this, the present writer would advocate some caution and more imagination. There is a danger, especially through the private members' bill procedure, that the language of the ADA 1990 is being adopted almost wholesale without proper regard for differences in terminology, culture and interpretation in the two jurisdictions. The lessons of the comparative method must be heeded. The experience and examples of Canadian and Australian legislation provide a deeper mine of raw materials that can be quarried in the production of any new legislation. The strengths and weaknesses of these laws elsewhere must be recorded, and the best of the comparative models should be recruited to the development of disability discrimination measures in Britain. This would require not simply the transplantation of the non-discrimination principle, but also the borrowing of techniques in affirmative action, contract compliance and equal opportunity planning.

If anti-discrimination and equal opportunity legislation is the way ahead for disabled workers' rights, the limitations of legal formulae must be recognized. Legislation cannot hope completely to redress the vulnerability of disabled people in the labour market, and political and economic power must be used to enfranchise disabled workers. The anti-discrimination model may only be capable of containing overt discrimination while defusing social pressure for radical change in favour of disabled persons. As in the USA, recognition in law that disabled persons are a disadvantaged group in the employment field is a necessary, but not sufficient, condition to mandating remedial action and equal rights. Statutory commitment to equal opportunities and equal treatment can assist the integration of this minority group, but the limits of the law must be understood and accounted for.

In the USA, many writers believe that the law has only partly succeeded in empowering disabled people, largely because of inadequate enforcement, conflicting interpretation and limited scope.[5] That is certainly a criticism that can be levelled at the RA 1973. Commenting on the ADA 1990, a statute in which so much hope is invested, Yelin notes that the legislation

> bars discrimination against persons with disabilities in employment, but it may not convince employers that such persons will be productive or [that they should] purchase the equipment to help them do their jobs. In short, *the law cannot guarantee work.*[6]

He regards section 504 of the RA 1973, upon which the 1990 legislation was modelled, as a 'bellwether for the ADA', but observes that section 504 produced mixed results for the employment of disabled persons in the federal employment sector.[7] Yelin's analysis suggests that the disability anti-discrimination legislation

> was not successful in ensuring that persons with disabilities shared in the employment gains occurring . . . when government employment was expanding. Later, the legislation did not prevent workers with disabilities from bearing a disproportionate share of the retrenchment in government employment.[8]

That is borne out by the statistical data. Between 1970 and 1982, the US federal government workforce grew from 4.5 million to over 6 million strong, increasing its proportional representation in the national workforce from 5.7 to 5.8 per cent (a growth of 2 per cent in relative terms). In contrast, the number of disabled persons in government employment increased from 0.45 million to 0.62 million, increasing its proportion of the government workforce from 9.9 to 10.2 per cent (a growth of 3 per cent in relative terms). However, from 1982 to 1987, the government workforce shrank by 11 per cent in absolute terms and by 19 per cent in relative terms. The impact of this shrinkage was disproportionately felt by disabled workers. The number of disabled government employees declined by 18 per cent in absolute terms and by 8 per cent in relative terms (compared with a decline of 10 per cent in the absolute numbers of government employees without disabilities and a 2 per cent *increase* in relative terms for that group). The best that might be said is that the legislation might have had a role to play in ensuring that disabled workers in the federal employment sector fared less badly than their disabled counterparts in the economy as a whole.[9]

From an economist's viewpoint, the limits of the law must also be marked. For example, Johnson, although sympathetic to the notion of disability discrimination laws, shows an economist's caution to the costs–benefits analysis of such laws. In the context of reasonable accommodation, Johnson propounds the view that

> Case-by-case determinations of the effect of an impairment on the capacity to perform a job are difficult to generalize. Decisions must be influenced by the combined, idiosyncratic effects of an individual's qualifications and impairment compared to the workplace and job of one employer. This type of decision does not establish strong precedents that would inform employers and impaired workers of their respective rights and responsibilities . . . Although the question of the costs of case-by-case determinations relative to the benefits of reducing discrimination is an empirical one, it seems likely that the costs of enforcing laws relating to handicap discrimination are high relative to enforcement costs for other forms of discrimination.[10]

He argues that a concept of reasonable accommodation that would comport with efficiency would lead employers to invest in accommodations to the point where the marginal cost of the accommodations is equal to the marginal benefit as measured by the increase in the productivity of the accommodated disabled worker. However, beyond that point an employer's taste for positive discrimination (or, more accurately, fair treatment) in favour of disabled workers must in principle become sated. As a result, we might expect that disability discrimination laws will only assist those disabled workers whose profile accords most closely with 'able-bodied' employees, and that severely disabled persons, or workers with unusual or radical disabilities, will be excluded from the law's protection in practice.

None the less, these arguments as to the limits of disability discrimination law merely counsel us to address and scrutinize the detail and scope of any law reform that might be proposed. It is clear from the experience of the ADA 1990 that any disability rights legislation in Britain must aim for a high level of statutory specificity. The development of new legal standards should not be left to chance or to the vagaries of judicial interpretation. Burgdorf observes that

> the impetus for statutory specificity stems from idiosyncrasies of disability discrimination, which demand more statutory guidance than general mandates not to discriminate.[11]

However, the same observer notes that specificity is a 'double-edged sword'. Detailed legislation creates rigid law requiring legislative intervention to amend unforeseen interpretations of substantive provisions, a problem that is less insurmountable in 'legislation' through regulations or codes of practice. Furthermore, detailed guidance as to the spirit of the law is perhaps best left to regulatory agencies or commissions. Burgdorf also points out that legislators may find it more difficult to disagree with statements of broad principle, but easier to pick holes in precisely defined legal standards.[12]

With those words of caution ringing in our ears, nevertheless, it is right to end upon a note of optimism and positive expectation. Equal rights for disabled workers is an idea and ideal whose time has come. Lessons from abroad must be learnt before any new disability discrimination law can be made to work. In the context of discrimination law at large, the means to enforce the non-discrimination principle will need to be looked at afresh, and reforms in respect of disability provide a ripe opportunity for such reassessment. It may be also that the enactment of disability discrimination legislation will influence the shape of sex and race discrimination laws, or inspire the development of legal responses to other forms of social discrimination. In particular, the reasonable accommodation concept might be one that could be usefully expressed as a component part of gender and race discrimination directives. The case for disability discrimination law is a compelling one. The comparative method assists us to make that case and to design the law's response to the disadvantage and vulnerability of a once forgotten minority.

NOTES

1. *Garrity* v *Gallen* (1981) 522 FSupp 171 at 206.
2. Daunt, 1991: 63 (emphasis in original).
3. *Ibid.*: 60.
4. Louis Harris and Associates, 1986.
5. See, for example: Flaccus, 1986a; McCluskey, 1988; Tucker, 1989a.
6. Yelin, 1991: 130 (emphasis added).
7. *Ibid.*: 136.
8. *Ibid.*: 137.
9. It is also noteworthy that Canadian employment equity laws have had only a marginal impact upon the labour market share and employment opportunities of disabled workers.
10. Johnson, 1986b: 259. Some answers to the empirical questions posed by economists like Johnson in the context of the ADA 1990 might well be answered in due course by on-going, longitudinal research into the before and after effects of the new legislation. See: Blanck, 1991, 1992.
11. Burgdorf, 1991: 510.
12. *Ibid.*: 511.

Postscript

In January 1995 the British government published the Disability Discrimination Bill backed by a White Paper (*Ending Discrimination Against Disabled People*: Cm 2729). The Bill is expected to become law by Autumn 1995. It introduces a right of access for disabled persons to goods, facilities and services, while the White Paper promises consultation on further measures in the areas of transport and education. However, the immediate effects of these proposals are likely to be felt in the employment field in both the public and private sectors.

The Bill will repeal the disabled workers' quota and designated employment schemes, and will abolish the disabled persons' register. In their place, Part II of the draft statute seeks to make it unlawful for an employer to discriminate against disabled persons in recruitment and selection, in employment offers, in terms and conditions, in employment opportunities generally, and in dismissal, or by subjecting a disabled person to any other employment detriment. Discrimination for this purpose refers to the less favourable treatment of a person for a reason relating to that person's disability and which is without justification. Victimization is also outlawed. The Bill places a legal duty on employers to make reasonable adjustments to employment arrangements, or to any physical features of premises, in order to overcome the effects of any substantial disadvantage faced by a disabled person as a result of those arrangements or features. A failure to comply with a duty to make reasonable adjustments is a discriminatory act, but the Bill makes it clear that the duty does not require positive discrimination in favour of disabled persons. The extent of the duty is to be amplified in regulations and cost may become a relevant factor.

It is noteworthy that the Bill does not include the concept of *indirect* discrimination. However, the White Paper makes it clear that the imposition of a condition or requirement, having the effect of excluding disabled persons, will be covered by the basic right of non-discrimination and the reasonable adjustment duty. This is achieved, nevertheless, by the inclusion of a justification defence to less favourable treatment, conditions for the operation of which are made explicit in the legislation. These features of the new Bill distinguish it from the model of existing race and sex discrimination laws in Britain. The justification defence is introduced in order to allow employers to discriminate on the basis of ability and merit but, as is argued in this book elsewhere, if discrimination theory is understood properly, such a defence is otiose and may weaken the prohibition on direct discrimination.

The Bill provides for industrial tribunals to have jurisdiction over disability discrimination complaints. Where a complaint is well founded, the tribunal may make a declaration of rights, order the payment of compensation based upon the ordinary tortious measure (including injury to feelings) plus interest, and recommend remedial action (subject to increased compensation in default). Provision is also made for the establishment of a National Disability Council that will advise the government on disability issues and prepare codes of practice to underpin the legislation. The Council is a purely advisory body and does not assume the powers and duties of the existing commissions under the other discrimination statutes. Codes of practice may also be prepared by the Secretary of State and will be relevant in legal proceedings.

The new law addresses persons with a disability as defined in Part I of the Bill. This means that an individual is covered if he or she has a physical or mental impairment that has a substantial and long-term adverse effect on ability to carry out normal day-to-day activities. Tribunals and courts will be required to take account of guidance to be issued by the Secretary of State as to the meaning of these definitional terms which are also expanded upon in Schedule 1. Only employers with 20 or more employees will be subject to the non-discrimination principle, although provision may be made for varying that threshold. Exception is also made for charities and in respect of supported employment.

Although not as comprehensive in its scope as the private member's Civil Rights (Disabled Persons) Bill – which has also been reintroduced by its sponsors – the Disability Discrimination Bill is an important concession that will make some inroads into the employment problems faced by disabled persons. Nevertheless, the Bill represents half measures and reluctant reform; cf. the more imaginative and contemporaneous proposals made to the Northern Ireland Office by the Standing Commission on Human Rights (Cm 2740). It is unlikely to produce reforming law of the depth and breadth desired by disability rights activists and disabled people themselves. The experience and lessons of similar laws in other common law jurisdictions have been largely ignored. Moreover, the Bill does not reveal a commitment of public funding that will be necessary to bring about the structural changes needed to promote disabled equal opportunity. The White Paper also indicates that the timetable for implementing the new measures is likely to be a leisurely one. Disability may be on the agenda, but it is obviously not starred business.

Brian Doyle
Salford
18 January 1995

Bibliography

Acton, N. 1981. Employment of disabled workers: where are we going? 120 *International Labour Review*, 1–14.

Adelman, D. 1986. Employment discrimination. Section 501 of the Rehabilitation Act of 1973: finally a legal standard. 18 *Arizona State Law Journal*, 147–60.

Albeda, W. 1985. *Disabled People and Their Employment.* Luxembourg: EC.

Alexander, L. 1990. AIDS in the workplace: a legal guide. 22 *Connecticut Law Review*, 943–1008.

Anti-Discrimination Board (New South Wales). 1979. *Discrimination and Physical Handicap.* Sydney: Government Printer.

Anti-Discrimination Board (New South Wales). 1981. *Discrimination and Intellectual Handicap.* Sydney: Government Printer.

Astor, H. 1988. Discrimination in employment on the ground of physical impairment. 1 *Australian Journal of Labour Law*, 79–84.

Astor, H. 1990. Anti-discrimination legislation and physical disability: the lessons of experience. 64 *Australian Law Journal*, 113–28.

Baker, J. 1982. Rehabilitation Act of 1973: protection for victims of weight discrimination? 29 *University of California Los Angeles Law Review*, 947–71.

Banking, Insurance and Finance Union. 1987. *Opening Doors: a Report by BIFU Disablement Advisory Committee.* London: Banking, Insurance and Finance Union.

Barlow, W. and Hane, E. 1992. A practical guide to the Americans with Disabilities Act. 71(6) *Personnel Journal*, 53–60.

Barnard, T. 1990. The Americans with Disabilities Act: nightmare for employers and dream for lawyers? 64 *St John's Law Review*, 229–52.

Barnes, C. 1991. *Disabled People in Britain and Discrimination: a Case for Anti-Discrimination Legislation.* London: Hurst.

Barnes, C. 1992. Institutional discrimination against disabled people and the campaign for anti-discrimination legislation. 12 *Critical Social Policy*, 5–22.

Barrett, T. 1989. Employing disabled persons: *bona fide* occupational requirement or qualification, reasonable accommodation and the tolerance of safety risk. 9 *Windsor Yearbook of Access to Justice*, 154–82.

Bassen, N. 1977. Synopsis of state laws regulating employment of the handicapped. 4 *Journal of College and University Law*, 293–333.

Bayler, M. 1992. Dulling a needle: analyzing federal employment restrictions on people with insulin-dependent diabetes. 67 *Indiana Law Journal*, 1067–90.

Bazemore, L. 1986. Employment discrimination against cancer victims: a proposed solution. 31 *Villanova Law Review*, 1549–75.

Bercusson, B. 1978. *Fair Wages Resolutions*. London: Mansell.

Berkowitz, M. and Hill, M. (eds). 1986a. *Disability and the Labor Market: Economic Problems, Policies and Programs*. New York: ILR Press.

Berkowitz, M. and Hill, M. 1986b. *Disability and the labor market: an overview*. In *Disability and the Labor Market: Economic Problems, Policies and Programs* (eds M. Berkowitz and M. Hill). New York: ILR Press, 1–28.

Berlin, M. 1985. Reasonable accommodation: a positive duty to ensure equal opportunity. *Canadian Human Rights Yearbook 1984–1985*, 137–67.

Berns, B. 1986. Interpreting qualified handicapped person under section 501 of the *Rehabilitation Act of 1973: Mantolete* v *Bolger*. 28 Boston College Law Review, 187–95.

Berthoud, R., Lakey, J. and McKay, S. 1993. *The Economic Problems of Disabled People*. London: Policy Studies Institute.

Bhatia, G. 1990. The role of the Canadian Human Rights Commission in protecting the rights of mentally disabled persons. 4(2) *Canadian Journal of Rehabilitation*, 107–12.

Bible, J. 1990. When employers look for things other than drugs: the legality of AIDS, genetic, intelligence and honesty testing in the workplace. 41 *Labor Law Journal*, 195–213.

Bierman, D. 1990. Employment discrimination against overweight individuals: should obesity be a protected classification? 30 *Santa Clara Law Review*, 951–76.

Birkett, K. and Worman, D. 1988. *Getting on with Disabilities: an Employer's Guide*. London: Institute of Personnel Management.

Black, E. 1988. So you think you have a drug problem: drug testing in the workplace. 14 *Employee Relations Law Journal*, 475–85.

Blanck, P. 1991. The emerging workforce: empirical study of the

Americans with Disabilities Act. 16 *Journal of Corporation Law*, 693–803.

Blanck, P. 1992. Empirical study of the employment provisions of the Americans with Disabilities Act: methods, preliminary findings, and implications. 22 *New Mexico Law Review*, 119–241.

Bogaards, P. 1982. The Rehabilitation Act of 1973: who is handicapped under federal law? 16 *University of San Francisco Law Review*, 653–80.

Bolderson, H. 1980. The origins of the disabled persons employment quota and its symbolic significance. 9 *Journal of Social Policy*, 169–86.

Bolderson, H. 1991. *Social Security, Disability and Rehabilitation: Conflicts in the Development of Social Policy 1914–45*. London: Kingsley.

Boller, H. 1982. Unlawful treatment of the handicapped by federal contractors and an implied private cause of action: shall silence reign? 33 *Hastings Law Journal*, 1293–358.

Bordieri, J. and Comninel, M. 1987. Competitive employment for workers with disabilities: an international perspective. 53(3) *Journal of Rehabilitation*, 51–7.

Bowe, F. 1978. *Handicapping America: Barriers to Disabled People*. New York: Harper and Row.

Brigham, D. 1985. Affirmative action policy in the United States. In *Economics and Equity in Employment of People With Disabilities: International Policies and Practices* (eds R. Habeck, D. Galvin, W. Frey, L. Chadderdon and D. Tate). East Lansing: University Centre for International Rehabilitation, Michigan State University, 116–19.

British Deaf Association. 1984. *Deaf Discrimination: a Challenge to the Hearing Community*. Carlisle: British Deaf Association.

Britton, A. 1987. Evaluating legislation: regulation of pre-employment enquiries. 37 *DePaul Law Review*, 1–26.

Brooke-Ross, R. 1984. The disabled in the Federal Republic of Germany. 18 *Social Policy and Administration*, 172–8.

Brooke-Ross, R. and Zacher, H. 1983. *Social Legislation in the Federal Republic of Germany*. London: Bedford Square Press.

Buckle, J. 1971. *Handicapped and Impaired in Great Britain Part II: Work and Housing of Impaired Persons in Great Britain*. London: HMSO.

Bunting, C. 1981. *Public Attitudes to Deafness*. London: HMSO.

Bureau of National Affairs. 1990. *The Americans with Disabilities Act: a Practice and Legal Guide to Impact, Enforcement and Compliance*. Washington, DC: Bureau of National Affairs.

Burgdorf, R. (ed.). 1980a. *The Legal Rights of Handicapped Persons: Cases, Materials and Text.* Baltimore: Brookes.

Burgdorf, R. 1980b. Who are handicapped persons? In *The Legal Rights of Handicapped Persons: Cases, Materials and Text* (ed. R. Burgdorf). Baltimore: Brookes, 1–52.

Burgdorf, R. 1991. The Americans with Disabilities Act: analysis and implications of a second-generation civil rights statute. 26 *Harvard Civil Rights–Civil Liberties Law Review*, 413–522.

Burgdorf, R. and Bell, C. 1984. Eliminating discrimination against physically and mentally handicapped persons: a statutory blueprint. 8 *Mental and Physical Disability Law Reporter*, 64–71 and 75.

Burgdorf, R. and Burgdorf, M. 1975. A history of unequal treatment: the qualifications of handicapped persons as a suspect class under the equal protection clause. 15 *Santa Clara Lawyer*, 855–910.

Burgdorf, R. and Falcon, B. 1980. Employment. In *The Legal Rights of Handicapped Persons: Cases, Materials and Text* (ed. R. Burgdorf). Baltimore: Brookes, 317–438.

Burkhauser, R. 1990. Morality on the cheap: the Americans with Disabilities Act. 13 *Regulation*, 47–56.

Burkhauser, R., Haveman, R. and Wolfe, B. 1990. *The Changing Economic Condition of the Disabled: a Two Decade Review of Economic Well-being.* Washington, DC: National Council on Disability.

Butler, D. 1980. *Southeastern Community College* v *Davis*, section 504 and handicapped rights. 16 *California Western Law Review*, 523–55.

Bynoe, I., Oliver, M. and Barnes, C. (eds). 1991. *Equal Rights for Disabled People: the Case for a New Law.* London: Institute for Public Policy Research.

Campbell, T. and Heginbotham, C. 1991. *Mental Illness: Prejudice, Discrimination and the Law.* Aldershot: Dartmouth.

Canadian Human Rights Commission. 1986. *Effects of the Bhinder Decision on the Canadian Human Rights Commission: a Special Report to Parliament.* Ottawa: Can HRC.

Canfield, L. 1987. Cancer patients' prognosis: how terminal are their employment prospects? 38 *Syracuse Law Review*, 801–29.

Canter, E. 1984. Employment discrimination implications of genetic screening in the workplace under Title VII and the Rehabilitation Act. 10 *American Journal of Law and Medicine*, 323–47.

Carr, J. 1987. *New Roads to Equality: Contract Compliance for the UK?* (Fabian Tract No. 517). London: Fabian Society.

Chirikos, T. 1991. The economics of employment. 69 *Milbank Quarterly*, Supplements 1/2, 150–79.

Cohen, W. 1992. An economic analysis of the issues surrounding

AIDS in the workplace: in the long run, the path of truth and reason cannot be diverted. 41 *American University Law Review*, 1199–242.

Colker, R. 1995. *The Law of Disability Discrimination: Cases and Materials.* Cincinnati, OH: Anderson Publishing Co. (in press).

Collignon, F. 1986. The role of reasonable accommodation in employing disabled persons in private industry. In *Disability and the Labor Market: Economic Problems, Policies and Programs* (eds M. Berkowitz and M. Hill). New York: ILR Press, 196–241.

Collins, R. 1988. Reliance on state law: protecting the rights of people with mental disabilities. 13 *Vermont Law Review*, 305–21.

Columbia Human Rights Law Review. 1973. Methadone maintenance program participation as a hiring criterion. 5 *Columbia Human Rights Law Review*, 421–36.

Combs, I. and Omvig, C. 1986. Accommodation of disabled people into employment: perceptions of employers. 55(2) *Journal of Rehabilitation*, 42–5.

Commission of the European Communities. 1984. *Workshop on the Employment of Disabled People.* Brussels: Directorate-General for Employment, Social Affairs and Education.

Commission of the European Communities. 1988. *Report from the Commission on the Application of Council Recommendation 86/379/ EEC of 24 July 1986 on the Employment of Disabled People in the Community* (COM(88) 746 final). Luxembourg: EC.

Commission of the European Communities. 1992. *Second Report from the Commission to the Council, the European Parliament and the Economic and Social Committee on the application of the Community Charter of the Fundamental Social Rights of Workers* (COM(92) 562 final 23 December 1992). Luxembourg: EC.

Commission of the European Committees. 1994. European Social Policy: A Way Forward for the Union (COM(94) 333 final). Luxembourg: EC Commission on Social Justice. 1994. *Social Justice: Strategies for National Renewal.* London: Vintage.

Committee on Rights of Persons with Handicaps (South Australia). 1978. *The Law and Persons with Handicaps.* Adelaide: Government Printer.

Commonwealth Disability Anti-Discrimination Legislation Committee. 1991. *National Disability Discrimination Legislation: a Discussion Paper.* Canberra: The Committee.

Cook, T. 1977. Nondiscrimination in employment under the Rehabilitation Act of 1973. 27 *American University Law Review*, 31–75.

Cook, T. 1991. The Americans with Disabilities Act: the move to integration. 64 *Temple Law Review*, 393–469.

Cooper, J. 1991. Overcoming barriers to employment: the meaning of reasonable accommodation and undue hardship in the Americans with Disabilities Act. 139 *University of Pennsylvania Law Review*, 1423–68.

Cornes, P. 1984. *The Future of Work for People with Disabilities: a View from Great Britain.* New York: World Rehabilitation Fund.

Council of Europe. 1990. *Legislation on the Rehabilitation of Disabled People in Sixteen Members States of the Council of Europe* 4th edn. Strasbourg: Council of Europe.

Craft, J., Benecki, T. and Shkop, Y. 1980. Who hires the seriously handicapped? 19 *Industrial Relations*, 94–9.

Creasman, R. and Butler, P. 1991. Will the Americans with Disabilities Act disable employers? 42 *Labor Law Journal*, 52–6.

Crespi, G. 1990. Efficiency rejected: evaluating 'undue hardship' claims under the Americans with Disabilities Act. 26 *Tulsa Law Journal*, Fall, 1–36.

Crow, S. 1992. Anti-drug programs under the ADA: business as usual or harassment of a protected class? 43 *Labor Law Journal*, 117–24.

Croxen, M. 1984. *Overview: Disability and Employment.* Luxembourg: EC.

Cunningham, I. 1993. *Disability and Employment.* Stockton-on-Tees: Jim Conway Foundation.

Daunt, P. 1991. *Meeting Disability: a European Response.* London: Cassell.

DeJong, G. 1979. *The Movement for Independent Living: Origins, Ideology and Implications for Disability Research.* East Lansing: Michigan State University.

DeLury, B. 1975. Equal job opportunity for the handicapped means positive thinking and positive action. 26 *Labor Law Journal*, 679–85.

Department of Economic Development. 1986. *Equality of Opportunity in Employment in Northern Ireland: Future Strategy Options. A Consultative Paper.* Belfast: HMSO.

Department of Employment. 1973. *The Quota Scheme for Disabled People: Consultative Document.* London: Department of Employment.

Department of Employment. 1986. Explanatory Memorandum on European Community Document: Council Document 4673/86 of 4 February 1986 Concerning a Commission Proposal for a Recommendation on the Employment of Disabled People in the European Community (10 March, unpublished). London: Department of Employment.

Department of Employment. 1990. *Employment and Training for People with Disabilities: Consultative Document.* London: Department of Employment.

Department of Social Security. 1994. *Disability on the Agenda: Consultation on the Government's Measures to Tackle Discrimination against Disabled People.* London: Department of Social Security.

Disabled People's International. 1981. *Proceedings of the First World Congress.* Singapore: Disabled People's International.

Dolatly, G. 1993. The future of the reasonable accommodation duty in employment practices. 26 *Columbia Journal of Law and Social Problems,* 523–53.

Doyle, B. 1987a. Employing disabled workers: the framework for equal opportunities. *Equal Opportunities Review,* No. 12, March–April, 5–10.

Doyle, B. 1987b. Disabled workers, employment vulnerability and labour law. *Vulnerable Workers in the UK Labour Market: Some Challenges for Labour Law* (eds) P. Leighton and R. Painter. 9(5) *Employee Relations,* 20–9.

Doyle, B. 1991. Disabled workers: legal issues. In *Vulnerable Workers: Psychosocial and Legal Issues* (eds M. Davidson and J. Earnshaw). London: John Wiley & Sons, 93–117.

Doyle, B. 1993a. Employment rights, equal opportunities and disabled persons: the ingredients of reform. 22 *Industrial Law Journal,* 89–103.

Doyle, B. 1993b. Disability, discrimination and equal opportunities: a comparative study of legal models addressing the employment rights of disabled persons, with particular reference to Britain and the United States, unpublished PhD thesis, University of Salford.

Doyle, B. 1994a. *New Directions Towards Disabled Workers' Rights.* London: Institute of Employment Rights.

Doyle, B. 1994b. Disabled employees. In *Tolley's Employment Law.* London: Tolley Publishing Co. Ltd, D40/1–D40/15.

Driedger, D. 1989. *The Last Civil Rights Movement: Disabled People's International.* London: Hurst.

Drimmer, J. 1993. Cripples, overcomers and civil rights: tracing the evolution of federal legislation and social policy for people with disabilities. 40 *University of California Los Angeles Law Review,* 1341–410.

Du Pont and Company. 1990. *Equal to the Task,* 2nd edn. Wilmington, DE: E.I. Du Pont de Nemours and Company.

Dworkin, T. and Stegger, E. 1989. AIDS victims in the EC and the US: are they protected from unjustified discrimination? 24 *Texas International Law Journal*, 295–329.

Economic and Social Committee of the European Communities. 1981. *Problems of the Handicapped.* Brussels: Economic and Social Committee.

Egan, B. 1979. Civil rights: handicapped individuals. Rehabilitation Act of 1973 does not require affirmative action: *Southeastern Community College* v *Davis.* 13 *Creighton Law Review*, 607–18.

Employment and Immigration Canada. 1986. *Employment Equity Act and Reporting Requirements.* Ottawa: Minister of Supply and Services Canada.

Employment and Immigration Canada. 1991a. *Annual Report: Employment Equity Act.* 1991. Ottawa: Minister of Supply and Services Canada.

Employment and Immigration Canada. 1991b. *Consultations in Preparation for the Review of the Employment Equity Act.* Ottawa: Minister of Supply and Services Canada.

Employment and Immigration Canada. 1992. *Annual Report: Employment Equity Act.* 1992. Ottawa: Minister of Supply and Services Canada.

Epstein, R. 1992. *Forbidden Grounds: the Case Against Employment Discrimination Laws.* Cambridge, MA: Harvard University Press.

Equal Opportunities Commission for Northern Ireland. 1986. *Response to the Consultative Document. Equality of Opportunity in Employment in Northern Ireland: Future Strategy Options.* Belfast: EOC.

Equal Opportunities Review. 1989. Only people with disabilities need apply. 23 *Equal Opportunities Review*, January–February, 22–5.

Equal Opportunities Review. 1992. Positive action on disability: three case studies. 43 *Equal Opportunities Review*, May–June, 11–18.

Ervin, J. 1991. Reasonable accommodation and the collective bargaining agreement under the Americans with Disabilities Act of 1990. 1991 *Detroit College of Law Review*, Fall, 925–72.

European Communities. 1991. *Disabled Persons: Statistical Data Volume 1.* Luxembourg: EC.

European Communities. 1993. *Disabled Persons: Statistical Data Volume 2.* Luxembourg: EC.

European Industrial Relations Review. 1988. Employment of the disabled. *European Industrial Relations Review*, No. 175, 17–23.

Fagot-Diaz, J. 1988. Employment discrimination against AIDS victims: rights and remedies available under the federal Rehabilitation Act of 1973. 39 *Labor Law Journal*, 148–66.

Fair Employment Agency. 1987. *Comments of the Fair Employment Agency for Northern Ireland on the Government Consultative Paper on Future Strategy Options for the Promotion of Equality of Opportunity in Northern Ireland.* Belfast: Fair Employment Agency.

Feldblum, C. 1991a. Medical examinations and inquiries under the Americans with Disabilities Act: a view from the inside. 64 *Temple Law Review,* 521–49.

Feldblum, C. 1991b. The Americans with Disabilities Act definition of disability. 7 *Labor Lawyer,* 11–26.

Feldblum, C. 1991c. Employment protections. 69 *Milbank Quarterly,* Supplements 1/2, 81–110.

Finkelstein, V. 1991. Disability: an administrative challenge? In *Social Work: Disabled People and Disabling Environments* (ed. M. Oliver). London: Kingsley.

Fitzpatrick, R. 1991. Alcoholism as a handicap under federal and state employment discrimination laws. 7 *Labor Lawyer,* 395–430.

Flaccus, J. 1986a. Discrimination legislation for the handicapped: much ferment and the erosion of coverage. 55 *University of Cincinnati Law Review,* 81–116.

Flaccus, J. 1986b. Handicap discrimination legislation: with such inadequate coverage at the federal level, can state legislation be of any help? 40 *Arkansas Law Review,* 261–326.

Floyd, M. and North, K. 1986. Quota schemes and the assessment of employment handicap in Britain and West Germany. 1 *Disability, Handicap and Society,* 291–9.

Forsyth, T. 1981. Protections for the handicapped in federally financed programs and *Southeastern Community College* v *Davis.* 54 *Southern California Law Review,* 1053–75.

Fox, J. and Davison, B. 1989. Smoking in the workplace: accommodating diversity. 40 *Labor Law Journal,* 387–402.

Fredman, S. and Morris, G. 1989. *The State as Employer: Labour Law in the Public Services.* London: Mansell.

Frierson, J. 1992a. An analysis of ADA provisions on denying employment because of risk of future injury. 17 *Employee Relations Law Journal,* 603–22.

Frierson, J. 1992b. An employer's dilemma: the ADA's provisions on reasonable accommodation and confidentiality. 43 *Labor Law Journal,* 308–12.

Fry, E. 1986. *An Equal Chance for Disabled People? A Study of Discrimination in Employment* (Occasional Paper No. 4). London: Scope.

Gardner, R. and Campanella, C. 1991. The undue hardship defense to the reasonable accommodation requirement of the Americans with Disabilities Act of 1990. 7 *Labor Lawyer,* 37–51.

Garner, D. 1993. Protecting job opportunities of smokers: fair treatment for the new minority. 23 *Seton Hall Law Review*, 417–58.

Georgetown Law Journal. 1973. Abroad in the land: legal strategies to effectuate the rights of the physically disabled. 61 *Georgetown Law Journal*, 1501–23.

Gittler, A. 1978. Fair employment and the handicapped: a legal perspective. 27 *DePaul Law Review*, 953–87.

Goh, J. 1991. 'Smokers need not apply': challenging employment discrimination against smokers under the Americans with Disabilities Act. 39 *University of Kansas Law Review*, 817–43.

Gooding, C. 1994. *Disabling Laws, Enabling Acts: Disability Rights in Britain and America.* London: Pluto Press.

Gostin, L. 1991. Genetic discrimination: the use of genetically based diagnostic and prognostic tests by employers and insurers. 17 *American Journal of Law and Medicine*, 109–44.

Graham, P., Jordan, A. and Lamb, B. 1990. *An Equal Chance? Or No Chance? A Study of Discrimination Against Disabled People in the Labour Market.* London: Scope.

Grasso, C. 1993. Are employers who refuse to hire smokers discriminating within the meaning of the Americans with Disabilities Act of 1990? 66 *St John's Law Review*, 1109–25.

Gray, W. 1992. The essential-functions limitation on the civil rights of people with disabilities and John Rawls' concept of social justice. 22 *New Mexico Law Review*, 295–352.

Habeck, R., Galvin, D., Frey, W., Chadderdon, L. and Tate, D. (eds). 1985. *Economics and Equity in Employment of People With Disabilities: International Policies and Practices.* East Lansing: University Centre for International Rehabilitation, Michigan State University.

Haber, L. 1985. Trends and demographic studies on programs for disabled persons. In *Social Influences in Rehabilitation Planning: Blueprint for the 21st Century* (eds L. Perlman and G. Austin). Alexandria, VA: National Rehabilitation Association, 27–37.

Hadler, N. 1986. Criteria for screening workers for the establishment of disability. 28 *Journal of Occupational Medicine*, 940–5.

Haggard, L. 1993. Reasonable accommodation of individuals with mental disabilities and psychoactive substance use disorders under Title I of the Americans with Disabilities Act. 43 *Washington University Journal of Urban and Contemporary Law*, 343–90.

Hahn, H. 1983. Paternalism and public policy. 20 *Society*, No. 3, March/April 1983, 36–47.

Hahn, H. 1984. *The Issue of Equality: European Perceptions of Employment for Disabled Persons.* New York: World Rehabilitation Fund.

Hahn, H. 1987. Adapting the environment to people with disabilities: constitutional issues in Canada. 10 *International Journal of Rehabilitation Research*, 363–72.

Haines, A. 1983. *EE Black Ltd* v *Marshall*: a penetrating interpretation of 'handicapped individual' for sections 503 and 504 of the Rehabilitation Act of 1973 and various state equal employment opportunity statutes. 16 *Loyola of Los Angeles Law Review*, 527–66.

Harris, A., Cox, E. and Smith, C. 1971. *Handicapped and Impaired in Great Britain Part I*. London: HMSO.

Harvard Law Review. 1984. Employment discrimination against the handicapped and section 504 of the Rehabilitation Act: an essay on legal evasiveness. 97 *Harvard Law Review*, 997–1015.

Harvard Law Review. 1986. The constitutional rights of AIDS carriers. 99 *Harvard Law Review*, 1274–93.

Harvard Law Review. 1987. Facial discrimination: extending handicap law to employment discrimination on the basis of physical appearance. 100 *Harvard Law Review*, 2035–52.

Haveman, R., Halberstadt, V. and Burkhauser, R. (eds). 1984. *Public Policy Toward Disabled Workers: Cross-National Analyses of Economic Impacts*. Ithaca, NY: Cornell University Press.

Hearne, P. 1991. Employment strategies for people with disabilities: a prescription for change. 69 *Milbank Quarterly*, Supplements 1/2, 111–28.

Heshizer, B. and Muczyk, J. 1988. Drug testing at the workplace: balancing individual, organizational and societal rights. 39 *Labor Law Journal*, 342–57.

Hoffman, B. 1986. Employment discrimination based on cancer history: the need for federal legislation. 59 *Temple Law Quarterly*, 1–45.

Holtzman, G., Jennings, K. and Schenck, D. 1992. Reasonable accommodation of the disabled worker: a job for the man or a man for the job? 44 *Baylor Law Review*, 279–311.

Honey, S., Meager, N. and Williams, M. 1993. *Employers' Attitudes towards People with Disabilities*. Brighton: Institute of Manpower Studies.

House of Commons Committee of Public Accounts. 1988. *Employment Assistance to Disabled Adults* (21st Report, Session 1987–8, HC Paper 144). London: HMSO.

House of Commons Employment Committee. 1981. *The MSC's Review of the Quota Scheme for the Employment of Disabled People* (2nd Report, Session 1981–2, HC Paper 27). London: HMSO.

House of Commons Employment Committee. 1982. *The MSC's*

Review of the Quota Scheme for the Employment of Disabled People: Observations by the Government on the 2nd Report of the Committee in Session 1981–82 (6th Special Report, Session 1981–82, HC Paper 556). London: HMSO.

House of Commons Employment Committee. 1990a. *Disability and Employment* (1st Report, Session 1990–91, HC Paper 35). London: HMSO.

House of Commons Employment Committee. 1990b. *The Work of the Equal Opportunities Commission: Minutes of Evidence* (Session 1989–90, HC Paper 364-i). London: HMSO.

House of Commons Employment Committee. 1991. *Recruitment Practices. Volume 2: Minutes of Evidence, Appendices and Index* (2nd Report, Session 1990–91, HC Paper 176-II). London: HMSO.

House of Commons Employment Committee. 1994. *The Operation of the Disabled Persons (Employment) Act 1944: Minutes of Evidence* (Session 1993–94, HC Paper 281). London: HMSO.

Human Rights Commission (Australia). 1985. *Epilepsy and Human Rights.* Canberra: Australian Government Publishing Service.

Income Data Services Ltd. 1981. *Employing Disabled People* (IDS Study No. 255). London: Income Data Services Ltd.

Income Data Services Ltd. 1992. *Employing Disabled People* (IDS Study No. 508). London: Income Data Services Ltd.

Industrial Relations Review and Report. 1986. Contract compliance and equal opportunities. 381 *Industrial Relations Review and Report,* 2–6.

Institute of Personnel Management. 1987. *Contract Compliance: the UK Experience.* London: Institute of Personnel Management.

International Labour Organisation. 1923. *Employment of Disabled Men.* Geneva: ILO.

Janis, R. 1986. A unified theory for section 504 employment discrimination analysis: equivalent cost-based standards for 'otherwise qualified' and 'reasonable accommodation'. 43 *Washington and Lee Law Review,* 63–87.

Job Accommodation Network. 1987. *Evaluation Survey April 1987.* Washington, DC: President's Commission on Employment of People with Disabilities.

Jochheim, K. 1985. Quota system policy in the Federal Republic of Germany. In *Economics and Equity in Employment of People With Disabilities: International Policies and Practices* (eds R. Habeck, D. Galvin, W. Frey, L. Chadderdon and D. Tate). East Lansing: University Centre for International Rehabilitation, Michigan State University, 106–10.

Johnson, L. and Associates Inc. 1980. *Reasonable Accommodations:*

Research and Remedies (Report for the US Department of Education, Office of Civil Rights).

Johnson, W.T. 1986a. Handicap discrimination and workers' compensation rights. 12 *Employee Relations Law Journal*, 162–73.

Johnson, W.T. 1986b. The Rehabilitation Act and discrimination against handicapped workers: does the cure fit the disease? In *Disability and the Labor Market: Economic Problems, Policies and Programs* (eds M. Berkowitz and M. Hill). New York: ILR Press, Cornell University, 242–61.

Johnstone, R. 1988. Pre-employment health screening: the legal framework. 1 *Australian Journal of Labour Law*, 115–46.

Johnstone, R. 1989. Physical disability in employment. *Law Institute Journal*, August, 728–9.

Jones, N. 1991a. Overview and essential requirements of the Americans with Disabilities Act. 64 *Temple Law Review*, 471–97.

Jones, N. 1991b. Essential requirements of the Act: a short history and overview. 69 *Milbank Quarterly*, Supplements 1/2, 25–54.

Jones, P. and Cullis, J. 1988. Employment of the disabled: a rationale for legislation in the United Kingdom. 8 *International Review of Law and Economics*, 37–49.

Justice. 1987. *Industrial Tribunals: a Report*. London: Justice.

Kaufman, M. 1987. Federal and state handicapped discrimination laws: towards an accommodating legal framework. 18 *Loyola University of Chicago Law Journal*, 1119–48.

Kavka, G. 1992. Disability and the right to work. 9 *Social Philosophy and Policy*, 262–90.

Kelly, R. 1986. Reasonable accommodation in the federal sector: an examination of the application of the Rehabilitation Act to the federal employer. 29 *Howard Law Journal*, 337–69.

Kenney, J. 1988. AIDS in the workplace: termination, discrimination and the right to refuse. 11 *Dalhousie Law Journal*, 581–611.

Krauss, H., Mehnert, T., Nadler, R. and Greenberg, R. 1993. Perceiving oneself as 'disabled' or as having a 'disabling condition': a discriminant function analysis. 16 *International Journal of Rehabilitation Research*, 119–31.

Kriegel, L. 1969. Uncle Tom and Tiny Tim: some reflections on the cripple as negro. 38 *American Scholar*, 412–30.

Kulkarni, M. 1983. *Quota Systems and the Employment of the Handicapped*. East Lansing: University Centre for International Rehabilitation, Michigan State University.

Kushen, R. 1988. Asymptomatic infection with the AIDS virus as a handicap under the Rehabilitation Act of 1973. 88 *Columbia Law Review*, 563–86.

Kussner, B. 1989. AIDS-based discrimination in the workplace: issues and answers. 47 *University of Toronto Faculty of Law Review*, 383–419.

Labour Research Department. 1989. *Workplace Health: a Trade Unionists' Guide*. London: Labour Research Department.

Labour Research Department. 1990. Fit for danger? – facing the health test. 79 *Labour Research*, No. 2, 15.

Lang, J. 1978. Protecting the handicapped from employment discrimination: the job-relatedness and *bona fide* occupational qualification doctrines. 27 *DePaul Law Review*, 989–1012.

LaPlante, M. 1991. The demographics of disability. 69 *Milbank Quarterly*, Supplements 1/2, 55–77.

Large, P. 1982. *Report of the Committee on Restrictions Against Disabled People*. London: HMSO.

Larson, D. 1986. What disabilities are protected under the Rehabilitation Act of 1973? 37 *Labor Law Journal*, 752–66 (also published in 16 *Memphis State University Law Review*, 229–54).

Larson, D. 1988. Mental impairments and the Rehabilitation Act of 1973. 48 *Louisiana Law Review*, 841–74.

Lavelle, L. 1991. The duty to accommodate: will Title I of the Americans with Disabilities Act emancipate individuals with disabilities only to disable small businesses? 66 *Notre Dame Law Review*, 1135–94.

Law and Contemporary Problems. 1982. From wanderers to workers: a survey of federal and state employment rights of the mentally ill. 45(3) *Law and Contemporary Problems*, 41–65.

Law Reform Commission of Victoria. 1989. *Review of the Equal Opportunity Act* (Discussion Paper No. 17). Melbourne: LRCV.

Law Reform Commission of Victoria. 1990a. *Review of the Equal Opportunity Act* (Discussion Paper No. 19). Melbourne: LRCV.

Law Reform Commission of Victoria. 1990b. *Review of the Equal Opportunity Act* (Report No. 36). Melbourne: LRCV.

Law Society Employment Law Committee. 1992. *Disability, Discrimination and Employment Law*. London: Law Society Employment Law Committee.

Leach, B. 1989. Disabled people and the implementation of local authorities' equal opportunities policies. 67 *Public Administration*, 65–77.

Leap, T. 1979. State regulation and fair employment of the handicapped. 5 *Employee Relations Law Journal*, 382–405.

Leonard, A.M. 1987a. AIDS in the workplace. *AIDS and the Law: a Guide for the Public* (eds H. Dalton, S. Burris and the Yale AIDS Law Project). New Haven: Yale University Press, 109–25.

Leonard, A.M. 1987b. *Pyrrhic Victories: Winning Sex Discrimination and Equal Pay Cases in the Industrial Tribunals* 1980–84. London: HMSO.

Leonard, A.M. 1987c. *Judging Inequality: The Effectiveness of the Industrial Tribunal System in Sex Discrimination and Equal Pay Cases.* London: Cobden Trust.

Leonard, J. 1984. The impact of affirmative action on employment. 2 *Journal of Labor Economics*, 439–63.

Lepofsky, D. 1983. Representing handicapped persons' claims under the Ontario Human Rights Code and the Canadian Charter of Rights and Freedoms. 4 *Health Law Canada*, 43.

Lepofsky, M. 1985. Equality rights for handicapped persons in the Charter: putting the accent on individual ability. *Cambridge Lectures*, 117–52.

Lepofsky, M. 1992. The Canadian judicial approach to equality rights: freedom ride or roller coaster? 55 *Law and Contemporary Problems*, 167–99.

Lepofsky, M. and Bickenbach, J. 1985. Equality rights and the physically handicapped. *Equality Rights and the Canadian Charter of Rights and Freedoms* (eds A. Bayefsky and M. Eberts). Toronto: Carswell, 323–80.

Liberty. 1994. *Access Denied: Human Rights and Disabled People.* London: Liberty.

Lips, J. and Lueder, M. 1988. An employer's right to test for substance abuse, infectious disease and truthfulness versus an employee's right to privacy. 39 *Labor Law Journal*, 528–34.

Livneh, H. 1982. On the origins of negative attitudes toward people with disabilities. 43 *Rehabilitation Literature*, 338–47.

Lonsdale, S. and Walker, A. 1984. *A Right to Work: Disability and Employment* (Low Pay Unit Pamphlet No. 32). London: Disability Alliance/Low Pay Unit.

Louis Harris and Associates. 1986. *The International Center for the Disabled Survey of Disabled Americans: Bringing Disabled Americans into the Mainstream.* New York: Louis Harris and Associates.

Louis Harris and Associates. 1987. *The International Center for the Disabled Survey of Disabled Americans II: Employing Disabled Americans.* New York: Louis Harris and Associates.

Lunt, N. and Thornton, P. 1993. *Employment Policies for Disabled People: a Review of Legislation and Services in Fifteen Countries* (Research Series Paper No. 16). London: Department of Employment.

Lyth, M. 1973. Employers' attitudes to the employment of the disabled. 47 *Occupational Psychology*, 67–70.

McCarry, G. 1989. Landmines among the landmarks: constitutional aspects of anti-discrimination laws. 63 *Australian Law Journal*, 327–42.

McClure, T. 1978. The equal protection and due process clauses: two means of implementing 'integrationism' for handicapped applicants for public employment. 27 *DePaul Law Review*, 1169–97.

McCluskey, M. 1988. Rethinking equality and difference: disability discrimination in public transportation. 97 *Yale Law Journal*, 863–80.

McCrudden, C. 1986. Rethinking positive action. 15 *Industrial Law Journal*, 219–43.

McDonnell, R. and Weale, A. 1984. Regulating for equal employment opportunities: the case of the disabled quota. 11 *Journal of Law and Society*, 105–14.

McEvoy, S. 1988. Left-handed compliment: *de la Torres* v *Bolger* and the Rehabilitation Act of 1973. 39 *Labor Law Journal*, 358–71.

McEvoy, S. 1990. Cancer and employment discrimination: fighting job bias is worse than fighting the disease. 41 *Labor Law Journal*, 323–36.

McEvoy, S. 1992. Fat chance: employment discrimination against the overweight. 43 *Labor Law Journal*, 3–14.

McKenna, I. 1992. A proposal for legislative intervention in Canadian human rights law. 21 *Manitoba Law Journal*, 325–39.

Maffeo, P. 1990. Making non-discriminatory fitness-for-duty decisions about persons with disabilities under the Rehabilitation Act and the Americans with Disabilities Act. 16 *American Journal of Law and Medicine*, 279–327.

Mangin, G. 1983. *The Handicapped and Their Employment: Statistical Study of the Situation in the Member States of the European Communities*. Luxembourg: EC.

Manpower Services Commission. 1978. *Developing Employment and Training Services for Disabled People*. London: MSC.

Manpower Services Commission. 1979. *The Quota Scheme for the Employment of Disabled People: a Discussion Document*. London: MSC.

Manpower Services Commission. 1981. *Review of the Quota Scheme for the Employment of Disabled People: a Report*. Sheffield: MSC.

Manpower Services Commission. 1982. *Review of Assistance for Disabled People: a Report to the Commission*. London: MSC.

Manpower Services Commission. 1985. *Quota Scheme for the Employment of Disabled People: Working Group Report on Suggestions for Improving the Scheme's Effectiveness*. Sheffield: MSC.

Manpower Services Commission. 1986. *Jobcentre Staff's Perception of Their Services to Disabled People.* Sheffield: MSC.

Martin, J., Meltzer, H. and Elliot, D. 1988. *The Prevalence of Disability among Adults* (OPCS Surveys of Disability in Great Britain Report 1). London: HMSO.

Martin, J. and White, A. 1988. *The Financial Circumstances of Disabled Adults Living in Private Households* (OPCS Surveys of Disability in Great Britain Report 2). London: HMSO.

Martin, J., White, A. and Meltzer, H. 1989. *Disabled Adults: Services, Transport and Employment* (OPCS Surveys of Disability in Great Britain Report 4). London: HMSO.

Martin, M. 1980. Accommodating the handicapped: the meaning of discrimination under section 504 of the Rehabilitation Act. 55 *New York University Law Review,* 881–906.

Maselek, R. 1992. Employee medical screening under the Americans with Disabilities Act of 1990. 26 *Suffolk University Law Review,* 653–95.

Mason, K. 1982. Employment discrimination against the overweight. 15 *University of Michigan Journal of Law Reform,* 337–62.

Massie, B. 1994. *Disabled People and Social Justice.* London: Institute for Public Policy Research.

Mayerson, A. 1991a. The Americans with Disabilities Act: an historic overview. 7 *Labor Lawyer,* 1–9.

Mayerson, A. 1991b. Title I: employment provisions of the Americans with Disabilities Act. 64 *Temple Law Review,* 499–520.

Mello, J. 1993. Employing and accommodating workers with disabilities: mandates and guidelines for labor relations. 44 *Labor Law Journal,* 162–70.

Michigan Law Review. 1981. Implying a cause of action under section 503 of the Rehabilitation Act of 1973. 79 *Michigan Law Review,* 1093–112.

Mikochik, S. 1991a. Foreword: a celebration of equality. 64 *Temple Law Review,* 371–3.

Mikochik, S. 1991b. The constitution and the Americans with Disabilities Act: some first impressions. 64 *Temple Law Review,* 619–28.

Miller, P. 1987. Coming up short: employment discrimination against little people. 22 *Harvard Civil Rights–Civil Liberties Law Review,* 231–73.

Moreton, T. 1992. European support for people with disabilities. 21(6) *Personnel Review* 74–87.

Morrell, J. 1990. *The Employment of People with Disabilities: Research into the Policies and Practices of Employers* (Research Paper No. 77). London: Department of Employment.

Morris, A. and Nott, S. 1991. *Working Women and the Law: Equality and Discrimination in Theory and Practice.* London: Routledge.

Murphy, R. 1991. Reasonable accommodation and employment discrimination under Title I of the Americans with Disabilities Act. 64 *Southern California Law Review,* 1607–44.

Nagi, S. 1965. Some conceptual issues in disability and rehabilitation. *Sociology and Rehabilitation* (ed. M. Sussman). Washington, DC: American Sociological Association.

Nagi, S. 1969a. *Disability and Rehabilitation: Legal, Clinical and Self-Concepts and Measurements.* Columbus, OH: Ohio State University Press.

Nagi, S. 1969b. Congruency in medical and self-assessment of disability. 38 *Industrial Medicine,* 27–83.

Nagi, S. 1975. *An Epidemiology of Disability Among Adults in the United States.* Columbus, OH: Mershon Center, Ohio State University.

Nagi, S. 1991. Disability concepts revisited: implications to prevention. In *Disability in America: toward a National Agenda for Prevention* (eds A. Pope and A. Tarlov). Washington, DC: National Academy Press, Appendix A.

Napier, B. 1989. AIDS, discrimination and employment law. 18 *Industrial Law Journal,* 84–96.

Napier, B. 1991. AIDS sufferers at work and the law. In *Vulnerable Workers: Psychosocial and Legal Issues* (eds M. Davidson and J. Earnshaw). Chichester: Wiley, 139–58.

National Advisory Council on the Employment of Disabled People. 1986. *Report of the Working Party on the Principles Underlying Employment Provisions for Disabled People.* London: NACEDP.

National Advisory Council on the Employment of Disabled People. 1990. *Response to the Government's Consultative Document 'Employment and Training for People with Disabilities'*. London: NACEDP.

National Audit Office. 1987. *Department of Employment and Manpower Services Commission: Employment Assistance to Disabled Adults. Report by the Comptroller and Auditor General* (HC Paper 367). London: HMSO.

National Council on the Handicapped. 1986. *Toward Independence: an Assessment of Federal Laws and Programs Affecting Persons with Disabilities – with Legislative Recommendations.* Washington, DC: Government Printing Office.

National Council on the Handicapped. 1988. *On the Threshold of Independence: Progress on Legislative Recommendations toward Independence.* Washington, DC: Government Printing Office.

National Council on Intellectual Disability. 1989. *The Rights of People with Disabilities: Areas of Need for Increased Protection. A Discussion Paper.* Sydney: Human Rights and Equal Opportunities Commission.

Neal, B. 1992. The proper standard for risk of future injury under the Americans with Disabilities Act: risk to self or risk to others? 46 *Southern Methodist University Law Review*, 483–512.

New York University Law Review. 1974. Employment discrimination against rehabilitated drug addicts. 49 *New York University Law Review*, 67–86.

Nicolai, D. and Ricci, W. 1977. Access to buildings and equal employment opportunity for the disabled: survey of state statutes. 50 *Temple Law Quarterly*, 1067–85.

Nothdurft, J. and Astor, H. 1986. Laughing in the dark: anti-discrimination law and physical disability in New South Wales. 28 *Journal of Industrial Relations*, 336–52.

O'Dea, K. 1980. Protecting the handicapped from employment discrimination in private sector employment: a critical analysis of section 503 of the Rehabilitation Act of 1973. 54 *Tulane Law Review*, 717–64.

Olenick, D. 1980. Accommodating the handicapped: rehabilitating section 504 after *Southeastern.* 80 *Columbia Law Review*, 171–91.

Oliver, M. 1985. Discrimination, disability and social policy. In *Year Book of Social Policy in Britain 1984–85* (eds C. Jones and M. Brenton). London: Routledge and Kegan Paul, 74–99.

Oliver, M. 1990. *The Politics of Disablement.* Basingstoke: Macmillan.

Oliver, M. and Barnes, C. 1991. Discrimination, disability and welfare: from needs to rights. In *Equal Rights for Disabled People: the Case for a New Law* (eds I. Bynoe, M. Oliver and C. Barnes). London: Institute for Public Policy Research, 7–16.

O'Neill, D. 1976. *Discrimination Against Handicapped Persons: the Costs, Benefits and Inflationary Impact of Implementing Section 504 of the Rehabilitation Act of 1973 Covering Recipients of HEW Financial Assistance.* Arlington, VA: Public Research Institute.

Ontario Human Rights Commission. 1990. *Discrimination Because of Handicap.* Toronto: Ontario Human Rights Commission.

Ontario Ministry of Citizenship. 1989. *Guidelines for Assessing Accommodation Requirements for Persons with Disabilities under the Ontario Human Rights Code 1981 as Amended.* Toronto: Ministry of Citizenship.

Paolicelli, D. 1979. Employment discrimination against the handicapped: can *Trageser* repeal the private right of action? 54 *New York University Law Review*, 1173–98.

Parker, S. 1983. *The Disabled Unemployed: a Survey Carried out on Behalf of the Manpower Services Commission.* London: Office of Population Censuses and Surveys.

Parliament of the Commonwealth of Australia. 1992. *Employment of People with Disabilities: Report of the Senate Standing Committee on Community Affairs.* Canberra: Senate Printing Unit.

Partlett, D. 1977. The Racial Discrimination Act 1975 and the Anti-Discrimination Act 1977: aspects and proposals for change. 2 *University of New South Wales Law Journal,* 152–74.

Pati, G. and Adkins, J. 1980. Hire the handicapped: compliance is good for business. 58(1) *Harvard Business Review,* 14–22.

Peck, C. 1983. Employment problems of the handicapped: would Title VII remedies be appropriate and effective? 16 *University of Michigan Journal of Law Reform,* 343–85.

Percy, S. 1989. *Disability, Civil Rights and Public Policy: the Politics of Implementation.* Tuscaloosa: University of Alabama Press.

Perlin, M. 1987. State constitutions and statutes as sources of rights for the mentally disabled: the last frontier? 20 *Loyola of Los Angeles Law Review,* 1249–327.

Perras, R. and Hunter, W. 1986. Handicap discrimination in employment: the employer defense of future safety risk. 6 *Journal of Law and Commerce,* 377–400.

Phelan, G. 1992. Essential functions of a job under the ADA: determining if a disabled individual is 'qualified'. 39(1) *Federal Bar News and Journal,* 46 and 63–6.

Piercy. 1956. *Report of the Committee on the Rehabilitation, Training and Resettlement of Disabled Persons* (Cmd 9883). London: HMSO.

Pitt, G. 1992. Can reverse discrimination be justified? In *Discrimination: the Limits of the Law* (eds B. Hepple and E. Szyszczak). London: Mansell, 281–99.

Poirier, D. 1991. La protection juridique des personnes âgées ou handicapées et la charte canadienne des droits et libertés. 23 *Ottawa Law Review,* 553–79.

Posner, R. 1989. An economic analysis of sex discrimination laws. 56 *University of Chicago Law Review,* 1311–35.

Postol, L. and Kadue, D. 1991. An employer's guide to the Americans with Disabilities Act. 42 *Labor Law Journal,* 323–42 (also published in 24 *John Marshall Law Review,* 693–729).

Premus, R. and Carnes, D. 1982. *Regulation and Small Business Participation in the Federal Contract Market: the Effect of Section 503* (Report for the United States Small Business Administration). Dayton, OH: Wright State University School of Business Administration.

Prescott-Clarke, P. 1990. *Employment and Handicap.* London: Social and Community Planning Research.

Presidential Commission on the Human Immunodeficiency Virus Epidemic. 1988. *Report of the Presidential Commission on the Human Immunodeficiency Virus Epidemic.* Washington, DC: The Commission.

Rains, R. 1992. A pre-history of the Americans with Disabilities Act and some initial thoughts as to its constitutional implications. 11 *St Louis University Public Law Review,* 185–202.

Rand, J. 1988. Employment protection for the substance abuser: a comparison of the Swedish and American approaches. 9 *Comparative Labor Law Journal,* 450–74.

Rasnic, C. 1992. A comparative analysis of federal statutes for the disabled worker in the Federal Republic of Germany and the United States. 9 *Arizona Journal of International and Comparative Law,* 283–336.

Ratushny, E. 1986. Implementing equality rights, standards of reasonable accommodation with legislative force. In *Righting the Balance: Canada's New Equality Rights* (ed. L. Smith). Saskatoon: Canadian Human Rights Reporter, 255–72.

Ravaud, J-F., Madiot, B. and Ville, I. 1992. Discrimination towards disabled people seeking employment. 35 *Social Science and Medicine,* 951–8.

Rebell, M. 1986. Structural discrimination and the rights of the disabled. 74 *Georgetown Law Journal,* 1435–89.

Rehabilitation International. 1981. *Charter for the 80s.* New York: Rehabilitation International.

Research Surveys of Great Britain Ltd. 1978. *Attitudes of the Disabled to Employment Legislation: Main Report* (unpublished research report prepared for Employment Services Division, Manpower Services Commission). London: MSC/Research Surveys of Great Britain Ltd.

Richards, R. 1985. Handicap discrimination in employment: the Rehabilitation Act of 1973. 39 *Arkansas Law Review,* 1–72.

Richman, D. 1978. Applying the constitutional doctrine of irrebuttable presumption to the handicapped: *Gurmankin* v *Costanzo.* 27 *DePaul Law Review,* 1199–218.

Rickard, T., Triandis, H. and Patterson, C. 1963. Indices of employer prejudice toward disabled applicants. 47 *Journal of Applied Psychology,* 52–5.

Rickard, T., Triandis, H. and Patterson, C. 1977. Indices of employer prejudice toward disabled applicants. In *Social and*

Psychological Aspects of Disability: a Handbook for Practitioners (ed. J. Stubbins). Baltimore: University Park Press, 523–9.

Rioux, M. 1994. Towards a concept of equality of well-being: overcoming the social and legal construction of inequality. VII(1) *Canadian Journal of Law and Jurisprudence*, 127–47.

Robbins, A. 1991. Employment discrimination against substance abusers: the federal response. 33 *Boston College Law Review*, 155–209.

Rockey, P., Fantel, J. and Omenn, G. 1979. Discriminatory aspects of pre-employment screening: low-back x-ray examination in the railroad industry. 5 *American Journal of Law and Medicine*, 197–214.

Ronalds, C. 1990. *National Employment Initiatives for People with Disabilities: a Discussion Paper.* Canberra: Australian Government Publishing Service.

Ronalds, C. 1991. *National Employment Initiatives for People with Disabilities: Report of the National Consultations with People with a Disability.* Canberra: Australian Government Publishing Service.

Rothstein, M. 1983. Employer selection based on susceptibility to occupational illness. 81 *Michigan Law Review*, 1379–1496.

Rothstein, M. 1987. Screening workers for AIDS. *AIDS and the Law: a Guide for the Public* (eds H. Dalton, S. Burris and the Yale Law Project). New Haven, CT: Yale University Press.

Rothstein, M. 1992a. Genetic discrimination in employment and the Americans with Disabilities Act. 29 *Houston Law Review*, 23–84.

Rothstein, M. 1992b. Discrimination based upon genetic information. 33 *Jurimetrics Journal*, 13–18.

Rouault, G. 1978. *The Handicapped and their Employment: a Statistical Study.* Luxembourg: EC.

Roussos, G. 1990. Protections against HIV-based employment discrimination in the United States and Australia. 13 *Hastings International and Comparative Law Review*, 609–78.

Royal National Institute for the Deaf. 1987. *Communication Works: an RNID Inquiry into the Employment of Deaf People.* London: RNID.

Sainsbury, S. 1970. *Registered as Disabled.* London: Bell.

Sainsbury, S. 1973. *Measuring Disability.* London: Bell.

Sales, B., Powell, D., Vanduizend, R. and Associates. 1982. *Disabled Persons and the Law.* New York: Plenum Press.

Schaffer, D. 1991. Tax incentives. 69 *Milbank Quarterly*, Supplements 1/2, 293–312.

Schau, J. 1986. Handicapped workers: who should bear the burden of proving job qualifications? 38 *Maine Law Review*, 135–84.

Schiff, M. and Miller, D. 1993. Reasonable accommodation under the Americans with Disabilities Act. 28 *Gonzaga Law Review*, 219–34.

Schoenfeld, B. 1980. Civil rights for the handicapped under the constitution and section 504 of the Rehabilitation Act. 49 *University of Cincinnati Law Review*, 580–610.

Schoon, E. 1979. Private rights of action for handicapped persons under section 503 of the Rehabilitation Act. 13 *Valparaiso University Law Review*, 453–500.

Schreiber, S. 1984. Rights of the handicapped to be otherwise qualified: when does section 504 of the Rehabilitation Act protect the handicapped?; *Nelson* v *Thornburgh*. 57 *Temple Law Quarterly*, 179–202.

Schroedel, J. and Jacobson, R. 1978. *Employer Attitudes towards Hiring Persons with Disabilities: a Labor Market Research Model*. Albertson, NY: Human Resources Center.

Scotch, R. 1984. *From Good Will to Civil Rights: Transforming Federal Disability Policy*. Philadelphia: Temple University Press.

Scotch, R. 1987. *Disability Politics and Disability Rights: a Perspective from Great Britain*. New York: World Rehabilitation Fund.

Scotch, R. 1989. Politics and policy in the history of the disability rights movement. 67 *Milbank Quarterly*, Supplement 2, 380–400.

Sculco, T. 1992. Smokers' rights legislation: should the state 'butt out' of the workplace? 33 *Boston College Law Review*, 879–902.

Scutt, J. 1977. The Anti-Discrimination Act (New South Wales). 15 *Law Society Journal*, 241–5.

Shakespeare, T. 1993. Disabled people's self-organisation: a new social movement? 8 *Disability, Handicap and Society*, 265–80.

Shaller, E. 1991. 'Reasonable accommodation' under the Americans with Disabilities Act: what does it mean? 16 *Employee Relations Law Journal*, 431–51.

Shaller, E. and Rosen, D. 1991. A guide to EEOC's final regulations on the Americans with Disabilities Act. 17 *Employee Relations Law Journal*, 405–30.

Shapiro, B. 1991. The heavy burden of establishing weight as a handicap under anti-discrimination statutes. 18 *Western State University Law Review*, 565–77.

Shelley, M. 1991. *National Disability Discrimination Legislation: Report of the National Consultation with People with a Disability*. Canberra: Australian Government Publishing Service.

Sherman, S. 1989. An individualized definition of 'handicap' and its application to HIV. 22 *University of California Davis Law Review*, 653–88.

Sigel, C. 1984. Legal recourse for the cancer patient-returnee: the

Rehabilitation Act of 1973. 10 *American Journal of Law and Medicine*, 309–21.

Simon, P. 1984. Employment discrimination: analyzing handicap discrimination claims: the right tools for the job. 62 *North Carolina Law Review*, 535–71.

Sklar, H. 1986. An employer's duty to reasonably accommodate handicapped employees and applicants under the Rehabilitation Act of 1973. 2 *Labor Lawyer*, 733–50.

Sluzas, A. 1981. Civil rights: employment discrimination. Presumptive back pay extended to the handicapped discriminatee under section 1983: *Gurmankin* v *Costanzo*. 54 *Temple Law Quarterly*, 190–211.

Smith, F. 1989. AIDS-based employment discrimination in the American and Canadian workplace. 10 *Comparative Labor Law Journal*, 531–62.

Smith, J. 1992. Accommodating the Americans with Disabilities Act to collective bargaining obligations under the NLRA. 18 *Employee Relations Law Journal*, 273–85.

Smith, S. 1992a. Disabled in the labour market. 7 *Employment Policy Institute Economic Report*, No. 1.

Smith, S. 1992b. *Wasted Opportunities*. London: Scope.

Snowdon (Earl of). 1976. *Integrating the Disabled: Volume 1. Report of the Working Party on Integration of the Disabled*. Horsham: National Fund for Research into Crippling Diseases.

Snowdon (Earl of). 1979. *Integrating the Disabled: Volume 2. Evidence to the Working Party on Integration of the Disabled*. Horsham: National Fund for Research into Crippling Diseases.

Snyder, D. 1993. Qualified individuals with disabilities: defining the ADA's protected class. 44 *Labor Law Journal*, 101–9.

Southam, C. and Howard, G. 1987. *AIDS and Employment Law*. London: Financial Training Publications.

Stahlhut, E. 1993. Playing the trump card: may an employer refuse to reasonably accommodate under the ADA by claiming a collective bargaining obligation? 9 *Labor Lawyer*, 71–96.

Standing Advisory Commission on Human Rights. 1990. *Religious and Political Discrimination and Equality of Opportunity in Northern Ireland: Second Report* (Cm 1107). London: HMSO.

Stevens, G. 1986. Exploding the myths about hiring the handicapped. 63(12) *Personnel*, 57–60.

Stickler, D. and Sebok, A. 1992. Legal issues surrounding preemployment physical examinations in the coal industry. 94 *West Virginia Law Review*, 811–34.

Stine, M. 1992. Reasonable accommodation and undue hardship

under the Americans with Disabilities Act of 1990. 37 *South Dakota Law Review*, 97–120.

Stolker, B. 1992. Weigh my job performance, not my body: extending Title VII to weight-based discrimination. 10 *New York Law School Journal of Human Rights*, 223–50.

Streicher, K. 1987. Cancer-based employment discrimination: whether the proposed amendment to Title VII will provide an effective anti-discrimination remedy. 62 *Indiana Law Journal*, 827–56.

Stubbins, J. 1982. The quota system for the employment of disabled persons. 43 *Rehabilitation Literature*, 141–5.

Stuhlbarg, S. 1991. Reasonable accommodation under the Americans with Disabilities Act: how much must one do before hardship turns undue? 59 *University of Cincinnati Law Review*, 1311–48.

Sullivan, M. 1991. From personal tragedy to social oppression: the medical model and social theories of disability. 16 *New Zealand Journal of Industrial Relations*, 255–72.

Sullivan, R. 1985. Balancing the rights of the alcoholic employee with the legitimate concerns of the employer: reasonable accommodation versus undue hardship. 46 *Montana Law Review*, 401–18.

Taras, D. 1992. The duty to accommodate disabled employees. 47 *Relations Industrielles*, 709–27.

Tarnopolsky, W. 1983. The equality rights in the Canadian Charter of Rights and Freedoms. 61 *Canadian Bar Review*, 242–64.

Tarnopolsky, W. and Pentney, W. 1985. *Discrimination and the Law in Canada* (loose-leaf with 7th Cumulative Supplement 1991). Toronto: de Boo.

Tate, K. 1989. The federal employer's duties under the Rehabilitation Act: does reasonable accommodation or affirmative action include reassignment? 67 *Texas Law Review*, 781–849.

Thompson, M. 1986. *Employment for Disabled People*. London: Kogan Page.

Thompson, P., Lavery, M. and Curtice, J. 1990. *Short Changed by Disability*. London: Disablement Income Group.

Thornburgh, D. 1991. The Americans with Disabilities Act: what it means to all Americans. 64 *Temple Law Review*, 375–85 (also published in 41 *Labor Law Journal*, 803–7).

Thornton, M. 1990. *The Liberal Promise: Anti-discrimination Legislation in Australia*. Melbourne: Oxford University Press.

Tomlinson. 1943. *Report of the Interdepartmental Committee on the Rehabilitation and Resettlement of Disabled Persons* (Cmnd 6415). London: HMSO.

Townsend, P. 1979. *Poverty in the United Kingdom: a Survey of Household Resources and Standards of Living.* Harmondsworth: Penguin.

Trades Union Congress. 1993. *Disabled People Working in the Public Sector* (Report by Equality and Social Policy Department). London: TUC.

Tucker, B. 1989a. Section 504 of the Rehabilitation Act after ten years of enforcement: the past and the future. 1989 *University of Illinois Law Review,* 845–921.

Tucker, B. 1989b. The Americans with Disabilities Act: an overview. *University of Illinois Law Review,* Fall, 923–39.

Tucker, B. 1992. The Americans with Disabilities Act of 1990: an overview. 22 *New Mexico Law Review,* 13–117.

Tudor, K. 1989. The politics of disability in Italy: *La Lega per il Diritto al Lavoro degli Handicappati.* 25 *Critical Social Policy,* Summer, 37–55.

Tyler, M. 1993. Law and change: the Disability Discrimination Act 1992: genesis, drafting and prospects. 19 *Melbourne University Law Review,* 211.

United Nations. 1990a. *Report on National Legislation for the Equalization of Opportunities for People with Disabilities: Examples from 22 Countries and Areas.* New York: United Nations.

United Nations. 1990b. *Disability: Statistics Compendium* (Department of International Economic and Social Affairs: Statistical Office: Statistics on Special Population Groups: Series Y, No. 4). New York: UN.

US Bureau of Labor Standards. 1961. *Workmen's Compensation and the Physically Handicapped Worker* (Bulletin No. 234). Washington, DC: US Department of Labor.

US Civil Service Commission. 1975. *Employment of Handicapped Individuals in the Federal Government* (Report prepared for the Senate Committee on Labor and Public Welfare and House Committee on Education and Labor). Washington, DC: CSC.

US Commission on Civil Rights. 1981. *Civil Rights Issues of Handicapped Americans: Public Policy Implications.* Washington, DC: Government Printing Office.

US Commission on Civil Rights. 1983. *Accommodating the Spectrum of Individual Abilities.* Washington, DC: Government Printing Office.

US Department of Labor. 1948. *The Performance of Physically Impaired Workers in Manufacturing Industries.* Washington, DC: Government Printing Office.

US Department of Labor. 1980. *Affirmative Action for the Handicapped.* Washington, DC: Government Printing Office.

US Department of Labor. 1982. *A Study of Accommodations Provided to Handicapped Employees by Federal Contractors: Final Report* (2 vols) (a study carried out by Berkeley Planning Associates). Washington, DC: Government Printing Office.

US Equal Employment Opportunity Commission. 1986. *Annual Report on the Employment of Minorities, Women and the Handicapped Individuals in the Federal Government, Fiscal Year 1986.* Washington, DC: EEOC.

US House of Representatives. 1990a. *Report of the House Committee on Education and Labor* (House of Representatives Report No. 101-485(II), 101st Congress, 2nd Session) reprinted in *United States Code Congressional and Administrative News* (101st Congress, 2nd Session, 1990) Vol. 4, 303–445.

US House of Representatives. 1990b. *Report of the House Committee on the Judiciary* (House of Representatives Report No. 101-485(III), 101st Congress, 2nd Session) reprinted in *United States Code Congressional and Administrative News* (101st Congress, 2nd Session, 1990) Vol. 4, 445–511.

US Senate. 1989. *Report of the Senate Committee on Labor and Human Resources* (Senate Report No. 101-116, 101st Congress, 1st Session).

Vaughn, D. 1988. Smoking in the workplace: a management perspective. 14 *Employee Relations Law Journal*, 359–86.

Vizkelety, B. 1991. Reasonable accommodation revisited: *Alberta Human Rights Commission* v *Central Alberta Dairy Pool.* 70 *Canadian Bar Review*, 335–51.

Vogel-Polsky, E. 1984. *The Economic Integration of the Disabled: an Analysis of Measures and Trends in Member States.* Luxembourg: EC.

Waddington, L. 1995. *Disability, Employment and the European Community.* London: Blackstone Press (forthcoming).

Walker, A. 1982. *Unqualified and Underemployed: Handicapped Young People and the Labour Market.* London: Macmillan.

Ware, H. and Neale, R. 1986. *Affirmative Action for People with Disabilities* (Discussion Paper No. 11). Canberra: Human Rights Commission (Australia).

Wasson, R. 1987. AIDS discrimination under federal, state and local law after *Arline.* 15 *Florida State University Law Review*, 221–78.

Waters, P. 1990. The coverage of AIDS-related discrimination under handicap discrimination law: the US and Australia compared. 12 *Sydney Law Review*, 377–419.

Watt, R. 1992. HIV, discrimination, unfair dismissal and pressure to dismiss. 21 *Industrial Law Journal*, 280–92.

Weicker, L. 1991. Historical background of the Americans with Disabilities Act. 64 *Temple Law Review*, 387–92.

Weirich, C. 1991. Reasonable accommodation under the Americans with Disabilities Act. 7 *Labor Lawyer*, 27–36.

Weiss, S. 1974. Equal employment and the disabled: a proposal. 10 *Columbia Journal of Law and Social Problems*, 457–96.

West, J. 1991a. *The Formation of National Disability Rights Policy in the 100th Congress.* Washington, DC: National Institute on Disability and Rehabilitation Research.

West, J. 1991b. The social and policy context of the Act. 69 *Milbank Quarterly Supplements* 1/2, 3–24.

West, J. (ed.). 1991c. *The Americans with Disabilities Act: from Policy to Practice. 69 Milbank Quarterly*, Supplements 1/2.

Whaley, J., Mattison, C., Dodd, A. and Mullins, D. 1986. *A Sense of Purpose: a Study of Visually Handicapped People and Their Search for Work.* London: RNIB.

White House Conference on Handicapped Individuals. 1977. *Summary and Final Report.* Washington, DC: Government Printing Office.

Wightman, P. 1991. *Costs of Disability: a Survey of the Costs of Disabilities in Labour Force Related Activity* (Social Policy Division, Policy Research Paper No. 59). Canberra: Department of Social Security.

Wilkie, T. 1993. *Perilous Knowledge: the Human Genome Project and Its Implications.* London: Faber.

William and Mary Law Review. 1992. Employing the alcoholic under the Americans with Disabilities Act of 1990. 33 *William and Mary Law Review*, 895–947.

Williams, C. 1972. Is hiring the handicapped good business? 38 *Journal of Rehabilitation*, March–April, 30–4.

World Health Organization. 1980. *International Classification of Impairments, Disabilities and Handicaps: a Manual of Classification Relating to the Consequences of Disease.* Geneva: WHO.

World Health Organization. 1990. *Is the Law Fair to the Disabled? A European Survey.* Copenhagen: WHO.

Yelin, E. 1991. The recent history and immediate future of employment among persons with disabilities. 69 *Milbank Quarterly*, Supplements 1/2, 129–49.

Yuker, H., Block, J. and Young, J. 1966. *The Measurement of Attitudes toward Disabled Persons.* Albertson, NY: Human Resources Center.

Zadny, J. 1979. *Employer Reactions to Efforts to Place Disabled and Disadvantaged Workers.* Portland, OR: Regional Rehabilitation Research Institute, Portland State University.

Index